www.wadsworth.com

www.wadsworth.com is the World Wide Web site for Wadsworth and is your direct source to dozens of online resources.

At *www.wadsworth.com* you can find out about supplements, demonstration software, and student resources. You can also send email to many of our authors and preview new publications and exciting new technologies.

www.wadsworth.com

Changing the way the world learns©

The American Bureaucracy

The Core of Modern Government

Third Edition

Richard Stillman II
University of Colorado, Denver

THOMSON
™
WADSWORTH

Australia • Canada • Mexico • Singapore • Spain •
United Kingdom • United States

THOMSON

WADSWORTH

Publisher: Clark Baxter
Executive Editor: David Tatom
Technology Project Manager: Melinda Newfarmer
Assistant Editor: Amy McGaughey
Editorial Assistant: Reena Thomas
Marketing Manager: Janise Fry
Advertising Project Manager: Nathaniel Bergson-Michelson
Project Manager, Editorial Production: Catherine Morris

Print/Media Buyer: Doreen Suruki
Permissions Editor: Elizabeth Zuber
Producton Service: Carlisle Publishers Services
Copy Editor: Barbara Somogyi
Cover Designer: Brian Salisbury
Cover Image: Photodisc
Compositor: Carlisle Communications, Ltd.
Text and Cover Printer: Webcom

Printed in Canada
1 2 3 4 5 6 7 07 06 05 04 03

For more information about our products, contact us at:
Thomson Learning Academic Resource Center
1-800-730-2214
For permission to use material from this text, contact us by: **Phone:** 1-800-730-2214
Fax: 1-800-730-2215
Web: http//www.thomsonrights.com

Library of Congress Control Number 2003100991

ISBN 0-534-61420-5

Wadsworth/Thomson Learning
10 Davis Drive
Belmont, CA 94002-3098
USA

Asia
Thomson Learning
5 Shenton Way #01-01
UIC Building
Singapore 068808

Australia/New Zealand
Thomson Learning
102 Dodds Street
Southbank, Victoria 3006
Australia

Canada
Nelson
1120 Birchmount Road
Toronto, Ontario MIK 5G4
Canada

Europe/Middle East/Africa
Thomson Learning
High Holborn House
50/51 Bedford Row
London WC1R4LR
United Kingdom

Latin America
Thomson Learning
Seneca, 53
Colonia Polanco
11560 /Mexico D.F.
Mexico

Spain/Portugal
Paraninfo
Calle/Magallanes, 25
28015 Madrid, Spain

Contents

Preface

This is a third and thoroughly revised edition of a book first published in 1987. Readers will note that in this edition considerable updated factual material, with new charts and tables, and helpful pedagogical aids at the end of every chapter were added and portions, such as Chapter 6, were entirely rewritten in order to address the issues of the twenty-first century. Nonetheless, the basic thesis of this book remains unchanged.

In the recent decades Americans ironically have exhibited intense hostility towards public bureaucracy and, at the same time, increasing dependence upon its services. Certainly government bureaucracy is unloved and unwanted but it also is very much a fact of contemporary life. American government, the society, and its citizens are now dependent upon vast, interconnecting webs of complicated administrative systems, processes, and procedures. In the routine visit to the county hospital, the simple delivery of a personal letter, in NASA's projects putting men and women in space, or the National Institutes of Health's long-term projects for discovering a cure for cancer, public bureaucracies are at work. Large, complex administrative machinery, often hidden from public view, carries out these tasks through formal and informal hierarchies of experts using advanced technologies and diverse skills. Public agencies are decisively reshaping our lives, for today and into the distant future, through the public policies they implement, the services they perform (or fail to perform), and the regulations and research they develop. The exercise of this authority over the public and private sectors comes from diverse sources of power, both granted and acquired by public bureaucracies.

The following pages in this new edition, just like the previous editions, introduce students and general readers to public bureaucracy in the United States and seek to answer such questions as: What is the nature of modern public bureaucracy? How has it grown and acquired such influence over our lives? What are its formal aspects? Informal elements? Internal dynamics? External sources of power? What are the tasks it performs? The impacts on our lives? How are these outputs fashioned and made to happen? What are the major trends in public bureaucracy in the twenty-first century? And its future?

First and foremost, as in the prior editions this book provides an introductory overview of public bureaucracy in the United States for general readers and students new to the field. It focuses upon government *bureaucracy,* not private or not-for-profit or other varieties. It assumes no prior background or understanding of the topic. As in any introductory text, some details are omitted in order to paint a broad picture of the whole. Since the topic is large and the literature is vast, further readings are suggested at the end of each chapter.

Second, this edition, like the previous ones, argues throughout that public bureaucracy is now *the core* of modern U.S. government. Although no mention of bureaucracy is made in the U.S. Constitution, the heart of every public function, at every level of government today, depends largely upon the work of public bureaucracies and bureaucrats. For better or worse—or better *and* worse—it is the way public policies get accomplished. Examining how bureaucracy works and influences the directions of public policies will be the principal focus of this book. To use Harold Lasswell's famous phrase, this text looks at how bureaucracy determines "who gets what, when, how." In brief, a study of bureaucracy as our modern central institution for making political choices and carrying them out.

Third, this new edition, like the first and second ones approaches the institutions of public bureaucracy as open, dynamic *systems* with the essential elements of inputs, outputs, formal structures, internal dynamics, feedback mechanisms, and environmental influences. Successive chapters are organized around an explanation of the systems' essential features and explore the nature of the bureaucratic system, its components, and their interrelationship with the whole. Review questions and listings of key terms at the end of each chapter further serve to underscore its key points. What a bureaucratic system is and how it can be understood as a dynamic whole will be discussed in the opening chapter.

Finally, this text studies the subject of public bureaucracy from an analytical and descriptive point of view, rather than from an advocacy or prescriptive standpoint. It makes no case *for* bureaucracy, or *against* bureaucracy. The text is written primarily to help students and the general public understand this important and central governing institution and how it affects their everyday lives. Therefore, the author aims to describe public bureaucracy as it is, not as it ought to be. Obviously, this task can be difficult because of the pejorative connotations of the term, "bureaucracy." The reader should be cautioned from the outset that this word is used throughout the text in its neutral, descriptive, and analytical meaning, that is, as an institution of government. Furthermore, to avoid boring repetition, "bureaucracy" is used interchangeably in this text with other terms such as "public agency," "executive branch," "government organization," "bureau" and "public enterprise" (even though the author realizes all too well that these words do not denote precisely the same meanings).

One last point: this writer might reasonably be asked why he spent so many years laboring over this book on a subject that many regard at best as "dull" and at worst as "noxious." My reply is to remind the reader of a delightful scene in the *Wizard of Oz* where Dorothy and her companions glimpse the wizard behind a curtain. He is busy running the gears, wheels, and machinery that create the steam clouds and awesome illusions of the magician. Dorothy scolds, "You are a very bad man," to which the wizard replies, "Oh, no, my dear, I'm really a very good man; but I'm a very bad wizard." The underlying premise of this text is much the same: bureaucracies are not the results of some inherent evil or of "bad men," but perhaps only of *our own* ineffective wizardry. It is hoped that this text will make a small step in the direction of improving our understanding of public bureaucracy—"glimpsing the wizard behind the curtain" and maybe even our wizardry in dealing with "the wizard."

A word of special thanks must specifically go to three people who aided the author immensely in the difficult task of researching new data and factual material for this revision: Professor James P. Pfiffner and Professor Tim Conlan at George Mason University; and Erin Collard, a UCD graduate and research assistant. Their help was greatly appreciated and invaluable to the author.

Thanks also go to the following group who acted as reviewers for this book: Mark Hoffman, Grand Valley State University-Grand Rapids; Raymond Pomerleau, San Francisco State University; and James Simmons, University of Wisconsin.

"Sure we have our bad apples, but most of our bureaucrats are pretty decent. In fact, our federal bureaucrats are to capitalism what the New York Police and Fire Departments were to 9/11—the unsung guardians of America's civic religion, the religion that says if you work hard and play by the rules you'll get rewarded and you won't get ripped off . . . much of America's moral authority to lead the world derives from the decency of our government and its bureaucrats."

Thomas L. Friedman, *The New York Times* (July 28, 2002), p. K 13.

"I would remark how rarely additions to the public sector have been initiated by the demands of voters or the advocacy of pressure groups or platforms of political parties. On the contrary, in the fields of health, housing, urban renewal, transportation, welfare, education, poverty, and energy, it has been, in very great measure, people in government service, or closely associated with it, acting on the basis of their specialized and technical knowledge, who first perceived the problem, conceived the program, initially urged it on the President and Congress, went on to help lobby it through to enactment, and then saw to its administration."

Samuel Beer, Presidential Address before the American Political Science Association, "Federalism, Nationalism, and Democracy in America," *American Political Science Review,* vol. 72, no. 1 (March 1978).

"The modern state is operated by technicians according to the hierarchical model of administrative management, rather than by equal participants according to a model of deliberation and persuasion."

Sheldon Wolin, "Reagan Country," *New York Review of Books* (December 18, 1980), p. 9.

"For better or worse—or better and worse—much of our government is now in the hands of professionals. . . ."

Frederick C. Mosher, *Democracy and the Public Service,* 2nd ed., Chapter 5 (1982).

". . . public administration exists, massively, centrally, and often decisively for our individual and collective lives."

Dwight Waldo, "A Conversation with Dwight Waldo," in *Public Administration Review,* vol. 35, no. 4 (July/Aug. 1985), p. 465.

"All realistic study of government has to start with an understanding of bureaucracy . . . because no government can function without it."

Carl J. Friedrich, *Constitutional Government and Democracy,* 4th ed., Chapter II (1968), p. 57.

"The work of government will henceforth be too vast and varied, the sum of money too great, the details with which it will have to deal too complicated to render it possible to perform without a staff of trained officials, furnished with the usual motives to behave well and make the public service the whole and sole business of their lives."

Senator Charles Sumner (R, MA.) in offering the first civil service proposal to Congress in 1864 as quoted in the *New York Times* (May 10, 1864), p. 4.

About the Author

Richard Stillman II is a Professor of Public Administration at the Graduate School of Public Affairs, University of Colorado at Denver and is the author or editor of several books including: *Preface to Public Administration, The Modern State, and its Study* (with Walter Kickert), *Creating the American State,* and *Basic Documents of American Public Administration Since 1950.* His textbook, *Public Administration: Concepts and Cases,* 7th edition, is used at over 400 universities and colleges. His books have been translated into Chinese, Korean, and Hungarian, and he is an elected fellow in the National Academy of Public Administration.

1

■

The American Public Bureaucracy

Public Bureaucracy Defined
Some of Our Negative Ideas about Bureaucracy
Some Myths and Realities about U.S. Public Bureaucracy
What Is U.S. Public Bureaucracy?
Why Study American Public Bureaucracy?
How This Text Approaches American Public Bureaucracy
Summary of Key Points
Key Terms
Review Material
Notes
Further Reading
Web Sites

On September 11, 2001, the United States experienced the worst foreign attack since Pearl Harbor, December 7, 1941. Al Qaeda terrorists hijacked four commercial passenger jets, which they smashed into the New York City World Trade Center Twin Towers and the Pentagon near Washington, D. C., killing nearly 3,000 Americans. Much like Pearl Harbor, there had been advanced intelligence warnings about a possible terrorist strike that were ignored by authorities. On August 16, nearly a month earlier, the FBI field office in Minneapolis, Minnesota, arrested Moroccan-born Zacarias Moussaoui in a suburban motel near the Twin Cities. Moussaoui had triggered the suspicions of a local flight instructor at the Pan Am International Flight Academy in Eagan, Minnesota. The instructor reported Moussaoui's odd behavior to the FBI because he had paid in cash for training on a Boeing 747 flight simulator in order to learn only how to take off, not land. Further, he had failed to solo a single-engine Cessna after 50 hours of practice, yet he wanted to fly 747 jets.

FBI agents investigated then confronted the belligerent, uncooperative Moussaoui. They turned him over to immigration authorities for visa violations and impounded his possessions, which included a laptop computer, two knives, binoculars, a hand-held aviation radio, and a notebook. The field agents next asked FBI headquarters for search warrants to examine the contents of the suspect's laptop, but FBI headquarters denied the request, even though local field agents were convinced that this known Muslim Radical was involved with a terrorist plot to hijack U.S. planes. Washington headquarters claimed that there was insufficient evidence to tie Moussaoui to a foreign threat, even though the French Government earlier had given the CIA evidence that he had ties to Muslim Terrorists and his notebooks contained phone numbers of a Yemeni individual, who turned out to be the paymaster financing the entire 9/11 attack.

As Ms. Coleen Rowley, the FBI field office agent in Minnesota who led the investigations of Moussaoui, later told a Congressional Investigating Committee, "The agents in particular believed that Moussaoui had signaled he had something to hide in the way he refused to allow them to search his computer." However, she added that her Washington superiors "continued to throw up roadblocks and undermine the efforts to obtain a warrant." "HQ personnel brought up almost ridiculous questions in their apparent effort to undermine probable cause." In other words, the FBI field office failed to convince their Washington supervisors that a search warrant was necessary which, in turn, blocked discovery of the 9/11 surprise attack. In short, public bureaucracy's flawed operation allowed this horrid disaster to happen.

For better or worse, or better *and* worse, we as a society, like all victims of 9/11, are dependent upon various public bureaucracies at times for protecting our lives and livelihoods.

Today no institution is more vital to our daily existence and well-being as a nation, a community, a neighborhood, or as individuals. Though we cannot often see it or touch it, public bureaucracy plays a major role, perhaps even a life and death role, in deciding such questions as:

What is the quality of the air we breathe?

How safe are our city streets?

Is the water we drink and the food we eat pure?

Are highways planned and maintained properly?

Will there be parks, playgrounds, and recreation for our leisure time?

How well will the next generation be educated?

Do the aged, infirm, poor, and unemployed receive adequate public assistance?

Are our communities well designed for living?

Where should research next explore—the frontiers of space, the oceans, the land, or the human body?

Will a first-class letter we mail arrive promptly?

Is the U.S. nuclear arsenal controlled and commanded properly?

How safe and healthy are the job sites we work at?

Are doctors, nurses, and hospitals capable of healing the sick?

Or, for that matter, is the hairstylist, tradesperson, or any professional certified to perform work for his or her customers?

Can we be sure the house we live in or the car we drive is well constructed?

Will the U.S. economy—its currency, trade, and fiscal matters—be managed fairly and efficiently?

And, yes, are we well-defended from future terrorist attacks?

Public bureaucrats not only perform such jobs but also help to make critical policy choices about whether or not these jobs ought to be done. Indeed, our fate as a nation and people depends upon complicated networks of a vast and pervasive bureaucratic system that, though largely unseen, is central to our individual and collective lives. Yet these very attributes—pervasiveness, invisibility, and centrality—make public bureaucracy exceedingly difficult to define as a phenomenon. What is "it," if "it" is everywhere?

PUBLIC BUREAUCRACY DEFINED

No precise definition of public bureaucracy exists, but for the purposes of this text it is defined as *the structure and personnel of organizations, rooted in formal laws and informal processes, that collectively function as the core system of U.S. government and that both determine and carry out public policies using a high degree of specialized expertise and technologies.*

Note that this definition of public bureaucracy contains several elements:

- *Structure and personnel of organizations* refers to both the formal and informal attributes of public agencies and the people who are employed in them
- *Rooted in formal laws and informal processes* means that bureaucracies are ultimately based on written laws, codes, and statutes as well as informal politics, interests, and actions
- *Core system* is a set of elements that together function as the central network for operating the U.S. government
- *U.S. government* involves the three branches (executive, legislative, and judicial) as well as the three levels (federal, state, and local)

- *Determine and carry out public policies* means that the organizations help to both decide and implement choices in governmental affairs
- *High degree of specialized expertise and technologies* concerns specific professional skills, knowledge, and advanced training as well as a vast array of techniques and tools to perform bureaucratic work

The definition above is an analytical, descriptive, and neutral one that identifies public bureaucracy as a central institution in U.S. government. This text explores the topic of public bureaucracy from the standpoint of that definition. However, the word *bureaucracy* often has a highly emotional, negative, *prescriptive* meaning. And here lies the source of much confusion. The word has a double meaning that defines essentially the same phenomenon as something that is *both good and bad*. The double meaning implied in the word *bureaucracy* leads to a number of popular myths and misconceptions about it. This chapter will begin by outlining some attitudes toward bureaucracy and bureaucrats. It will next sketch aspects of the realities of modern U.S. bureaucracy that frequently stand in sharp contrast to our popular beliefs and ideas about U.S. bureaucracy. The rationale and design for this book will emerge from discussion about the myths and realities of U.S. public bureaucracy.

SOME OF OUR NEGATIVE IDEAS
ABOUT BUREAUCRACY

Few things are more disliked in our modern society than bureaucracy; hardly any other occupation is held in lower esteem than that of a bureaucrat. Both bureaucracy and bureaucrats are subject to contempt and criticism in both the press and private conversation. "Inefficient," "full of red tape," "big," "unresponsive," "unproductive," "inhumane," and "inept" are frequently among the emotionally charged criticisms regularly leveled at bureaucracy and bureaucrats.

Maybe we hold bureaucracy in such low esteem because of firsthand experiences. Most of us are familiar with standing in long lines at a post office waiting to mail a letter and with filling out long forms for motor vehicle registrations, or for God knows what purposes. Every April 15 we gripe at paying what may seem higher taxes to Uncle Sam in return for fewer and fewer visible public services.

Whatever the cause or source of our perpetual criticisms of those nameless, faceless bureaucrats, these views have become part and parcel of our American folklore. It is no wonder that popular dictionary definitions echo our profound dislike of bureaucracy. *The American Heritage Dictionary's* definition of bureaucracy reads in part: "numerous offices and adherence to inflexible rules of operation; . . . any unwieldy administration." According to *Webster's New World Dictionary of the American Language,* "bureaucracy is governmental officialism or inflexible routine." *Roget's Thesaurus* gives equally demeaning synonyms for *bureaucracy:* "officialism," "officiousness," and "red tape."

Scholars have likewise damned it. Max Weber, the great German scholar of bureaucracy, was horrified by what he saw as the irreversible trend of "bureau-cratization" in human affairs, and he mourned the concomitant loss of human dignity and freedom: "It is horrible to think that the world could one day be filled with nothing but those little cogs, little men clinging to little jobs and striving towards bigger ones. . . . This passion for bureaucracy is enough to drive one to despair."[1] A French scholar Michel Crozier, in *The Bureaucratic Phenomenon,* argues that "the vulgar and frequent sense of the word 'bureaucracy'. . . evokes the slowness, the ponderousness, the routine, the complication of proce-dures, and the maladapted response of 'bureaucratic' organizations to the needs which they should satisfy, and the frustrations which their members, clients or subjects consequently endure."[2] The English scholar C. N. Parkinson gained an international reputation by developing his "laws" of bureaucratic practice; such as, "Work expands to fill the time allotted."[3]

American scholars have been little kinder over the years. E. Pendleton Her-ring saw bureaucracies as rigid and run by "special interests."[4] In his *Bureaucra-tization of the World,*[5] Henry Jacoby dismally pictures bureaucracy's worldwide spread as the central cause of decline in democratic values. Many of the writ-ings of sociologist Robert Merton focus on the "dysfunctions" of bureaucracy[6] by cataloguing its various shortcomings and inadequacies in modern life. In *Bu-reaucratic Government USA,*[7] David Nachmias and David Rosenbloom paint an equally unhappy portrait of the spreading of bureaucratic control over most as-pects of life in the United States and the subsequent loss of control by Ameri-cans over bureaucracy.

For the most part, politicians echo our critical sentiments about bureau-cracy. Democratic presidential candidate Jimmy Carter in 1976, Republican candidates Ronald Reagan in 1980 and 1984 and George Bush in 1988, as well as his son, George W. Bush, in 2000 ran against "bureaucracy." In 1993 one of President Bill Clinton's first actions as a new president was to appoint his Vice President Al Gore to head a task force, which produced a report, *The National Performance Review* (NPR), aimed at recommending fundamental reforms in the federal bureaucracy and cutting federal personnel by 250,000. Presidents in re-cent decades have promised to "cut it," "trim it," "reform it," and "clean it up." In future elections, no doubt, similar campaign slogans for the reform of bu-reaucracy are likely to appear. Politicians mirror our popular disgust. From left to right in the political spectrum, bureaucracy is a target, as reflected by the fol-lowing popular opinions expressed by the man on the street—"it's the prob-lem with government"; "it's too big"; "full of lame-brained, overpaid pencil-pushers"; "it's where everyone stays on for life"; "it's out of touch with the grass roots"; "it grows relentlessly"; "it produces only red tape"; "it's all-powerful"; "it's inefficient."

Glancing at the book titles of several polemics against bureaucracy only un-derscores the ongoing intense hostility: *The Federal Rathole, Fat City: How Wash-ington Wastes Your Taxes, Burning Money, Alice in Blunderland, The Spending Cancer, The Government Racket, The Bureaucratic Syndrome,* and *America by the Throat.* Typ-ical of such books, Martin Gross's *A Call for a Revolution: How Washington Is*

Strangling America has chapter titles such as "More Pork, More Waste," "The Tax Monster," "Welfare Slavery," and "The Great Budget Game." From the air waves as well issues a daily drumbeat of complaints. For example, Denver, Colorado, alone has two radio talk shows that give cash awards to people who phone in to report government waste and inefficiencies. Nationally, popular daytime talk show hosts on radio, like Rush Limbaugh, or nighttime TV hosts like Jay Leno frequently feature government agencies as the "butt of their jokes." The highest rated and longest running TV weekly news journal, *60 Minutes,* often highlights bureaucratic bungling as major stories.

In a nutshell, such "polemics" reflect the hostile ideas many people, from august scholars to the man on the street, *believe* about bureaucracy. Charles Goodsell summed it up well when he observed: "The employee of bureaucracy, that lowly bureaucrat, is seen as lazy or snarling or both. The office occupied by this pariah is viewed as bungling or inhuman or both. The overall edifice of bureaucracy is pictured as overstaffed, inflexible, unresponsive, and power-hungry, all at once."[8]

These "myths" are even perpetuated by those who should know better, as Beverly A. Cigler and Heidi L. Neiswender discovered in a careful context analysis of 18 current American government introductory texts at the college level. Not only was the overall coverage of bureaucracy skimpy (see Table 1.1),

Table 1.1 Subject Areas Covered in American Government Introductory Textbooks (N = 18) and the General Complaints Featured About Bureaucracy

Topics Covered in Basic Texts	
The President/Presidency	33.3%
Federalism/Constitution	22.2
Congress/Legislators	16.6
Foreign Policy	12.1
Domestic/Social Policy	10.6
Bureaucracy	5.1

Type and Frequency of Complaints in Bureaucracy Chapter	Number
Not accountable	11
Too large	11
Paperwork/red tape	8
Inefficient/wasteful	7
Citizen complaints/lack of satisfaction	5
Incompetent	3
Difficult to fire bureaucrats	3
Negative comparison between bureau and democracy	2
Patronage	1
Corruption/whistle-blowing	0

SOURCES: Beverly A. Cigler and Heidi L. Neiswender, "Bureaucracy in the Introductory American Government Textbook," *Public Administration Review,* 51(5) (Sept./Oct. 1991): 443. Reprinted by permission and updated by Beverly A. Cigler and Richard D. White, "Bureaucracy in the Introductory American Textbook Revisited," unpublished paper delivered at NASPAA Conference, Oct. 14–17, 1998, Boise, Idaho, pp. 2–3.

but a majority simply repeated the old myths about this subject, leading the authors to conclude "that significant omissions or inaccurate information may contribute to a general public uninformed about the role of the public service in governance."[9]

But there is another side to the discussion, namely, the reality—what is U.S. public bureaucracy actually like? Let's examine some popular myths a little more closely in order to gain a clearer and more accurate understanding of U.S. public bureaucracy. Let's begin our discussion by separating the facts from fiction about bureaucracy. Now, will the *real* bureaucracy please stand up (or step forward)?

SOME MYTHS AND REALITIES ABOUT U.S.
PUBLIC BUREAUCRACY

Bureaucracy is criticized on television shows, on radio, in books, by presidents, the press, the public, and academics. Indeed, almost everyone takes a shot at bureaucracy. It is blamed for a variety of social ills from wrongly causing "red tape" to rightly failing to stop the 9/11 terrorist attack on the New York City Twin Towers and the Pentagon. Again, in the words of Charles Goodsell, "Bureaucracy stands as a splendid hate object."[10]

What is bureaucracy in the United States really like? What are its forms and elements? There are, as previously outlined, many popular beliefs concerning bureaucracy, and we might begin this discussion by clearing the air, so to speak, by examining some popular notions about bureaucracy.

Myth 1: Bureaucracy Is the Problem
with U.S. Government

Ask almost anyone about bureaucracy, and the response "It's THE PROBLEM with U.S. government!" comes almost automatically. The presidency, the Supreme Court, and Congress often receive far greater, and more charitable, press coverage than the bureaucracy (though they too have received hard knocks in recent years). Presidents, courts, and Congress are generally associated with what U.S. government is *and* does. These institutions are seen as the places where the *real* decisions and actions of government take place, often for the good of all citizens. But the president is merely one individual; the Supreme Court, simply nine judges; and Congress, only 535 individuals, compared with governmental bureaucracy, which is composed of roughly 18 million federal, state, and local employees. In the words of Carl Friedrich, these people and their organizations form "the core of modern government," for it is here where the bulk of government work gets done—"where the rubber meets the road," so to speak.[11]

Public bureaucracies educate 47 million public school children every day, pass out 7 million unemployment checks every week, deliver 45 million Social Security retirement checks every month, maintain 300,456 miles of interstate highways (and another 4 million miles of public roads), run 123 veterans

A little JOG with the PRESIDENT'''''

Government bureaucracies are frequently pictured as "overwhelmingly large" and needing "a trim-down."

By Jim Morin. Copyright 1993 by *The Miami Herald.* Reprinted with special permission of King Features Syndicate.

hospitals serving 950,000 persons, serve in 175 embassies and delegations overseas, put astronauts into space, award 4 percent of the population welfare assistance, handle 208 billion letters and packages every year, register and license 216 million autos, fund one-third of all research done in America, and much more. Whether this work is done efficiently, wisely, or well—or whether it should be done at all—is open to argument. These questions aside, public bureaucracies carry out most of the work of government and so are central to the operations of the U.S. government. Therefore, bureaucracy is not only THE PROBLEM with government—it makes government—indeed civilized society—possible. Bureaucracy is how most things get done in government, and so it is "the core" of governmental operations. It is the way society carries out the purposes of government; the way much of government actually governs and acts in *both* "good" and "bad" ways. Thus bureaucracy creates *both* problems as well as makes society run, indeed makes modern civilization possible by providing the "basics" such as roads, schools, police, and fire protection. Its influences are profound yet always two-sided.

At the heart of bureaucracy's influence upon everyday life is its ability to make political choices—sometimes critical life and death choices—for society *and* for all its citizens—to determine, in Harold Lasswell's view of politics, "who gets what, when, how."[12] Government bureaucracies exercise important administrative choices—to decide and act in ways that affect all of us—through essentially four routes, according to Theodore Lowi;[13] that is, by regulatory activities, redistributive policies, distributive policies, and constituent services.

Regulatory activities concern the making and enforcing of rules and regulations. There is a broad array of regulatory agencies involved with rule-making and rule-enforcing activities such as the Federal Communications Commission, which regulates telephone, TV, radio, and Internet providers; the Security Exchange Commission, which regulates securities and stock exchange activities; and the Food and Drug Administration, which ensures the purity of foods and the safeness of drug and medical practices.

Redistributive functions involve the transfer of tax benefits from one group of citizens to another: the Social Security Administration annually transfers billions of dollars from working citizens to retired and disabled persons; and state and local welfare agencies transfer billions of dollars from the general population to the poor, sick, and disabled.

Distributive policies are developed by public agencies that use general revenues to provide goods and services to entire populations, regardless of class of group: police, public schools, and the U.S. Postal Service "distribute" services to everyone.

Constituent services involve the work of those agencies and departments that service government as a whole. A municipal budget office's decision can affect the whole of city government; or the State Department's foreign policy choices influence the entire nation. These are "constituent-type" bureaucracies.

More will be said in Chapter 2 about the nature, quality, and scope of these different types of bureaucratic policies and how they impact our lives in the United States. The important point for now is that bureaucracy plays a huge role in the way government works and in determining how society is governed. Hence, bureaucracy creates *both* problems and progress. It can be the source of much good and much ill. It is always a two-edged sword.

Myth 2: Government Bureaucracy Is Overwhelmingly Large and Monolithic

Much of the criticism directed at U.S. public bureaucracy involves its size. "It's overwhelming." "It's too big." "It's overpowering." Statistics are frequently cited to shore up this argument: data that indicate that U.S. bureaucracy is the largest employer in the country, consuming a quarter of the Gross National Product, and that it is the fourth-largest bureaucracy in the world—behind only Russia, China, and India in numbers of employees. United States public bureaucracy spends more than a trillion dollars annually. All such data are accurate—but only partly.

United States bureaucracy is not one massive organization but numerous small units, mostly very small ones situated at the grass roots. Actually, as Table 1.2 points out, there are 87,504 U.S. bureaucracies—or, more precisely, 1 federal government, 50 state bureaucracies, and 87,453 local public bureaucracies. As Table 1.2 shows, the bulk of public employees work in local bureaucracies with 19,372 municipalities; 16,629 townships; 34,683 special districts; 3,043 counties; and 13,726

Table 1.2 Number of U.S. Governments by Type in 1998

Federal Government	1
State Governments	50
County Governments	3,043
Municipalities	19,372
Towns	16,629
School Districts	13,726
Special Districts	34,683
Total	87,504

SOURCE: *Statistical Abstract of the United States,* 1998.

Table 1.3 Numbers of Federal Bureaucracies by Employment Size Range

Size Range	Number Units in 20 Agencies	Number Post Offices	Total Number Units	Percent Units in This Range
1–4	5,652	20,340	25,992	57.2
5–9 (P.O. 5–10)	1,762	5,255	7,017	15.4
10–24 (P.O. 11–25)	3,145	2,644	5,789	12.7
25–49 (P.O. 26–50)	1,573	1,061	2,634	5.8
50–99 (P.O. 51–99)	924	578	1,502	3.3
100–199	617	360	977	2.2
200–299	254	118	372	.8
300–399	253	78	331	.7
500–999	250	88	338	.7
1,000–1,999	173	45	218	.5
2,000–4,999	156	33	189	.4
5,000–9,999	37	10	47	.1
10,000 and up	22	3	25	.06
Totals	14,818	30,613	45,431	99.9

SOURCE: U.S. Office of Personnel Management, and Charles T. Goodsell *The Case for Bureaucracy,* 3rd ed. (Chatham, NJ: Chatham House, 1994), p. 136. Reprinted by permission.

school districts. Of these, 30,913 public organizations have *no* full-time employees. And only 1,159 have more than 1,000 employees—and nearly one-third or 493 of these are school districts, which means that the bulk of "big" bureaucracy is in reality made up of very small organizational units located at the grass roots. Many of the big public organizations on the local level are school systems.

But what about the federal level? Approximately 2.7 million civilian employees and nearly the same number of military add up to a large and impressive figure, but here, too, as Table 1.3 points out, these are scattered throughout 45,431 units with 57.2 percent of them employing fewer than four people. Only

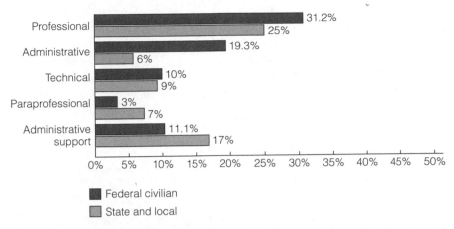

FIGURE 1.1   Percentages of white collar full-time civilian workers in the state and local versus federal governments, 1999

Source: *Statistical Abstract of the United States,* 2000, p. 331 and U.S. Office of Personnel Management, 2000.

25 or .06 percent employ more than 10,000 personnel. Contradicting Max Weber's view of bureaucracy as "overtowering," data show that even the federal level is composed mostly of small, fragmented organizations. Chapter 2 will deal with the variety and types of bureaucratic structures in the United States.

Myth 3: Bureaucrats Are All Alike

We hear talk of the typical bureaucrat, as if bureaucrats were a homogeneous mass of green-eye-shaded underachievers or nonachievers. The evidence, however, points to considerable diversity in public bureaucrats; it is impossible to speak of "a typical bureaucrat." Bureaucrats do many jobs, and so there are many varieties of public employees. There are over 9,000 federal job categories describing tasks such as drug enforcement, flying space shuttles, and delivering mail. People engaged in these occupations are individually and collectively far from being "lame-brains." As Figure 1.1 points out, more than 25 percent of full-time state/local and 31.2 percent of federal employees work at professional occupations (by comparison, only 12 percent of private sector workers are classed as "professionals").

At the federal level over the past two decades, the total percentage of professional, administrative, and technical jobs has risen from roughly half to two-thirds of the civilian work force, while the shares of clerical dropped from 24 percent to 19 percent and blue collar from 24 percent to 19 percent. The U.S. Health and Human Services Department alone employs 4,000 biologists, physicists, and chemists; 17,000 medical doctors, and health specialists; 2,000 mathematicians, statisticians, and engineers; 5,000 public health officers; and 30,000 legal claims or benefits personnel.

Increasingly, public employees are highly trained engineers, scientists, dentists, doctors, nurses, biological and physical scientists, mathematicians, teachers,

Table 1.4 Personnel Turnover Rates within the Federal Civil Service, 1985–1997

Year	ACCESSIONS		SEPARATIONS	
	Total	New Hires	Total	Quits
1985	541,787	451,516	484,742	185,453
1989	515,759	435,911	483,850	172,376
1993	382,399	253,374	423,830	127,140
1997	283,517	208,725	333,431	81,574

SOURCE: U.S. Office of Personnel Management, *Monthly Report of Federal Civilian Employment.*
Turnover data exclude Legislative and Judicial branches, U.S. Postal Service, Postal Rate Commission.

librarians, archivists, accountants, and so on. As Frederick Mosher points out, public service is in fact "a professional state."[14] Numerous highly skilled blue collar personnel and craftspeople are also employees of the public services. Today, for instance, a firefighter, while he or she may not be categorized as a professional, has to have increasing and specialized expertise in the use of a wide assortment of new techniques and complex substances in order to fight fires in houses, highrises, factories, and offices. Chapter 4 will further describe the professionalization of employees inside U.S. public bureaucracy.

Myth 4: Bureaucrats Stay on Forever

The popular image of a bureaucrat is of someone tenured for life in a comfortable job. The old adage says, once a bureaucrat, always a bureaucrat. Here, too, statistics tell a different story. Public bureaucrats are in reality quite mobile, having turnover rates equal to and sometimes exceeding those of private business. As Table 1.4 indicates, 12 percent of total federal workers were "separated" in 1997: but as the table also points out, this statistic varies considerably by year. Turnover rates from public service vary considerably from jurisdiction to jurisdiction, by job function, and according to level of government. Turnover rates, however, at the state and local levels are roughly the same overall as the "Feds," though rates in individual state and municipal bureaucracies by job category and at various grade levels differ widely. Cutbacks at the federal level between 1990 and 2001 varied from agency to agency (indicated in Table 1.5). Even those who remain within a single agency frequently change jobs (averaging only 2.3 years in one slot at the federal level), often moving laterally or upward across a wide range of government positions. The point is that unlike the Washington Monument, bureaucrats, individually and collectively, are not permanent fixtures on the landscape. More will be said about their transitory nature in Chapter 4.

Myth 5: All Bureaucrats Live in Washington, D.C.

The bulk of civil servants are local, not federal, workers—15.4 million are employed by states or localities and therefore are scattered throughout the 50 states. As Figure 1.2 shows, local bureaucracy has grown from 40.5 percent (1950) to

Table 1.5 Changes in Federal Civilian Workforce in Selected Departments, 1990–2001

Departments	1990	2001	Change
Agriculture	122,594	100,084	22,510 (−)
Defense	1,034,152	670,568	363,584 (−)
Energy	17,731	15,689	2,042 (−)
HHS	123,959	63,323	60,636 (−)
HUD	13,596	10,154	3,442 (−)
Labor	17,727	16,016	1,711 (−)
State	25,228	28,054	2,826 (+)
Transportation	67,364	64,131	3,233 (−)

SOURCE: Monthly Report of Federal Civilian Employment, Office of Workforce Information, May 2001.

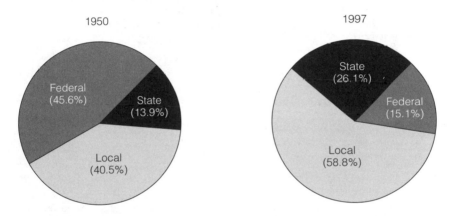

FIGURE 1.2 American bureaucracy—1950 vs. 1997 (percent of federal, state, and local bureaucrats)

Source: *Statistical Abstract of the United States*, 1993, p. 318 with update.

58.8 percent (1997) of the total number of public employees. Of the total federal work force of 2.7 million civilian federal personnel, as indicated in Figure 1.3, only 11.9 percent are stationed in Washington, D.C. Or, put another way, 88.1 percent live elsewhere. The distribution of the federal civilian workforce is roughly uniform across the United States, depending upon population. Large states such as California and New York have greater concentrations by comparison with smaller states. There tends to be a higher concentration of local bureaucrats in state capitals and county seats—as would be expected—but the overall distribution of the bureaucratic work force shows a fairly even spread geographically; hence bureaucrats are hardly removed physically from the grass roots. Indeed, as several studies show, bureaucrats are probably more closely representative of the overall characteristics of the U.S. population than employees of other institutions, such as Congress, labor unions, and big business.

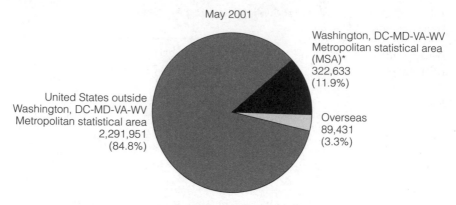

May 2001

Washington, DC-MD-VA-WV
Metropolitan statistical area
(MSA)*
322,633
(11.9%)

United States outside
Washington, DC-MD-VA-WV
Metropolitan statistical area
2,291,951
(84.8%)

Overseas
89,431
(3.3%)

Total Employment: 2,704,015

*Washington, DC-MD-VA-WV MSA includes the District of Columbia; Calvert, Charles, Frederick, Montgomery, and Prince George's counties in Maryland; Arlington, Clarke, Culpeper, Fairfax, Fauquier, King George, Loudon, Prince William, Spotsylvania, Stafford, and Warren Counties, and the Cities of Alexandria, Fairfax, Falls Church, Fredericksburg, Manassas Park in Virginia; and Berkley and Jefferson Counties in West Virginia.

FIGURE 1.3   Distribution of federal civilian employment by major geographic area, May 2001

Myth 6: Bureaucracy Operates in Secret

This "myth" is answered asking another question: "Compared to what?"

A case in point: in planning, organizing, and executing the Gulf War operations for Desert Storm in late 1990 and early 1991, General H. Norman Schwarzkopf, as Commander in Chief of the Central Command, exercised constraints over press coverage. For example, he declined often to answer journalists' questions that could aid the enemy by his responses. He had no alternative throughout the Iraqi–Kuwait crisis, for he would risk the death and destruction of his own troops if the enemy knew his position, capabilities, and plans ahead of time. *But* compared to other wars throughout history, press coverage was extensive, aggressive, and round-the-clock, especially thanks to satellite TV news coverage such as CNN, ABC, CBS, and NBC. Reporters not only were allowed at the Central Command Headquarters in Riyadh, Saudi Arabia, but when the Saudis requested they leave, the Central Command insisted the press stay "in pools" and even cover the front lines. Journalists were permitted to remain in Baghdad, reporting from behind enemy lines for the duration of the combat. Likewise, on the home front, debates in Congress and the administration were freely aired in public.

Certainly, sectors of government such as defense, intelligence, and law enforcement require secrecy to operate, but compared to other governments, past and present, few work in the glare of public scrutiny as does American Bureaucracy. The rise of aggressive investigative reporters, armed with new tools of access such as the Federal Freedom and Information law and local "sunshine laws," as well as instant TV/radio "hook ups" and armies of lobbyists (in 1999 numbering 6,135 lobbying firms in Washington, D.C., along with 686 registered "foreign agents") make for few "bureaucratic secrets," at least in the long term. Chapter 3 will discuss more fully the open and porous qualities of modern American bureaucracy.

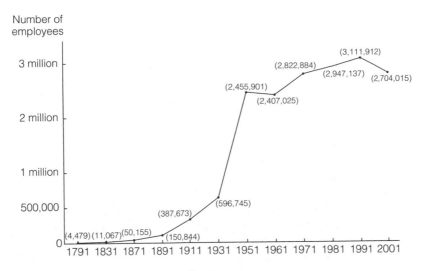

FIGURE 1.4   Growth of the federal civilian bureaucracy

Source: *Historical Statistics of U.S.* and *Statistical Abstract of the United States,* 2001.

Myth 7: Bureaucracy Grows Relentlessly

Actually, the bureaucratic growth rate has been highly uneven, as Figure 1.4 shows. In 1930 there were slightly over a half million federal employees and there were about 2.5 million in 1950. During the 20 years between 1930 and 1950, three critical changes forced the quadrupling of federal bureaucracy: Hot war and cold war demands caused the formation of new large public bureaucracies (Department of Defense, Veterans Administration, Central Intelligence Agency, Agency for International Development, U.S. Information Agency, National Security Council) and the growth of existing ones. *New technologies* also spawned postwar growth in new agencies (Atomic Energy Commission, National Science Foundation, the Air Force, Federal Aviation Administration, and Federal Communications Commission). The need for *regulating the economy and dealing with the economic hardship* caused by the Great Depression during the 1930s stimulated the creation of other new agencies (Security Exchange Commission, Farm Credit Administration, Social Security Administration, National Labor Relations Board, and others).

Since 1950, however, the total federal workforce has remained relatively stable at roughly 2.7 million civilians and 2.5 million military—give or take a few hundred thousand workers. Indeed, the federal employees dropped from 4 percent of the total work force in 1950 to 2 percent in 2001 or 31 employees (federal, civilian, and military) per 1,000 U.S. population in 1957, down to 21 per 1,000 in 1999. During the early 1980s the federal workforce dropped in absolute numbers in many agencies because of President Reagan's budget and personnel reductions, but overall since the early 1950s it has been fairly stable in absolute numbers (refer to Figure 1.4). Though as Table 1.5 stresses there have been considerable changes in the size of the federal workforce within various departments during the last decade.

Local–level public employment, however, grew from 6 million in 1960 to 10.8 million in 1981. This increase is the result of categorical, block grant, and revenue–sharing funds that were made available by the federal government during the 1960s and 1970s. Since 1980 state and local personnel continue to experience major employment increases from 10.8 million to 15.4 million (1997) as the public have asked local governments to assume greater roles and responsibilities. The point is that U.S. bureaucracy over the years has both grown and declined at uneven rates and is not "ever-growing." Moreover, some public agencies expand while others decline. Wartime pressures alone caused marked changes in the size of bureaucracy because of the changing pressures of defense requirements. Task demands for public services, such as defense, change over time, as does the size of public agencies. Indeed, some agencies even go out of business entirely. Herbert Kaufman, who examined federal organization survival rates since 1923, found that 15 percent of public organizations had disappeared, for an organizational death rate of 27.6 per 10,000 (one-half the death rate for business firms, which stands at 56.8 per 10,000 businesses). Bureaucracies, then, do die like other organizations.[15] Furthermore, recent studies indicate that when public bureaucracies grow it is largely because of legislative pressures. According to Gary J. Miller and Terry M. Moe, bureaucratic growth "depends upon conditions reflecting the way the legislature organizes itself for decision making. In particular, through the design of its committee system, the operation of rules of thumb, and the adoption of characteristic modes of oversight, the legislature sets the parameters of governmental growth. It is this structure imposed by the legislature that most fundamentally shapes the size of government, the performance of bureaucracy, and the impact of reforms."[16] Chapter 2 will describe U.S. bureaucracy's growth and change.

Myth 8: Bureaucracy Produces Only Red Tape

Rules and regulations or "red-tape" are part and parcel of every organization, including large and small businesses as well as large and small public agencies. A private doctor must follow the rules—both formal and informal—of his or her profession, just as a public employee must. Whether government has more or less red tape is by no means clear. Certainly there is no clear evidence one way or another. Furthermore, what may be red tape or needless regulation to one person may not be so for another. The Federal Aviation Administration's (FAA) 1990 rule banning smoking on domestic airplane flights may be both a boon to nonsmokers and a blow to smokers. An annual state-required auto emissions checkup may be a waste of time for an individual driver, but the annual test certainly helps to clean up air and can result in health benefits to an entire community. Securing a municipal business license or a zoning variance to operate a small business at home may well be a headache for the businessperson, but the enforcement of licensing and zoning laws also helps to maintain neighborhood privacy, community attractiveness, and public health. It may well be red tape to require a police officer to read a person his or her rights prior to making an arrest, but it is a very important legal means for protecting individual rights. Red tape can be viewed both ways—as needless bureaucratic rules and regulations and as essential requirements for health, happiness, and security. Much depends on an individual's perspective.

Yet, more importantly, red tape is not the major product of bureaucracy: U.S. bureaucracies and bureaucrats are incredibly diverse, doing many jobs that society deems essential. Some bureaucracies *are* regulatory agencies, such as the FAA, which regulates the airline industry, and the Federal Communications Commission (FCC), which regulates the airwaves. Some involve distributive or redistributive services, while others provide constituent services. The list of their activities is long and complex and will be discussed further in Chapter 2.

Myth 9: Bureaucracy Is All-Powerful and Out of Control

While bureaucracy is indeed the core system of U.S. government, as this text argues, in general, individual bureaus and bureaucrats have exercised enormous unchecked power and unfettered influence only for brief historical periods and within specific functional fields. As examples one can cite General Eisenhower's command of the D-Day invasion forces of Europe on June 6, 1944; General MacArthur's postwar occupation of Japan in the late 1940s; Admiral Rickover's development of the nuclear navy during the 1950s; Allen Dulles's direction of the CIA during the 1950s; and J. Edgar Hoover's tenure as the head of the FBI until the early 1970s. Such examples of unchecked bureaucratic power, however, are quite rare and are generally confined to unique individuals with forceful personalities operating in unusual times of stress or crisis. The truth is that power varies enormously from agency to agency and from policy field to policy field. The bulk of U.S. bureaucracy is composed of small, fragmented organizations exercising limited influence over the lives of the general population (see Tables 1.2 and 1.3). What effective power do the 450 employees at the American Battle Monuments Commission or the dozen bureaucrats at the Kern County Mosquito Abatement District have over our lives? Not much. But others are powerful, such as the Federal Reserve System, which regulates interest rates and other monetary matters, or, say, a particular state highway department, and they very well may be a source of both political clout and big-ticket public expenditures.

Yet, even these agencies certainly are not all-powerful or out of control, for every public agency operates within the political context of numerous external checks placed upon it by the legislature, the chief executive, the courts, and outside pressure groups. All agencies in government are dependent and interdependent upon a variety of other political institutions for their enabling legislation, annual budgets, personnel authorizations, and policy oversight. Indeed, as Figure 1.5 shows, so many federal agencies share in trade-environmental policy-making and implementation that no *one or few* can control policy overall in these fields. Fragmentation and lack of coordination due to dispersion of authority are critical problems today in shaping policy. Chapter 5 will discuss this problem in more detail.

U.S. Trade Representative (USTR)
Leads interagency task force on trade/environment
Represents United States at GATT
Cochairs (with EPA) U.S. delegation to trade/environment discussions at OECD
Leads negotiations on North American Free Trade Agreement (NAFTA)

Environmental Protection Agency (EPA)
Participates in interagency trade/environment task force
Cochairs (with USTR) U.S. delegation to trade/environment discussions at OECD
Coordinates with Mexico on U.S.-Mexico border environmental matters
Participates in NAFTA working groups
Receives recommendations from the Trade and Environment Committee of the National Advisory Council for Environmental Policy and Technology

State Department
Leads U.S. delegation at most international environmental negotiations
Participates in interagency trade/environment task force

Commerce Department
Participates in interagency trade/environmental task force
Has administrative units with specialized responsibility, including:
International Trade Administration
National Oceanic and Atmospheric Administration

Other departments and agencies with specific missions as relevant:
Agriculture Department
Treasury Department
Justice Department
Labor Department
Interior Department
Energy Department
Food and Drug Administration
U.S. International Trade Commission
Specialized export promotion and foreign assistance agencies:
U.S. Agency for International Development (US AID)
Export-Import Bank of the United States (Eximbank)
Overseas Private Investment Corporation (OPIC)
U.S. Trade and Development Program (US TDP)

FIGURE 1.5   Key federal agencies with responsibilities pertinent to trade and environment policy today

Source: Office of Technology Assessment, 1992.

Myth 10: Governmental Bureaucracy Is Inefficient and Wastes Resources

The most frequent charge leveled at bureaucracy is that it is inefficient. However, efficiency must be measured against something. Normally it is defined by the achievement of the greatest returns for the least amount of resources or energy expended. As Clarence Ridley and Herbert Simon determined in their classic book *Measuring Municipal Services* (1940), efficiency of public enterprise depends upon what goals or objectives are established and which resources and personal energies are expended. Certainly in the private sector, where the goal is the production of one or more types of goods and services and where the bottom line is quantifiable, profit and loss statements can be relatively good indicators of corporate efficiency or inefficiency. In the public sector, where goals are diverse and outputs are often nonquantifiable, the efficiency of public agencies proves much harder to determine. Is the U.S. Army efficient? It is hard to say, because there is only *one* U.S. Army, and its missions are multiple, frequently nonquantifiable, and certainly not concerned with producing more goods for the least cost. What are the "returns" for winning a battle? Or preventing a war? Here, achieving the safety and security of the nation through preventing or winning wars is more important than simply the efficient use of military resources (i.e., counting the numbers of guns fired or bullets used or reducing body counts or weapons costs—to take such logic to the absurd!).

Indeed, efficiency is only one of the goals, priorities, and values of most governmental bureaucracies. Government agencies are often mandated by law to emphasize other values than the bottom line. Take, for instance, the Federal Express Company vs. the U.S. Postal Service. Federal Express pioneered overnight parcel delivery service in the United States. Today it is a thriving multimillion-dollar business. However, Federal Express became successful by selectively servicing high-volume markets, namely, big cities, not small out-of-the-way places. The post office, by contrast, is mandated by law to provide daily mail service to *everyone,* regardless of location. Efficiency and profitability are not the sole aims of the post office, nor can they be, as long as Congress requires the post office to service *everyone equally.* Here equity is emphasized as a clear priority over efficiency. Certainly the postal service could make much more money by closing small post offices, by ending rural mail delivery, and by concentrating solely upon high-volume—and high-revenue—post offices. But neither Congress nor the general public would tolerate such selective service. Fairness, equity, and democracy are key critical values that public agencies must be concerned with, not just efficiency (though efficiency *is* an important value). Much of what government does cannot be measured only by the yardstick of efficiency, because of the multiple values that come into play in the public arena.

But the accusation of inefficiency is usually tied to the problem of wasted resources or, more specifically, wasted monies. No doubt waste can be found in many areas of governmental bureaucracy, especially in budgets with the magnitude of the federal budget, which stands at well over one trillion dollars, and with governmental spending of over one-quarter of the Gross National Product. But increasingly fewer goods, services, and activities are actually being provided and performed by the federal government. One-half of the annual federal budget is today expended on interest payments for the national debt, on direct payments to individuals, such as military pensions or social security benefits, and on direct transfers to others (entitlement programs). One-third of the remainder goes to grants-in-aid to states and localities, and another third goes to other institutions and businesses in exchange for various contracted services. That means that only 5 to 7 percent of the entire federal budget is being used by the government to run its own programs *and to waste at its own discretion!* In other words, a comparatively small amount of the federal budget is discretionary funding used to run civilian agencies. Most federal expenditures are expenditures *mandated* through entitlements, contracts, direct grants, debt servicing, and so on. Limited funds are available for bureaucrats to use for their own purposes— either efficiently or inefficiently! Chapter 6 will discuss some of these factors and their implications and complexities in light of the problems associated with the contemporary bureaucratic system.

Myth 11: Bureaucrats Are Unrepresentative of the U.S. Population

The rebuttal to this statement largely turns on the meaning of *unrepresentative*. If the term is used to describe bureaucracy's numerical similarity with the entire U.S. population, then U.S. bureaucrats are probably more representative of the country as a whole than any other institution in U.S. society—Congress, the Judiciary, labor unions, businesses, churches, and so on. As Figure 1.6 shows, minority and gender diversity has increased since 1990. But, public agencies vary considerably in the percentages of females, minorities, and handicapped individuals they employ. Some, such as Health and Human Services and the Treasury, exceed those particular groups' percentages in the general population. In 1990 HHS had 64 percent of its work force made up of females; 36 percent were minorities, and about 1 percent handicapped. More than half of some combat units in the U.S. military are made up of blacks (compared to 12 percent of blacks in the entire U.S. population). And some agencies clearly "underrepresent" the total population, as in the case of females (51 percent of the entire population), who are employed by the U.S. Postal Service and the Department of the Interior in percentages of 25 and 32.7, respectively. Or at the local level, two-thirds of protective services are made up of white males, whereas 70 percent of black females are employed in three categories: office, clerical, and paraprofessional work.

These statistics, nevertheless, can be highly deceptive because they tell us little about the *actual* composition of each agency's workforce much beyond very simplistic totals in terms of percentages of ethnic, racial, or sexual identification. As Chapter 4 of this text will discuss, each bureau or agency generally reflects the characteristics of the major clientele it serves. The Bureau of Land Management, for example, which manages the federal grazing land in western states, is heavily "stocked" with employees from the West, who are mostly graduates of land-grant agricultural schools, and thus is highly reflective of its principal "users," western cattlemen and ranchers. By contrast, the U.S. Foreign Service within the State Department tends to be dominated by Ivy-League, liberal arts graduates from generally upper-middle-class families, again reflecting the chief characteristics of its clients, namely, international corporations, diplomatic organizations, and foreign governments. The truth is that the *overall* composition of U.S. bureaucracy is perhaps more representative of the population than any

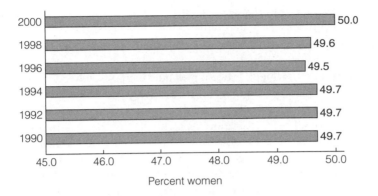

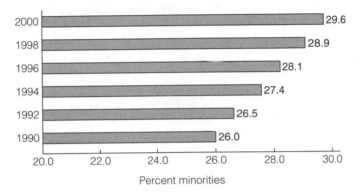

FIGURE 1.6   Trends in percentage of women and minorities in federal government white-collar occupations, 1990–2000

Source: *U.S. Office of Personnel Management, Central Personnel Data File.*

other U.S. institution, but particular bureaus and agencies often reflect the peculiar characteristics, traditions, and demands of the clientele they service. More will be said about this subject in Chapter 4.

Myth 12: Bureaucracy Is the Same Everywhere in the World

The last five decades of rich and intensive research into comparative politics and administration have taught us much about the uniqueness of the U.S. bureaucratic system. According to these studies, none in the world quite matches the U.S. bureaucracy in structure, design, personnel, and controls.

The United States, according to Gabriel A. Almond and Sidney Verba, has a unique "civil culture" characterized by "broad-based pluralism and mass participation," including "communications and persuasion, a culture of consensus and diversity, a culture that permitted change but moderated it." In their words, the

United States stands out as "a participant civic culture" by comparison with the rest of the world.[17]

Six features of U.S. political culture mark its bureaucratic system as being distinctive.

First, whereas continental European bureaucracies tended to be created "overnight," normally by "a great leader" (i.e., Frederick the Great in Prussia or Napoleon in France), the development of U.S. bureaucracy took place gradually over two centuries. The most important effect of such gradualism on public administration, as Ferrel Heady observes: "was that the administrative system was able to take shape feature by feature in a way that reflected the political changes and was consonant with them. Political and administrative adaptations were concurrent and fairly well balanced, but the political theme was dominant. At no time has the administrative apparatus been called upon to assume the whole burden of government because of a breakdown of the political machinery."[18]

Second, the United States, largely because it was and is "a participant civic culture," treated professional bureaucrats throughout much of its history with a contempt uncharacteristic of other nations. In most other societies, working for government is considered a high-status job, but it certainly is not in the United States. Jobs in public bureaucracy carry far less prestige than jobs in the largely private sector fields of law, medicine, and business. As a result, the United States was slow to professionalize its public services and relied heavily upon mass citizen participation to do much of the government work normally assigned to professional careerists in other countries. Not until 1883 did the U.S. Congress pass a civil service law (covering then only 10 percent of the federal workforce), nearly 30 years *after* the British Northcote-Trevelyn Report of 1854 had substantially professionalized their civil service and more than two centuries after the French minister Richelieu had created an intendant system, a rudimentary civil service, for collecting taxes for King Louis XIII. As Frederick Mosher has argued, it was not until the mid-twentieth century that the United States could claim to have a "professionalized civil service,"[19] considerably later than any other western nation. Even today U.S. bureaucracy contains widespread participation by amateurs and volunteers, as will be described in Chapter 6.

Third, the structure of U.S. bureaucracy likewise shows remarkable differences from that in the rest of the world. The bureaucracies in most other countries operate with uniformly structured ministries that are clearly differentiated from the legislature and responsible to top-level elected officials, who in turn are responsible to an elected parliament. Top ministerial posts are political, but just a rung below them are permanent senior civil servants who run ministry affairs over the long term. In the United States on the other hand, executive departments, again as Ferrel Heady notes, are "the major entities but included in the executive branch are a plethora of regulatory commissions, government corporations and other units. Decisions as to executive reorganization as well as many other matters about their operations are basically legislative matters."[20] In the United States, furthermore, relationships between the senior political officials and permanent careerists in agencies are often highly ambiguous. They are very often temporary, fluid situations leading to what Hugh Heclo calls "a government of strangers."[21]

Fourth, much of the development of western bureaucracies is based upon class lines, often rigid ones that allow little mobility between different classes inside bureaucracies. The British Civil Service is divided into three major classes—clerical, executive, and administrative (in ascending order of class "eliteness" and functional responsibilities). The French have their highly meritocratic "grands corps," drawn largely from their elite civil service training academy, Ecole National d' Administration. Germany divides its civil service into lower, medium, and higher classes. The United States operates its bureaucracy without an apparent class system. There is no "Oxbridge" or "Grands Corps" tradition in this country. Certainly there is a hierarchy of officialdom imposed by a government service (GS) rating structure, but securing a GS slot is based upon open, competitive exams that are practical, specialized, and directly related to the ability to perform specific tasks necessary for fulfilling the duties of the post. Task, not class, is the chief determinant of personnel assignments in the system. Thus the U.S. bureaucratic system reflects a far greater degree of mobility than others. If there tend to be rigidities inside the U.S. system, they are blockages horizontally—for various reasons there may be fewer personnel transfers between agencies than elsewhere in the world.

Fifth, on the whole, European bureaucracies remain much more closed, prone to secrecy, and controlled from the top down than those in the United States. As Brian Chapman and James B. Christoph point out, in Great Britain and on the Continent, the attention of civil servants is focused on the political minister in charge of the department as "the key political referent in their lives as officials."[22] The political ministers set policy and speak to "the outside world." Loyalty from subordinates is expected. Ministerial responsibility, coupled with hierarchical loyalty to the person at the top, is the chief way of securing administrative control. By contrast, control over the U.S. bureaucracy issues from diverse sources—legislature, judiciary, chief executive, other agencies, outside special interests, internal rules, procedures, and professional norms. United States bureaucratic involvement in policy-making processes is prized, even rewarded, which leads to considerably more openness and participation by bureaucrats in what most foreign observers would regard as "the political arena." As Wallace Sayre remarks, "The American civil servant who earns high and lasting prestige in his society is usually one who most completely breaks the mask of anonymity and becomes a public figure."[23] As a result, the U.S. system is less "closed" and more "noisy" than its European counterparts and even third world and former communist bureaucracies. Controls are also exercised less from the top down and more from the bottom up, from the inside to the outside, and from the outside to the inside.

Finally, as Figure 1.7 indicates, compared to other Western nations, the United States operates with one of the leanest bureaucracy per capital, comprising 15 percent of the total U.S. employment and is the most decentralized bureaucratic system. Whereas German and the Netherlands local governments employ 28 percent and 30 percent, respectively, of total government employees, 58 percent of the government workforce in the United States is located in cities, counties, and special districts.

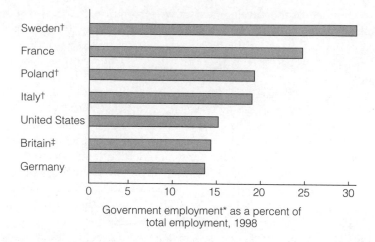

FIGURE 1.7   Government employment* as a percent of total
employment, 1998

Source: As cited in *The Economist* January 15, 2000, p. 53.

In sum, U.S. bureaucracy is very different from bureaucracies in other parts of the world. Most other bureaucracies, as Sayre remarks, opt for "a more orderly and symmetrical, a more prudent, a more cohesive and more powerful bureaucracy," whereas the United States has chosen instead "a more internally competitive, a more experimental, a noisier and less coherent, a less powerful bureaucracy within its own governmental system, but a more dynamic one."[24]

What sources have created this unique U.S. system? What are the varieties of its "experimental" forms? Its less coherent arrangements? Its "less powerful" but "more dynamic" functions and roles in society? Its distinguishing features? These questions will be discussed in the next chapters.

WHAT IS U.S. PUBLIC BUREAUCRACY?

Some basic patterns and contours of U.S. public bureaucracy emerge from the foregoing discussion. Puncturing some of the popular myths and describing some of the major realities of U.S. bureaucracy tell us a good deal about its basic attributes. To characterize briefly its salient features, U.S. public bureaucracy:

- Is made up of roughly 87,000 separate units rather than one massive whole
- Is a heterogeneous variety of organizations, some large, like the Department of Defense, but most quite small, employing relatively few people

- Is broken up among federal, state, and local levels, with the bulk of public organizations found at the local level
- Is sometimes expanding in size and sometimes contracting
- Is geographically distributed fairly evenly across the nation
- Performs a variety of central functions deemed useful or necessary by society: the bulk of the federal bureaucracy is defense-related while much of the local level is heavily education-oriented
- Consumes a major share of the Gross National Product, though increasingly at the federal level these monies go for "contracting-out" services with only a very small percent of federal budgets spent on work done "in-house"
- Is made up of several thousand occupational categories containing increasingly professional employees
- Is neither "all-powerful" nor "out of control" but very much dependent, bounded, and controlled by several institutions such as legislatures, courts, elected chief executives, and other agencies as well as by special interests and political groups outside government
- With rare exceptions operates with a significant degree of openness to the public and the press, by comparison with other nations
- Is hard to measure "its outputs" in terms of its efficiency or inefficiency because of unique, nonquantifiable outputs and diverse goals, purposes, and activities
- Is highly representative of the U.S. population though particular agencies reflect salient features of their specific clientele groups
- Is very different from other public systems in the world because of its fragmented, decentralized and diverse structures, its experimental nature, its political participation, and its gradual development
- Is involved with "core functions" in government, particularly in making decisions involving four kinds of critical policy issues: regulative, distributive, redistributive, and constituent
- Along with Congress, the president, and the courts is actively engaged in the entire spectrum of duties and responsibilities of public policy making and the governing of the United States

In brief, U.S. public bureaucracy is composed of fragmented, heterogeneous, dispersed, fluid, open, professionalized, and "localized" organizations that come in numerous and diverse shapes and sizes and have varied powers and purposes and exercise various degrees of influence over the lives of citizens. United States public bureaucracies stand at the very heart of the policy-making and governing processes, for along with Congress, the presidency, and the courts, they actively engage in shaping and making public policies affecting the lives of all Americans.

WHY STUDY AMERICAN PUBLIC BUREAUCRACY?

Precisely because U.S. bureaucracy stands at the very heart of the governing processes and influences the ways we live, work, and act, bureaucratic institutions are worth knowing about. Students of U.S. government devote considerable attention to the study of the legislative processes and to an examination of how the presidency influences decisions in government and how the courts use their interpretative functions to affect lives and livelihoods. But frequently the most critical element of bureaucracy's role within U.S. government is neglected or mentioned only in passing. A typical U.S. government textbook devotes only a few pages, if that, to bureaucracy's roles and influences, while the presidency, the Congress, and the Supreme Court may be given several chapters of commentary, description, and analysis. Although those institutions attract more attention from the media, a well-rounded understanding of governmental processes also necessitates a study of bureaucracy. Bureaucracy is not merely the passive, routine implementor of the laws enacted elsewhere in government. It is not a machine. It is an active partner in the political processes and as such is involved in deciding "who gets what, where, when, and how." Understanding how these decisional processes work, why they work the way they do, the manner in which they affect our lives, and their possibilities for change and reform is not only intellectually satisfying, it is a basic step to becoming knowledgeable about how modern U.S. government operates.

Further, bureaucracy is an increasing source of employment. Knowing about possibilities for employment in this area and about the setting where many work today—the possibilities and constraints of working within U.S. public bureaucracy—will be helpful to those thinking about careers in this field.

For those who never will set foot in a public agency, it can be useful to know about bureaucracy. Few professionals, businesses, non-profits, or unions are unaffected today by a government agency's licensing, policing, regulation, contracts, or prohibitions. We all, sooner or later, for better or worse—or for better *and* worse—are influenced by the activities of U.S. public bureaucracy. It is to our own advantage to know how public bureaucracy works. It serves our self-interest to be as informed as we can be about this subject, which is so vital to our lives and livelihoods. It is also a part of being a responsible citizen.

HOW THIS TEXT APPROACHES
AMERICAN PUBLIC BUREAUCRACY

Several years ago Stephen Bailey wrote a delightful essay in *Public Administration Review* entitled "A Structured Interaction Pattern for Harpsichord and Kazoo."[25] His essay was partly whimsical, partly autobiographical, and very much true to life. In essence, it recounted a day in the life of a political science professor (Bailey) who suddenly found himself elected mayor of Middletown, Connecticut. During the day, Professor Bailey taught the *theory* of U.S. government, in which he often stressed its neat, rational, ideal format. At night he served as the part-time leader of a mid-sized, complex municipality. As its chief administrator, he regularly had to cope with the messy, often irrational difficulties of dealing with irate citizens who did not get their garbage picked up or snow removed and with city hall employees who wanted better pay. By day, Bailey could be the detached outside observer (the harpsichord approach to viewing ideally what is government); by night he often found himself being the "artful improviser" on the inside (the kazoo approach actually running government).

Bailey's article stressed an important point: Things look different from the inside of municipal bureaucracy than they do from the outside. This is not to say that one view is necessarily superior to the other. A general, theoretical overview is essential to a grasp of the panorama of bureaucracy, whereas the insider's perspective is equally useful in appreciating the hard realities of making government operate and in sensing that the parts of the whole do not always fit neatly together.

This book is different from others on bureaucracy. It will attempt to capture *both* dimensions of U.S. bureaucracy—the big picture as well as the reality of its operations. Each chapter will discuss an important theoretical component of U.S. bureaucracy based upon a systems model—the grand view from the outside. Each chapter through numerous examples will relate how the theoretical elements discussed *actually operate*. An attempt will be made to appreciate both the theoretical and practical realities of U.S. bureaucracy *and* how both dimensions interrelate. In this manner, students will be exposed to both the theory and practice of U.S. public bureaucracy—the view from outside *and* from within.

What theoretical model is most useful in gaining a sense of the whole from the outside? What model will provide an overview of the structure and a framework for analysis? How can we make sense out of the whole as well as the parts?

While there are numerous approaches to the study of bureaucracy, this book will utilize an open systems perspective to guide the general discussion of U.S. public bureaucracy. What is an open systems model? Why select this methodological framework? Basically, a systems model provides an effective way of viewing the whole as well as the parts and how they interrelate. Systems models are utilized in many fields—engineering, medicine, physics, and chemistry and in economics and the other social sciences—as a tool for understanding the components of a field and how these components of a system work together and interact as an ongoing process. Some systems models are highly complex and methodologically quantified, such as those purporting to describe how the entire U.S. economy operates, but a simplified, nonquantifiable systems model will suffice for illustrating how U.S. public bureaucracy works. This systems model will include, as Figure 1.8 illustrates, a discussion of (1) the forms of bureaucratic institutions and the sources that gave rise to U.S. bureaucracy; (2) the environment within which these units operate and the basic inputs into the bureaucratic system that are the chief sources for agency growth, decline, and stability; (3) the internal conversion processes or the elements and activities inside bureaucratic structures by which inputs are turned into outputs; (4) the outputs (goods, services, and activities) of bureaucracy; (5) the manner by which these various outputs are "fed back" into the general environment; and (6) future of the bureaucratic system as a whole and how it shapes society's future.

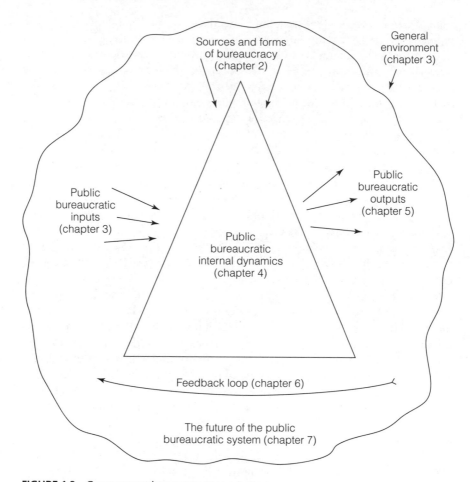

FIGURE 1.8 Government bureaucracy as a system

Each of the next six chapters will examine one of the aforementioned elements of U.S. public bureaucracy. Chapter 2 will look at the rise of U.S. bureaucracy—the sources, structures, and variety of public bureaucracies in the United States. What gave rise to U.S. bureaucracy? Why there are so many various kinds of organizations? What are the contemporary forms and functions through which U.S. public bureaucracy operates today? Its formal policy–making roles? Its formal processes?

Chapter 3 focuses upon the major types of inputs into bureaucracy: What is the general environment of public organizations? What are the major sources of growth, decline, and stability? How do contemporary socioeconomic factors, political actors, and institutional processes influence every public agency?

Chapter 4 looks inside bureaucracy: its basic internal structures, subsystems, major groups, and the political and professional elites that direct its activities and outputs. How do these elements influence the work that public agencies perform in society?

Chapter 5 examines the types of bureaucratic outputs: What are the major products of U.S. bureaucracy? How are these produced? What gamesmanship is involved? What are the institutional forces and the political situations that support or impede these outputs? How do these outputs influence our lives?

Chapter 6 studies the "feedback loop." What are the major varieties of bureaucratic feedback? Their sources? Their impacts on the departments, agencies, and priorities in government?

Chapter 7 will view the future of U.S. bureaucracy from the standpoint of the overall bureaucratic system. What are the major trends influencing bureaucracy in the twenty-first century? What forces strengthen or weaken its role and institutions within society? Given the contemporary dynamics of the bureaucratic system as a whole, how can bureaucracy tomorrow best be made to serve and be responsive to the public interest? What will ensure that it is controlled by citizens and remains responsible to those individuals it serves?

SUMMARY OF KEY POINTS

Public bureaucracy plays a central role in governing the 21st century United States, and it therefore has been described throughout this chapter as "the core system of U.S. government." It decisively determines important policy questions in U.S. life today and is the chief institution for implementing those policy choices. However, bureaucracy, even though it is pervasive and critical to running our society, often cannot be seen, recognized or easily comprehended. Partly for these reasons many myths surround its purposes, structure, and activities. Several of these myths have been examined and exploded in this opening chapter, such as the myths that state that bureaucracy is "too large," "out of control," "produces only red tape," and so on. From this discussion about bureaucratic myths emerges bureaucracy's general modern characteristics as well as a systems model for comprehending its elements and its totality. The following chapters will discuss these major elements of the bureaucratic system and how public bureaucracy operates today as the central system of U.S. governance.

KEY TERMS

public bureaucracy	formal rules	core system of U.S. government
myths about bureaucracy	bureaucratic representation	
bureaucratic system		bureaucratic inefficiency
policy-making roles	turnover rates	bureaucratic secrecy
public vs. private bureaucracy	red tape	feedback loop
	bureaucratic inputs	bureaucratic outputs

REVIEW MATERIAL

Review Questions

1. How would you describe the major characteristics of U.S. bureaucracy? Its actual practice and operation?

2. What are some of the popular notions or "myths" about bureaucracy you have expressed or heard expressed in discussions with friends, family, and others?

3. What are the sources of these opinions? Are these beliefs well founded?

4. In general, can you describe in what ways U.S. public bureaucracy plays a central role in society? And more specifically in your life?

5. Based on your reading of this chapter, how do you define public bureaucracy? And why is it worth studying?

Class Debate

Pro/Con—Resolved that Americans' intense dislike of their bureaucracy would stop if bureaucrats were referred to by their specific names like police, fire fighters, the military, foreign service officers, or teachers.

Student Homework Assignment

Randomly interview five people about their views on bureaucracy: What do they associate with the term "bureaucracy"? Is it a positive or negative point of view? Are these views related to any of the myths discussed in this chapter? Where do their ideas about this topic derive from? Based upon your small sample survey, how would you recommend that the public might be better educated about bureaucracy, or at least gain a more realistic understanding of its work and influence on their lives?

Case Analysis

Read "The Blast in Centralia No. 5" in any edition of Richard Stillman's *Public Administration: Concepts and Cases.* From the vantage point of the major characters in the case study, how do you think each one saw public bureaucracy and, in turn, how did that definition influence their own actions in the case? Inspector Scanlon? Director of the Department of Mines and Minerals Medill? Governor Green? District UMW Union Leader "Spud White"? Centralia Mine Manager Brown? The Centralia Miners of Local 52 who wrote "The Save Our Lives Letter"? Can you generalize whether or not myths about bureaucracy that each individual held played a role in the mine disaster?

NOTES

1. As quoted in Reinhard Bendix, *Max Weber: An Intellectual Portrait* (New York: Doubleday, 1960), p. 464.

2. Michel Crozier, *The Bureaucratic Phenomenon* (Chicago, IL: University of Chicago Press, 1964), p. 3.

3. C. N. Parkinson, *Parkinson's Law and Other Studies in Administration* (Boston, MA: Houghton Mifflin, 1957), p. 16.

4. E. Pendleton Herring, *Public Administration and the Public Interest* (New York: McGraw-Hill, 1936), p. 10.

5. Henry Jacoby, *The Bureaucratization of the World* (Berkeley: University of California Press, 1973), p. 32.

6. Robert K. Merton et al., *A Reader in Bureaucracy* (New York: Free Press, 1952), p. 6.

7. David Nachmias and David H. Rosenbloom, *Bureaucratic Government USA* (New York: St. Martin's Press, 1980), p. 18.

8. Charles Goodsell, *The Case for Bureaucracy* (Chatham, NJ: Chatham House, 1983), p. 2.

9. Beverly A. Cigler and Heidi L. Neiswender, "Bureaucracy in the Introductory American Government Textbook," *Public Administration Review* 51(5) (Sept./Oct. 1991): 444.

10. Goodsell, *Case for Bureaucracy,* p. 14.

11. Carl J. Friedrich, *Constitutional Government and Democracy,* 4th ed. (Waltham, MA: Blaisdell, 1968), p. 38.

12. Harold Lasswell, *Politics: Who Gets What, When, How* (New York: McGraw-Hill, 1936), p. 7.

13. Theodore Lowi, "Four Systems of Policy, Politics and Choice," *Public Administrator Review* 32 (July/Aug 1972): 298–310.

14. Frederick C. Mosher, *Democracy and the Public Service,* 2d ed. (New York: Oxford University Press, 1982), chapter 5.

15. Herbert Kaufman, *Are Government Organizations Immortal?* (Washington, DC: Brookings Institution, 1976), pp. 73–77.

16. Gary J. Miller and Terry M. Moe, "Bureaucrats, Legislators, and the Size of Government," *American Political Science Review* (1983), p. 320.

17. Gabriel A. Almond and Sidney Verba, *The Civic Culture* (Princeton, NJ: Princeton University Press, 1963), p. 8.

18. Ferrel Heady, *Public Administration: A Comparative Perspective,* 3d ed. (New York: Marcel Dekker, 1985), p. 207.

19. Frederick C. Mosher, *Democracy and the Public Service,* 2d ed. (New York: Oxford University Press, 1982), chapter 5.

20. Heady, *Public Administration,* p. 209.

21. Hugh Heclo, *A Government of Strangers* (Washington, DC: Brookings Institution, 1977). Heclo's entire book relates to this theme and the problems it raises for U.S. government.

22. As quoted in Heady, *Public Administration,* p. 214.

23. Wallace Sayre, "Bureaucracies: Some Contrasts in Systems," *Indian Journal of Public Administration,* 10 (2) (1964): 228.

24. Ibid., p. 223.

25. Stephen K. Bailey, "A Structured Interaction Pattern for Harpsichord and Kazoo," *Public Administration Review* 14 (Summer 1954): 202–4.

FURTHER READING

The term *bureaucracy* has eighteenth-century French origins: *bureaucratie,* apparently from the woolen cloth (burel) used to cover writing desks; thus the term for the place of such activity—bureaus, or, more broadly, bureaucracy. For an interesting review of the history of the idea of bureaucracy, read Martin Albrow's *Bureaucracy* (1970).

Serious scholarly study of bureaucracy began in the twentieth century largely because of the work of the German scholar Max Weber (1864–1920). His fragments of writings on this subject were published posthumously and did not become widely available in the United States until after World War II via such books as H. H. Gerth and C. Wright Mills (eds.), *From Max Weber* (1946), and Reinhard Bendix, *Max Weber: An Intellectual Portrait* (1960). Marianne Weber's biography of her husband, *Max Weber: A Biography* (1975), provides an especially good review of his life and ideas, and more recently, John P. Diggins, *Max Weber* (1996).

Taylor Cole and Carl Friedrich's *Responsible Bureaucracy* (1932) was probably the first book published in the United States with *bureaucracy* in the title and that heavily drew upon Weberian thinking. During the postwar era sociologists in particular studied this subject extensively with numerous fruitful results. See especially Peter M. Blau and Marshall W. Meyer, *Bureaucracy in Modern Society*, 2d ed. (1971) and Robert K. Merton et al., *A Reader in Bureaucracy* (1952) as worthy heirs of Weberian traditions.

The post–World War Two literature in public administration, though not titled as books on bureaucracy, contains several distinguished and diverse contributions to our understanding of bureaucracy. Included in this literature are: Herbert Simon, *Administrative Behavior* (1947); Charles Hyneman, *Bureaucracy in a Democracy* (1950); Paul Appleby, *Big Democracy* (1945); Dwight Waldo, *The Administrative State* (1948); Fritz Morstein Marx (ed.), *Elements of Public Administration,* 2d ed. (1959); Paul Appleby, *Policy and Administration* (1949); John Gaus, *Reflections on Public Administration* (1947); Harold Stein (ed.), *Public Administration and Policy Development* (1952); and Frederick C. Mosher, *Democracy and the Public Service,* 2d ed. (1982).

Political science literature since the 1960s has produced a varied, rich, and distinguished literature on bureaucracy that includes Anthony Downs, *Inside Bureaucracy* (1967); Graham Allison, *Essence of Decision* (1971); Henry Jacoby, *The Bureaucratization of the World* (1973); David Beetham, *Bureaucracy* (1987); Harold Seidman, *Politics, Position and Power,* 5th ed. (1997); Francis E. Rourke, *Bureaucracy, Politics, and Public Policy,* 4th ed. (1996); Donald P. Warwick, *A Theory of Public Bureaucracy* (1975); Peter Woll, *American Bureaucracy,* 2d ed. (1977); Gary L. Wamsley and Mayer N. Zald, *The Political Economy of Public Organizations* (1973); Kenneth Meier, *Politics and the Bureaucracy* (1979); Douglas Yates, *Bureaucratic Democracy* (1982); David Nachmias and David H. Rosenbloom, *Bureaucratic Government USA* (1980); James Q. Wilson, *Bureaucracy* (1989); Gerald Garvey, *Facing the Bureaucracy* (1993); and B. Dan Wood and Richard W. Waterman, *Bureaucratic Dynamics: The Role of Bureaucracy in a Democracy* (1994). For useful surveys of recent literature on the topic, see Donald Kettl, "Public Administration," in Ada W. Finifter, *Political Science* (1993), as well as the opening essay in Larry B. Hill (ed.), *The State of Public Bureaucracy* (1992).

The past decade or so has seen numerous publications dealing with specialized perspectives on public bureaucracy. Themes of bureaucratic reform are found in Michael Barzelay, *Breaking through Bureaucracy* (1992); William T. Gormley, *Taming the Bureaucracy;* Jack H. Knott and Gary Miller, *Reforming Bu-*

reaucracy (1987); and Patricia Ingrahm and Donald Kettl (eds.), *Agenda for Excellence*. On the other hand, a good account of the limits of reform is George W. Downs and Patricia D. Larkey's *The Search for Government Efficiency* (1986). Issues of accountability and control are developed in Dennis Riley, *Controlling the Federal Bureaucracy* (1987); Judith Gruber, *Controlling Bureaucracies* (1987); and Bernard Rosen, *Holding Bureaucrats Accountable* 3rd ed. (1998). For a feminist perspective on the subject, read Kathy Ferguson, *The Feminist Case Against Bureaucracy* (1984).

Street-level studies of bureaucrats are discussed in Jeffery Prottas, *People-Processing* (1979) and Michael Lipsky, *Street-Level Bureaucracy* (1980). The broad comparativist overview is outlined in Joel D. Alerbach and Robert D. Putnam, *Bureaucrats & Politicians in Western Democracies* (1981); Ferrel Heady, *Public Administration,* 5th ed. (1995); and Metin Heper (ed.), *The State and Public Bureaucracies* (1987). The specific problems of legislative-bureaucratic relationships are developed in Cathy M. Johnson, *The Dynamics of Conflict between Bureaucrats and Legislators* (1992) and Douglas R. Arnold, *Congress and the Bureaucracy* (1980); relationships between bureaucracy and markets in Donald Kettl, *Sharing Power* (1993) and Charles Wolf, *Markets or Governments* (1988); relations between bureaucrats and professionals in Jeffrey Glanz, *Bureaucracy and Professionalism* (1991); and relationships with citizens in Bryan D. Jones, *Service Delivery in the City* (1980) and Eugene Lewis, *American Politics in a Bureaucratic Age* (1988). For two useful readers in this field, see Frederick S. Lane (ed.), *Current Issues in Public Administration* 6th ed. (1999) as well as Camilla Stivers, (ed.), *Democracy, Bureaucracy, and the Study of Administration* (2000).

For a sampling of the harsh critics of bureaucracy read: Albert Jay Nock, *Our Enemy the State* (1935); Ludwig von Mises, *Bureaucracy* (1944); C. Northcote Parkinson, *Parkinson's Law and Other Studies in Administration* (1957); William A. Niskanen, *Bureaucracy* (1971); J. Peter Grace, *Burning Money* (1984); Martin L. Gross, *The Government Racket* (1992); and George Roche, *America by the Throat* (1983).

For a good counter to such polemics, read: Charles and William Beard, "The Case for Bureaucracy" (1993), reprinted in the *Public Administration Review* (1986); Harlan Cleveland, "The Case for Bureaucracy," *New York Times Magazine* (1963); Ralph Hummel, "The Case for Public Servants," and Charles Goodsell, "The Case against Deduced Pathology," both in *The Bureaucrat* (1988); and especially, Charles Goodsell, *The Case for Bureaucracy,* 3rd ed. (1993).

For more recent analytical writings probing distrust in government, read: Joseph Nye, et.al., *Why People Don't Trust Government* (1997); Gary Wills, *A Necessary Evil: A History of American Distrust in Government* (1999); Chery S. King and Camilla Stivers (eds.), *Government is US* (1998); and NAPA Report, *A Government to Trust and Respect* (1999).

Some of the great "classics" of literature that can tell us much more than most social science texts on this topic include: Norman Mailer's *The Naked and the Dead* (1948), James Gould Cozzens's *Guard of Honor* (1948), James Jones's *From Here to Eternity* (1951), and Herman Wouk's *The Caine Mutiny* (1951).

One should not overlook contemporary scholarly journals that cover the bureaucracy, such as *Public Administration Review, The American Review of Public*

Administration, Administrative Theory, and *Praxis,* and *Administration and Society,* as well as major government studies such as *Leadership for America* (1989), *Creating a Government That Works Better and Costs Less* (1993), and *Revitalizing State and Local Public Service* (1993).

WEB SITES

http://www.analytictech.com/mb021/bureau.htm: General subject overview with reference to Weber

http://www.pushback.com: "Pushing Back the Bureaucracy"

http://www.aspanet.org/: American Society for Public Administration home page

http://www.aspanet.org/publications/index.html: ASPA list of journals

http://www.house.gov/hoekstra/myth/home.html: The Myth of the Magical Bureaucracy

http://www.npr.gov/npr/library/nprrpt/annrpt/wrkcst94/create.html: Creating a Government that Works Better and Costs Less (1994)

http://www.outsights.com/systems/bop/bop.htm: Bureaucracy & Organizational Politics essay

http://plsc.uark.edu/plsc3253/public%20trust.htm: Ambivalence about "the" Bureaucracy

http://www.thisnation.com/bureaucracy.html: The Bureaucracy

http://www.usatoday.com/news/comment/2002/02/06/ncoppf.htm: Bureaucracy hurts reform

http://www.utoledo.edu/~ddavis/weber.htm: Max Weber brief

http://www.wf.net/~connally/blinks.html: Bureaucracy links

http://www.literature.org/authors/de-balzac-honore/bureaucracy/: Balzac's *Bureaucracy*

2

■

The Rise of American Bureaucracy

The United States did not always have much of a bureaucracy. Nor did it need one. When the United States began in 1789 as a "new nation," the population was under 4 million (compared with over 285 million today). The average American was a farmer. Nine out of ten people lived directly off the land (now less than 5 percent are farmers). Given the social simplicity and rural autonomy of 1789, few demands were made upon government. No autos meant that no roads had to be built, no drivers' licenses granted, no taxes raised for these purposes. There were no telephones, airlines, or television stations to regulate. No sewage, water, or utilities were provided for homes. Nor were clean air, pure food, and good public health then considered "essentials." Compulsory education through high school was unheard of. Geographic isolation of the "first new nation" prompted little need for a standing army, navy, and air force to defend "global American interests"; nor were there orbiting space shuttles, lunar landings, COMSAT weather satellites, social security retirement benefits, and medicare/medicaid protection. There was no need of a big bureaucracy to provide such services.

Now our 285 million population is over 70 times larger, more heterogeneous, more technologically dependent and interdependent, making greater and more complex demands upon government for a wide variety of goods and services. In particular, urbanization increased dependence upon government activities. In 1789 New York City had a population of 33,000; today it contains more than 8 million people, bringing enormous new demands upon municipal government for basic services. Fire, police, schools, welfare, zoning, water, sewage, and housing are just a few "basics" required by modern urban life. A complex social environment today promotes the development of complex bureaucratic services.

THE GROWTH AND EMERGENCE OF ORGANIZED FUNCTIONS OF GOVERNMENT BUREAUCRACY

Much as the hull of a ship gradually acquires barnacles, the United States acquired its bureaucratic institutions and services gradually as layers upon layers of responsibilities were added over the course of two hundred years. Different types of social pressures spawned, over a long time, bureaucracy's organizations. These new bureaucratic services or tasks were added slowly and unevenly. Sometimes the buildup of public bureaucracies was almost imperceptible; sometimes it was quite swift. First, the basic core bureaucratic service functions were created at the start of the new nation's existence; second, those involved with national economic development evolved in the nineteenth century; third, service-oriented tasks came into being in the late nineteenth century; fourth, the rise of regulatory agencies and government corporations services developed in the progressive period of the early twentieth century; fifth, surges in social service organizations arose during the Great Depression; sixth, the development of the large standing defense establishment appeared during World War II and the postwar Cold War era; and seventh, new forms of staff services as well as state and local bureaucracies grew throughout the twentieth century (see Figure 2.1). Each of these basic types of bureaucratic organizations will be examined in turn.

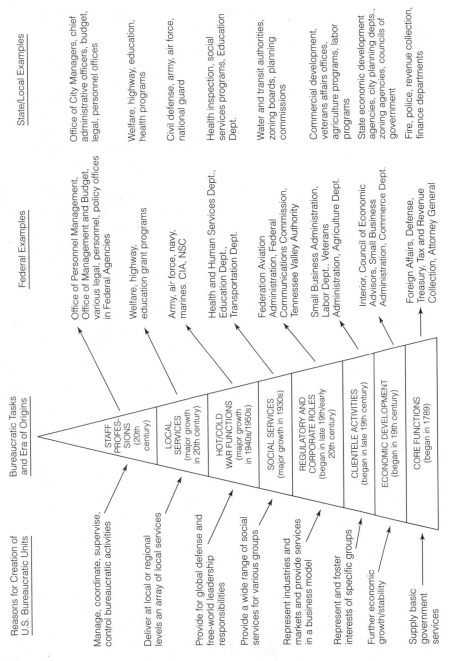

Figure 2.1   Modern U.S. bureaucracy

Creation of the Basic Core Service Functions

At the inception of the U.S. government in 1789, little bureaucracy was needed. Nevertheless, a few public agencies were necessary. Congress created the first executive departments to perform the essential core service functions. Core tasks are those which every nation (or state or municipality) develops in order to be a nation (or state or municipality). The United States set up five units in 1789 to carry out its core functions: the State Department to conduct its external affairs with other nations; the War Department and later the Navy Department (now combined into the Defense Department) to provide protection from threats from other nations; the Treasury Department to collect revenues, pay bills, settle accounts, and establish broad economic policies; the Attorney General's Office (now the Department of Justice) to represent legal cases and offer legal advice to the president and his Cabinet; and the Postal Services Department to run the national mail system, which was and still is essential for internal communications (the U.S. Postal Service now operates as an independent government corporation).

As indicated in Figure 2.2, the *department* (with the exception of the Office of the Attorney General, which became a department in 1870) was the key bu-

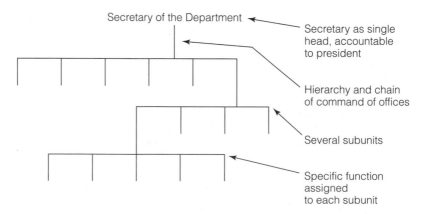

Figure 2.2   Boards or councils and departments organizational chart

reaucratic building block from the start. It was the basic organizational arrangement for providing critical national services, and departments still remain one of the basic organizational building blocks at federal, state, and local levels.

Why? Largely because the founding fathers had several unhappy experiences throughout the Revolutionary War in conducting administrative business with councils, boards, and legislative committees. These had proved to be slow, unresponsive, and irresponsible. General George Washington, as commander-in-chief of the Continental Armies during the Revolutionary War, continually complained about the inability of these committees to reach agreements and to decide and act expeditiously on critical military matters. When Washington became president, it was no small wonder that he, along with others in Congress who had experienced similar frustrations, instituted departments that were responsible to a single chief executive. The founding fathers had learned one bitter lesson from the Revolution—some*one* should be held responsible for doing the work of government, and the department format, they saw, was the most effective organizational model to facilitate that end.

The departmental head would be called a secretary (following the British model) and would be appointed, with the consent of the Senate, by the president and would serve at his pleasure. It was this last point that stirred the only real debates in Congress relative to the formation of these early departments. Some representatives argued that only with the consent of the Senate should the president be able to remove Cabinet officials, but the arguments of Congressmen James Madison (Virginia), Fisher Ames (Massachusetts), and others won out. They stressed the need for executive accountability for departmental affairs. One individual, the president, should be held responsible for executive affairs, and thus the president, not Congress, should be entrusted with the power to remove his key assistants. For a period after the Civil War, the Tenure of Office Act of 1867 restricted presidential powers of removal, but since the Supreme Court decision reached in *Myers v. the United States* (1926), the president has been given an essentially free hand in removing political appointees.

While small and informally run, the early departments were created to perform specific tasks, as evidenced by their enabling legislation, that were vital to the nation's well-being. The tasks at hand involved the basic work of the new nation. In short, defense, diplomacy, and functional necessities stimulated the creation and subsequent structure of these first bureaucracies. The State Department was established to conduct foreign affairs, maintain embassies and ambassadors abroad, and advise the president on international policies. Thomas Jefferson, the first secretary of state, not only managed diplomatic affairs but had multiple, often unrelated duties (as is the case today with many Cabinet secretaries). He was in charge of issuing copyrights and patents, minting currency, and taking the national census (largely because of Jefferson's interest in these subjects and because no one else wanted to assume responsibility for them). As Figure 2.3 indicates, the actual *title* of the act establishing the State Department did not even mention "foreign affairs." All this Jefferson performed with the assistance of just one chief clerk, seven assistant clerks, and one messenger.[1]

DEPARTMENT OF STATE
AN ACT TO PROVIDE FOR THE SAFE-KEEPING OF THE
ACTS; RECORDS AND SEAL OF THE UNITED STATES,
AND FOR OTHER PURPOSES, SEPTEMBER 15, 1789*

Section 1. *Be it enacted by the Senate and House of Representatives of the United States of America in Congress assembled,* That the Executive department, denominated the Department of Foreign Affairs, shall hereafter be denominated the Department of State, and the principal officer therein shall hereafter be called the Secretary of State.

Sec.2. *And be it further enacted,* That whenever a bill, order, resolution, or vote of the Senate and House of Representatives, having been approved and signed by the President of the United States, or not having been returned by him with his objections, shall become a law, or take effect, it shall forthwith thereafter be received by the said Secretary from the President; and whenever a bill, order, resolution, or vote, shall be returned by the President with his objections, and shall, on being reconsidered be agreed to be passed; and be approved by two-thirds of both Houses of Congress, and thereby become a law or take effect, it shall, in such case, be received by the said Secretary from the President of the Senate, or the speaker of the House of Representatives, in whichsoever House it shall last have been so approved; and the said Secretary shall, as soon as conveniently may be, after he shall receive the same, cause every such law, order, resolution, and vote, to be published in at least three of the public newspapers printed within the United States, and shall also cause one printed copy to be delivered to each Senator and Representative of the United States, and two printed copies duly authenticated to be sent to the Executive authority of each State; and he shall carefully preserve the originals, and shall cause the same to be recorded in books to be provided for the purpose.

Sec.3. *And be it futher enacted,* That the seal heretofore used by the United States in Congress assembled, shall be, and hereby is declared to be, the seal of the United States.

Sec.4. *And be it further enacted,* That the said Secretary shall keep the said seal, and shall make out and record, and shall affix the said seal to all civil commissions, to officers of the United States, to be appointed by the President by and with the advice and consent of the Senate, or by the President alone. *Provided,* That the said seal shall not be affixed to any commission, before the same shall have been signed by the President of the United States, nor to any other instrument or act, without the special warrant of the President therefore.

*1 Stat. 14 (1789). Sections 5, 6, and 7, providing procedural details, are here omitted.

Figure 2.3 From the very beginning, U.S. government bureaucracy was rooted in specific public laws approved by the legislature that established its mission(s), structure, and personnel. The law Congress enacted in 1789 created the Department of State, but note that the title of the act actually covered other duties as is the case for many agencies today.

The War Department supervised at first both the army and navy, but in 1798 the navy "spun off" into a separate department in order to prepare for the then-expected naval warfare with Great Britain: Here is an early example of how a crisis precipitated the formation of a new, independent department; in a similar fashion two centuries later, in 1977, the Energy Department, forged from bits and pieces of several smaller agencies, came into existence because of a national energy crisis and in 2001, after the 9/11 terrorist attacks, the Department of Homeland Security was created. Like the State Department, the War and Navy departments were small operations, having few ships, less than 4,000 soldiers, and only 80 civilian employees. The following account by a prominent foreign visitor of his meeting with Secretary of War James McHenry in 1796 gives a sense of the informality of these departments' daily operations.

> The government officials were as simple in their manners as ever. I had occasion to call upon McHenry, the Secretary of War. It was about eleven o'clock in the morning when I called. There was no sentinel at the door, all the rooms, the walls of which were covered with maps, were open, and in the midst of the solitude I found two clerks each sitting at his own table, engaged in writing. At last I met a servant, or rather *the* servant, for there was but one in the house, and asked for the Secretary. He replied that his master was absent for the moment, having gone to the barber's to be shaved. Mr. McHenry's name figured in the State Budget for $2,000, a salary quite sufficient in a country where the Secretary of War goes in the morning to his neighbor, the barber, at the corner, to get shaved. I was as much surprised to find all the business of the War Office transacted by two clerks, as I was to hear that the Secretary had gone to the barber's.[2]

While informality was a characteristic of early departmental activities, pronounced differences between the departments were even then apparent. The Treasury Department, partly because of the vigorous personality and leadership of Alexander Hamilton, was given the broadest mandate and widest latitude in its original enabling legislation: "to digest and prepare plans for the improvement and management of revenue"; "to superintend the collection of the revenue"; "to execute such services relative to the sale of the lands belonging to the United States"; and "to perform all such services relative to the finances."[3] And indeed Hamilton exercised broad, sweeping powers in his efforts to raise and collect new sources of national revenues, supervise and direct disbursement of funds, control public debts, and create a national bank. He even drew up the first economic blueprint of national economic growth in his *Report on Manufacturers*. As is also true today, personalities and intellectual capacities of leaders combined with the departmental legal authority and day-to-day responsibilities create wide variations *between* government organizations, even if they can all be broadly defined as departments.

The attorney general, as noted earlier, was different in that his authority was represented by an office, not a department. Until well into the nineteenth century, attorneys general were part-timers. They acted more or less as legal advisors to presidents and as chief litigators for the United States. This tradition continues to this day. Attorneys general have been often close personal friends, indeed personal attorneys, of presidents they have served—witness two Carter and Reagan appointees, Griffin Bell and William French Smith. Early attorneys general were expected to continue their private legal practices to support themselves. The same was true for local postmasters who worked for the postmaster general. They were also unsalaried and were expected to charge customers for services (a tradition that also holds true today in an altered form, since the U.S. Postal Service is now an independent government corporation and is expected to be a self-supporting enterprise).

For the most part, these core service functions—diplomacy, national defense, finance, legal advice, and internal communications—with minor variations remain today core service functions of U.S. bureaucracy, but with one important difference. Each federal department that performs these basic tasks has multiplied its scope, activities, and size enormously over the past two hundred years.

Figure 2.4 shows the State Department's present organization. It is a far cry from the way it was in Thomas Jefferson's day when it had 8 clerks, 1 messenger, and 25 agents! Today State's bureaucracy comprises more than 55,000 persons, staffing 175 embassies around the world, and representing the United States in over 50 international organizations and at more than 800 international conferences annually. The tasks that Figure 2.4 shows are only the very "tip of the iceberg" of State's incredibly complex functional responsibilities. Many of these tasks were not even conceived of in 1789. They include descriptors like "oceans," "human rights," "refugee programs," "international narcotics matters," and "international organization affairs." The same expansion of roles and responsibilities has taken place in other core departments—Treasury, Defense, and Justice. Though these departments' activities have greatly enlarged, as in the case of the State Department, their basic structures remain much the same as when they were first organized—having a cabinet secretary in charge, a chain of command, a hierarchy and functionally differentiated activities, and some responsibilities that do not fit in clearly with their overall basic missions.

At the state and local levels, bureaucratic development in this era mirrored the federal level. First, until the twentieth century, professionalism was rare. Most core public services such as police and fire functions were provided through volunteers. Welfare, streets, and water were maintained by citizens or private contractors—or not at all. Elected officials often mixed their representative duties with administrative functions. Often elected city councils or state representatives served on specialized committees to oversee and perform local/state activities, such as patrolling the town or serving in the state militia.

Second, administrative oversight therefore was communal and collective, rather than lodged in a single elected or appointed official. Mayors and governors, like U.S. presidents throughout the nineteenth century, served more or less as ceremonial figureheads, rather than administrative managers. Mayors participated in council deliberations and voted, but they rarely led or managed as "strong mayors" or "city managers" do today. Policy and administrative direction derived largely from legislative committees in city hall as well as the state house.

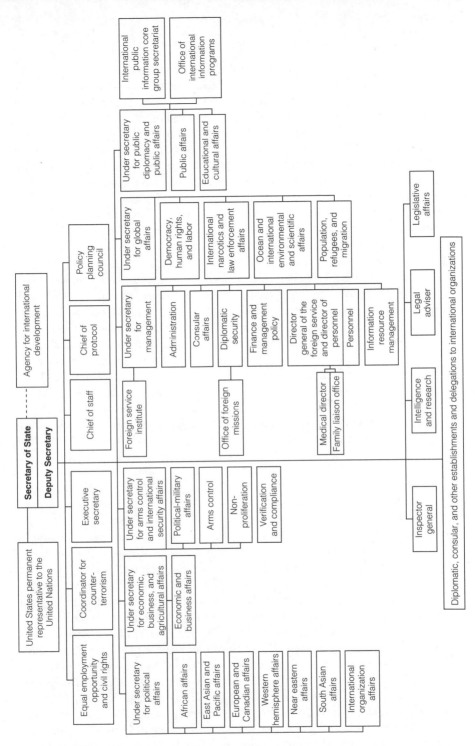

Figure 2.4 Department of State

Source: *U.S. Government Manual.*

Third, functional administrative roles were ill-defined, mixed with politics, and frequently overlapped with several activities. Elected sheriffs and judges, for instance, had not only law enforcement and judicial duties, but often they were also assigned other functions such as caring for the poor, widows and orphans, or collecting public revenue. In Boston in 1813, the city council finance committee not only selected the city treasurer, oversaw the financial accounts, set tax collection rates, dealt with the details of public expenditures and finance administration, but also was responsible for poor relief and public health. State legislatures frequently assumed and carried out what nowadays would be viewed as routine local duties such as for health or safety. Rational division of bureaucratic responsibilities, with clear-cut specializations and neat, well-ordered chains-of-command had to await the dawn of the twentieth century when the Progressive Era ushered in modernized state and local reorganization.

Finally, throughout most of the nineteenth century, there was simply little need for many state/local services that are deemed essential today. Self-sufficiency and volunteerism were the norm. Until 1889 Baltimore and New Orleans operated without public sewage treatment, relying instead on private cesspools and privies. Many communities like Charleston and Newark during the same era had no paved roads. Since little was known about the relationship between clean drinking water and public health, drinking water was drawn from household pumps, nearby streams, or from privately financed water works. Mass compulsory public education had to await the twentieth century. Without autos, electricity, and other modern technological inventions, there was little need for huge, complex state and local regulatory bureaucracies.

National Economic Development
in the Nineteenth Century

The first governmental organizations in the United States were created to service the essential core functions of the new nation and were organized in the form of departments and offices. But the nineteenth century saw the emergence of other organizational arrangements. The Interior Department, the only federal department created between 1789 and 1870, was established in 1849 to foster domestic growth and national development. This was the era of rapid westward expansion. As the population shifted west, a new department was necessary to serve new national needs. Proposals to create a "Home Office," along the lines of a British Home Office (essentially a department for domestic affairs), had repeatedly been raised since 1789. However, local pressures to resist federal involvement in this area, coupled with the worries of a growing bureaucracy (even then), had blocked any moves in this direction until 1849, when the need for greater coherence and policy direction became imperative. The Interior Department emerged as an amalgam of bits and pieces of several other agencies then in existence—all involving domestic concerns: Bureau of Indian Affairs (from the War Department); Military Pensions (from War); Patent Office (from State); Census Bureau (from State), and Land Office (from Treasury). Note that the bureau became the organizing principle at Interior. Interior's scattered and somewhat unrelated collection of domestically oriented agencies with a mix of names containing the words *bureau* and *office* remain to a large extent its basic pattern and mode of operation to this very day.

Some of the old functions are still important at Interior (see Figure 2.5), such as the Bureau of Indian Affairs and the Bureau of Land Management (formerly Land Office), but many new functions have been added, including the Bureau of Mines, for the inspection of mines and enforcement of safety rules; the National Park Service, for running the national parks; and the U.S. Fish and Wildlife Service, devoted to the protection and improvement of fish and wildlife. Many more functions that were not even envisioned in 1849 are now included in Interior, such as the Ocean Mining Administration.

While the domestically oriented and service-directed tasks have greatly expanded at Interior, its original coupling of disconnected, hodgepodge tasks remains intact. What this organizational pattern created, unlike the original core service departments, was a greater degree of subunit autonomy within its structure (the name *bureau* may therefore imply a greater degree of subunit independence—but not always). Generally, oversight from the Cabinet secretary or president of, say, the Land Office within Interior (now the Bureau of Land Management) was less evident even from the start because of the "pulls" of congressional subcommittees and interest groups. Again, this historic pattern holds true today. Even now a president or a secretary of Interior often finds it difficult, if not impossible, to impose long-term policy direction and coherence on diverse Interior service functions such as parks, recreation, wildlife management, resource management, and Indian affairs. Particularly as these domestic functions develop strong domestic constituencies, bureau fragmentation and independence increase.

New service functions were also added to old-line departments in the nineteenth century, along with other varieties of organizational designs. The Civil War and its aftermath forged a diversity of new public activities. The War Department added the Freedmen's Bureau (1866) to aid newly freed slaves; the Treasury added the Internal Revenue Service (1866), the controller of the Currency (1863), and the Secret Service (1865)—all formed to supervise the collection of revenue and the regulation of currency. The attorney general became an officer with Cabinet rank in 1870 and was put in charge of the Justice Department to handle growing numbers of post–Civil War civil suits, legal controversies over natural resources, and taxes. The Justice Department's subunits were called *divisions,* for example, the Civil Division and the Tax Division. Why this occurred and why their chiefs were called assistant attorneys general is unclear, though here as elsewhere the pressures of dealing with problems resulting from national growth and development fostered new service functions and an enlarged bureaucracy. Bureaucratic institutions grew quickly in the late nineteenth and early twentieth centuries. But note how the new names utilized to distinguish the subunits in bureaucracy varied widely, for example, *bureau, service, controller,* and *division.* Each term denoted important subunits within major departments performing specified public tasks, yet the names varied principally because of different departmental traditions. *Divisions* were utilized, for instance,

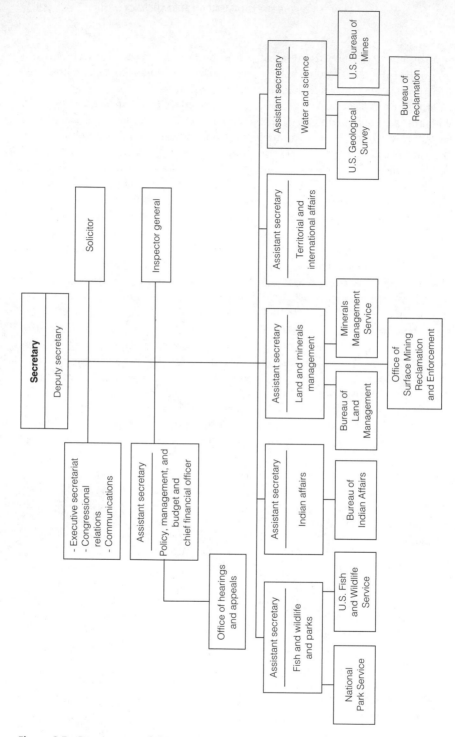

Figure 2.5 Department of the Interior, 1993–1994

Source: *U.S. Government Manual*, 1993–1994.

to designate Justice's subdivisions, but not elsewhere. Historic accident and unique departmental traditions caused the multiplication of subunit names and variations of U.S. organizational patterns.

An important deviation from the standard organizational pattern occurred with the creation of the Smithsonian Institution in 1846. In 1829 the will of James Smithson of England bequeathed to the United States his entire estate, "to found at Washington, under the name of the Smithsonian Institution, an establishment for the increase and diffusion of knowledge among men."[4] Congress wanted to accept the gift, but the purpose of the grant did not fit neatly into any of the existing departmental activities. Consequently, Congress created the first independent government agency in the form of a "foundation," vesting control of this agency outside the traditional executive branch chain of command by giving it to the Smithsonian Board of Regents. The board is composed of the chief justice, the vice president, three U.S. senators, three House members, and nine private citizens. The Smithsonian Institution began an important trend of bureaucratic autonomy, for today there are more than 60 independent agencies operating outside the 15 traditional federal departments (see Figure 2.6). Some are quite large, like the General Services Administration (GSA) or the National Aeronautics and Space Administration (NASA). Other independent agencies, like ACTION, which consist of a loose collection of voluntary agencies such as the Peace Corps, Job Corps, Foster Grandparent Program, Volunteers in Service to America (VISTA), and the Drug Use Prevention Program, are quite small by comparison, with only a few thousand employees and a several hundred million dollar annual budget. ACTION's independence was due to presidential initiative. President Kennedy emphasized at its inception that the Peace Corps' mission should be distinct and separate from such traditional diplomatic agencies as the State Department. Traditional international agencies like State have never wanted to merge with ACTION.

The Clientele Service Functions

The latter half of the nineteenth century saw the formation of distinctly new forms of U.S. bureaucracy. These responded in large part to new pressures and requirements of society. As Richard Schott has observed, "Whereas earlier federal departments had been formed around specialized governmental functions (foreign affairs, war, finance and the like), the new departments of this period— Agriculture, Labor and Commerce—were devoted to interests and aspirations of particular economic groups. Their emergence testified to the growing specialization and occupational differentiation occurring in American Society."[5] In Schott's view, the growing and powerful economic blocks of interest groups in the late nineteenth and early twentieth centuries spawned new and powerful bureaucracies catering to specific clientele service needs.

The largest and most powerfully organized clientele group of this era was made up of farmers. Three-fourths of Americans at the time were living off the land. The U.S. Department of Agriculture (USDA) was created in 1862. It was at first headed by a commissioner, who then assumed full Cabinet status in 1889 as

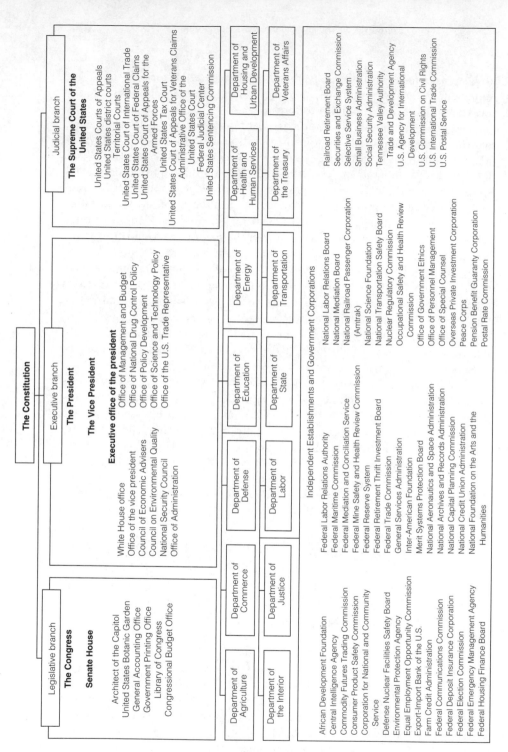

Figure 2.6 The government of the United States

Source: *U.S. Government Manual, 2001–2002.*

a departmental secretary. The USDA was established in the same year Congress passed the Morrill Act, which granted land for agricultural colleges to western states, and the Homestead Act, which opened public land to homesteaders. As Leonard White points out, these acts and the USDA "were the three major statutory foundations of federal agricultural policy for nearly a century."[6] At first the functions of the USDA were principally research and education. Development of new farming techniques and dissemination of these methods throughout the country were its early departmental priorities. As the charter of the USDA outlined, its initial goals were "to acquire and diffuse among people useful information on subjects connected with agriculture," "to conduct practical and scientific experiments," and "to appoint persons skilled in the natural sciences pertaining to agriculture."[7] The USDA was a federal bureaucracy that, quite unlike core departments such as State, which saw to the needs of the nation as a whole, catered directly to the needs and interests of a single group, farmers.

Today, although less than 5 percent of Americans live on farms, the USDA has grown into one of the largest federal departments because it conducts a variety of agricultural service functions considerably broader and more pervasive than those outlined by the original charter. As Figure 2.7 indicates, over the years the activities of the USDA have expanded into economic forecasting, nutritional programs, food stamps, consumer services, rural development, international affairs, natural resources, and environmental protection. Note how the original scientific and educational programs of the department are now headed only by a director, not an assistant secretary, signaling their relative decline in importance within the overall scheme of current departmental activities. Also, while the USDA's clientele is still predominantly the farm population, the department serves many other groups, such as consumers, international markets, and environmentalists. The number of the USDA's "clienteles" has multiplied during the last century, as have its functional tasks.

The Rise of Regulatory Agencies
and Government Corporations

The late nineteenth and early twentieth centuries saw the development of two other forms of governmental bureaucracies outside the traditional departmental structures: regulatory agencies and government corporations. Regulatory agencies have been viewed by some as "the fourth" or "hidden" branch of government because they play such powerful, yet unpublicized, roles in shaping policies and agendas. Much of the growth of regulatory bureaucracies was, like that of earlier types of federal bureaucracies, the result of new societal needs for public services.

The basic social fabric of the United States was rapidly changing in this era. By the end of the nineteenth century, huge corporate structures, "the trusts," began to control, even monopolize, large segments of markets as diverse as oil, steel, railroads, and other manufacturing enterprises. Trusts had become able to control markets and rig market prices by the late 1800s. Both their enormous economic size and political influence precipitated vigorous demands from the

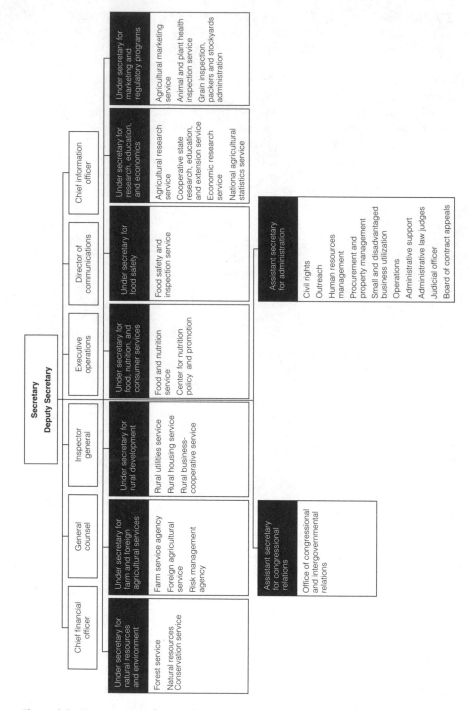

Figure 2.7　Department of Agriculture

Source: *U.S. Government Manual, 2002–2003.*

public, particularly western farmers and small businesses, that checks be placed on trusts' unrestrained powers.

Government responded with two measures to control these giant corporations. First, "busting the trusts" by legislation. The aim of the Sherman Antitrust Act of 1890 was to break up these large trusts by assigning new enforcement powers to the Justice Department. Second, regulatory commissions created permanent legal machinery to oversee and regulate corporate trust activities. Independent regulating began at the federal level in 1887 with the Interstate Commerce Commission (ICC), which was set up to regulate railroad rates, then a major economic issue for western farmers. The monopolistic practices of many railroads servicing the West and Midwest had "squeezed" many farmers, who, in turn, demanded government action. Help came in the form of this new type of bureaucracy, the ICC.

The ICC was modeled on early state regulatory commissions. Three-, five-, or seven-person boards were given legal autonomy and political independence (at least in theory) by being placed outside the formal executive departments. These boards were given quasilegal and executive powers to regulate prices in specific economic markets to curb monopolistic and unfair practices by industrial giants.

Today, more than a century after the creation of the ICC, there are several regulatory commissions or boards at federal and state levels, as reflected in Figure 2.8. These commissions or boards regulate a diverse number of critical economic fields, as well as professions and trades, and they now constitute a major and influential part of bureaucracy.

Figure 2.9 shows an organization chart of the Federal Trade Commission, which was established to regulate broad areas of trade practices. Note that its format is essentially the same as the first one established, the ICC. In the words of Professor Marver Bernstein, such commissions involve "location outside an executive department; some measure of independence from supervision by the President or a Cabinet Secretary; immunity from the President's discretionary power to remove members of independent commissions from office."[8] It should be added that while Congress has given many regulatory powers to independent commissions, over the years it has also assigned many regulatory functions to regular departments. For example, under the Packers and Stockyards Act of 1921 regulatory functions were assigned to the secretary of agriculture rather than to the Federal Trade Commission. Regulatory activities today are carried out by many executive departments, and not only within independent commissions. Again, historic accident rather than deliberate design frequently determines the location and degree of authority assigned to bureaucracy by Congress.

The Progressive Era also saw the creation of another important form of public bureaucracy: the government corporation. As Harold Seidman, a well-known scholar in this field, has written, the government corporation was "essentially an empirical response to problems posed by increasing reliance on government-created business enterprise and business-type operations to accomplish public purposes."[9] The government corporation was modeled on the private corporation. It had a board of directors, which was given a degree of

EXAMPLES OF MAJOR FEDERAL REGULATORY COMMISSIONS/BOARDS	EXAMPLES OF MAJOR STATE REGULATORY COMMISSIONS/BOARDS
Federal Communications Commission	Accountancy State Board
Federal Energy Regulatory Commission	Acupuncturists Registrations
National Telecommunications and Information Administration	Administrator of Nursing Homes Board of Examiners
National Transportation Safety Board	Anticompetitive Conduct Committee
Nuclear Regulatory Commission	Architects Board of Examiners
Postal Rate Commission	Barber-Cosmetology State Board
Rural Electrification Administration	Chiropractic Examiners State Board
Securities and Exchange Commission	Dental Examiners State Board
Federal Trade Commission	Electrical State Board
	Engineers and Land Surveyors State Board
	Manufactured Housing Board
	Marriage and Family Therapist Examiners State Board
	Medical Examiners State Board
	Mental Health Grievance Board
	Nursing State Board
	Optometric Examiners State Board
	Outfitters and Guides Registrations
	Passenger Tramway Safety Board
	Pharmacy State Board
	Physical Therapy Registrations
	Plumbers Examining Board
	Podiatry Board
	Professional Counselor Examiners State Board
	Psychologist Examiners State Board
	Social Work Examiners State Board
	Veterinary Medicine State Board

Figure 2.8 At the federal and state levels, numerous regulatory commissions and boards exercise powerful influences over specific economic markets.

independence from civil service rules and annual budgetary processes in order to enable it to carry out its corporate activities with greater flexibility in personnel and finances. The corporate format was especially appealing because it *did not* look like, nor was it called by any name resembling, "a public bureaucracy." It was, rather, "a corporation." Given the strong appeal of business values—that is, values associated with efficiency, economy, and effectiveness—throughout U.S. history, such labeling was highly attractive to the electorate and its representatives. Business values were especially popular during the Progressive Era (the "city manager plan," which modeled local government along business lines, was also created at that time).

The corporate model was an effective device for implementing new programs with speed and efficiency. Government was being asked to perform many new public services. The public wanted these tasks done quickly and efficiently. New roads, schools, and utilities were needed. The government corporation therefore found favor precisely because it could execute these new tasks expeditiously and effectively. When the U.S. government purchased the Panama

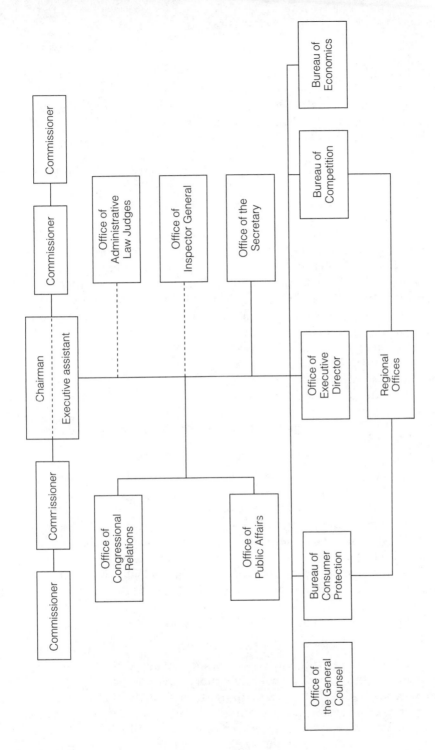

Figure 2.9 Federal Trade Commission

Source: *U.S. Government Manual.*

Railroad Company from the French Canal Company in 1904, a government corporation (the first one) was created to operate the canal railway. It was notably successful in aiding the building of the canal. Over one hundred government corporations since 1904 have been established to undertake a wide variety of public tasks—from COMSAT, which operates communications satellites, to the Tennessee Valley Authority (TVA), which provides power, irrigation, recreational facilities, and economic development to the Tennessee Valley. Like regulatory commissions, government corporations, at least in theory, are isolated from politics through the appointment of bipartisan directors with overlapping terms. Such neutrality and independence is an important factor in government corporations' flexibility in decision-making, personnel compensation, and long-term planning capability, especially greater freedom from the Executive Office of the president in fiscal matters, personnel appointments, and capital planning. This rationale was used by President Nixon in 1970 when he proposed to transform the U.S. Postal Service from an executive department into a government corporation. This change was necessary, according to Nixon, "to free it from partisan political pressure" and to "improve its economy and efficiency."[10] The "corporate" form of the post office, (see Figure 2.10), and of many other public service organizations as well, is considered a preferable means of delivering services to the public.

For much the same reasons, the Resolution Trust Corporation format was created in 1989 to manage and resolve the $150 billion failure of Saving and Loan Associations. As in the past, Congress turned to this corporate format for "making efficient use of funds" and "maximize return on value" and "minimize the losses to government." Many other federal organizations are modeled along much the same lines: Federal Government National Mortgage Association, Commodity Credit Corporation, Federal Crop Insurance Corporation, Federal Home Loan System, Federal Deposit Insurance Corporation, Export-Import Bank of the United States, Overseas Private Investment Corporation, and Rural Telephone Bank. As their names signify, they perform many kinds of specific tasks for the public, generally along the lines of those performed by private business. Their work constitutes a major share of federal activities but is largely a "hidden" dimension of government bureaucracy.

Surges in Social Services in the New Deal
and the Great Society

As James Q. Wilson has written, much of our modern bureaucracy is a result of "majoritarian surges of popular demand for more government activity"[11] in the Progressive, New Deal, and Great Society eras. By popular demand, the Progressive Era brought into existence new varieties of regulatory and governmental corporations, yet the greatest source of civilian growth in U.S. bureaucracy occurred during the New Deal in the 1930s and the Great Society in the 1960s. Both eras ushered in new, diverse types of social service bureaucracies.

The New Deal stimulated unprecedented numbers of bureaucratic services: This was largely in response to an economic crisis—the Great Depression—that

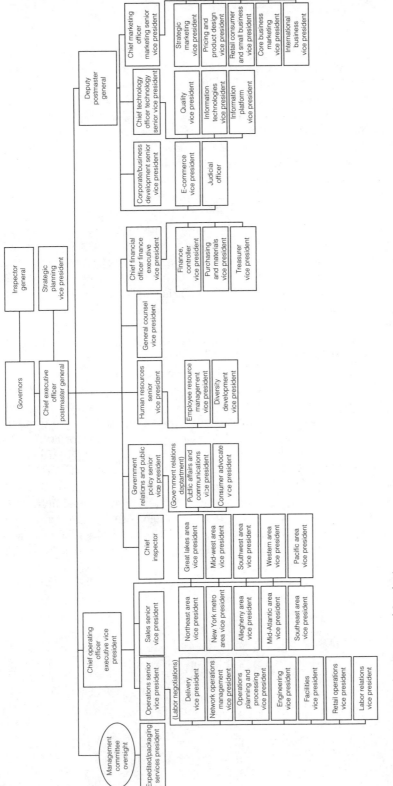

Figure 2.10 United States Postal Service*

*Since 1970 the U.S. postal service has been a government corporation with 788,000 employees, 38,000 post offices, handling 208 billion pieces of mail annually.

Source: *U.S Government Manual 2001–2002*, p. 553.

gripped the United States in the early 1930s. In 1933, 14 million Americans were out of work—one in four workers. In that same year, 5,000 banks closed their doors and industrial income fell from 85 to 37 billion dollars. Industry was at a standstill; breadlines formed; bankruptcies were common. The average of fifty industrial stocks on the New York Stock Exchange dropped from 252 to 61 between 1929 and 1933. Franklin Roosevelt was inaugurated as president on March 4, 1933. With vast support from the electorate and Congress, he moved quickly to set up a broad array of programs to cope with the economic disaster. The Federal Emergency Relief Administration (1933) was established to direct grants to localities for the support of poor and unemployed persons; the Civilian Conservation Corps (1933) put thousands of young men to work planting forest lands; the Farm Credit Administration (1933) extended farm loans and agricultural credit to bankrupt farmers; the Federal Deposit Insurance Corporation (1933) established protection for bank depositors; and the Works Progress Administration (1933) hired many men and women to build roads, schools, airports, and hospitals. Many other new public agencies were formed to deal quickly with the problems and impacts of this harsh economic emergency.

Most of the measures enacted in Roosevelt's first term were considered temporary. In his second term, however, many permanent public bureaucracies to alleviate or eliminate future economic crises like the Great Depression were created. The social security system created a mandatory retirement benefit program for workers as well as unemployment compensation and welfare programs for the blind, the handicapped, and dependent children, administered through the Federal Security Agency (1939). The Fair Labor Standards Act (1938) established a minimum wage and maximum work hours, and the National Labor Relations Act (1935) created a national system for labor-management collective bargaining that exists to this day. Another New Deal public agency, the Federal Crop Insurance Corporation (1938), established a system of minimum base prices for farmers—parity payments—that guaranteed farmers minimum base prices for their produce in depressed market years. Through the Rural Electrification Administration (1935), electric power was brought to many isolated households; and the Farm Security Administration (1937) sought to improve the health, safety, and working conditions of farm laborers. These and many other new social services added enormously to the size and scope of the federal bureaucracy. As Figure 2.11 shows, the United States developed a large, permanent bureaucracy to carry out these New Deal tasks.

If the New Deal concentrated on finding ways to put people back to work and to provide both "welfare basics" to millions and economic stability to various sectors of the economy, the Great Society in the 1960s sought to extend and expand the scope of these social programs to many areas that had been neglected by the New Deal. After the death of President John F. Kennedy on November 22, 1963, President Lyndon Johnson launched the Great Society, a vigorous new expansion of social service programs. The Medicare Program, for example, established in 1966, guaranteed medical insurance for the aged; the Office of Economic Opportunity (1964) administered "the war on poverty" through var-

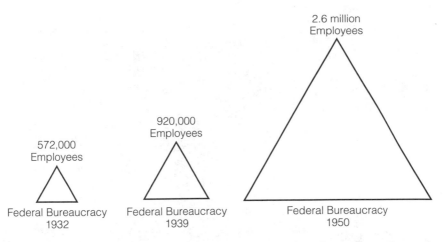

Figure 2.11   Rapid growth of federal bureaucracy, 1932–1950, due to depression and hot and cold wars

ious new programs that required "the maximum feasible participation" of the poor; the Department of Housing and Urban Development in 1965 brought together several existing urban-oriented federal agencies and several new ones such as the Model Cities Program, within a new Cabinet-level department, to attack problems of housing and urban development. The Department of Transportation was established in 1966 to coordinate and target mass transit and general transportation policies for the entire nation; several regional commissions, such as the Appalachian Regional Commission, were created to deal with specialized regional economic and social needs. Further, the Great Society saw the rapid expansion of numerous grants-in-aid and categorical programs for the support of specific public programs for hospital, school, and highway construction, largely administered with matching funds through state and local public bureaucracies. Many of these programs are still on the books today.

Hot War/Cold War Defense Organizations

The unique geographic isolation of the United States combined with its historical liberal opposition to standing professional military forces made large defense bureaucracies both unnecessary and unwanted for the first 150 years of its history. Even the large, bloody battles of the Civil War and World War I were waged mostly with temporary volunteer "citizen soldiers," not with professionals.

All this changed in World War II. The geographic isolation of the United States suddenly disappeared as military threats came to its doorstep. Japan attacked Pearl Harbor on December 7, 1941. Declarations of war from Hitler's Germany and Mussolini's Italy followed. These powerful totalitarian regimes, combined with new arms technology and the weakening of western democracies such as England and France, thrust onto the United States new responsibilities for defending its own interests as well as those of the free world. Overnight new defense agencies became necessary to plan, coordinate, mobilize, and administer the U.S. war effort. Twelve

BY SACK FOR THE STAR TRIBUNE

A new government organization can signal important shifts to new public priorities.

Source: Washington Post National Weekly Edition, June 24–30, 2002, p. 25. Reprinted by permission of Tribune Media Services.

million men and women served in the armed services during World War II, and between 1941 and 1945, 147 new bureaucratic units were established by powerful new institutions, such as the Office of Price Administration, which planned and directed the overall war economy, and the Selective Service System, which established and administered the draft. As Figure 2.11 points out, this war-related activity caused the greatest jump in the overall size of the federal bureaucracy in U.S. history.

After the war many of these new bureaucratic entities, such as the Office of Price Administration, were abolished, but many others remained because of continued threats from the Soviet Union and other communist regimes. The Cold War, which sometimes turned hot in out-of-the-way places such as Korea, meant that during the 1940s and 1950s defense readiness and preparedness were considered a high priority. Large, permanent public bureaucracies were created because of these new long-term defense requirements. The Department of Defense (DoD) was established in 1947 through merging both War and Navy departments and the creation of a new subunit, the Air Force. The National Security Act, which created DoD in 1947, also established the Central Intelligence Agency to collect, coordinate, and disseminate foreign intelligence information vital to U.S. security needs (see Figure 2.12). Foreign aid to friendly and neutral nations became an indispensable and undisputed part of U.S. strategic defenses. Military aid, offered to allies in substantial amounts during the 1940s and 1950s, was channeled through DoD's Military Area Assistance Group. Nonmilitary aid was dispensed through the Economic Cooperation Administration

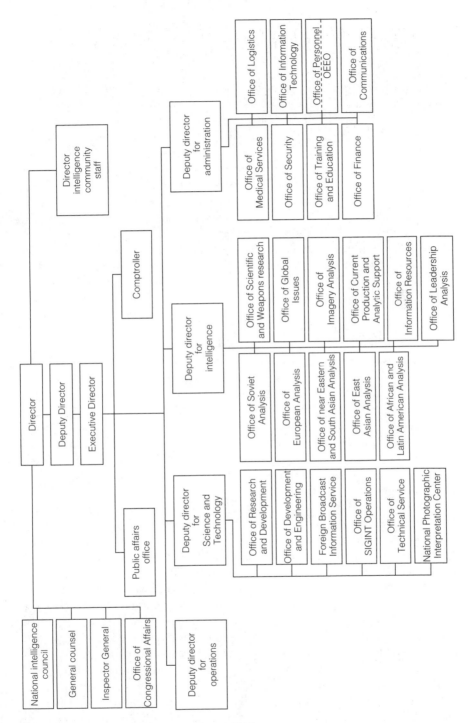

Figure 2.12   Central Intelligence Agency, 1991

Source: Central Intelligence Agency, 1991.

(ECA), which in 1961 became the Agency for International Development (AID). ECA and later AID sought to strengthen friendly and neutral countries economically, socially, and politically through a variety of grants, loans, and technical assistance programs.

Cold War defense programs spilled over into domestic issues and public programs. The need to harness science and scientific talent to serve the nation's Cold War needs became a vital preoccupation during this period. The Manhattan Project created the atomic bomb, which had brought a swift and dramatic end to hostilities in World War II, but after the war Congress was faced with the awesome task of controlling the future use and development of atomic energy. To this end, the Atomic Energy Commission was created in 1946. Basic and applied research was fostered and stimulated through a new grant system that Congress set up in 1950 through the National Science Foundation (NSF). NSF, an independent agency with its own staff of scientific panels whose function was to approve grants for scientific research, became an important new avenue for stimulating research capabilities in universities and private research laboratories. NSF maintained the independence of scientists within their "home" institutions while fostering research into "potential defense spinoffs" through extensive grants and other assistance. Direct links with scientific knowledge and defense department priorities during the 1940s and 1950s were further enhanced by the growing practice of "contracting out" for services to universities, not-for-profit "think tanks" such as the Rand Corporation, and large numbers of private businesses.

Similarly, Cold War pressures to keep pace with the Russians proded formation of the National Aeronautics and Space Administration (NASA) in 1958. The U.S.S.R.'s launching of Sputnik in October 1957 brought the United States overnight into an accelerated and extended space race with the Soviets. NASA throughout the 1960s, and even today, is designated as the "lead" agency in this effort to explore regions beyond the earth. NASA's role and prominence grew largely as a response to Cold War threats from the Soviets, just as AID's, the CIA's, the Atomic Energy Commission's, and NSF's did. Indeed, the spillovers and spinoffs into domestic programs from Cold War concerns were so numerous that it is difficult to describe them all succinctly. For example, the National Defense Highway Act (1955) created a vast, $100 billion plus highway program, perhaps the largest public works program in history, stimulated and promoted in part by "defense" concerns (as the legal title of its enabling legislation indicates). The National Defense Education Act of 1958 fostered an influx of loans and grants for mathematics and science education in high schools and colleges. This act was prompted by fears that the United States was falling behind the Soviets in these fields. External threats or fears of external threats to the United States have been a major enduring source of the formation, growth, and maintenance of many postwar public bureaucracies and government programs.

Staff and Local Service Functions

The rise of bureaucratic institutions in the twentieth-century United States spurred the concomitant growth of new layers of bureaucracies to oversee, coordinate, plan, and manage government. One of the earliest staff mechanisms created for these purposes was the General Staff. It was set up by Congress in 1903, upon the advice of Elihu Root, then secretary of war, to better plan and coordinate military activities and to prevent the repetition of the logistical calamities of the Spanish American War. Further, the Budget and Accounting Act of 1921 created an executive budget and added the Bureau of the Budget (first operating under the secretary of the treasury and later within the Executive Office of the President—EoP) as a key instrument for fiscal and budgetary planning. This act (perhaps *the* most critical contribution to federal bureaucracy's development) established the General Accounting Office to provide independent auditing oversight and controls.

The Brownlow Commission Report in 1937, which was the first major study of the organization of the presidency since 1789, recommended to President Franklin Roosevelt a substantial increase in staff assistance for the president. In the early 1930s, the president had only a few personal secretaries and special assistants, most "on loan" from other agencies, but by the 21st century EoP has since grown into a formidable bureaucracy in its own right. Today EoP is the "staff arm" of the president. It consists of several thousand employees, many of them long-term careerists, and comprises a number of powerful policy advisory organizations (see Figure 2.13). Some of them are: the Domestic Policy Advisor, which advises the president on domestic policy issues; the National Security Advisor, which counsels the President on international and defense issues; the Council of Economic Advisers, which sets macroeconomic policies; the Office of Management and Budget, which develops the annual executive budget; and the Director of Intergovernmental Affairs which assists in developing national intergovernmental policies. Even the vice president's office now has a sizable staff of 80, and the first lady's office, several dozen people.

Staff bureaucracies have further proliferated in each of the 14 federal executive departments, so that reporting to each Cabinet secretary are many large, specialized offices providing legal advice, policy analysis, personnel and budget recommendations, and much more (refer to Figures 2.4, 2.5, 2.7, 2.9, 2.10, and 2.12). Congress also has added enormous "overhead staffs" to its legislative advisory and planning capacities. For example, the Congressional Reference Service provides documentary and data reference for congressional activities; the Congressional Budget Office provides budget and economic advice to Congress; the Office of Technology Assessment helps legislators to plan, evaluate, and anticipate future impacts of technology upon U.S. society; and the General Accounting Office, already mentioned, is an important source of fiscal and programmatic oversight. Whereas three decades ago Congress had 5,000 employees, in 2001 it has approximately 23,000 staffers (more than some federal departments). Even the judicial bureaucracy has grown rapidly over the last 25 years. Ironically, members of Congress, who have been often the most vocal critics of federal bureaucracy, are part of the fastest-growing bureaucracy since 1970.

Furthermore, more than 1,500 advisory boards and 120 commissions at the federal level report to either the executive or legislative branches, or both, and provide government with a wide array of technical, expert, or lay

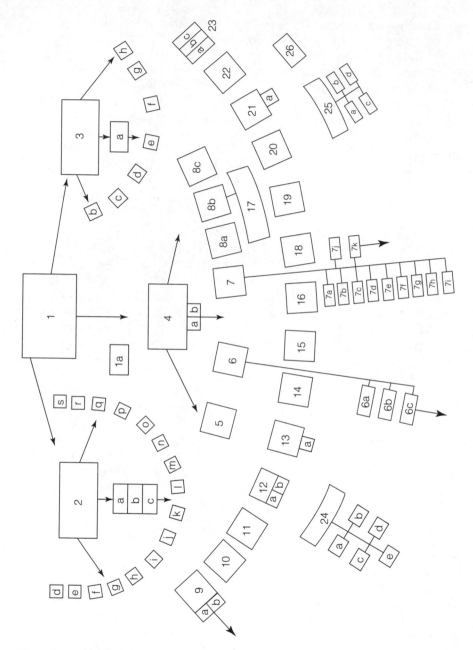

Figure 2.13   The Executive Office of the President

Source: Adapted from Bradley H. Patterson, Jr. *The White House Staff: Inside the West Wing and Beyond* (Washington, D.C.: Brookings Institution, 2000), pp. 44–46. Reprinted by permission of The Brookings Institution.

Key to the Organization Chart of the White House Staff

1   President
1a   Director of Oval Office Operations, the presidential aide, the president's , secretaries and the West Wing receptionist
2   Vice President
2a   Chief of Staff
2b   Deputy Chief of Staff
2c   Executive Assistant
2d   Counselor for Public Affairs
2e   Press Secretary
2f   Speechwriter
2g   Scheduling Office
2h   Advance Office
2i   Deputy Assistant for National Security Affairs
2j   Domestic Policy Adviser
2k   Executive Director, National Energy Policy Development Group
2l   Counsel
2m   Legislative Affairs Office
2n   Deputy Assistant for Operations
2o   Correspondence Office
2p   Photo Office for the Vice President
2q   Military Aides to the Vice President
2r   Residence Manager and Social Secretary
2s   Spouse of the Vice President
3   First Lady
3a   Chief of Staff
3b   Special Assistant
3c   Press Secretary
3d   Director of Correspondence
3e   Director of Projects
3f   White House Social Secretary and Social Aides
3g   Director of Scheduling and Advance
3h   Speechwriter
4   White House Chief of Staff
4a   Deputy Chief of Staff for Policy
4b   Deputy Chief of Staff for Operations
5   Secretary to the Cabinet
6   Staff Secretary
6a   Executive Clerk
6b   Office of Records Management
6c   Correspondence Office (includes ten specialized units)
7   Assistant to the President for Management and Administration
7a   White House Management Office
7b   Intern Program
7c   Photography Office
7d   Telephone Service
7e   Travel Office
7f   Visitors Office
7g   White House Conference Center
7h   Personnel Office

7i   Support services from the Office of Administration (database, libraries)
7j   Service Delivery Team of the General Services Administration
7k   White House Military Office (eleven units, including the White House Communications Agency, the Medical Unit, Camp David, *Air Force One, Marine One,* food service, transportation, Ceremonies Coordinator)
8a   Senior Adviser for Policy and Strategy
8b   Counselor for Communications
8c   Office of Homeland Security
9   National Security Adviser and three Deputy National Security Advisers
9a   Executive Secretary
9b   Situation Room (plus fifteen specialized NSC Senior Directors and staffs)
10   Assistant for Economic Policy
11   Assistant for Domestic Policy
12   Assistant for Legislative Affairs
12a Deputy for Legislative Affairs (Senate)
12b Deputy for Legislative Affairs (House)
13   Counsel to the President
13a Security Office
14   Director of Political Affairs
15   Director for Intergovernmental Affairs
16   Director of Presidential Personnel
17   Director of Communications/Media Affairs
18   Press Secretary
19   Director of Public Liaison
20   Director of Speechwriting
21   Director of Presidential Scheduling
21a Presidential Diarist
22   Director of Advance
23   Special Assistants for Special Purposes
23a Office of Strategic Initiatives
23b Office of Faith-Based and Community Initiatives
23c National AIDS Policy Coordinator
24   White House units of the U.S. Secret Service
24a Presidential protective detail
24b Vice Presidential protective detail
24c Technical Security Division
24d Protective Research Division
24e Uniformed Division
25   Chief Usher and the staff of the Executive Residence
25a Curator
25b Family Theater
25c White House Liaison Office of the National Park Service
25d Graphics and Calligraphy Office
26   President's Commission on White House Fellows

Figure 2.13 Continued

Table 2.1   Total U.S. Bureaucracy Workforce, 1991–2001

| | EMPLOYMENT (MILLIONS) | | | | |
	1991	Percentage	2001	Percentage	Change
Federal Civilians	3.1	25.20%	2.7	18.30%	−0.4
Military	2.1		1.4		−0.7
State & Local	15.4	74.70%	18.3	81.70%	2.9
Total	**20.6**	**100%**	**22.4**	**100%**	**1.8**

SOURCE: *2001 Statistical Abstract of the United States.*

advice. Most are small and staffed with temporary personnel, but some have important duties and exert strong influence on government. For example, the National Security Council, through its staff expertise and coordinative role, is immensely important in charting the future course of defense policies.

Concomitant with the growth of staff services at the federal level has been the rise of local and state bureaucracies during this century. Throughout much of the nineteenth century, local bureaucracies were limited or nonexistent. Most Americans lived on farms or in small towns where private businesses or voluntary cooperation were the chief routes for getting things done—hence volunteer fire brigades, locally "raised" schools, church-supported charities for the poor, aged, and infirm, and privately built and run transit systems, utilities, and housing.

Urbanization, new technologies, industrialization, and demands for new and improved public services brought a rapid growth in state and local bureaucracies throughout the twentieth century. State and local bureaucracies developed around the necessity for core functions, such as police and safety services. Continued economic development, regulatory functions, and corporate forms such as housing and transit authorities added new tasks. Educational needs in particular spurred the development of local public bureaucracies throughout this century. Urbanization and industrialization of the United States in the early 1900s created demands for an educated workforce with vastly improved skills and expertise. State compulsory education laws enacted largely in the twentieth century required, in turn, the development of massive, complex local education systems to educate the young from kindergarten through high school. State-supported universities and colleges became commonplace by the 1960s. The popularity of the automobile stimulated state highway construction and the establishment of policing, vehicle licensing, and registration programs. After the Great Depression, state and local welfare bureaucracies, funded increasingly through federal grants, replaced voluntary sources for aiding the poor. Fire and police services expanded in size, scope, and sophistication in response to new technological requirements and to demands for better public protection. Federal categorical grants to localities, combined with block grants and revenue sharing enacted in the 1970s, funneled more fiscal aid to states and localities, spawning the rapid growth of these bureaucratic institutions in a wide variety of areas. Mass transit systems, for example, are found in many medium-sized and large municipalities, thanks to various amounts of dis-

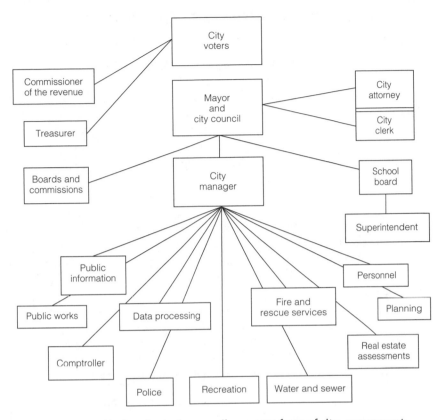

Figure 2.14 Organization chart of a council-manager form of city government

cretionary and categorical grants from the federal government (mainly from UMTA, Urban Mass Transit Administration). Food stamps also are locally administered but, for the most part, are federally funded (from the USDA programs). As Table 2.1 indicates, since 1950 the most sizable increases in public employment have occurred at state and local levels. Further, much like the federal government, state and local bureaucracies have developed large staffs—"budgeters," "personnelists," and lawyers, as well as expert and lay advisory boards and commissions—to oversee and manage their activities.

As Figure 2.14 shows, the formal executive departments as well as the many staffs, commissions, and boards of federal bureaucracies are mirrored in local bureaucracies. Local bureaucracy also has core agencies (fire and police functions), economic development activities, social service agencies, even regulatory and corporate enterprises (zoning and planning boards and housing and transit authorities). These tasks, like those at the federal level, have grown over time and have been sustained both by environmental needs and bureaucratic inertia. More will be said in Chapter 3 about the specific inputs that foster growth and changes within individual bureaucracies. Later chapters will also dwell upon the recent trends in the twenty-first century affecting bureaucratic organizations.

GENERAL CHARACTERISTICS OF THE RISE OF U.S. BUREAUCRACY: GRADUALISM, EXPERIMENTALISM, MAJORITARIANISM, AND COMPLEXITY

As this chapter has underscored, U.S. bureaucracy was not built overnight. It developed gradually, without plan, over more than two hundred years of history, although, as Table 2.2 indicates, there were seven critical periods where spurts of bureaucratic growth occurred: Washington's presidency, the mid-nineteenth century, the Gilded Age, the Progressive Era, the New Deal, World War II and the Cold War, and the Great Society, where new national experiences, such as war and depression, fostered new demands for public actions and activities.

In each of these eras, however, there was no standard format for public organizations. Rather, there was considerable diversity in formal structures. Americans have been remarkably experimental in creating new types of organizations to fulfill various functional needs. Perhaps no other nation has developed such a wide range of bureaucratic forms—from steeply hierarchical formal executive departments under the strict control of the chief elected official (a president, governor, or mayor) to autonomous agencies outside the structure and authority of the executive branch and exhibiting comparatively "flat" organizational forms. Throughout U.S. history, experimentalism has certainly been one of the hallmarks of the rise of bureaucracy. That tradition, as Chapter 6 of this text describes, continues today.

Table 2.2 also demonstrates a third important feature of the rise of U.S. bureaucracy: its majoritarian sources. The bulk of U.S. bureaucracy, contrary to the belief of many, was not caused by pressure groups. Rather, there were specific periods when strong surges of majoritarian influence overrode special interests, resulting in the creation of public organizations that promoted national goals in the name of the public interest. The Federalist Era saw the demand for the formation of "the core departments" of the executive branch to carry out the work of "the first new nation." Similar "majoritarian surges" significantly expanded governmental programs during the Progressive, New Deal, World War II and Cold War, and Great Society eras, though certainly for different reasons and with different results. Only throughout the nineteenth century were major bureaucratic innovations largely caused by special interest (i.e., farmer, labor, and business groups) rather than majoritarian surges.

Finally, over more than two centuries in the life of bureaucratic institutions, an increasing complexification of the entire system can be observed. Each succeeding wave of "majoritarian surges" formed a new layer of complexity, which in turn increased the size and diversity of the entire administrative system. Much of the general public's frustration with modern-day bureaucracy may well be caused by a lack of comprehension of such diverse, complex institutions—their functions, structures, or purposes. Understanding these institutions is, of course, the subject of this text.

Table 2.2 Rise of U.S. Public Bureaucracy since 1789: The Seven Critical Eras of Growth

Key Period in Bureaucracy's Development	Public Demands and National Requirements	Major Source of Political Support	Sample Types of Public Agencies Established
Federalist Era 1789–1802	"Core Functions" of U.S. Government	Early Nationalism and Federalist party	State, War, Treasury, Justice Depts.
Mid-nineteenth century	Nation-state economic development	Jacksonian-Democratic-Whig parties	Interior Dept. and various public works projects
"Gilded Age"—late nineteenth century	Assistance for farmer, labor, business, and other key political interests	Special interest pressures of agriculture, labor, and business	Clientele depts. of Agriculture, Labor, and Commerce
Populist and progressive eras of late nineteenth and early twentieth century	Regulation of business and new forms of public action	Progressive reform led by presidents Theodore Roosevelt and Woodrow Wilson	Regulatory agencies (such as FTC, ICC, and government corporations (such as Panama Canal Authority))
New Deal in 1930s	New social regulations and services for coping with the Great Depression	Democratic party led by President Franklin Roosevelt and New Deal coalition	Regulatory units like Farm Credit Administration or Federal Deposit Insurance Corp. and new social services like the Social Security Administration
World War II (1940–1945) and Cold War Era in 1940s and 1950s	Global defense requirements	Wartime and postwar national consensus for strong defense	DoD, CIA, NASA, and AID
"Great Society," 1960s	"War on Poverty" and vast new social programs	President Lyndon Johnson's "Great Society" programs forged from Liberal-Democratic coalitions in the 1964 election	HUD and DoT, as well as poverty and social programs like Head Start, VISTA, and Medicare

FORMS, FUNCTIONS, POLICIES, AND PROCESSES
OF CONTEMPORARY U.S. BUREAUCRACY

How do the formal elements of U.S. bureaucracy appear today? Table 2.3 summarizes most of the basic forms of present-day federal, state, and local-level bureaucracy. Altogether, these forms represent a composite of over two hundred years of U.S. bureaucratic development. The range today, as Harold Seidman notes, is "staggering" and "defies classification."[12] It is a product of gradualism, experimentalism, majoritarianism, and complexification. Who knows for sure whether some of these units can even properly be termed public bureaucracies? For instance, the Rand Corporation, which is a largely publicly funded, legally chartered private organization, occupies a twilight zone between public and private bureaucracy. Some public bodies are essentially publicly funded but are run like private corporations, as are many local "special district governments." Are these "public" or "private" bureaucracies? Indeed, can such distinctions between "public" and "private" be made, given the mixing and blending of the two categories today?

Equally problematic are their functional assignments. As Table 2.3 also illustrates, many serve traditional executive roles, carrying out tasks assigned by the chief executive and approved by the legislature and judicial branches, although some fulfill entirely quasi-judicial or quasi-legislative functions. The Indian Claims Commission, for example, acts much like a court. Independent regulatory commissions, such as the Food and Drug Commission, have quasi-legislative roles in that Congress has granted to them significant authority to make rules, an essentially legislative function of government. The traditional view, therefore, that public bureaucracies perform only "executive functions" is wrong. Most agencies are involved in the work of all three branches of government—executive, legislative, and judicial.

The policies that are promulgated as a result of these activities have been well summarized and classified by Theodore Lowi in a four-cell matrix.[13] Lowi sees public sector outputs of administrative units as the making of public policies that *actually* force things to happen to people or groups of people throughout society. Public organizations are not only purposeful but also perform actions that legitimately require actions or inactions on the part of either individuals or the whole environment. The policy outputs of government are unique by comparison with other private or nonprofit organized outputs, according to Lowi, because public agencies have the ability to coerce actions on the part of others. Such coercion may be *immediate* (throwing criminals in jail) or *remote* (administering a sales tax to every customer in an entire state). Lowi uses the polar dimensions of individual versus environment *and* immediate versus remote coercion to develop a four-cell matrix in which he summarizes the four basic varieties of public policy outputs of governmental organizations (see Table 2.4).

First, *regulative policies* involve both immediate and individual-oriented outputs of government units, such as the Federal Trade Commission (FTC) actions to stop unfair market competition by business or Federal Communications Commission (FCC) and Federal Drug Commission (FDC) actions to eliminate

Table 2.3 Major Forms and Functions of U.S. Bureaucracy

Bureaucratic Form	Examples of Form	Major Functions
Executive Department (all levels)	State Department, Education Department, Defense Department	Principally implement tasks assigned, with some advisory and regulatory duties
Executive Offices of President, Governor, or Mayor (all levels)	Office of Management and Budget, National Security Council, Council of Economic Advisors	Principally advisory and staff support roles for chief executive
Foundations (mainly federal level)	National Science Foundation	Promotion of research through grants; some advisory roles
Institutions and Institutes (mainly federal)	Smithsonian Institution, National Cancer Institute (HHS), Foreign Service Institute (State), Institutes for Environmental Research (Commerce)	Promotion of research-in-house and through grants; education and teaching function
Independent Agencies (all levels)	ACTION (headed by one person), CIA (headed by one person), Merit Systems Protection Board (committee governed), Transportation Safety Board (committee governed)	Perform a wide variety of executive quasi-judicial, quasi-legislative, and advisory functions *outside* formal executive department—either single headed or committee governed
Commissions on Claims (mainly federal)	Indian Claims Commission, Foreign Claims Settlement Commission	Largely judicial functions
Regulatory Agencies (all levels)	Interstate Commerce Commission, Federal Trade Commission, Nuclear Regulatory Commission	Largely regulatory functions
Government Corporations (all levels)	Tennessee Valley Authority, U.S. Railway Association, Federal Prisons Industries, Inc., Federal Crop Insurance Corporation, St. Lawrence Seaway Development Corporation	Carry out a wide variety of functions either within an executive dept. or independent of the executive branch; may be mix public-private ownership
Boards, Councils, and Committees (all levels)	Federal Records Council, Water Resources Councils	Largely coordinative and advisory duties

Continued

Table 2.3 *Continued*

Bureaucratic Form	Examples of Form	Major Functions
Advisory Bodies (all levels)	National Historical Publications Commission, Advisory Board of St. Lawrence Seaway Development, Advisory Council on Vocational Education	Advisory group of primarily private citizens but legally constituted permanent bodies
Intergovernment Units (all levels)	Great Lakes River Basin Commission, Ozarks Regional Commission, Local Council of Government	National and regional planning, coordinating, and advisory bodies
Joint Executive-Congressional Units (all levels)	Migratory Bird Conservation Commission, Advisory Commission on Low Income Housing	Primarily advise both legislature and executive
Legislative Organizations (all levels)	General Accounting Office, State Auditor, County Auditor	Primarily advisor, research, oversight, and audit role for legislature
Special Districts (local only)	School District, Water and Sewer District, Fire District	Performs a wide range of county and municipal services independent of general government
Private Organizations, funded and set up by government (all levels)	Rand Corporation, Institute for Defense Analysis, MITRE, Los Alamos Labs, County Hospitals	Independent units funded partly or almost entirely by government and chartered by governor to perform specific types of contractual service
Public Organizations, privately funded with mixed public-private directorship and highly autonomous (all levels)	Federal Reserve Board, Corporation for Public Broadcasting, Legal Services Corporation	Autonomous public units, largely privately supported, with a wide variety of tasks

Table 2.4 Varieties of Policy Products of Public Bureaucracies

	Individual Effects	Environment Effects
Immediate Coercion	Regulatory Policies, e.g., Federal Trade Commission and Federal Communications Commission	Redistributive Policies, e.g., Federal Reserve Board, Internal Revenue Service, Social Security Administration, Federal Housing Administration
Remote Coercion	Distributive Policies, Veterans Administration, Agriculture Department, Department of Energy, National Science Foundation	Constituent Policies, e.g., Defense Department, State Department, Justice Department, Office of Management and Budget

fraudulent advertising, or Immigration and Naturalization Service (INS) en-forcement of immigration laws, or the Drug Enforcement Agency's efforts to combat illicit drug activities. By contrast, *redistributive policies,* according to Lowi's matrix, are immediate but influence society only as a whole. The Federal Reserve Board (FRB) establishes its bank reserve requirements and prime rates, causing, in turn, general inflationary or deflationary trends throughout society. The administration of the progressive income tax by the Internal Revenue Service (IRS) redistributes monies from one group of citizens in society to an-other, which affects the entire nation. The Social Security Administration (SSA) likewise redistributes monies from younger workers to pensioners.

Third, *distributive policies* are those public outputs that are remote *and* individual-oriented. Tariffs influence buying habits of individual consumers but are usually administered far from where these consumers live and work. Similarly, direct government subsidies to industry or to particular social groups, such as farmers or veterans, are distributive forms of public policies, according to Lowi. Finally, the fourth cell of Lowi's matrix contains *constituent policies,* which are both re-mote and aimed at all of society. The Department of Defense's (DoD) policy outputs are, for the most part, in this category—defense of the national inter-ests against foreign enemies. No one group of Americans gains more or less (at least in theory) from preserving national security, freedom, and liberty. Yet the work of DoD is remote from the daily life of the average citizen.

Obviously, real-world public agencies do not always fit neatly as pure types within the Lowi four-cell matrix. Many agencies promulgate multiple types of public policies at the same time. DoD, for example, may be primarily involved in defending the nation, but it is also very much engaged in distributional and redistributional policy making via its huge $300 billion-plus annual budgets. The EPA regulates air, water, and land quality in the United States, though it also acts to distribute grants to state, local, and private organizations and there-fore is very much engaged in distributive policy making. The Department of Agriculture (DoA), which was founded as a clientele department to serve the needs of farmers, can properly be viewed as a distributive agency, but it also reg-ulates the entire food chain to ensure the health and safety of Americans. Most agencies thus contain a mix of Lowi's categories.

However, the formal policy-making processes that are found within public agencies often are significantly shaped upon the dominant policy activity of an agency as is indicated in Table 2.5. Each variety of policy-making activity tends to have associated with it distinctive internal formal processes and procedures es-sential for carrying out these policies. As one would expect, regulatory policy-making bodies involve highly legalized internal processes, often associated with the legislative or judicial branches of government, rule making, adjudication, law enforcement, and investigation/review processes. Constituent services require more traditional forms of managerial processes to carry out tasks for their agen-cies: program development, program implementation, policy revision, program review, and evaluation. Redistributive bureaucracies contain normally a mix of le-galistic and managerial processes (adjudication, policy development, program im-plementation, and advisory). The internal processes of distributive organizations

Table 2.5 Major Formal Processes of U.S. Bureaucracy

AGENCY BY TYPE OF POLICY PROCESS

	Regulatory	Distributive	Redistributive	Constituent
Major Types of Formal Processes Involved in Agency Policy-Making Roles	*Rule Making* Quasi-legislative process of establishing agency rules for agency jurisdiction that covers everyone	*Distribution of Benefits* Specific distribution of cash, goods, services to groups, individuals, state or local government with or without restrictions	*Adjudication* Determination of whether or not individual can receive benefits that are due under law	*General Program Development* Designing new programs to meet constituent service needs
Key Elements of Formal Policy-Making Processes	*Adjudication* Quasi-judicial of charging violations of agency rules and effects only single case one at a time *Law Enforcement* Quasi-executive function of selected application of laws and rules to groups and individuals *Investigation and Review* Process of examining complaints to see if merits remedying as well as review regulatory actions in order to revise or change rulings	*Public Sponsored Research* In-house or contracted programs for research and development on distributive programs *Information Gathering and Dissemination* Collect, process, and send out data and information to groups and individuals involving benefits *Initiation of New Programs* Assists in development of new goods or changes old ones for distribution of benefits	*Policy Development* Creation of new proposals to change or readjust distribution of goods and services to individuals *Program Implementation* Carrying out of specifically mandated activities according to legislative standards *Advisory Processes* Assisting legislative and executive branches in programming new legislation, revising or proposing new laws, particularly using legislative clearance process	*Program Implementation* Carrying out specific legislative statutes and executive orders mandating service activities *Policy Revision and Creation* Creation or redesign of policies affecting program activities through advice to legislatures and executive *Program Review and Evaluation* Examination and investigation of programs in order to improve or change actions of agency

focus upon those processes that relate directly to the distribution of benefits, publicly sponsored research activities, information gathering and dissemination, and advisory processes. The type of policy activities, therefore, significantly influence the type of formal internal policy-making processes found in every agency.

Much of this chapter traced the development of the formal structures of modern U.S. bureaucracy. What *really* shapes public bureaucracies' directions and impacts upon society for the most part comes from a variety of formal and informal inputs from the outside. These bureaucratic inputs will be the subject of the next chapter.

SUMMARY OF KEY POINTS

This chapter outlined, in brief, the historical development of U.S. bureaucracy. A variety of societal demands over the past two hundred years contributed significantly to the growth of diverse types of bureaucratic institutions. At its creation in 1789 the United States required the formation of the first core functions to conduct diplomacy, wage war, mint currency, and so on. Western expansion brought about new bureaus and agencies, like the Interior Department, to cope with the country's internal economic/social development. Clientele agencies, such as the Agriculture, Commerce, and Labor departments, arose in the late nineteenth century as responses to specialized needs and pressures of important occupational interest groups. At roughly the same time, regulatory agencies and government corporations were created to protect the public interests in new policy areas and were organized with new types of administrative authority. The greatest increases in the size and scope of U.S. bureaucracy occurred as a result of the Great Depression of the 1930s, the defense requirements of the 1940s and 1950s, and the Great Society in the 1960s. Local bureaucracies mirrored the federal model in forms and functions and specialized in providing social services at the grass roots. Because of the surge in federal block grants, categorical aid, and revenue-sharing programs, public bureaucracy in states and localities grew rapidly in the 1960s and 1970s. Gradualism, experimental design, majoritarian surges, and complexity, coupled with the inertia of bureaucratic institutions, sustain the size and scope of U.S. bureaucracy. United States bureaucracy comes in a variety of forms—executive departments, agencies, bureaus, regulatory commissions, government corporations, boards, and many others. Despite the popular view, there is no *one* typical public bureaucracy or bureaucrat in the United States today.

KEY TERMS

core functions	executive departments	Great Society
clientele agencies	staff agencies	constituent policies
regulatory agencies	New Deal	distributive policies
government corporations	Cold War Era	redistributive policies

REVIEW MATERIAL

Review Questions

1. Why did the United States have little in the way of a government bureaucracy until the twentieth century? What were its major organizational forms until the twentieth century?

2. What key factors prompted the growth of bureaucracy in the twentieth century?

3. Why did diverse forms of bureaucratic organizations develop in America?

4. How can we generalize about the overall development of U.S. bureaucracy?

5. What is meant by bureaucratic policy making? Its four types? How is the type of policy making activity related to internal agency policy-making processes?

Class Debate Pro/Con

Resolved that the unique characteristics of U.S. bureaucracy's historic development, that is, gradualism, experimentalism, majoritarianism, and complexity, are the very sources of the American public's inability to comprehend how it operates and cope with it effectively in their daily lives.

Student Homework Assignment

Select a state or local public agency or unit of government and outline its history: Why was it created? Its evolution? Sources of growth or decline? Its forms, functions, policy outputs, and processes? Does its overall development conform or fail to conform to the bureaucratic history outlined in the chapter? Why or why not?

Case Analysis

Read "The Blast in Centralia No. 5" in any edition of Richard Stillman's Public Administration: Concepts and Cases. In many respects this case study unfolds like a Greek Tragedy, as if the mine disaster was destined from the start to occur—or was it? At what key points in the case study's history might the mine explosion have been prevented? What needed to happen at these historic points to stop the events that led to the catastrophe? Can participants within the historic stream of bureaucratic events, as depicted within this case, understand and then do something about their direction? If so, how? Or, are we, like the miners in Centralia No. 5, entrapped in bureaucratic actions we can neither comprehend nor alter?

NOTES

1. Leonard D. White, *The Federalists: A Study in Administrative History* (New York: Macmillan, 1948), pp. 22–23.

2. Ibid., p. 147.

3. Frederick C. Mosher (ed.), *Basic Documents of American Public Administration, 1776–1950* (New York: Holmes and Meier, 1976), pp. 36–38.

4. *The U.S. Government Manual* (Washington, DC, 1980), p. 733.

5. Richard L. Schott, *The Bureaucratic State: The Evolution and Scope of the American Federal Bureaucracy* (New York: General Learning Press, 1972), p. 9.

6. Leonard D. White, *The Republican Era, 1869–1901* (New York: Macmillan, 1958), p. 232.

7. Ibid.

8. Marver H. Bernstein, *Regulating Business by Independent Commission* (Princeton, NJ: Princeton University Press, 1955), p. 130.

9. Harold F. Seidman, *Politics, Position and Power*, 2d ed. (New York: Oxford University Press, 1975), p. 254.

10. House Document, pp. 91–313.

11. James Q. Wilson, "The Rise of the Bureaucratic State," *Public Interest* (Fall 1975), p. 90.

12. Seidman, *Politics*, p. 236.

13. Theodore Lowi, "Four Systems of Policy, Politics, and Choice," Inter-University Case Program, Case No. 110 (Syracuse, NY: Syracuse University, 1972), p. 27.

FURTHER READING

Students can learn much by reading Leonard White's now-classic four-volume history of the growth of U.S. bureaucracy: *The Federalists* (1948), *The Jeffersonians* (1951), *The Jacksonians* (1954), and *The Republican Era* (1958). Shorter but equally distinguished works include: Matthew A. Crenson, *The Federal Machine* (1975); Frederick C. Mosher, *Democracy and the Public Service*, 2d ed. (1982); and Robert H. Wiebe, *The Search for Order, 1877–1920* (1967). Useful interpretative pieces can be found in Richard Schott's brief monograph, *The Bureaucratic State* (1972), James Q. Wilson's "The Rise of the Bureaucratic State" in *The Public Interest* (Fall 1975), Herbert Kaufman's "Emerging Conflicts in the Doctrines of Public Administration," in *American Political Science Review* (1956), as well as John C. Beach et al. "State Administration and the Founding Fathers During the Critical Period," *Administration and Society* (February 1997) pp. 511–530.

For other theoretical conceptions of the rise of bureaucratic institutions, read Stephen Skowronek, *Building a New American State: The Expansion of National Administrative Capacities, 1877–1920* (1982); Don K. Price, *America's Unwritten Constitution* (1983); E. N. Gladden, *A History of Public Administration*, two volumes (1972); Ernest Barker, *The Development of Public Service in Western Europe, 1660–1930* (1944); Martin Albrow, *Bureaucracy* (1970); Brian Chapman, *The Profession of Government* (1959), and Sidney H. Aronson, *Status and Kinship in the Higher Civil Service* (1964); John Rohr, *To Run a Constitution* (1986); Richard Stillman, *Creating the American State* (1998); H. H. Gerth and C. Wright Mills (eds.), *From Max Weber* (1946); Alfred D. Chandler, *The Visible Hand* (1977); Dwight Waldo, *The Administrative State*, 2d ed. (1984); Theodore Lowi, *The End of Liberalism*, 2d ed. (1979); Martin J. Schiesl, *The Politics of Efficiency* (1977); Otis

L. Graham, *Toward a Planned Society* (1976); Barry Karl, *The Uneasy State* (1983); Samuel P. Huntington, *American Politics: The Promise of Disharmony* (1981); Camilla Stivers, *Bureau Men, Settlement Women* (2000); and Paul C. Light, *Tides of Reform* (1997).

Serious students of bureaucracy should examine primary materials—executive orders, congressional acts, and official reports—as found in Frederick C. Mosher (ed.), *Basic Documents of American Public Administration, 1776–1950* (1976) and Richard J. Stillman, *Basic Documents of American Public Administration since 1950* (1982).

For an outstanding reference book containing well-written, short essays on the development of many individual government agencies, see Donald R. Whitnah (ed.), *Government Agencies* (1983). Look especially at the references in this book for other useful books and essays on these agencies' development. The annual *U.S. Government Organization Manual* is an equally important reference book.

One should not neglect several excellent works on the growth of particular key governmental sectors and units: Thomas K. McCraw, *Prophets of Regulation* (1984); Frederick C. Mosher, *A Tale of Two Agencies* (1984); Samuel P. Huntington, *The Soldier and State* (1957); Larry Berman, *The Office of Management and the Presidency, 1921–1979* (1979); Jane S. Dahlberg, *The New York Bureau of Municipal Research* (1966); Barry Karl, *Executive Reorganization and Reform in the New Deal* (1963); Frederick C. Mosher, *The GAO* (1979); Don Kettl, *Leadership at the Fed* (1986); James Q. Wilson, *The Investigators* (1978); Darrell L. Pugh, *Looking Back—Moving Forward* (1988); David H. Rosenbloom, "Public Administration Theory and the Separation of Powers," *Public Administration Review* (1983); Paul Van Riper, *History of the United States Civil Service* (1958); Stephen Ambrose, *Upton and the Army* (1964); Martha Derthick, *The National Guard in Politics* (1965); Otto Nelson, *National Security and the General Staff* (1946); Robert Cushman, *The Independent Regulatory Commissions* (1941); Martha Derthick, *Agency Under Stress* (1990); Paul Light, *Monitoring Government* (1993); Jerry Mitchell, *The American Experiment with Government Corporations* (1999); Michael P. Riccards, *A Republic If You Can Keep It* (1987); and Richard J. Stillman II, *The Rise of the City Manager* (1974).

Comprehensive bibliographical guides to this literature are Daniel W. Martin, *The Guide to the Foundations of Public Administration* (1989); Jos C. N. Raaschelders, *Handbook of Administrative History* (1998); as well as Donald F. Kettl, "Public Administration," in Ada W. Finifter, *Political Science* (1993). Larry B. Hill (ed.), *The State of Bureaucracy* (1992) provides 11 essays by leading scholars of this topic that review the literature and current research issues in this field.

WEB SITES

http://www.fedstats.gov/: federal agencies

http://www.uncle-sam.com/independent.html: quasi-official agencies

http://www.theorator.com/bills107/issues/bureaucracy.html: Bills Concerning the Growth or Reduction of the Federal Bureaucracy in the 107th Congress

http://www.whitehouse.gov/government/independent-agencies.html: federal agencies and commissions—listed alphabetically

http://www.analytictech.com/mb021/histbur.htm: Historical Forces Behind Bureaucratization

3

■

External Forces Shaping
Modern Bureaucracy

George Will observed that "government generally is a dance, a minuet, of small minorities." He might have said much the same thing about public bureaucracy: "It's generally a dance, a minuet, of special interests around government agencies." This chapter will examine this "dance." More precisely, this chapter explores the large variety of external forces shaping modern U.S. bureaucracy. What is the general environment of public bureaucracies today? What are the major inputs that shape U.S. bureaucratic agencies? The external sources of their growth? Stability? Decline?

It is not easy to differentiate *external* forces from *internal* factors that affect every administrative unit. Modern public agencies are made up of multiple offices, layered one upon another. Historically, this layering occurs as new units are added to older ones or as old ones subdivide responsibilities. For example, the Federal Bureau of Investigation (FBI) was established as an autonomous agency 38 years after the Justice Department was created in 1870. Today it is a subunit of the Justice Department; therefore, from the standpoint of the Justice Department, the FBI is an internal unit. But from the perspective of the director of the FBI, the department is external to the bureau's operations. Similarly, at the local level, the fire department as a distinct agency is normally created *after* the incorporation of a municipality and is inside, or internal to, a city government. But from the vantage point of the fire chief, the city is external to its operations.

The perspective or organizational standpoint from which one views a bureau, office, or agency determines whether forces are considered internal or external to its operations. The emphasis in this chapter, however, will be to point out the major external factors that shape the future of every unit of bureaucracy at the federal, state, and local levels. External inputs are the powerful forces influencing every agency's growth, continuation, or decline. These inputs can determine the fate of a local police department or a state welfare office or a federal regulatory agency. Because of their importance to an agency's future, these inputs should be carefully examined.

As Figure 3.1 indicates, the external forces "dancing around" every public bureaucracy can be divided into four types. First is the general environment, consisting of the broad milieu of U.S. values, constitutional structure, and functional requirements. This general environment is the most fundamental and long-term factor influencing context within which all U.S. public organizations operate.

Second, the socioeconomic factors involving specific shifts in population, technology, and the economy directly affect the growth, stability, and decline of individual bureaucratic institutions. These socioeconomic inputs influence the types of services and levels of services bureaucracy performs for a society. Socioeconomic forces create "the market" for public services rendered by government bureaucracy. In short, they determine the overall task demands and levels of resources available for bureaucracy.

The third level of input includes political forces, that is, the major external political groups and interests surrounding public agencies. They may be created and fostered by the socioeconomic factors, or they may be autonomous and independent of socioeconomic factors. They include public opinion, clientele groups, media coverage, public interest groups, and power elites. All these in various yet critical ways influence an agency's survival, stability, and decline.

The fourth level, institutional inputs, come from within government and involve institutions nearest and most directly influential to the bureaucracy itself: chief executives and their staffs, legislatures and their staffs, courts and judges, as well as other offices, agencies, bureaus, and departments at every level of government. Often the political level of inputs registers its influence upon bureaucracy through this institutional level. Nonetheless, institutional inputs are often

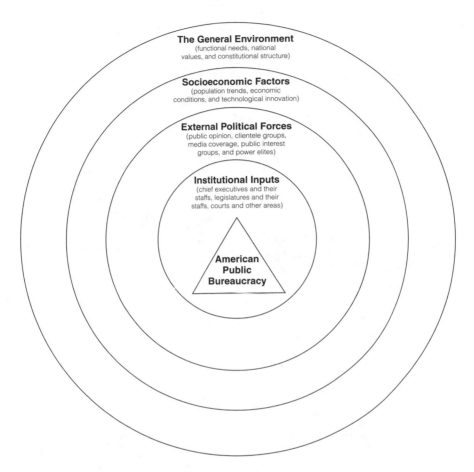

FIGURE 3.1   External forces shaping public bureaucracy: four types of inputs

most immediately germane and necessary to any bureaucracy's survival, especially in regard to establishing the goals to be accomplished, budget appropriations, personnel levels, laws and rules, top leadership, and the formal/informal degrees of independence or dependence.

While the general environment and the three levels of inputs—socioeconomic, political, and institutional—will be discussed separately, in reality they rarely act separately. Rather, they more often "dance" in concert with one another. Changing public opinion may stimulate media coverage, which in turn may cause legislative action or reaction regarding an individual public agency. Further, levels and the patterns of inputs change within different situations; therefore, not all the forces outlined here influence *every* bureaucracy. Some forces influence any given agency more than others; some come into play while others do not, depending on the time, place, and circumstances. Much, therefore, depends on the relationship between the actual situation and the

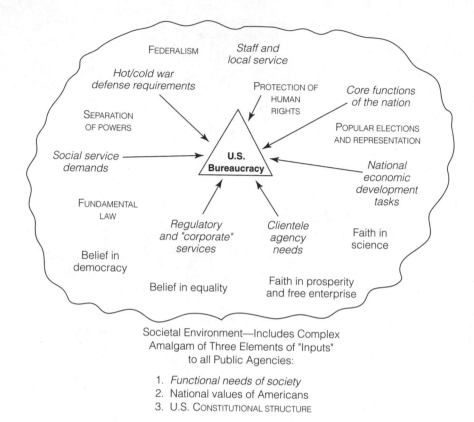

Societal Environment—Includes Complex
Amalgam of Three Elements of "Inputs"
to all Public Agencies:

1. *Functional needs of society*
2. National values of Americans
3. U.S. CONSTITUTIONAL STRUCTURE

FIGURE 3.2   Societal environment—first-level inputs

special amalgam of external factors that may affect any one particular bureaucracy. The nature of these inputs, how they shape the future of public organizations, and their basic forms and configurations of power are the central
questions addressed in this chapter.

THE GENERAL ENVIRONMENT OF AMERICAN PUBLIC
BUREAUCRACY: FIRST-LEVEL INPUTS

Public bureaucracy operates within the general environment of U.S. society,
and within this particular milieu (see Figure 3.2) three important and constant factors surround bureaucratic institutions: persistent functional needs of
society, fundamental national values that the American people hold near and
dear, and the constitutional structure of government within which public bureaucracy operates.

The Functional Needs of Society

In Chapter 2 we learned that U.S. public bureaucracy grew up to service the essential functional needs which persist to this day.

Core Functions The first duty of bureaucracy is to perform very essential core functions of government necessary for the survival of the nation, state, or city, such as diplomacy, defense, and internal security at the national level; and police, fire, and other functions at the local level.

National Economic Development Tasks The economic requirements necessary to build a nation and provide for industrial growth and prosperity are considered equally fundamental in modern society. Today this remains a major functional activity of several units of bureaucracy, such as the Council of Economic Advisors and the departments of Commerce and the Interior.

Clientele Agency Needs Since the late nineteenth century, a major function of U.S. bureaucracy has been to represent the needs, concerns, and interests of key diverse occupational and social groups within government.

Regulatory and Corporate Services Regulating the national economy and performing many types of activities through public corporate enterprises also remain fundamental functions of government.

Social Services Particularly since the Great Depression of the 1930s, bureaucratic agencies have assumed a variety of important social service tasks, including the care of the aged, the infirm, the poor, the unemployed, and the homeless.

Global Hot and Cold War Requirements Since World War II, the U.S. position of leadership in the free world has created important and enduring bureaucratic tasks involving international organizations, defense capabilities, and foreign diplomacy.

Staff and Local Services The managerial responsibilities of running large and complex bureaucracies are sources of its further development and of the provision of various local services at the state, county, and municipal levels of government.

National Values

Behind these constant demands upon bureaucracy are important fundamental national values peculiar to the United States, within which bureaucracy operates. These values and structures are critical to shaping contemporary bureaucracy. Some of the major civic values are worth outlining in brief.

Belief in Democracy Faith in democracy, freedom, and popular participation as a basis of government are considered fundamental to the heritage of the United States. The democratic ideal is a deeply ingrained tradition. It makes its impact upon bureaucratic institutions in numerous ways, from the public's insistence upon specific devices for control of bureaucracy to the broader conceptions that public bureaucracy should ultimately serve "the people" and "the popular will."

Belief in Equality Like democracy, equality is also a basic belief of Americans, stemming from Jefferson's ringing statement in the Declaration of Independence that "all men are created equal." Much of the work today within bureaucracy is concerned with promoting equality and equity. Its services must be provided for *all* Americans fairly and equably.

Faith in Prosperity and Free Enterprise American culture has largely been shaped by commercial enterprises. Over the years the United States has maintained a strong commitment to the promoting of material prosperity through the free enterprise system. "The business of America is business," a U.S. president once commented, and U.S. bureaucracy today is deeply involved with as well as committed to the promotion of a free market economy and national prosperity. Indeed, some U.S. bureaucratic institutions (i.e., the government corporation or council manager governments) have been shaped in the corporate model because of the popularity of business ideals.

Faith in Science and Education Science as well as education in general are also fundamental ideals. These ideals hold a special place of honor, bordering almost on religious devotion. Partly this devotion is based upon the belief that science and education can advance material progress and democratic ideals. As a result, roughly half of local and state budgets are devoted to supporting education, grades K through 12 as well as higher education. A substantial portion of federal budgets go to support scientific and educational goals.

The U.S. Constitution

The general environment within which the U.S. bureaucracy operates has also been shaped by elements of the U.S. Constitution.

The Fundamental Law The U.S. Constitution itself serves as the fundamental law for the United States. It sets forth the purposes and basic framework of government and also stresses that the government should be rooted *in law.* Indeed, the basic construct of public bureaucracy is itself framed in laws, rules, and statutes. Laws both help to insure bureaucratic actions are responsive ultimately to the general electorate and their representatives as well as make U.S. bureaucracy operate fundamentally in a different way compared to private businesses.

Separation of Powers Basic to the Constitution in Articles I, II, and III is the "scatteration of power" through the vertical division of constitutional authority into three separate branches: executive, legislative, and judicial. This division of power has posed special complexities and dilemmas for U.S. bureaucracy since it fragments bureaucracy's structures, activities, and oversight, by holding government agencies accountable not only to the executive branch but to the courts and the legislature as well.

Federalism The federal Constitution further divides power horizontally among the federal, state, and local governments, thus giving some degree of institutional autonomy to each level of government. Federalism "scatters power" in order to prevent concentration of authority and to safeguard human liberty. Like the concept of separation of powers, the federal design of the U.S. Constitution required by the Tenth Amendment in the Bill of Rights adds further complexity and unique dilemmas to U.S. bureaucracy.

Protection of Human Rights The first 10 amendments to the Constitution, the Bill of Rights, extend basic liberties to every citizen, such as the freedoms of speech, the press, and religion and the right to due process. These basic protections place limits upon what bureaucracy can and cannot do to individuals, thus further complicating bureaucratic tasks. The Bill of Rights requires that bureaucratic activity hold the rights of human beings as a high priority, even, at times, higher than the needs of society as a whole.

Periodicity of Popular Elections and Representation According to the Constitution, federal elections must be held at 2-, 4-, or 6-year intervals. This constitutional requirement provides the avenue for popular participation in governmental affairs as well as the major mechanism for popular oversight of government. Popular elections are also a chief source of top-level direction and leadership—elected *and* appointed—of public bureaucracy. These elections also create complex issues involving the changing relationships *between* popularly elected officials and permanent bureaucratic officials.

It is important to recognize that the three elements of functional needs, national values, and constitutional structure work together to make up a unique and complex general environment within which American public bureaucracy operates today. This environment directly shapes what bureaucracy can and cannot accomplish. Specific bureaus, agencies, and offices are also influenced by socioeconomic, political, and institutional factors.

SOCIOECONOMIC FACTORS: SECOND-LEVEL INPUTS

As Max Weber, one of the great scholars of bureaucracy, once pointed out, bureaucratic institutions arose first under conditions of sufficient populations, particularly urban populations, combined with a "monied economy."[1] Concentrations of people who trade with currency rather than barter are fertile soil for the development of bureaucratic institutions. While Weber was taking "the grand world view" to explain the rise of bureaucracy during the early Roman empire, in fifth-century China, and during the late Middle Ages in Europe, much the same could be said today about U.S. bureaucracy. Bureaus, agencies, and departments are fundamentally dependent upon socioeconomic conditions that create various demands for such institutions.

Three factors in particular are important for creating market demand for bureaucratic services and institutions. First are population shifts. Rising or declining populations as well as different demographic mixes of classes, especially income classes, determine to a large extent the levels and types of bureaucratic services rendered and institutions required. Second, economic conditions are critical. The GNP (the total of all goods and services produced in the nation), regional economic growth or decline, increasing or decreasing tax/revenue bases, and general levels of employment, inflation, and interest rates either encourage or retard bureaucracy's development. Finally, technological innovation is a vital element. Much of modern bureaucracy is a response to new technology which must be regulated or accommodated by infrastructure (roads, railroad tracks, telephone poles, and the like). The speed of technological innovation and the kind and quantity of technology developed can decisively influence the growth or stagnation of public bureaucracy.

The following three types of socioeconomic factors involving population shifts, economic changes, and technological inventions can combine in differing ways to influence the future of particular bureaucratic institutions.

Regional/National Socioeconomic Growth
Situations: High Task Demands

Many Rocky Mountains and Northwest cities and states have experienced enormous growth in the last decade or more. Populations have grown rapidly; their regional economies have boomed as industries moved south and new ones have opened their doors; jobs became plentiful, attracting more people to these areas. In certain areas of Colorado, Utah, and Washington state the rapidity of technological innovation by computer, hi-tech, and Pacific rim trading firms has been an important factor in promoting this economic boom. Workers and their families have moved from the North to these areas for jobs, and retirees have gone there for the recreation and retirement. Population growth, economic expansion, and technological innovation have created strong market demands for public services provided by governmental bureaucracy. Roads and schools are needed; water and sewage facilities and utilities must be built; planning, zoning, and other public services considered essential to industrial and community development are necessary. Local bureaucracies have had to expand to cope with the needs of population growth, industrial expansion, and technological change. The "boom town" or "boom region" syndrome creates, in turn, revenue and tax surpluses that finance very real demands for more public services, particularly social services, physical infrastructures, and economic regulation, which must be supplied by government bureaucracy. Silicon Valley, California, for example, is one area that exemplifies how successive waves of innovation since 1950 promoted regional economic growth (see Figure 3.3).

Socioeconomic boom periods generate bureaucratic expansion for the nation as a whole. One such era was the post–World War II period in the United States. Economic conditions—low inflation rates, favorable trade and budget surpluses, and strong growth rates—all provided adequate budget resources for

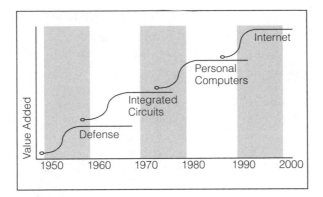

FIGURE 3.3   Evolution of Silicon Valley

funding the large defense and foreign assistance programs described in Chapter 2. Population expansion, particularly the postwar baby boom, stimulated nationwide needs for improved educational, recreational, highway, and housing facilities. These services came to be provided by large federal departments, such as Health and Human Services, Housing and Urban Development, Transportation, and many others. The automobile, computers, television, mass transit, and other such modern conveniences created needs for new public agencies.

Think about the effect of the car on bureaucracy. In the postwar United States, the automobile necessitated the paving of hundreds of thousands of miles of federal, state, and local roadways; caused the out-migration of millions of people to suburbia, which in turn caused the creation of numerous local governments; and necessitated massive and complex state regulatory machinery to license vehicles as well as to control the environment. The state highway patrol and licensing bureaus were also products of the automobile age. There are many other indirect spinoffs from the development of the auto (some claim even the postwar baby boom can be attributed to the backseats of autos).

It is difficult, if not impossible, to sort out exactly which variables are more or less critical to bureaucratic growth. Generally, new bureaucratic activities are stimulated by one or more of the following socioeconomic factors: (1) an expanding population with new needs for services; (2) a changing demographic mix, such as a baby boom, that creates particular demands for new types of public goods and services; (3) a growing revenue and tax base fueled by an expanding regional or national economy. (A growing economy permits more and better social services); (4) little or no inflation and low interest rates that allow for adequate capital formation and infrastructure development by public agencies; and (5) technological change and scientific innovation spurring the development of public works projects (i.e., highways) or of government regulations (i.e., the Federal Communications Commission's regulation of radio and television frequencies).

Socioeconomic Stability: Constant
Bureaucratic Task Demands

Under stable conditions, bureaucratic growth may be limited or nonexistent. Regions or cities where the economy is relatively stable, the population unchanging, and technological innovation constant create markets where demands for bureaucratic services vary little. In small towns, in some suburban communities, and even in some regions where the population-economy-technology variables are stable, few new sorts of public services are needed or demanded. The prime emphasis may well be on keeping the costs of government down and the size of bureaucracy constant: If there is no rapid increase in total numbers of people, there are no new demands for new bureaucratic services. If there is no changing demographic cohort of populations, such as a baby boom, there are no sudden new requirements for specific public services for particular groups of citizens. If there is no jump in consumer incomes, there are few new wants and demands on bureaucracy and no enriched tax and revenue bases for rendering such services. If there are few new technological innovations, little demand for government intervention is stimulated. Under such stable socioeconomic conditions, in a small town, for example, the city government may simply concentrate upon "keeping its doors open" and do little else. The municipal bureaucracy of an affluent, stable suburban community or region concentrates on providing good schools, roads, and safe and quiet streets, at reasonable costs, emphasizing *no* growth in total size of government. The community's goal is efficient, effective, and stable public services and an environment that fosters an unchanging community lifestyle. Hence, there are insignificant new demands for more public tasks and public agencies. This same situation can hold true for state- or regional-level bureaucracies as well.

The United States has rarely, if ever, experienced prolonged eras of socioeconomic stability. Change has been a major part of its history. But some federal activities have experienced stable task demands because of relatively stable socioeconomic conditions surrounding these agencies. The U.S. Battle Monuments Commission, in charge of taking care of battle sites, has been relatively stable in size, except in wartime. Many other public agencies also have few new task demands to stimulate their growth. They thus remain relatively stagnant in activity and static in size.

Socioeconomic Decline: Reduced Task Demands

A declining socioeconomic situation can have two very different effects upon bureaucratic institutions. At the national level, but not at the state and municipal levels, a precipitous socioeconomic decline can be a driving force for rapid expansion of bureaucratic institutions because of the U.S. government's ability to incur massive deficits. The Great Depression prompted massive increases in federal expenditures for a wide range of new social services, primarily to alleviate the chronic unemployment and impoverished social conditions of the 1930s. Such "pump-priming" or "countercycle expenditures," based upon New Deal experimentation and Keynesian economic doctrines, increased federal expenditures to offset industrial unemployment and economic decline. "Pump-priming" throughout the 1930s also fueled a dramatic and unprecedented jump in size, scope, and intensity of bureaucratic activities.

At the state and local levels, where such fiscal policy of countercyclical expenditures is impossible or prohibited by strict local/state debt limitations and revenue ceilings, the reverse generally occurs under declining socioeconomic conditions (except where federal help is provided). For example, during the late 1970s and early 1980s, the northeastern frostbelt and midwestern rustbelt regions of the United States experienced just such a downturn. The "oil shocks" of the 1970s—a tenfold jump in oil prices, from less than $3 to nearly $40 per barrel—produced a rapidly rising double-digit inflation rate. Industrial productivity slowed. Some sectors of the economy, such as northeastern smokestack industries—steel, rubber, and autos—were particularly hard hit by foreign competition, which caused some plants to slow down production or, in some cases, to close altogether. Unemployment jumped to nearly 11 percent of the total workforce. Massive out-migrations to sunbelt states occurred in the late 1970s and early 1980s as people sought work and better living conditions. Likewise, in the early 1990s, earthquakes, riots, defense cuts, and floods in California as well as the dawn of the twenty-first century produced a massive "hi-tech" slump due to oversupply and falling demand in many regions produced an economic downturn resulting in a severe state-wide recession and unemployment as well as cutbacks in state social services and bureaucratic activities.

The direct effects of declining socioeconomic conditions bring about sharp cutbacks in state and local public services. Population declines create less need for bureaucratic services; industrial slowdowns and plant closings dry up regional and local revenue bases and taxing powers; technological innovation slows or shifts elsewhere. Such socioeconomic declines translate into bureaucratic reductions that in some states or regions become quite severe.

In Massachusetts, for example, hard hit by the economic downturn, voters in 1978 passed Proposition 2½, which slashed property tax revenues from 8 to 2½ percent of the market rate, cut excise tax revenue, held regional authorities to 4 percent budget increases, and eliminated binding arbitration for police and fire personnel. The direct impact of Proposition 2½ was a loss of 20,000 public service jobs at the local level and 8,000 at the state level. Bureaucratic services were reduced across the board. Massachusetts residents either did without some public services or were asked to pay for others that had been performed free of charge or at little cost. Similar cutbacks occurred elsewhere in declining states or regions, although how the cutbacks were handled and their degree of intensity vary widely from state to state and locality to locality.

George E. Peterson and Thomas Muller, Urban Institute scholars, assert: "There can be little doubt that substantial population loss compounds the fiscal pressure on city governments. Population decline tends to bring an automatic loss of tax-raising capacity; corresponding economies in city expenditures

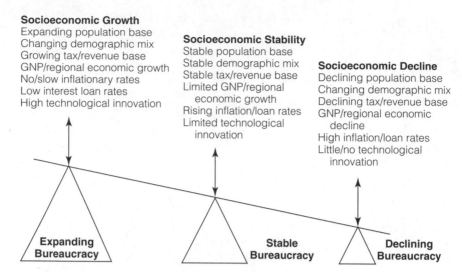

FIGURE 3.4   Socioeconomic forces influencing bureaucracy

are much more difficult to achieve.[2] In these situations local bureaucracy is frequently forced to contract.

The federal level is not immune to socioeconomic pressures, either. The early 1980s due to Reagan's Presidential initiatives saw federal social service cutbacks, prompted in part by fiscal pressures on the federal budget. Or, in the 1990s with the end of the Cold War defense cutbacks were severe. The social security program in the twenty-first century especially faces critical socioeconomic pressures in the future. Figure 3.5 points out that as the large baby boom cohort grows up, the total population ages. The executive summary of a recent report of the Population Reference Bureau highlighted the effects of such aging on the social security program: "The social security system is in poor financial health in part because of the aging of the U.S. population, the changing face of the American household, improved life expectancy, earlier retirement, large increases in benefits, and slow economic growth combined with rapid inflation."[3] These factors prompted Congress in the 1990s to raise social security taxes and to delay benefits to certain categories of individuals in order to save the system from bankruptcy.

The Reality of Present-Day Socioeconomic Pressures
upon Bureaucracy: A Mixed Set of Futuristic Influences

In reality, changing socioeconomic factors outlined on Figure 3.4 create mixed effects that neither totally accelerate nor shrink bureaucratic size. A Cabinet Council on Economic Affairs report on shifting socioeconomic trends in the United States over the next 10 to 15 years points out that "the changing demographics will have positive overall effects on the economy, but the necessary ad-

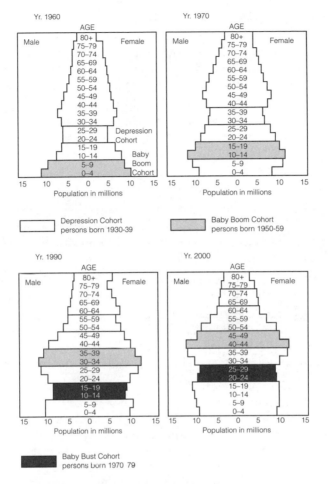

FIGURE 3.5   U.S. population age-sex pyramids, 1960–2000

Sources: 1960–1970: U.S. Bureau of the Census: 1980–1990: Unpublished tabulations prepared by Leon Bouvier for the Select Commission on Immigration and Refugee Policy, 1980.

justments may be difficult for specific sectors and individuals."[4] Among the many probable effects on bureaucratic activities cited by the report are:

- The decline of the youthful population will make our ability to maintain all volunteer armed forces difficult over the next few decades.

- To attract the diminishing pools of young people, military wages may have to be increased by 12 percent to compete with higher real wages paid in the private sector.

- Decline in the number of young workers will lessen the need for job training and other federal programs targeted at employment for the young.

- As the overall school-age population declines, some schools will be shut, but greater percentages of students will be minorities and immigrants in center cities, creating substantial local needs for specialized educational training.

- Today, 25 percent of federal outlays go to the aged (over 65). But as the United States "grays," this number could increase to 32 to 63 percent by 2025, putting increasing pressures on social security, medicaid, medicare, and other programs for the elderly.

- As the population matures, productivity and savings rates generally go up, causing positive effects on tax revenues, interest rates, and credit markets, all sources of possible government revenue.

- As the population ages, there will be greater pressures for increased varieties of social services and retirement systems.

- As the youth cohort (18–25) in the population declines, so might crime, auto accidents, and the student population, resulting in less demand for police-related services, public hospitals, and public educational institutions.

- Leisure time activities, particularly recreational services for the elderly and retired, will increase as the population matures.

- As family formation rates decline because of the decline in the number of youths and the increase in the number of elderly, fewer single-family homes and more apartment and condo dwellings will be needed, thus shifting community governments' emphasis in urban planning and development.

No doubt such predictions are highly speculative and open to challenge, but what is clear from such forecasts is that socioeconomic factors can have many major influences upon bureaucratic institutions. Particularly, as Figure 3.6 emphasizes, the rapid growth projected in the over 85-year-old age category may pose the most critical new burdens facing American public bureaucracy in the future for welfare, medical, and nursing home services.

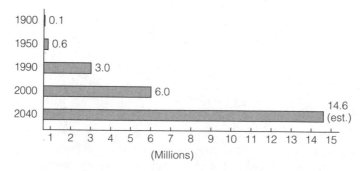

FIGURE 3.6 Total number of americans (in millions) 85 years old or older

Source: U.S. Bureau of the Census.

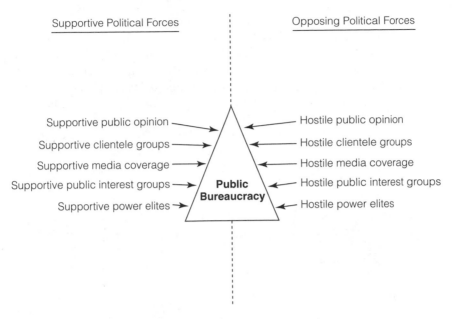

Supportive Political Forces   Opposing Political Forces

Supportive public opinion ⟶   ⟵ Hostile public opinion

Supportive clientele groups ⟶   ⟵ Hostile clientele groups

Supportive media coverage ⟶   ⟵ Hostile media coverage

Supportive public interest groups ⟶   **Public**   ⟵ Hostile public interest groups
                              Bureaucracy
Supportive power elites ⟶   ⟵ Hostile power elites

FIGURE 3.7   Supportive/opposing political forces surrounding bureaucracy

EXTERNAL POLITICAL ACTORS: THIRD-LEVEL INPUTS

The third level of inputs are external political actors that significantly shape the purposes, processes, and actions of bureaucracy. External groups can be highly visible, vocal, and immediately attentive to what public agencies do or don't do. As Figure 3.7 indicates, they can be divided into essentially two groups—supporters and opponents of agencies. For the most part, neutral political groups make no significant impacts upon public agencies (though their lack of involvement can indeed give others latitude for taking action).

Administrative organizations do not exist in a vacuum; that is, without some degree of this external public support or hostility exercised either directly upon the agency or through intermediaries such as lawyers and lobbyists. At the widest level, public support (or hostility) is registered upon agencies by public opinion as reflected in polls, surveys, or a barrage of angry letters to an agency head; by contrast, the most direct and explicit pressures on bureaucracy may be from specific powerful clientele groups that surround many agencies. For example, veterans groups like the American Legion and the Veterans of Foreign Wars have vital stakes in the operations of the Department of Veterans Affairs. Other external political actors include the media (newspapers, radio, television), public interest groups (Common Cause and Ralph Nader's groups), power elites (often informal but highly powerful networks of influential citizens and advisors, such as consulting firms, contractors, and special counsels). This chapter will examine the specific types of critical inputs each of these makes upon bureaucratic processes and institutions.

Public Opinion

Generally public opinion is too transitory and amorphous to have much influence on the typical public agency. Most agencies simply do not operate in the direct gaze of the public eye. How many citizens care about the County Records Management Office or the Federal Property Resource Service? Most do not even know of their existence. John Q. Public is frequently too busy, too ill-informed, or too uninterested to pay much attention to administrative matters that are frequently technical, arcane, and obscure. As Walter Lippmann wrote, "It is not fair to expect too much of the common man. . . . The public will arrive in the middle of the third act and will leave before the last curtain, having stayed just long enough perhaps to decide who is the hero and who is the villain of the piece."[5]

Public opinion expresses itself at the polls every 2 or 4 years after highly charged political campaigns. Public opinion directly influences the selection of legislators and chief executives, but rarely does it pay direct, sustained attention to specific administrative actions. But this is not to suggest that public opinion *never* involves itself with bureaucracy. Like a great unseen presence, it exerts tremendous strength at certain moments—perhaps only fleeting ones—creating enormous pressures on particular administrative activities.

Generally, public support or hostility is triggered by three factors: first, a dramatic event such as the 9/11 terrorist attack on the New York World Trade Center and the Pentagon in Washington, D.C., the disaster at Three Mile Island in 1980, the U.S.S.R.'s launching of Sputnik in 1957, Hurricane Andrew in South Florida in 1992, or the 1994 Los Angeles Earthquake can evoke a strong and immediate public demand for new or increased bureaucratic activities—beefed-up National Security, more rapid emergency relief to hurricane or earthquake victims, better nuclear regulation in the Three Mile Island case, and increased funding for U.S. space projects in 1957. A catastrophe like 3,000 deaths in 9/11 led to rapid expansion of Defense and Homeland Security expenditures; the deaths of 240 marines in Lebanon in October 1983 prompted severe public criticism and resulted in new military efforts to protect U.S. soldiers' safety, eventually leading to the marines' total withdrawal from Lebanon by February 1984. Similarly, accidental deaths of 18 U.S. Army Rangers and the wounding of 75 in Somalia, East Africa, on October 3, 1992, led to President Clinton's promise to withdraw all American forces by the end of March 1994 and turn operations over to the United Nations. In such cases, widely publicized catastrophes can produce sharply expanded or curtailed or reformed agency actions almost overnight.

Second, certain highly visible agencies have over the years made special efforts to curry public favor and develop positive public images. The FBI and the U.S. Marine Corps throughout much of their recent histories have paid particular attention to generating favorable coverage from the media. Their PR efforts in the long run pay these agencies rich dividends, especially in recruitment of personnel and budget allocations. The U.S. Marine Corps' annual Toys for Tots Program and spit-and-polish drill teams help maintain overall public confidence, which then can be translated into legislative support for their activities.

Third, public opinion can produce long-term external influences on public agencies. It is no accident, for example, that Los Angeles developed one of the earliest and strongest air pollution control programs in the nation. Beginning shortly after World War II, Los Angeles initiated local air pollution controls because of growing popular support for clean air. Air pollution abatement still remains a high priority for people living in Southern California, and it is therefore a vital concern of local government. Public perceptions, however, can swing rapidly one way or another as external threats increase or decrease. For example, over the past four or more decades public support for defense expenditures has generally coincided with actual increases in defense appropriations. In 1952, in the midst of the Korean War, 80 percent of the U.S. public opposed cuts in the defense budget, which then grew by almost 60 percent. By contrast, in 1972, as more and more Americans wanted their government to withdraw from Vietnam, only 25 percent of the public opposed defense cuts, and the defense budget grew little. In 1982, 60 percent of Americans opposed defense cuts. New concerns about defense preparedness arose largely because of events such as the 1980 Iran hostage crisis and President Reagan's 1980 political campaign promises, and in 1982 the defense budget grew 20 percent. Similarly, at the end of the Cold War in the 1990s, public support for defense spending waned and major defense cuts were initiated by both the Bush senior and Clinton administrations but then after the 9/11 2001 tragedy rose sharply again. Big swings in public opinion about defense issues have, over the long term, directly affected trends in defense budget allocations and the size and quality of the entire National Security establishment.

The Media

Since the 1980s, as illustrated by Figure 3.8, which shows that as the AIDS epidemic spread, AIDS attracted increasing media attention and public outcry, especially with graphic details and photos of death and dying youth. As a result, the federal appropriation for AIDS research was rapidly increased by Congress, much of it thanks to vivid images portrayed on TV and in the press. Like public opinion, the media ignore much of the work of administrative units in government. Except for large-city papers like the *New York Times,* the *Washington Post,* and the *Los Angeles Times,* and public radio or television news, the media give only fleeting attention to administrative agencies. The exceptional heroism of local firefighters in putting out a three-alarm blaze or a governor's education budget may be highlighted, but the media cover most bureaucratic work with little depth or detail. Why? There are many contributing factors.

First and foremost, the media are in business to sell advertising space, newspapers, and air time. Thus the media are often compelled to cover news that is of interest to local audiences at the moment. A popular superbowl game thus preempts a report on an obscure regulatory agency or on a budget allocation, even though the latter events may have far-reaching and more profound effects on everyday life. Tight deadlines, too few staffers, poorly trained and poorly paid reporters, and limited space, combined with uninformed or careless readers, diminish interest in administrative details that are often boring and complex. Further, competition for readers' attention is fierce in most media markets today among TV, radio, and various print sources. Thus, editors give "play" to the most exciting stories to keep or attract a greater market share, which in turn affects their profit margins. All these factors serve to limit, distort, or simplify coverage.

Other factors influence coverage as well. Norton Long once told the story of a New York City mayor who, after returning from a whirlwind European vacation, was badgered by the press to tell about what he had learned on his trip. Trying to make his trip seem important and productive, he said, "I was impressed with the antinoise campaign in Paris." This gave the reporters something to write about and got the mayor off the hook. But the editorial staff at one paper was having a slow news day and needed a story to generate copy. So they picked up the antinoise idea and even brought out a special edition of the paper with a headline, "Mayor Favors Anti-Noise Campaign." Soon other city papers took up the hue and cry for an antinoise campaign, and before long city agencies were mobilized to carry out just such a crusade—all because the mayor had to think of something fast off the top of his head to tell local reporters who needed something to print.[6]

While this story points out that media coverage can indeed be trivial, episodic, and lacking in depth, the media can nonetheless influence administrative activities by (1) creating new problems for agencies to solve where none had previously existed or had not been perceived as important—for example, a municipal antinoise crusade; (2) helping to direct or redirect the existing priorities of departments or agencies through editorials, "the slant of the news," and the intensity of coverage of certain issues or events; and (3) giving sustained support or criticism to public programs and thus influencing *how* these bureaucratic programs are delivered, as well as when, where, and to whom they are delivered—again through the intensity and slant of coverage.

As Brookings scholar Walter G. Held has noted, different media are important to different agencies, depending on the markets served by particular media: "Bureau leaders in the Department of Agriculture are less concerned with efforts by the *New York Times* to affect their decision making than with the editorial views and interpretive reporting of the newspapers in the farmbelt and in rural communities because the *Times* is oriented to the urban dweller rather than toward those in rural areas. On the other hand, the bureau leaders in the State Department find the *Times* of considerable significance when it attempts to influence decisions in international affairs."[7] Indeed, specialized publications like *The American Hunter,* published by the National Rifle Association, and *Today's Education,* prepared by the National Education Association, while not having wide daily circulations can target enormous *and sustained* special interest pressures on particular agency decisions. The latter journal is by far more critical to leaders of the roughly 15,000 local school districts, and the former impacts decisions of the Bureau of Alcohol, Tobacco, and Firearms that administers America's gun laws and the Bureau of Land Management that oversees 270 million acres of public land used by hunters.

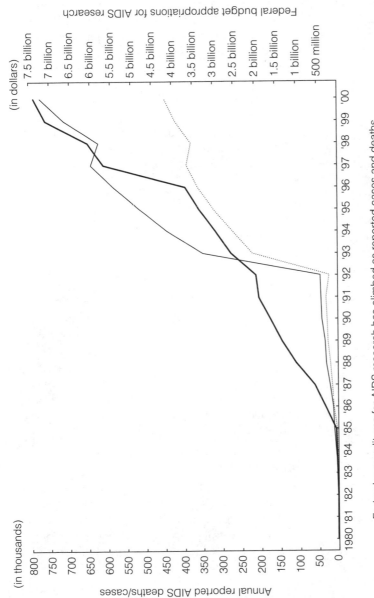

FIGURE 3.8 Federal budget appropriations for AIDS research, reported AIDS cases, and deaths from AIDS

Federal expenditures for AIDS research has climbed as reported cases and deaths from AIDS attracted attention from the media and the public in the 1980s

.... Deaths from AIDS
——— Reported cases of AIDS
——— Dollars appropriated for AIDS research by federal government

Source: 2002 U.S. budget and national statistics on AIDS-related death rates published by U.S. Public Health Service.

By contrast, a highly rated television investigative news program like *60 Minutes* can bring about a brief but sometimes overwhelming public reaction to an agency's actions or inaction. A story on *60 Minutes* about a young black man imprisoned in Dallas for a robbery he did not commit brought about his immediate release by the governor. But whether the story will have any long-term impact on the administration of Dallas's criminal justice system is open to doubt. Neither *60 Minutes* nor its viewers can sustain long-term interest in the complicated and difficult details of criminal justice administrative reform. The rise of popularity of similar "TV news magazines" like *60 minutes II* only accentuates the episodic criticism of public agencies.

Though perhaps the most difficulty that the media pose for bureaucracy by the controversies that are engendered from their coverage is simply the time diverted away from managing urgent operational tasks at hand. For instance, at the height of running the air war against the Serbs, May 30, 1998, NATO Commander General Wesley K. Clark, writes in his 2001 autobiography, *Waging Modern War.*

> I was also fighting another battle, one that was threatening to break out in the open, as the press became increasingly aware of the tensions between the Pentagon and me. I was doing my best to contain the damage, but it was clear to reporters on both sides of the Atlantic that the distance I was kept from the President and even from the Secretary of Defense was complicating efforts to move the campaign forward. On my recent trip to Washington I fended off two Wall Street Journal reporters pursuing a potentially damaging story concerning the Secretary of Defense's restrictions on me. On May 30, Steven Lee Myers and Eric Schmitt published an inflammatory article in The New York Times, asserting that my staff derisively call the Secretary "Senator" Cohen. So far as I knew, there was no truth to the story, and we had tried to head it off. Once published, we tried to deny it, without drawing more attention to it. But a recurring theme was obvious—for whatever reason, the Pentagon and the National Command Authority had kept their distance from the operation, rather than embracing it at the outset.[8]

Clientele and Special Interest Groups

Perhaps the most important and influential external political influences upon agency activities are clientele groups. Special interests surround every agency and try to convince the administrative organization to act, indeed that it has a *duty to act,* in the interests of the clientele group it serves. The National Cooperative Milk Producers once told its membership about the duties of the Agriculture Department:

> Eleven months from now the people will go to the polls. They will decide important issues. One of the greatest issues which farmers will help decide will be on the question of who controls the Department of Agriculture. We believe that the organized farmers of America will demand of both political parties that they will provide a reconstituted Department of

Agriculture to serve agriculture. Other Departments of Government serve the groups for which they are named. The Department of Agriculture today is not being permitted to function for farmers. We call for definite pledges on this great fundamental issue.[9]

Most special interest groups have a similar view of government departments, a view that may be characterized as narrow, self-serving, and self-promoting. This is reflected in Figure 3.9 by a full page ad appealing to military/civilian retirees to write their Congresspersons to protect their COLA. Particularly new information technology is employed to locate voters to pressure bureaucracy. For example, to locate allies beyond its 4 million members, the National Rifle Association buys government and business lists of pickup truck owners, people with hunting licenses, weapons owners, gun show exhibitions, and outdoor magazine subscribers. The data are fed into NRA computers to draw up "clean lists" of non-NRA members who might be contacted by mail or phone to aid future NRA political campaigns. This trend of data-triggered targeting is much more efficient with greater impacts than older, more interest group campaigns for politicking. Only at their own peril can agencies ignore such special interests, for they are vital to the survival of agencies in most cases. Or, as Herbert Simon, Victor Thompson, and Donald Smithburg wrote: "For some administrative organizations there are groups within society whose support, working through their representatives in the legislature, can guarantee the survival of the organization against almost any odds and whose opposition, in like fashion, is tantamount to the death of the organization or at least considerable modification of its objectives and methods."[10]

As one would suspect, the clientele groups surrounding any government organization vary considerably according to the nature and purposes of the agency. Farm groups are keenly interested in the work of the Department of Agriculture; businessmen in that of the Commerce Department; organized labor in the Department of Labor; pilots and airline companies in the Federal Aviation Administration, and so on.

These clientele groups' power and influence over public agencies have fascinated political scientists and sociologists for many years. In one of the earliest and now-classic studies of this subject, *TVA and the Grass Roots,* by Philip Selznick, the author describes the development of the TVA, a New Deal program to develop the Tennessee Valley region by means of building dams for hydroelectric power, flood control, and recreational activities. The TVA became a model for many government-sponsored regional developments. Yet, as Selznick's study shows, the TVA's success really came from the development of its "administrative constituency." The TVA worked hard and effectively to nurture and develop this regional support, what Selznick called "informal cooptation—a relation of mutual dependence develops, so that the agency organization must define its constituency and conversely."[11] In many respects, the TVA's clientele group was an ideal one to nurture, develop, and "co-opt" because first and foremost it was supportive of TVA activities. The TVA showered numerous economic benefits and privileges on the region.

Attention all Military Personnel

Act now! Ask Congress to stop the discriminatory
COLA treatment of military retirees
Call 1–800–392–5700

WESTERN
UNION

Dear Representative:

The Omnibus Reconciliation ACT (OBRA) of 1993 discriminates against military retirees. I am writing to seek your help to correct a gross inequity.

Of the more than 50 million retirees, annuitants and pensioners who receive cost-of-living adjustments (COLAs) based on service to country or who participate in income security like Social Security, only military and federal civilians were singled out for patently unfair COLA reductions. Even then, military retirees were hit more significantly than federal civilians. For example, under ORBA 1993, military COLAs will be delayed 39 months over the next five years, compared to a delay of nine months for federal civilians during the same time period.

It would send a strong, positive signal to members of the uniformed services if you were to champion the cause of COLA equity for military retirees by cosponsoring and actively promoting H.R. 3023. This bill would provide military retirees the same COLAs as those established for federal civilians by ORBA 1993.

Sincerely yours,

[A similar message will go to both of your senators]

Of the more than 50 million retirees, annuitants and pensioners who receive cost-of-living adjustments (COLAs), only military and federal civilian retirees were singled out for patently unfair COLA reductions in the Omnibus Budget Reconciliation Act (OBRA) of 1993. To make matters worse, military retirees were hit significantly harder than federal civilians, and they bear a disproportionate share of the burden. For example, under OBRA 1993, military COLAs will be delayed 39 months over the next five years, compared to a delay of nine months for federal civilians during the same time frame.

The radically different treatment of military retirees is an unconscionable breach of the longstanding commitment Congress has made to military retirees for almost 30 years. We must begin today to convince the Congress to correct this gross inequity by providing sufficient funds in the budget to continue our COLA linkage to federal civilians in fiscal year (FY) 1995 and beyond. To help us counter this discriminatory treatment, send The Military Coalition's COLA message to your senators and representative. Ask your representative to cosponsor and fight for enactment of H.R. 3023; ask your senators to sponsor similiar legislation in the Senate.

Take the following steps:

■ Dial Western Union's toll-free hot line number, 1–800–392–5700, and ask for the coalition's COLA action hot line. This service is available seven days a week, 24 hours a day.

■ Give the operator your full name, address, zip code and telephone number. Ask the operator to send our pre-stored COLA

FIGURE 3.9   Example of a cola advertisement

messages to your representative and senators. The operator has the correct names and addresses.

- The total cost of your three messages is $6.95. This fee can be charged to a VISA or MASTERCARD. In Alaska and Hawaii, it must be charged to a VISA or MASTERCARD.

- Those callers whose phone service is provided by U.S. West will receive an invoice directly from Western Union instead of changes on their phone bills.

- If you have any problems with the service or your bill, call 1-800-779-1111. An operator will answer Monday through Friday. 9:00 A.M. to 5:00 P.M.

- *Pass the word!!* Every message is critical if we hope to get the attention of those in the Congress.

COLA HOT LINE
1-800-392-5700

FIGURE 3.9 *Continued*

Source: From *The Retired Officers Magazine* (Jan/Feb, 1994). Reprinted by permission of the Military Officers Association of America (formerly TROA).

Support from clientele groups, however, is not always there. Sometimes agencies face large and powerful hostile groups. The National Rifle Association (NRA), for example, has one of the largest and most effective lobbies in Washington. Working on behalf of gun owners and hunters, it has consistently fought—and effectively curbed—its chief regulatory agency, the Bureau of Alcohol, Tobacco and Firearms, by keeping this bureau's budget small, its personnel demoralized, and its leadership on the defensive (in 1981–1982 the NRA very nearly succeeded in eliminating the Bureau entirely).

While basic clientele support or hostility is critical to an agency's prosperity, the size and location of the clientele group are important factors as well. The TVA has a ready-made regional constituency that includes almost everyone in the Tennessee Valley. The same is true of another regional agency, the Los Angeles Department of Power and Water (DPW). The DPW is perhaps the most influential public organization in all of southern California because of its captive constituency made up of every consumer of water and power in southern California. Because of its ability to supply its constituents with cheap, plentiful water and electrical power, it has had tremendous influence over the growth and economic development of the region, particularly in determining urban planning, patterns of land use, zoning, rights of way, and water distribution. The DPW has made many enemies in the process of using its influence, but its firm, wealthy, concentrated base of clientele support has permitted it to have its own way on most critical issues. A geographically dispersed clientele can be equally influential if its component groups are numerous and strategically situated. Nearly every town, large or small, contains, for example, a veterans' hall, an American Legion post, or clusters of reserve or retired military personnel. These dispersed veterans groups can have powerful effects on veterans' agencies at the state and federal levels, ensuring protection of veterans' privileges and military interests. Particularly they can aggressively support representatives in Congress

The National Rifle Association (NRA) holds very different views of itself, the government, and its influence on society.

Used by permission of Joe Sharpnack, © 1994.

or the state legislature who are favorable to their programs and administrative units of government (see Figure 3.9 for an example of their lobbying strategies).

Third, not only are size and location critical, but the level of intensity of the economic, organizational, and political resources that clientele groups can bring to bear on an agency is vital to their influence and effectiveness as well. For example, the concentrated economic-political wealth of the region has been used repeatedly to influence the future of the TVA. A sizable voting block of regional members of Congress combined with their strategic positions (Senator Howard Baker, minority and majority leader of the Senate for several years) kept alive for a decade the TVA's multibillion dollar Clinch River Breeder Reactor project in the face, even, of strong presidential opposition. Likewise a prosperous but small political lobby, the American Bankers Association, was able to mobilize savers across the country to defeat the proposed Internal Revenue Service dividend and interest withholding legislation, which would have closed a major loophole in the tax code and saved the government billions of dollars. The combination of wealth, expert legal advice, and effective media presentation has been instrumental in stopping government action. For example, contrast the organized clout of a bankers' lobby with that of a group of welfare mothers with little money, little time, and little organizational talent. The latter combination makes for a weak and ineffective lobby at the federal, state, and local levels.

Fourth, the autonomy of an agency has a direct bearing on the ease or lack of it with which a clientele group gains access to an agency. It is no accident that the TVA, for instance, remains an independent agency or that the Social Security Administration in 1994 became an independent government agency. Their powerful clientele groups generally find this independent organizational status preferable, since independent agencies are generally more open and available to interest groups than agencies that are sandwiched among hierarchical layers of federal, state, or local executive departments that are often—though not always—subject to greater executive oversight.

Indeed, clientele groups sometimes support reorganization in order to attain greater political influence over public agencies. The National Education Association (NEA) secured Jimmy Carter's campaign pledge and later his presidential support for setting up a separate Department of Education in 1979. In part, the NEA sought this new federal department as a means of gaining more direct control over educational policy making by separating these programs from health and welfare issues. At the Department of Health, Education and Welfare, the NEA had to jockey with a broader array of special interest health-welfare groups for policy-making authority.

The number of full-time clientele or special interest groups is estimated to be more than 100,000 just concentrated on the regulatory process in Washington alone; they are equally numerous in state capitals. They come in many shapes and sizes, some being no more than names on stationery letterheads. Depending upon the level of government, their influence over an administration varies in strength. A gay rights group exercises little influence over Congress; but it has a lot of political clout in cities with large gay populations, such as San Francisco. Other clientele groups, such as the AFL-CIO, comprise several million members and exercise enormous political-economic impact on Congress but may be ineffective in some public agencies that have little or no union membership or in some of the 22 right-to-work states, where compulsory unions are prohibited. Inputs and influences of clientele groups on bureaucratic institutions at the federal, state, and local levels are therefore extraordinarily diverse. These groups aid the election of friendly legislators, lobby for budget increases, sponsor favorable legislation, and secure higher personnel ceilings and favorable policy decisions from elected chief executives. They push for the expansion of existing programs or for the starting up of new administrative activities in their interest. But their inputs may be vast in some agencies and negligible in others, depending on their focus—the NRA may care a lot about guns but about little else.

There are also less obvious clientele inputs into agency actions. As Francis Rourke notes, "One of the major advantages that the support of interest groups have for an executive department is the fact that such groups can often do for a department things that it cannot very easily do for itself."[12] An army, navy, marine, air force officer, or noncommissioned officer on active duty, for example, cannot directly campaign for more divisions or air wings, but the Retired Officers Association or Air Force Association or Boeing Corporation can speak out on these topics. They actively wage media campaigns, hire lawyers and lobbyists to lobby Congress, leak favorable information to the press, and support election campaigns of "good candidates." Military personnel on active duty are prohibited from such activities (see Figure 3.9).

On the other hand, the risk, as Figure 3.10 points out, is that when an agency has one (or a few) big sponsoring clientele group(s), its activities come under so much scrutiny that it has little room to maneuver and can become what some have termed a captive agency. In other words, an interest group can have so much power over an agency's activities that it almost entirely controls the agency's destiny. By contrast, several strong, supportive groups may very well enhance an agency's flexibility, freedom of choice, and autonomy. If several groups surround an agency, the agency can selectively choose its supporters according to *its* interests and not be a captive to any single interest group. Conversely, weak interest group support may mean a weak bureau with either limited or wide autonomy. The size of an agency relative to its surrounding interests has a considerable influence over its autonomy also. No single business enterprise, not even WalMart, ExxonMobil, or General Motors, can match the annual $300 billion plus budget of the Department of Defense. DoD has, therefore, a greater degree of flexibility in dealing with General Motors. By comparison, a city bureaucracy in Pontiac, Michigan, a town in which GM's plant operations dominate life, has few choices since its economy and future are intimately connected with and dependent upon General Motors' activities there.

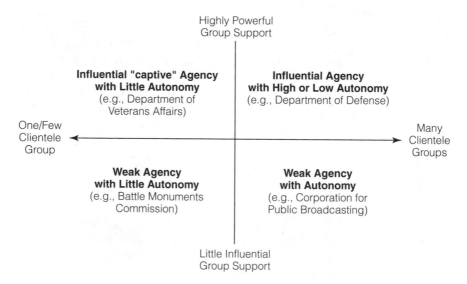

FIGURE 3.10   Relationship between number and size of interest group support and agency power

"Good Government" or Public Interest Groups

Good government groups purporting to promote the public interest have operated for some time at the local level. Unlike "special interests," "good government" groups generally do not advocate a particular party or single special issue but rather are more concerned with promoting improved democratic processes as a whole. Today, moderate-sized communities have scores of civic organizations promoting "the good of the community," and even the smallest towns have one or two groups that are at least nominally interested in the broad community welfare. These civic associations stress their nonpartisonship in elections and focus on a few themes, such as taxpayer associations that perennially call for reduced government spending. Other associations have broad agendas for reform and attract a cross section of individuals. The League of Women Voters and the National Civic League, for instance, act as lobbies for a broad array of "good government" causes. Many public interest groups may indeed be only "letterhead organizations" that operate with little more than post office mail drops, but others are well financed, have large memberships, and are highly visible in local, state, and federal activities.

Reformers have long been visible on the national level as well, but powerful and well-staffed public interest groups sprouted at the national level only during the 1960s. In this era John Gardner set up Common Cause, and Ralph Nader, Public Citizen, whose principal aim was to promote "the common cause" and "the public good." In the 1970s conservative "good government" groups, such as the Heritage Foundation and the American Enterprise Institute, emerged as powerful and well-organized forces. Staffed with eager, aggressive volunteers and a small cadre of professionals, these groups on the right, left, or in the center work full-time at fact finding, research, position taking, and generating publicity over a wide range of public issues. The use of FAXs, emails, computers, mass "targeted" mass mailings, television, and other hi-tech innovations in the 1980s and 1990s has made these groups highly influential forces in shaping public policies at all levels of government. Their emphases at both the local and national levels are directed at legislative activities; that is, at influencing legislation, budget priorities, and supporting sympathetic candidates.

But executive departments are not immune to their activities. First, much of these groups' activities involve monitoring executive agencies—collecting facts, publicizing wrongdoing, researching actions. Nader's organization is composed of several units, many devoted exclusively to exposing federal agencies' wrongdoings, researching their actions, and serving as "watchdogs." Nader units such as the Health Research Group, the Tax Reform Research Group, and the Critical Mass Energy Project aim at having input into government agencies. Nader's Visitor's Center arranges tours through many agencies to help publicize bureaucratic activities to interested citizens and visitors to Washington, D.C.

Second, these groups have played important legal roles in prodding executive agencies to litigate against industry. Nader's Raiders were instrumental in getting the Food and Drug Administration to ban certain unsafe food additives and in getting the Department of Transportation to tighten auto safety standards. They pushed hard for the Environmental Protection Agency investigation into the problems of acid rain and for the clean-up of ethylene dibromide. Nader's organizations successfully petitioned the Federal Aviation Administration to require nonsmoking on airplanes. They have been instrumental in prodding regulatory agencies to provide consumer groups with continuous representation in agency rule-making processes.

Third, these groups are not only confrontational but also cooperative; in some cases they actually do research for public agencies that the agencies cannot do for themselves. Some localities regularly rely upon Chambers of Commerce to collect and evaluate economic data for the community and region. Local chapters of the League of Women Voters often provide forums for the discussion and debate of salient administrative issues and opportunities for local public administrators to "educate" the public on particular issues. At the national level such respected institutions as the Council on Foreign Relations and the Brookings Institution are important sources of facts, public information, and policy analysis that are utilized by many federal agencies. Their services can be contracted-out for training agency personnel or doing important studies that can influence fundamental agency actions. This type of advisory service is an increasingly strong influence over bureaucratic activity.

Fourth, public interest groups can further aid bureaucracy by advocating policy positions. PTA groups at the local level argue for educational policies that education officials frequently are not able or are unwilling to openly advocate themselves. Environmental groups at the national level often become spokespersons for "good causes" that employees of the EPA cannot openly advocate.

Finally, in some cases these groups actually take over and run agencies. Jill Claybrook, one-time director of Nader's Congress Watch, was appointed by President Carter in 1977 to head the Highway Safety Administration. Dozens of the Heritage Foundation's policy specialists were channeled into the White House and numerous federal agencies after Bush Junior's election in 2000. Their transition papers and personnel expertise were key factors in directing Reagan's presidency. More recently, in 1993, Bruce Babbitt was appointed to head the Interior Department by President Clinton after serving as president of the League of Conservation Voters, an environmental activist "good government group." Indeed, these public interest groups have increasingly become the "shadow cabinet" of U.S. government. They serve as convenient places for out-of-power public officials to live, work, and criticize the incumbents. In the 1990s, various out-of-power prominent Republican officials from the Presidencies of Reagan, Bush Senior, and Bush Junior have found "homes" in such places as the CATO Institute, Heritage Foundation and the American Enterprise Institute.

Power Elites and Informal Influential Advisors

At every level of government there are informal leaders and advisors who also make important inputs into bureaucratic operations. On the national level it may be "wise old men" such as former Deputy Secretary of Defense Paul Nitze, who advised American presidents from Roosevelt to Bush on international security policies, or Lloyd Cutler, who served as White House legal counsel in the Carter administration and was brought back by President Clinton in the same capacity to sort out the "Whitewater Affair," or former Secretary of State Henry Kissinger who was asked to lead a commission on Central American policy and therefore on an ad hoc basis advise the State Department on its Central American policies, as well as Middle Eastern policies, or such as Robert Strauss, a powerful lawyer-lobbyist, who as former head of the Democratic National Committee can informally exert influence on public agency activities through numerous friendships and connections. Lawyers and lobbyists especially serve this role in municipalities and state capitals as well as in Washington, D.C. Strauss once spoke of himself as "a Washingtonian insider: You're sort of like an animal in the jungle. As you learn to move around the jungle, you develop a sense of trouble without knowing it's there. In Washington, I think I can sniff out the sides and dimensions of a problem."[13] Through his long, intimate acquaintance with the inner workings of Washington and his ties to money and influence as a partner in one of Washington's largest law firms (Akin, Gump, Strauss, Hauer and Felt), Strauss can inform his clients about key government decisions that have affected or will affect them. He is not only a source of insider tips but can also directly pressure agencies for favorable decisions on behalf of his clients. He can even secure the appointment of friends within key agencies, departments, and offices. As Strauss points out, a lot happens on the basis of these informal friendships with "people who run with me and I run with, and trust me, as I do them. We've been involved together over the years; we all ended up in the same orbit."[14]

On the local level, the "court house gang" or "East Side club" can exert these same types of pressures upon local bureaucracies in numerous hidden yet important ways. The extent of their power, however, varies considerably from city to city. As Edward Banfield found in Chicago when Richard J. Daley was mayor, the mayor and the Democratic Machine were clearly in charge of local government. They could decide upon or ratify almost every matter that went on in local agencies.[15] By contrast, in the classic study *Who Governs?*, Robert Dahl paints a very different portrait of New Haven's power structure under Mayor Richard Lee.[16] There power elites were fluid, open, and ever-changing; and who got involved was largely dependent upon the issue at hand. In short, New Haven's power elites were "pluralistic." No single group dominated the city government, but, rather, different individuals and groups became involved as issues and events changed. New Haven's power elite was neither uniform nor evident and thus had less clear or sustained influence inside city hall.

Whether power elites are open or closed, static or changing, concentrated or pluralistic depends to a great extent upon the locale and its peculiarities. Location determines, in other words, who they are and how they operate and what leverage they exert upon administrative organizations. In some places they may not even be able to fix a single parking ticket; elsewhere they might run the entire bureaucracy from behind the scenes. Floyd Hunter in his classic power study of Atlanta, *Community Power Structure,* found this to be the case in that city: "The [power] structure is a dominant policy-making group using the machinery of government as a bureaucracy for the attainment of certain goals coordinate with the interests of the policy-making group."[17] While Hunter's methodology remains controversial, his views of Atlanta's informal yet influential "hidden" power elites were probably correct, at least at the time of his study.

Local "influentials" may be propelled dramatically upward to the national scene. President Carter's staff from Georgia, "The Georgia Mafia," exercised considerable influence in formal bureaucratic posts (for example, the Office of Management and Budget's director, Bert Lance) and also in informal ones. President Reagan's "California Kitchen Cabinet" served in much the same role in the 1980s. Some of its members, such as Edwin Meese, Charles Wick, and William French, headed important federal organizations. Others exercised influence from informal advisory positions on the outside such as "The Texas Crowd" after George W. Bush's 2000 Presidential Election. Increasingly, wives of U.S. presidents seem to serve in this outside but very real and powerful advisory capacity, as Rosalyn Carter and Nancy Reagan demonstrated. In the 1990s, many of President Clinton's key appointments initially came from "F.O.B.s," the long-time informal network called "Friends of Bill." Bill Clinton's wife, Hillary, played an even greater policy-making role compared to that of other First Ladies, especially in formulating health-care reform.

On the whole, power elites exercise their influence through informal friendships and ties with government officials they work with, know, or grew up with. They can get friends appointed, remove enemies, thwart the careers of others. Through their superior knowledge of the rules of the game, they also can access bureaucratic data, knowledge, and inside bureaucratic processes. Further, they can more aggressively assert their rights, prerogatives, and privileges involving government services, perks, and benefits. This assertiveness stands in sharp contrast with the attitudes of the lower class individuals that Gideon Sjoberg, Richard Bryan, and Buford Farris studied: "The lower-class person stands in awe of bureaucratic regulations and frequently is unaware that he has a legal and moral claim to certain rights and privileges. More often, however, it is the lack of knowledge of the system's technicalities and backstage regions that is responsible for the lower-class person's inability to manipulate a bureaucratic system to his advantage."[18]

If certain individuals or groups tend to be excluded, some by contrast, precisely because of their skills, tend to wield far more influence over bureaucracy than others. As James Q. Wilson writes in *Bureaucracy:*

> Court procedures, like any political arrangements, tend to give more power to some and less to others. Access to the courts is expensive and requires legal skills; thus, as courts become more important to bureaucracies, lawyers become more important in bureaucracies. The management of the EPA often has been dominated by lawyers, much to the disgust of many engineers and scientists, because the key output of that agency, a regulation, is framed in a political environment that makes it more important to withstand legal attack than to withstand scientific scrutiny.[19]

And one should not overlook what Gerald Garvey in *Facing the Bureaucracy* refers to graphically as "The Day-Trippers," those "expert advisers, inside dopesters, and influence peddlers" from "prestige universities":

> The crowd from Harvard, at the Boston end of the major air shuttles, perhaps represents the elite of America's action intellectuals. From Harvard's law school, business school, and Kennedy School of Government they come. At the Washington end of the shuttle, they disgorge to a variety of assignments: on advisory panels of the National Academy of Sciences, in workshops on acid rain control or antitrust reform, as counselors to bureau chiefs or even cabinet officers. They will be on the 5:00 or 6:00 P.M. northbound plane from National Airport and home for supper.[20]

Finally, as Hugh Heclo observed, on the national level these power elites frequently exert influence through fluid, invisible chains of "issue networks."[21] From behind the scenes, they fund and build conservative think tanks like the Heritage Foundation which originally was developed by a conservative beer magnate, Adolph Coors, or those for more liberal groups; for example, the Brookings Institution, traditionally a home for out-of-power Democrats. These issue-advocating groups, foundations, associations, and institutions can exert powerful influences at the national level. They also, as has already been pointed out, help to set policies for public bureaucracy and are a source of its top administrative leadership.

MAJOR INSTITUTIONAL ACTORS:
FOURTH-LEVEL INPUTS

The first three levels of inputs to U.S. bureaucracy exert influence on bureaucracy from outside the government. The fourth level involves the critical inputs to bureaucracy from within government. These are the governmental institutions surrounding every public agency, office, department, and unit of executive bureaucracy—elected or appointed chief executives and their staffs, legislators and their staffs, courts and other offices, agencies, bureaus, and departments. Because of their frequently immediate proximity to public bureaucracy and their various influential inputs, they are perhaps the most important influences on growth, stability, and decline of an administrative organization. As Figure 3.11 shows, their inputs can be either supportive or hostile to an agency.

Chief Executives and Their Staff Inputs

Most units of U.S. bureaucracy report to an elected chief executive. In the federal government, it is the president of the United States; in a state, it is the governor; and at the local level, it is the mayor. Political appointees at all three levels of government can also be the chief executives to whom an agency, bureau, office, or

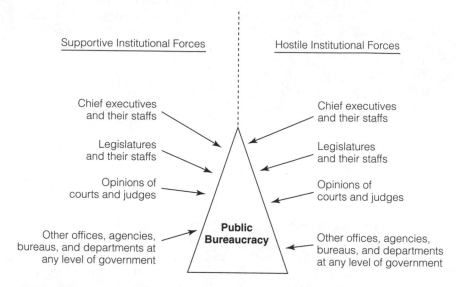

FIGURE 3.11 Supportive/hostile institutional forces surrounding bureaucracy

administrative unit reports. Normally, each of these chief executives, elected or appointed, has a very considerable staff that provides budget, personnel, and legal advice to their chief executive. A bureau within a major federal department might very well confront several levels of these overhead executive staffs. For instance, the director of the Bureau of Land Management within the Interior Department must deal with several levels of chief executives and their staffs—an assistant secretary for Land and Water Resources; the secretary of Interior and his staff; and the president and the executive office of the president. A simple budget or personnel request would have to be okayed upward through these staff levels, at times making for a lengthy and detailed review process. Opposition—or a veto—at any level may block the bureau's request. The same may be true within large state or local governments. Several executives and hierarchical staff levels exist through which an agency or bureau must report, and therefore they are critical sources of policy and administrative oversight.

In the years since the Brownlow Commission Report (1937) stated that "the president needs help," the Executive Office of the President (EoP) has grown into a bureaucracy of formidable proportions. Today EoP has 13 separate offices and over 5,000 employees, who exercise enormous influence over a wide range of budgetary, personnel, and policy fields within the executive branch. Indeed, other executive departmental staffs, EoP has become so large that it often does not speak with one voice. The Office of Management and Budget, for example, might work to cut the Department of Defense's budget while the National Security Council, also a part of EoP, might be working to increase it. EoP's Domestic Policy Advisor may actively work for a new Environmental Protection

Agency regulation while EoP's Council of Economic Advisers may oppose it because of its economic consequences. Thus executives and their staffs can make diverse and sometimes contradictory demands upon the same agency.

What sorts of specific key inputs do they make relative to public bureaucracies?

First and foremost, chief executives and their staffs establish broad policy mandates and priorities for public organizations. Presidents, governors, and mayors are elected as chief executives to do something. Their party platforms and campaign statements are full of promises (well over 600 were on record in 1976 for Jimmy Carter, 250 for Ronald Reagan in 1980 and in 1992, 350 for Bill Clinton). Normally these are broad promises, not necessarily specific details about a particular bureaucracy; for example, Reagan's pledges to "cut taxes," "strengthen defenses," and "cut government social programs." However, the year after Reagan became president these pledges were translated into very real changes in the federal bureaucracy—that is, expanded defense budget and programs, severe cuts in social programs, plus an overall three-year federal tax reduction, which in turn increased pressures for deeper cuts in social programs. Likewise, during the 1992 campaign, Bill Clinton pledged to concentrate on "a domestic agenda" (recall his campaign slogan, "It's the economy, stupid.") of job creation, balanced budgets, health reform, crime, and welfare reform, and his first years in office therefore concentrated on such policy initiatives. George W. Bush, Jr.'s 2000 campaign likewise had its priorities granted a narrow set (i.e., tax cuts, national security, and educational reforms) that he sought to initiate soon after his inauguration.

President Reagan, as had most presidents since John F. Kennedy, relied upon transition team task force reports in formulating the direction of the new administration. Transition teams study every federal agency in some depth in order to provide explicit policy directions to various agencies. They are also instrumental in building the cadre of their new leadership within bureaucracy. President Bush used this strategy particularly effectively by relying on his Vice President, Dick Cheney, with years of Washington insider experience, to head the transition team. For example, the sort of critical policy advice given to a new president by the transition team report on an agency can be read in the following principal recommendation to then-governor Ronald Reagan on May 19, 1980, from a senior consultant to his campaign, M. Peter McPherson, then a staff member at the Heritage Foundation, regarding what the Republican candidate should stress for the U.S. foreign aid program: "The United States foreign aid program should be changed to emphasize self-help and technology transfer rather than resource transfer. Studies have shown a higher 'rate of return,' for 'investments in the self-help/technology transfer programs.' "[22]

After the 1980 election McPherson became a top political appointee at the Agency for International Development and spent much of his time promoting just that policy recommendation within AID. McPherson's appointment demonstrates a second important input of chief executives to bureaucracy: namely, in hiring, firing, promoting, rewarding, and punishing personnel. A president of the United States appoints roughly 6,000 executive branch officials; a state governor, maybe two hundred or more cabinet and sub-Cabinet level officials; and a middle-sized community mayor, normally far fewer. As Figure 3.12 indicates, these appointed agency heads and staff officials are crucial to an elected executive's ability to shape and control the bureaucracy. They link the candidate's campaign potential with the office holder's actual performance. Normally, at the start of their terms, chief executives give these appointments their greatest care and attention. Joseph Califano, Jr., for instance, in his book *Governing America*[23] describes how making key personnel appointments was his first priority after his appointment as President Jimmy Carter's new secretary of Health, Education and Welfare. Califano could select the top two hundred of 150,000 employees at HEW. He gave priority to those "who shared his philosophy of government at HEW" and could bring skills that would complement his own. His appointment of Hale Champion, for example, as the deputy secretary, or number two man, was based upon Champion's reputed ability to implement HEW's programs at the state level, his administrative toughness, and his sense of humor, which Califano felt he needed at HEW. Champion, Califano later reflected, was a wise choice and one for which he, Califano, was much praised. But personnel appointments can become sources of great difficulties. Califano was criticized most severely over his appointment of a personal staff cook in the secretary's own executive dining room during a period when President Carter was preaching austerity in federal government spending. This appointment became an early source of scandal that dogged Califano with unwanted publicity until the cook was dismissed.

Not appointing personnel, though, can be useful as well to a chief executive. President Reagan's failure to appoint key agency heads for several months in social service departments such as Education, Health and Human Services, and Housing and Urban Development, weakened these agencies' abilities to defend themselves against the new administration's determination to cut their budgets and thus proved to be a highly effective strategy for implementing Reagan's overall philosophy and political agenda. On the other hand, his appointment of James Miller III to replace Michael Pertshuk as chairman of the Federal Trade Commission decisively moved that agency away from regulatory activism. In the 1990s, President Clinton was criticized for what many perceived as his delay in getting his appointees into key posts, which, in turn, inhibited his ability to "take charge" of key policy areas, notably defense and foreign policy making (though, unlike Reagan, it was less by choice and more because of inability to find and confirm able nominees). By contrast, President George W. Bush, Jr. "hit the ground running" so to speak by appointing his top National Security Team quickly (i.e., Secretary of State Colin Powell, Defense Secretary Donald Rumsfeld, National Security Advisor Condoleeza Rice and the like) because this policy issue was high on his political agenda.

Chief executives can direct the activities of bureaucracies through their personal involvement with their administrations. An activist mayor like former William Schaefer of Baltimore, Maryland, toured his city daily and then wrote memos to various city agencies about failures to perform such jobs as picking up the trash here, fixing that broken schoolyard swing, cutting down a dead tree limb there, checking on a citizen complaint over in a certain neighborhood. His frequent comment was, "If I can see it, why can't you?" But more often, especially in larger federal bureaucracies, chief executives cannot "eyeball" problems but must rely

The choices of top economists to guide national economic policies at the Council of Economic Advisors, OMB, and Federal Reserve over the last four decades have reflected presidential ideological and party commitments.

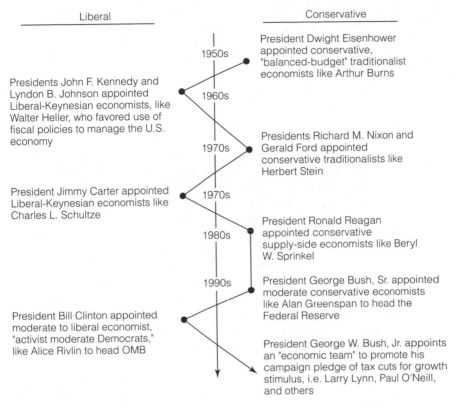

FIGURE 3.12   Political appointees selected for key posts in the administration is an important way a president controls the direction of bureaucracy.

upon their appointees and staffs to exercise procedural direction and management oversight of bureaucracies. Under many recent administrations, the Office of Management and Budget (OMB) increasingly exercises this powerful "micromanagement" of agency operations through OMB's policy procedures. OMB staffs have established detailed procedures to control bureaucratic actions of subordinates. A bureau chief that requests, for instance, policy changes that require legislative action forwards his request through OMB, which, in turn, indicate (1) that it has no objection and that therefore the agency can proceed with its proposal to Congress; (2) that it opposes the proposal and that therefore the agency cannot proceed; or (3) that the proposal is in accordance with the president's program and will have the full and active support of the president. Similarly, at the departmental level, various personnel including legal, budget, and management staffs exercise much the same policy oversight and "signoff" for actions of subordinate units.

Allocating scarce monetary resources is a fourth critical method by which chief executives can exercise their influence over public bureaucracy. The Budget and Accounting Act of 1921 gave to presidents the authority to present Congress with an executive budget. State and local governments have followed the practice of submitting annual executive budgets, which is perhaps the most direct way of controlling the bureaucracy. Executive budgets give presidents (or governors or mayors) the ability to set spending priorities and adjust funding levels for agencies. OMB at the federal level is charged with this responsibility of developing the president's annual budget, which must be approved by both houses of Congress. President Reagan quite effectively in 1981 used the executive budget process as his chief policy instrument for increasing defense expenditures and cutting back funding to social service departments and regulatory agencies. With supporters in Congress he was largely able to sustain these cuts in funding levels.

More recently George W. Bush, Jr.'s priorities to "beef up" homeland security has translated into rapid increases for a broad array of related security agencies, such as the FBI, INS, and Coast Guard. Over the years various budgetary reform techniques such as Performance Budgeting, Planning, Programming-Budgeting System, Management by Objectives, and Zero-based Budgeting have been introduced, by presidents and their OMB staffs precisely to improve oversight, efficiency, and control of funds to ensure that they are allocated in accordance with presidential policies likewise broader presidential organizational reform techniques such as Clinton-Gore's "Reinventing Government" proposals have been used strategically to shift resources and policy priorities as well as gain popular support for the Administration. These reforms have been used with various degrees of success by executives at the state and local level as well.

Other important methods of bureaucratic control by chief executives include: the power to reorganize—Congress has granted presidents limited powers to reorganize executive agencies; control over agency litigation—the Justice Department approves appeals and interprets statutory laws for federal agencies; control over whether or not to enforce vigorously laws—these decisions are also carried out mainly by the Department of Justice.

In general, stopping or vetoing agency actions is easier than getting them started, as President Carter discovered early in his administration:

> Even the President of the United States, with the august power of that imposing office can be overwhelmed by the incredible obdurateness of the organization. The *New York Times* relates how, after assuming office, Carter detected mice in the Oval Office, the very focal point of the presidency. He called the General Services Administration who then came and handled the matter. Shortly after Carter continued to hear mice, but worse, one died in the wall and the stench was quite noticeable during the formal meetings. However, when he again called the GSA, he was told that they had carefully exterminated all the mice; therefore, any new mice must be "exterior" mice, and exterior work is apparently the province of the Interior Department. They at first demurred but eventually a "joint task force" was mounted to deal with the problem.[24]

Agency action can be stymied not only by bureaucratic inertia and overlapping or confused jurisdictions but also by overlapping or confusing signals from the administration itself. An OMB directive may differ from that of a departmental secretary, assistant secretary, deputy assistant secretary, and so on. Rarely do all these multiple levels and their many staffs speak as one. A proposal by Reagan's secretary of the navy for recommissioning old battleships was supported by the secretary of defense but opposed by the DoD deputy secretary and OMB's director, thereby providing divided leadership on this issue. In such circumstances, what is a subordinate agency to do? Walter G. Held writes that in these cases, "bureau leaders . . . must be able to assess the importance of the various and often conflicting communications coming from the power structures in the presidential line of influence, which do not necessarily follow the organizational chain of command. The decision to respond favorably, to be inactive, or to take actions offsetting communications they judge to be harmful to the programs for which they are responsible is critical and requires the development of special skills."[25]

And where are we today in conceptualizing executive inputs? Contemporary scholarship on executive-bureaucratic relationships tends to stress its overall paradoxical nature. As presidential scholar James P. Pfiffner writes in *The Modern Presidency*:

1.   With respect to the cabinet: The best way for a president to "control" the executive branch is to delegate most issues that are clearly presidential to department and agency heads. Presidential involvement should be very selective.

2.   With respect to political personnel: The president should play a positive role in setting the tone for recruiting political appointees, but should delegate the selection of most subcabinet appointments to department and agency heads. Personal or ideological loyalty to the president does not guarantee the effective implementation of presidential priorities.

3.   With respect to the permanent bureaucracy: The career bureaucracy is often seen by new presidents as an obstacle to the achievement of presidential priorities. But cooperation with the career services is essential to accomplishing presidential goals, and enlisting the bureaucracy's enthusiastic support can enhance the probability of presidential success.[26]

Legislatures and Their Staff Inputs

The creation of agencies and their continued survival ultimately depend upon legislative bodies—Congress at the federal level, state legislatures for those agencies in state government, and in counties or cities, county boards of supervisors or city councils. Public bureaucracy at every level is ultimately a creature of the legislature and dependent on the legislature for its survival (see Figure 2.3). Although most elected legislators are all too prone to "damn the bureaucracy" on the campaign trail, they, in fact, provide the legal mandate for its existence by establishing not only its basic missions but also in many cases its fundamental organizational structure, staffing patterns, work rules, wage rates, top appointees, procurement procedures, accounting and auditing requirements, methods for citizen access to administrative information and various informal inputs into agency activities, and much more. In constitutional theory the executive and legislature are separate units, but administrative units in reality are significantly interdependent and interconnected with legislative decisions.

On these and most other matters, however, Congress rarely acts as a whole body, for as Robert S. Lorsch points out, "Congress has become so ponderous that it can hardly act on a significant legislation except under threat of calamity or force of overwhelming political pressure."[27] Rather, as Woodrow Wilson said nearly a century ago, "Congress at work is Congress in Committees."[28] Much the same is true for state legislatures and city councils; their work is done largely in committees. And it is in the committees and subcommittees of the legislature that the major inputs for bureaucracy are generated, decided on, and enacted.

At the federal level this process is a highly fragmented one. There are a large number of committees and subcommittees in the House and Senate, with numerous overlapping and competing influences. In practice, in any one executive unit or policy field there are several legislative committees and subcommittees with jurisdiction over a federal agency.

The annual funding requests of DoD, for example, are decided by the House and Senate Appropriations Committee (with the House reviewing first). The House and Senate Budget committees set the total budget ceiling as well as the ceiling for each functional area, such as defense. The House and Senate Armed Services Committee reviews the policies, programs, and activities of each agency in DoD and authorizes specific commitments for funding these choices. The House Government Operations and Senate Governmental Affairs committees examine how closely DoD agencies conformed to congressional mandates in performing their tasks and spending their funds. Here alone, eight committees and a large number of subcommittees are involved with the work of DoD. And there can be many other overseers as well: the House and Senate's Rules committees schedule hearings on defense issues; the House and Senate's Foreign Affairs committees involve themselves in overseas matters affecting the military, and the House and Senate Judiciary committees are concerned with many of DoD's legal matters.

A fragmented, particularistic, and specialized committee and subcommittee system leads to fragmented, particularistic, and specialized legislative inputs into federal bureaucracy. Except for controversial matters like funding for the B-1 bomber, the Panama Canal Treaty, the Gulf War, or the 9/11 terrorist attack, Congress rarely addresses a problem as a body. Congress generally accepts the decisions of its committees. The resulting inputs are frequently mixed and contradictory ones that chief executives and their staffs, offices, agencies, and bureaus must learn to read, then respond to or ignore.

The system leads not only to diverse inputs but also to bureaucratic conservatism and favoritism toward key committees and their members. For example, awhile ago the Pentagon proposed closing Fort Monroe, an antiquated army base in Hampton, Virginia. The fort is a relic from the War of 1812 and actually has a moat around it. It now has little use, and shutting down the base could save taxpayers $10 million annually. But Senator Paul S. Trible, Jr. (Rep.–Va.), the ranking Republican on a House subcommittee overseeing military facilities, inserted language in that year's appropriations bill barring the closing of Fort Monroe until the Pentagon had put together a detailed "socioeconomic impact statement" on how the closing of the base would affect the surrounding community. He challenged the Pentagon's estimated cost savings from its closure and secured the requirement that DoD would have to dig up and preserve all the historic artifacts in and around Fort Monroe before opening the base to the public as a kind of museum. This would cost an estimated $30 million, thus making it more expensive to close the base than to keep it operating. Fort Monroe remains today an active military base.[29]

Administrative leaders thus keep a watchful eye on the personalities and the particular constituent interests involved in congressional committees and subcommittees that oversee their organizations. Shifts in these personalities or in committee jurisdictions can significantly alter what happens to a given agency. Administrative agencies are also attentive to key members of these committees and their staffs, because the role and influence of congressional staffs have grown enormously over the past decades. Staffs not only are a source of technical advice to committee members, they also draft the bills that affect agencies and increasingly have provided key political appointees inside agencies through sponsorship by powerful House or Senate members. Furthermore, since 1970 large influential congressional oversight organizations, such as the Congressional Budget Office, have been established, and others such as the General Accounting Office and the Congressional Reference Service, have greatly expanded their oversight activities. As Louis Fisher, a noted scholar on this topic, writes: "The growth of agency and congressional staffs has placed a heavy strain on traditional techniques of legislative oversight and the dependence on good-faith agency efforts. Congress now has the resources to delve more deeply into administration. As the gap between the branches widens, because of staff build-up and turnover, Congress is less able and less willing to rely on customary methods of control. Oral agreements are being replaced by committee report language, which is giving way to statutory directives."[30]

Congressional oversight during the past three decades indeed shifted from informal to formal controls as Fisher suggests, though the formal controls exercised by legislators—particularly by committee and subcommittee members— over bureaucracy at every level of government have been the primary contemporary means of making legislative inputs into the administrative processes. Summing up, these methods include (1) establishing the organizations and their basic frameworks through legislation; (2) creating personnel policy covering a wide variety of areas: wages, classification of positions, hours, leaves, working conditions, and so on; (3) conducting investigations of particular agency activities and policies; (4) either formally advising administrative units as part of oversight commissions or informally advising their chief representatives through committee and subcommittee hearings and investigations;

(5) fixing budgets and appropriations annually; (6) requesting casework or enacting private bills that require agencies to perform specific tasks for congressional constituents; (7) passing resolutions and laws specifically requiring agency action or inaction on certain matters; and (8) confirming executive political appointments. These add up to powerful legislative sources of influence.

But it would be a mistake to think that the aforementioned eight legislative inputs work somehow mechanically or separately in "lock-step." These oversight influences often interact far more subtly upon public agencies (see Figure 3.13) in ways that recent thoughtful scholars of this subject refer to as "ironic." For example, Christopher H. Foreman, Jr. in his award-winning book *Signals from the Hill: Congressional Oversight and the Challenge of Social Regulation* writes:

> The irony . . . is this: the system works precisely by creating the impression of its failure. To galvanize congressional and public sympathy against some perceived abuse or excess, politicians and lobbyists tend to use extreme language, sounding the alarm against an unresponsive bureaucracy. Congressional policy entrepreneurs face a continued struggle to elevate their concerns and enlist the aid of others toward some preferred course of action. Rhetoric that plays on the perceived autonomy of renegade regulators is simply too useful to forgo. Thus aroused, Congress reins in the offending agency with an appropriation rider amended authorization, or embarrassing publicity. Or, perhaps, the mere threat of such action is enough to persuade the agency to reconsider its position. In either case, the system has done its job; the desired message has been effectively delivered. A lingering by-product, however, is the impression of rogue bureaucracy.[31]

Judicial Inputs

The historic 1803 *Marberry v. Madison* (1 Cranch 137) decision by the U.S. Supreme Court gave the courts authority to review executive decisions. Today federal and state court oversight of executive activities is a well-established tradition. The activities of bureaucrats and bureaucracy at all levels of government come under regular court scrutiny—and the scope of judicial review of administrative activity has expanded enormously since the 1960s. This growth has been fueled by three elements: first, the rapid increase in numbers of lawyers (particularly activist lawyers, such as Nader's Raiders, who are willing to take on "good government causes"); second, increasing numbers of activist judges willing to expand the scope of judicial oversight by hearing and deciding on novel matters with new local interpretations; third, the growth of public-interest law firms, store-front legal services for middle-class citizens, and government-sponsored legal services for the poor (such as the Legal Services Administration). These organizations have given many people their first opportunity to challenge bureaucracy in the courts.

Wider citizen access to courts results in more court cases against bureaucrats. Today educators, police, prison officials, social workers, and many other bureaucrats regularly find their behavior challenged and regulated by court decisions. While normally these involve individual cases affecting bureaucratic

OFFICE OF THE ASSISTANT SECRETARY OF DEFENSE
WASHINGTON, DC 20301-3040
October 7, 1992
MEMORANDUM FOR RECORD
SUBJECT: Telephone Call from Senator Kerry

At 12:30 PM on October 7, 1992 Senator Kerry, Chairman of the Senate Select Committee on POW/MIA Affairs, called for Assistant Secretary Andrews. As he was at lunch, Senator Kerry asked for me. This was a conference call and included Ms. Francis Zwenig, Staff Director of the Senate Select Committee on POW/MIA Affairs.

He cited the POW/MIA intelligence material released on NBC last evening (Dateline) and the leaks in the press (Evans & Novak, etc.) and said that he was very upset.

Senator Kerry was very emphatic that this has gone too far and that the Department has an obligation to take on the issue. We cannot continue to keep our arms tied behind our back. He said that we need to do at the hearing next week (October 15 and 16) what we did at the last meeting (Monday, October 5). Bring a blow up of the photographs of the "USA" and "K" symbols and show that the "K" is not a K and that it does not have walking feet. Have Mr. Gadoury explain how the USA could have been made. He stressed that unless we answer this attack directly the leakers will win and they will be able to claim "everyone knows" it was made by a POW. "We need to demonstrate reality," "Put a lie to it." The Secretary should make a one-time exception on the photography—show a blow up of the actual photograph (symbol portion) on TV.

He said that we have been repeatedly attacked by those who do not want to deal with reality. Each time we answer they find something new to raise. If we are ever going to stop this we need to demonstrate convincingly what the real thing looks like. Openness will take the wind out of their sails.

He urges the Department to come on very strong: "We are appalled. These leaks jeopardize any American in captivity who would try to signal. It is dishonest to leak information obtained in closed hearings knowing the Department cannot discuss intelligence sources and methods in public. We took responsible actions as soon as we found this symbol."

I raised our concern with discussing intelligence in public as we have global responsibilities that we cannot jeopardize. He agreed that this is difficult but that in this one case we need to find a way to take on the issue, find some way to lay out the issue.

Concerning the hearing, he agreed that a script would be unwise and recommended Mr. Andrews just "come on strong—appalled."

He stressed that he wants to work with us but reiterated that it is time for us to take on the issue.

FIGURE 3.13 Powerful members of Congress informally can put pressure on the bureaucracy as a key method for exercising legislative oversight.

clientele, at the extreme courts have taken over the operations of entire bureaucracies. This was apparent in numerous school busing cases during the 1960s and 1970s when an activist judge, Frank Johnson of the U.S. District Court in Alabama, directly supervised the state's prisons, mental health programs, and highway patrol for several years. As Donald L. Horowitz, a former research scholar at the Smithsonian Institution, has commented: "The frequency of litigation challenging governmental actions, especially in the federal courts, has increased," while "the scope of the exception to judicial review of matters committed to agency discretion has been steadily narrowed."[32]

While there are few administrative areas that courts have not ventured into, most often their influence tends to be: first, episodic and particularistic—that is, immediately concerned with remedying the administrative problem at hand (i.e., police brutality), rather than with setting broad, enduring administrative standards

and policies; second, courts more often than not are hostile to administrative activity, normally indicating what bureaucrats cannot do, as in cases involving, for
example, unfairness to welfare recipients. In brief, courts are good at vetoing bureaucratic actions but poor vehicles for laying down effective methods for carrying out or initiating administrative services; third, court decisions are by their very
nature legalistic, that is, based upon rules, legal reasoning, and precedent rather
than open-ended to cope with changing administrative reality and fluid complex
issues, as is illustrated by the finding that, "the personnel test in X agency was not
fair to minorities under the Civil Rights Act." Courts reason from *the* case and *the*
rule or *the* law, thus making their administrative inputs often very hard to transfer
elsewhere. For example, a remedy for the problems of Oakland's fire department
selection procedures may not be applicable to New York's problems. Finally court
decisions tend to be based on limited staff resources, analysis, and data (few courts
have much analytical staff), which also restricts their long-term oversight of how
public bureaucracy actually implements court decisions.

What impact, then, do courts have on the administrative process? While
sometimes it can be quite dramatic, as in the case of *Brown v. The Board of Education* (1953), which led to desegregation of the entire U.S. school system and
the advancement of equity and fairness of treatment for all citizens, courts, according to one authority:

> function on a basis that is too intermittent, too spotty, too partial, too ill-
> informed for them to have a major constructive impact on administrative
> performance. They can stop action in progress, they can slow it down, and
> they can make it public (their exposing function has been too little noted).
> Perhaps most important, they can bring moral judgment to bear, for moral
> evaluation is a traditional judicial strength. But courts cannot build
> alternative structures, for the customary modes of judicial reasoning are not
> adequate for this. . . . Nor can they interpret complex or specialized data, to
> secure expert advice, to sense the need to change course, and to monitor
> performance after decision. Courts can limit the discretion of others, but
> they find it harder to exercise their own discretion where that involves
> choosing among multiple, competing alternatives.[33]

In short, courts can and do make important inputs into bureaucracy, but
these tend to have both positive and negative influences. The "plus-side" of
court interventions into public agency affairs, as Gerald M. Pops and Thomas J.
Pavlak in *The Case for Justice* observe,

> supply public administration with many essential elements of justice. Due
> process serves as the foundation for treating people fairly in dispute
> settings, and it extends both procedural and many substantive rights that
> first emerged and were articulated during the Warren era. Administrative
> law generally has supplied incentives and the means to ensure that fair
> procedures are actually applied, not the least of which procedures is the
> potential for judicial review of administrative action.

But the authors quickly add important "negatives":

The lawyer's understanding of the world of administrative decisions, divided as it is into neat definitional compartments called "rulemaking," "adjudication," and "enforcement," and with its trust placed entirely in procedural safeguards to avoid administrative "abuse of discretion," is an artificial one at odds with the real world of politics and effective action. It is built on the notion that carefully conceived procedures will somehow secure justice.[34]

Other Offices, Bureaus, Agencies, and Departments Inputs

While courts may have weak long-term influences over administrative units, other bureaus, agencies, departments, and offices do have considerable control over their futures. As Herbert Kaufman has noted: "Every agency has natural enemies as well as natural allies."[35] The success of almost every action that an agency undertakes is dependent upon help from other agencies. No agency is entirely self-sufficient largely because of the functional division of authority by legislative bodies involving any policy field. Congress, for example, authorizes the Internal Revenue Service within the Treasury Department to collect taxes but authorizes the Tax Division within the Justice Department to prosecute tax law violators. Further, Congress has established the Council of Economic Advisers (CEA) within the White House to evaluate overall federal spending and revenues, which means that the CEA (along with the Treasury and other agencies) may recommend changes in tax policies. This situation creates considerable potential for both cooperation and rivalry.

A particularly intense conflict can ensue when agencies are given similar mandates. For example, the Bureau of Reclamation and the Army Corps of Engineers have been involved with water projects that have created agency rivalry. On the local level, police and fire departments sometimes clash over common public safety assignments or limited budgetary resources. Diametrically opposite philosophies create long-term rivalry, as with the EPA's "proconservation" ethos as opposed to Interior's generally "prodevelopment" outlook. Likewise, Presidents Clinton's as well as George W. Bush, Jr.'s economic initiatives created intense debates within their Cabinets among "probusiness," "prolabor," and "proconsumer" groups inside various agencies.

Particularly when budget cutbacks are common at many levels of government, these reductions generate fierce conflicts between bureaus. In the 1990s, Defense Department fiscal cutbacks brought out fierce interservice rivalries between the army, navy, and marines, who were all competing for fewer defense appropriations. Again citing Kaufman: "The federal treasury is not bottomless and they all draw from it. Some therefore gain at the expense of others. When the federal revenues increase rapidly, the conflicts are minimized. When they do not, the conflicts can grow very sharp. The economic assistance vis-à-vis domestic requirements, or city-oriented agencies versus agricultural and rural agencies, for example, are exceedingly divisive."[36]

Public agencies are in continuous competition with other government organizations over their missions, resources, autonomy, and clientele. Much like nations in the international arena of world politics, they engage in a struggle to survive, learning to forge alliances for mutual support and protection in order to fend off attacks from competitors and enemies. In an unstable and shifting political environment, where the stakes and outcomes are important for the very survival of bureaucratic units, there can be room for considerable conflict. But often, there is also the possibility of cooperation. At the local level, for example, city police, the country sheriff, the state highway patrol, and federal law enforcement agencies pool their data and engage in informal and formal cooperation on a wide range of law enforcement cases. At the national level, federal agencies assigned to tackle an immense problem of the 9/11 terrorist attacks cooperated effectively with one another. The AIDS epidemic also brought together, for example, public health units at several levels of government in a combined effort to deal with this killer disease.

BASIC PATTERNS OF INPUTS
SURROUNDING BUREAUCRACY

What sense can we make out of the welter of inputs described in this chapter that perpetually dance around public agencies at every level of government and determine their directions and destinies? Are there discernible patterns of inputs? In brief, how can we sum up this lengthy and complicated discussion?

One thing that should be clear is that inputs affecting agency actions come from many sources. Every public organization is influenced by diverse forces. The dynamics of the U.S. political landscape is pluralistic, pushing and pulling public agencies in many directions. The typical public agency sits in the midst of this fray involving four levels of inputs—general environment, socioeconomic impacts, and political and institutional forces.

Further, these forces do not affect any two agencies in exactly the same way. Situations vary widely from agency to agency. Inputs affect various parts of even a single agency in diverse and complex ways. For example, the support for or hostility to the major administrative units of the Department of Education exhibits an enormous variety, depending upon which major program one looks at: elementary or secondary education, civil rights, special education, bilingual education, and so on (see Figure 3.14). Each program is encircled by a cluster of different interests and forces that influence its work. Generalization is therefore risky.

How can we make sense out of the welter of vast "inputs" discussed in this chapter, which potentially or in fact "dance around" public agencies today? James Q. Wilson, a prominent political scientist, in his book *Bureaucracy,* offers one response in terms of thinking about "who gains" and who "feels the pain."[37] By viewing the problem from an essentially political-economizing perspective, Wilson argues that benefits from an agency's actions can accrue to one group or a few groups in society or to everyone. Likewise, costs or burdens from public bureaucracy's activities can fall on one or a few versus all or most people. Therefore, Wilson conceives of four varieties of environments in which government agencies work and which can in turn influence their actions (Figure 3.15).

First is the *client politics* situation, where most or all benefits go to a single agency but costs are born by all or most of the people. Here, one or a few groups, of course, strongly support the agency's activities, because they are the chief recipients of its goods and services. The Veterans Department is an example of this situation; veterans receive its services and hence strongly favor its ever-expanding actions, but its costs are distributed throughout society since its work is chiefly funded through general revenues from taxpayers. Clearly, the challenge for such an agency operating in this situation is to find and maintain some autonomy in its work from the client's interest(s) that get its services. As Wilson suggests, many don't succeed or don't even try.

Entrepreneurial politics is the opposite situation: benefits go to all or most people; costs go to a single group or a few groups. A case in point is the National Highway Safety Administration, created by the National Safety Highway Act of 1967 and aimed at promoting auto safety. Obviously, the NHSA benefits everyone through potentially improved auto safety, but its regulatory costs largely fall on one industry, specifically the auto makers. This situation pits the agency in a constant battle with a hostile regulated interest group, hence placing it in a precarious position where it must be entrepreneurial. Its actions must creatively and carefully navigate among many interests to maintain its very survival or risk capture by the groups that opposed its creation in the first place.

A third environment where bureaucracies can find themselves, according to Wilson's schema, is an *interest group* political situation, one confronting one group or a few groups that reap its benefits *and* pay its costs. OSHA, the Occupational Safety and Health Administration, serves mainly labor by regulating workplace conditions, and its regulatory costs fall mainly on businesses. In this position, OSHA is forced to constantly balance two competing major interests that are both concerned about the actions it takes or fails to take. An agency finding itself in this environment can become highly visible, since its activities are constantly being scrutinized and courted. According to Wilson, such an agency can achieve considerable "wiggle room" since its actions highly effect contending groups.

Finally, argues Wilson, agencies can operate in an environment of *majoritarian politics,* where both costs *and* benefits are spread over most or all of the population. These programs, as Chapter 2 points out, were created by vast majorities to initiate major societal reforms such as the Anti-Trust Division in the Justice Department established by the Sherman Act to curb monopolistic practices in the marketplace. In theory, at least, everyone benefits but also pays the costs of antitrust actions. This situation can result in a "neglected agency," says Wilson.

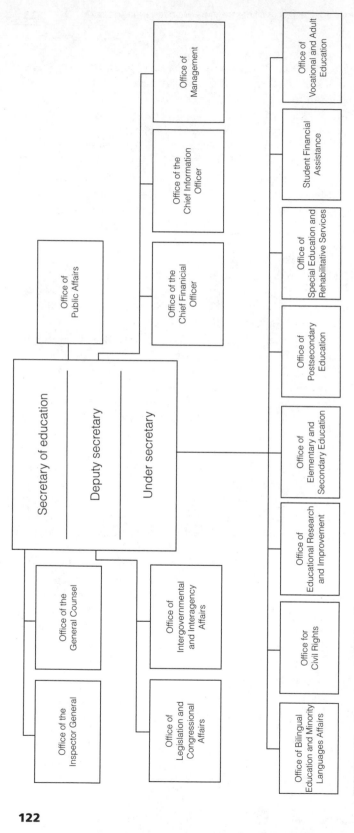

FIGURE 3.14 Department of Education

Source: U.S. Government Manual 2001–2002.

	Benefits go to one/few group(s)	Benefits go to many/all in society
Costs charged to one/few group(s)	Interest-group environment (e.g., OSHA)	Entrepreneurial politics environment (e.g., NHSA)
Cost charged to many/all in society	Client-politics environment (e.g., Veterans Department)	Majoritarian environment (e.g., Antitrust Division)

FIGURE 3.15   Four-fold typology summarizing the varieties of environmental situations

An agency can go about its business mostly unhampered by influences, and thus its leadership can have significant choices over the goals it pursues and the vigor with which the agency undertakes these goals.

Figure 3.15 summarizes Wilson's typology in a matrix and Figure 3.16 practically demonstrates a typical client politics situation. In this illustration, an executive bureau—the Peanuts and Tobacco Section of the Price Support Division within the Agricultural Stabilization and Conservation Service of the U.S. Department of Agriculture—takes its marching orders, for the most part, from special interest groups made up of tobacco growers and House and Senate subcommittees concerned with oversight of these affairs. The growers gain the benefits from the subsidies, and taxpayers pay the costs. Here the resulting "iron triangle" among a few "cozy relationships," in which most are cheerleaders for the agency, can potentially hurt the broader public good, that is, better health.

By contrast, as Maureen Hogan Casamayou reminds us (based on her extensive study of the 1986 Space Shuttle *Challenger* accident), at the other extreme, when there are too many dispersed interests and no stabilizing relationships in the bureaucratic environment, the public interest can be neglect, even lives can be lost if the overall external environment of an agency is not properly evaluated and then attended to. In the case of the *Challenger* accident, writes Professor Casamayou:

> There were too many cheerleaders in the agency's external environment and no countervailing pressures urging the agency toward increased caution on safety matters. Congress, the White House, and the media, for self-interested reasons, encouraged the agency to achieve its overly optimistic flight schedule. They were simply not sufficiently critical of NASA's ridiculous claims. At the same time, the agency's attentive interests simply assumed that the agency was adequately concerned about safety matters.[38]

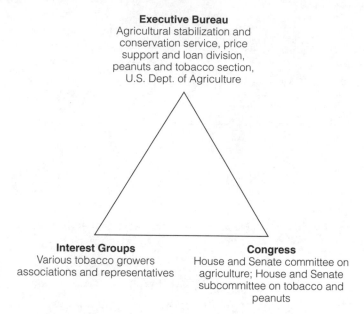

Executive Bureau
Agricultural stabilization and
conservation service, price
support and loan division,
peanuts and tobacco section,
U.S. Dept. of Agriculture

Interest Groups
Various tobacco growers
associations and representatives

Congress
House and Senate committee on
agriculture; House and Senate
subcommittee on tobacco and
peanuts

FIGURE 3.16 A classic client politics or "Iron Triangle" situation

SUMMARY OF KEY POINTS

Every government bureaucracy is surrounded by several external forces that influence its survival, growth, and decline. In this chapter the general environment of bureaucracy as well as three other levels of external pressures were outlined. Socioeconomic factors are the broadest, most pervasive of these external influences. Examples of these factors are population size, shifts in demographic groups, levels of economic activity, technological innovations, and the like. External political actors make up another level. Examples are public opinion, clientele groups, media coverage, and power elites. Yet another level consists of institutional actors within government, such as chief executives and their staffs, legislators and their staffs, courts and other offices, agencies, bureaus, and departments. These external factors come into play and prominence depending on the issue and situation at hand. One, a few, or all may get involved. The degree of involvement and level of intensity of inputs for any administrative organization depend on the circumstances and the situation. Several may push and pull in opposite directions simultaneously. They may work to promote and perpetuate the organization—or to decimate it.

Generally speaking; though highly complex, the patterns of inputs influencing public bureaucracies can be depicted as a four-fold typology, as illustrated by Figure 3.15, characterized by: Who gains? Who feels the pain? As a result, four varieties of environmental situations can be conceived: "client," "entrepreneurial," "interest group," and "majoritarian."

KEY TERMS

general environment

socioeconomic factors

institutional inputs

political forces

clientele groups

good government groups

iron triangles

issue networks

power elites

bureaucratic inertia

legislative oversight

entrepreneurial environment

informal cooptation

majoritarian environment

judicial inputs

client politics environment

interest group environment

REVIEW MATERIAL

Review Questions

1. Why is the external environment so influential overall in shaping U.S. bureaucratic institutions and the behavior of bureaucrats?

2. What are the distinctions between the four levels of inputs—general environment, socioeconomic, political, and institutional?

3. In your view, which ones are the most influential and the least influential? Why?

4. Why does this chapter argue that the critical legislative inputs to bureaucratic institutions come from committees and subcommittees? What factors cause these legislative inputs often to be diverse and contradictory?

5. What are four varieties of environmental situations that agencies confront according to James Q. Wilson? The criteria used to create this matrix? The strengths and weaknesses of each cell within the four-fold typology?

Class Debate Pro/Con

Resolve that irresponsible bureaucratic behavior results primarily from a public agency's "capture" by one or few narrow special interests.

Student Homework Exercise

Select a state or local public bureaucracy and chart the key socioeconomic trends that directly effected its growth, decline, or stability; for example, the movement of the general population, shifts in demographic groups, regional/ national economic changes, technological innovations, natural catastrophes, and major revenue increases or decreases. Which factor(s) do you judge to be most influential and why? Was the same factor(s) critical change-agents for other local/ state agencies in the region?

Case Study Analysis

Read "The Blast in Centralia, No. 5" in any edition of Richard Stillman, *Public Administration: Concepts and Cases.* Outline the major external forces influencing the outcome of this case. On a scale of 1 to 10, rank their power (10 being the most powerful influence): From the general environment? From socioeconomic factors? From political forces? From institutional inputs? What criteria did you use to rank their influence? And how do you define "power" in relationship to bureaucracy?

NOTES

1. For an excellent discussion of Max Weber and his views, read H. H. Gerth and C. Wright Mills, *From Max Weber: Essays in Sociology* (New York: Oxford University Press, 1946), particularly the introduction and essay on bureaucracy.

2. George E. Peterson and Thomas Muller, "The Economic and Fiscal Accompaniments of Population Change," in Brian J. L. Berry and Lester P. Silverman (eds.), *Population Redistribution and Public Policy* (Washington, DC: National Academy of Sciences, 1980), p. 110.

3. From an executive summary, "The U.S. in the 1980s: Demographic Trends" (Washington, DC: Population Reference Bureau, Inc., 1980), p. 16.

4. As cited in the *Washington Post,* Jan. 22, 1984, p. G7.

5. Walter Lippmann, *The Phantom Public* (New York: Macmillan, 1925), p. 77.

6. As recounted in Norton Long, *The Polity* (Chicago: Rarid McNally, 1962), p. 48.

7. Walter G. Held, "Decision Making in the Federal Government: The Wallace S. Sayre Model," in Frederick S. Lane (ed.), *Current Issues in Public Administration,* 2d ed. (New York: St. Martin's Press, 1982), pp. 38–55.

8. Wesley K. Clark, *Waging Modern War* (New York: Public Affairs, 2001), p. 335

9. As cited in V. O. Key, *Politics, Parties and Pressure Groups,* 4th ed. (New York: Thomas Y. Crowell, 1958), p. 744.

10. Herbert A. Simon, Donald W. Smithburg, and Victor A. Thompson, *Public Administration* (New York: Knopf, 1950), p. 384.

11. Philip Selznick, *TVA and the Grass Roots* (Berkeley: University of California Press, 1949), p. 145.

12. Francis E. Rourke, *Bureaucracy, Politics and Public Policy,* 2d ed. (Boston, MA: Little, Brown, 1976), p. 50.

13. James Conaway, "The Artful Persuader," *Washington Post Magazine,* Nov. 7, 1982, p. 13.

14. Ibid.

15. Edward C. Banfield, *Political Influence* (New York: Free Press, 1961).

16. Robert A. Dahl, *Who Governs?* (New Haven, CT: Yale University Press, 1962).

17. Floyd Hunter, *Community Power Structure* (Chapel Hill: University of North Carolina Press, 1953), p. 102.

18. Gideon Sjoberg, Ricard A. Brymer, and Buford Farris, "Bureaucracy and the Lower Class," *Sociology and Social Research* 50 (April 1966): 47.

19. James Q. Wilson, *Bureaucracy: What Government Agencies Do and Why They Do It* (New York: Basic Books, 1989), p. 284.

20. Gerald Garvey, *Facing the Bureaucracy: Living and Dying in a Public Agency* (San Francisco, CA: Jossey-Bass, 1993), p. 42.

21. Hugh Heclo, "Issue Networks and the Executive Establishment," in Anthony King (ed.), *The New Political System* (Washington, DC: American Enterprise Institute for Public Policy Research, 1978), pp. 87–124.

22. Unpublished transition memo from M. Peter McPherson, senior consultant to the presidential campaign of Governor Ronald Reagan, May 19, 1980, p. 1.

23. Joseph A. Califano, Jr., *Governing America* (New York: Simon and Schuster, 1981), chapter 1.

24. *The New York Times,* Jan. 8, 1978, p. 29.

25. Held, *Decision Making,* p. 9.

26. James P. Pfiffner, *The Modern Presidency* (New York: St. Martin's Press, 1994), p. 134.

27. Robert S. Lorsch, *Democratic Process and Administrative Law* (Detroit, MI: Wayne State University Press, 1969), p. 12.

28. Woodrow Wilson, *Congressional Government* (Boston, MA: Houghton-Mifflin, 1885).

29. Dale Russakoff, "Grace Panel Finds Pork Barrel Overflowing," *Washington Post,* Jan. 10, 1984, p. A3.

30. Louis Fisher, *The Politics of Shared Power: Congress and the Executive* (Washington, DC: Congressional Quarterly Press, 1981), p. 109.

31. Christopher H. Foreman, Jr., *Signals from the Hill: Congressional Oversight and the Challenge of Social Regulation* (New Haven, CT: Yale University Press, 1988), p. 183.

32. Donald L. Horowitz, "The Courts as Guardians of the Public Interest," *Public Administration Review* 37 (March/April 1977): 150.

33. Ibid.

34. Gerald M. Pops and Thomas J. Pavlak, *The Case for Justice: Strengthening Decision Making and Policy in Public Administration* (San Francisco, CA: Jossey-Bass, 1991), pp. 45–56.

35. Herbert Kaufman, *Are Government Organizations Immortal?* (Washington, DC: Brookings Institution, 1976), p. 15.

36. Ibid.

37. Wilson, *Bureaucracy,* pp. 75–83.

38. Maureen Hogan Casamayou, *Bureaucracy in Crisis: Three Mile Island, the Shuttle Challenger, and Risk Assessment* (Boulder, CO: Westview Press, 1993), p. 168.

FURTHER READING

A wealth of literature is available on the external environment and its influences upon U.S. bureaucracy. Classics on this subject are: E. Pendleton Herring, *Public Administration and the Public Interest* (1936); David B. Truman, *The Governmental Process* (1951), Emmette S. Redford, *Democracy in the Administrative State* (1969); Harold Seidman, *Politics, Position and Power,* 5th ed. (1991); Lawrence C. Dodd and Richard L. Schott, *Congress and the Administrative State* (1979); Louis Fisher, *The Politics of Shared Power* (1981); Paul Appleby, *Big Democracy* (1945); William W. Boyer, *Bureaucracy on Trial* (1963); Charles S. Hynneman, *Bureaucracy in a Democracy* (1950); Norton Long, *The Polity* (1962); Don K. Price, *The Scientific Estate* (1965); E. E. Schattschneider, *The Semi-Sovereign People* (1960); Emmette S. Redford, *Democracy in the Administrative State* (1969); and for an excellent recent overview of this topic, read Herbert Kaufman "Major Players: Bureaucracies in American Government," *Public Administration Review* 61, No. 1 (Jan/Feb 2001), pp. 18–42.

There are several solid case studies involving these issues, including: Stephen K. Bailey, *Congress Makes a Law* (1950); Raymond A. Bauer et al., *American Business and Public Policy* (1963); Daniel M. Berman, *A Bill Becomes a Law,* 2d ed. (1966); James W. Davis, Jr., *Little Groups of Neighbors* (1968); A. Lee Fritschler, *Smoking and Politics,* 2d ed. (1975); Philip Selznick, *TVA and the Grass Roots* (1949); Arthur W. Maass, *Muddy Waters—The Army Engineers and the Nation's Rivers* (1951); Herbert Kaufman, *The Forest Ranger* (1960); Laura Sims, *The Politics of Fat* (1998);

Karin Stabiner, *To Dance with the Devil* (1992); Martha Derthick, *Up in Smoke* (2001); and Jacob Hacker, *The Road to Nowhere* (1997).

More recent writings concerning various aspects of this vast subject include: James Q. Wilson, *Bureaucracy* (1989); Maureen Hogan Casamayou, *Bureaucracy in Crisis* (1993); Christopher H. Foreman, Jr., *Signals from the Hill* (1988); Gerald Garvey, *Facing the Bureaucracy* (1993); James A. Smith, *The Idea Brokers* (1991); Dennis D. Riley, *Controlling the Bureaucracy* (1987); Gerald M. Pops and Thomas J. Pavlak, *The Case for Justice* (1991); David Ricci, *The Transformation of American Politics* (1993); James H. Svara, *Official Leadership in the City* (1990); Jameson W. Doig and Erwin C. Hargrove, *Leadership and Innovation* (1990); James P. Pfiffner, *The Modern Presidency* (1994); Robert F. Durant, *The Administrative Presidency Revisited* (1992); Paul C. Light, *Monitoring Government* (1993); Charles Perrow and Maurio F. Guillen, *The AIDS Disaster* (1990); Garry C. Bryner, *Bureaucratic Discretion* (1987); Bradley H. Patterson, Jr., *The White House Staff* (2000); and Robert J. Waste, *Ecology of City Policy Making* (1988).

Several useful essays on interest groups and their influence on government are found in Allan J. Cigler and Burdett A. Loomis, *Interest Group Politics* 5th ed. (1998). Francis E. Rourke, *Bureaucracy, Politics, and Public Policy,* 4th ed. (1986), Frederick S. Lane, *Current Issues in Public Administration,* 6th ed. (1999). Camilla Stivers (ed.) *Democracy, Bureaucracy, and the Study of Administration* (2000) as well as Ronald Hrebenar (ed.) *Interest Group Politics in America* (1997). John Gaus's *Reflections on Public Administration* (1947) offers an especially good treatment of the relationship of general environment to public administration. For a more current view of this subject from a comparative perspective, read Ferrel Heady's *Public Administration: A Comparative Perspective,* 5th ed. (1996). One should not overlook the rich case studies exploring this subject that are available through the Inter-University Case Program, PO Box 229, Syracuse, NY 13210; the John F. Kennedy School of Government Case Program, Kennedy School of Government, Harvard University, 79 JFK Street, Cambridge, MA, 02138; and The Electronic Hallway, Graduate School of Public Affairs, the University of Washington, Seattle, WA. 98195.

WEBSITES

http://www.opensecrets.org/lobbyists/: Federal Lobbyist Database
http://www.alldc.org/: American League of Lobbyists
http://www.uncle-sam.com/executivedepts.html: Executive Departments
http://www.ncpa.org/pd/govern/govern8.html: Interest groups and lobbying

4

■

Inside Public Bureaucracy

Once a young aide to President William Howard Taft kept repeating the phrase "machinery of government" while briefing the president. Taft, so the story goes, became exasperated and turned to a friend and whispered, "My God, the man actually *believes* government is a machine!"

Taft had it right. United States government, especially its bureaucracy, is not an automated assembly line, devoid of human beings, lifeless and machinelike. Quite to the contrary, our public bureaucracy is composed of identifiable clusters of individuals who work and act in influential ways inside the bureaucracy. Each of these subsystems shapes the broad outcomes of bureaucratic institutions. Each competes for power and influence over its particular bureaucracy. These human subsystems perform different tasks in government. Through diverse strategies they aim to achieve different goals with different stakes or outcomes for bureaucracy. Each serves vitally important functions within bureaucracy and significantly determines in various ways what bureaucracy does or does not do and how well it performs these functions. The size and influence of each of these human subgroups vary considerably from agency to agency and locale to locale. Yet many public organizations contain several of these subsystems. Most public operations have all five subsystems, which jockey with one another for influence and status.

The boundary between each of the subsystems is not always clear. They tend to overlap with considerable gray areas between them. Subsystems in different agencies do not always exhibit the same exact dimensions, proportions, or precisely similar characteristics. Nor are all five groups necessarily found in every agency. Sometimes only one or two are represented. In other words, these subsystems are fairly open, fluid, and adaptive to differing organizational contexts and situations. They are also fundamentally *human and political, not machinelike in behavior.* Subsystems do have certain important similarities and differences in their roles, values, missions, power, status, functions, activities, and influence within public organizations. This chapter will examine the special characteristics of each subsystem within organizations and particularly how they affect the outputs of every agency from the inside. Brief descriptions of these five subsystems illustrated on Figure 4.1 follow.

Political appointees are those individuals who serve without tenure and whose appointments are based often, though not always, upon political ties or party loyalties.

Professional careerists are various groups of personnel with specialized expertise in specific fields. Positions occupied by these groups are usually based on advanced professional training. This subsystem offers lifetime careers and stresses "rank-in-person" rather than "rank-in-job."

The *general civil service* operates under "merit concepts." Characteristics of this subsystem are tenure, rank-in-position, and "classified" hierarchies of positions based upon the amount of tasks and responsibilities.

Unionized workers are blue collar and, increasingly, white collar workers whose employment is based upon negotiated contracts between union representatives and management within the jurisdictions they serve.

Contractual employees are untenured workers whose employment with government is directly or indirectly governed by various contractual agreements negotiated with individuals, private firms, nonprofit organizations, and universities for rendering specific services for a limited or specified time. They are not governed by civil service rules nor do they work under union contracts.

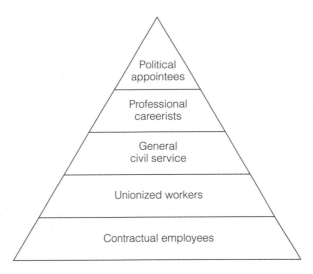

FIGURE 4.1   Internal dynamics of America's public bureaucracy as five subsystems

THE POLITICAL APPOINTEE SUBSYSTEM:
THE BIRDS OF PASSAGE

Most political appointees fill the top-level policy-making posts within federal, state, and local bureaucracies. These men and women serve in government without tenure, holding office at the pleasure of the chief elected official, who hires them, promotes them, or dismisses them. At the federal level, political appointees make up a fairly small group, with only 6,478 out of approximately 2.7 million federal civilian workers. As Table 4.1 shows, the federal political appointees are divided into four categories: (1) PASs, or presidential appointments with the consent of the Senate (1,355); PAs, or presidential appointments made by agency heads and approved by Office of Personnel Management (OPM) but not requiring Senate confirmation (1405); part-time appointees (2,349); and those made to the White House Staff (2,148). The number of PAS has remained fairly stable over the past two decades (roughly 636), but the number of noncareer category II political appointees has grown significantly. The number and categories of political appointees vary considerably in state and local jurisdictions. In some regions where there is no civil service system—particularly rural county governments or the machine-run cities—virtually all government jobs are handed out on the basis of party loyalty or political patronage. Today, however, most cities and states follow the federal pattern in reserving only top-level policy jobs for political appointees, who serve at the pleasure of a governor or mayor. Particularly in "reformed" or "clean" city and state governments, these posts are few and limited to only the very top levels. Colorado, for example, has only two dozen political appointees out of 5,000 manager-level posts. However, in Massachusetts

Table 4.1 Political Appointments Available to Presidents

Category I: full-time positions (almost all established by statute) that are filled by
personal presidential appointment

    Subcategory I-A (PAS): presidential appointees requiring Senate
    confirmation: cabinet secretaries and agency heads, deputy secretaries,
    undersecretaries, and assistant secretaries; plus members of regulatory
    commissions, 185 ambassadors, 94 district attorneys, 94 U.S. marshals,
    15 in international organizations, 4 in the legislative branch   1,125

    Subcategory I-B: presidential appointees not requiring Senate
    confirmation (PA)   20

    Subcategory I-C: federal judges to be appointed (the typical number of
    vacancies that need to be filled during a presidential term out of a
    total of 868 federal judges), all of which are PAS positions and most
    of which have lifetime tenure   200

Category II: full-time, nonpresidential, noncareer positions (appointments made by
agency heads but only with the sanction of the White House Office of Presidential
Personnel [OPP])

    Subcategory II-A: noncareer positions in the Senior Executive Service (SES)
    (upper-level positions; see description in "Some Facts about Noncareer
    Positions," below)   720

    Subcategory II-B: Schedule C positions (midlevel positions; see description
    in "Some Facts about Noncareer Positions," below)   1,428

Category III: part-time presidential appointee positions (established in
statute–members of advisory boards and commissions)

    Subcategory III-A: PAS   490

    Subcategory III-B: PA   1,859

Total of Categories I, II, and III: the noncareer universe of concern to the
White House OPP   5,842

Category IV: White House staff positions (only partially limited by statute)
(the OPP does not handle appointments in Category IV)

    Subcategory IV-A: receiving formal, signed commissions from the president
    (assistants to the president and deputy assistants to the president)   80

    Subcategory IV-B: appointed under presidential authority (special
    assistants to the president and below, that is, members of the White House
    staff, including the first lady's staff; the vice president's staff; and the
    domestic policy, economic policy, and national security council staffs)
    (excludes civilian and military detailees, secret service, and other
    professional support staffs, White House fellows, interns, volunteers)   556

The total noncareer universe: positions that can be filled by the White House
during a typical presidential term   6,478

SOURCE: Bradley H. Patterson and James P. Pfiffner, "The White House Office of Presidential Personnel,"
Presidential Studies Quarterly (September 2001), pp. 416–417. Copyright © 2001. Reprinted by permission of Sage
Publications, Inc.

all of the managers' positions in the state, some 3,500 jobs down to the supervi-
sor's lever, are considered "policy-making" positions and are available for the governor's appointees. Thus the range is quite wide, depending on the influence of
"reformism" found within the local/regional politics.

    Within federal bureaucracies, in particular, appointees' lack of tenure limits
the length of their employment. The average federal political appointee serves
only 22 months in office. Hugh Heclo has rightly observed that they are "birds
of passage"[1] who recognize from the start that they will not be around for very
long. The most they can look forward to is a 4-year term, and if a president is

Table 4.2 Backgrounds of Political Appointees from Truman's to Clinton's Administration

	Truman Through Carter	Reagan	Bush, Sr.	Clinton	Bush, Jr.
Education					
Advanced degree	69%	68%	80%	89%	83%
Law degree	40	26	40	67	43
Ivy League degree	48	58	50	50	52
Ph.D.	19	16	25	22	17
No college degree	0	0	0	0	0
Women	4%	5%	10%	17%	14%
Blacks	4%	5%	5%	17%	10%
Occupations					
Law	28%	11%	40%	5%	17%
Business	28	32	55	5	52
Government	16	16	5	67	22
Education	19	16	25	11	8
Military	3	5	10	0	1

SOURCE: *PS*, December 1993, p. 695, reprinted with permission of Cambridge University Press and updated by PAI demographic analysis, 2001.

reelected (and they are lucky) they *might* be reappointed for longer periods—though that is rare. Transience is their only common trademark. Most, therefore, set their sights and adapt their behavior for the short range by recognizing that if they are to accomplish *anything* in their jobs, they must move quickly. Short-term horizons, limited goals, and quick results tend to characterize their actions. This tendency among political appointees also probably characterizes state and local appointees within jurisdictions where there is a competitive party system. But elsewhere, if the top jobs have little or no turnover, political appointees can look forward to longer tenure in office, thus shifting their time horizons to somewhat longer perspectives.

Generally, though, appointees' job uncertainty means that they have to have another position, outside of government, to fall back on in case they fall out of favor or out of office (a good possibility given the hazards of these un-tenured posts today). Hence, as Table 4.2 demonstrates, many political ap-pointees at the federal level are drawn from law firms or are on leave from big businesses, government, or universities. The pool from which they are drawn is thus quite small and tends to be, but is not always, confined to upper-class individuals who can afford a short time away from their regular lines of work. This qualification, as Table 4.2 points out, also tends to drastically limit the so-cial characteristics of political appointees to white, urban, middle-aged males with advanced Ivy League educations and ambitions for high-status careers.[2] While President Jimmy Carter attempted to recruit greater numbers of women and minorities into these posts, the bulk of political appointees even in his administration in the late 1970s, and of Ronald Reagan's in the 1980s, was largely drawn from this very small pool. However, in the 1990s President Bill Clinton drew his top appointees from a slightly wider cross section of Americans with more advanced or law degrees, whereas President Bush, Jr.,

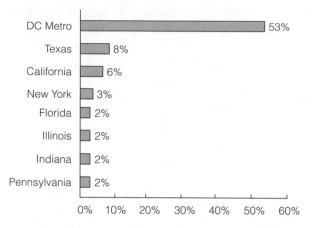

FIGURE 4.2 States where Bush Jr.'s appointees worked before joining administration

Source: PAI demographic analysis of Bush appointees.

Note: States with less than 2% not shown.

like his father, Bush, Sr., relied heavily on businessmen with greater prior private enterprise experience (see Table 4.2). Historically, as law firms, businesses, and universities tended to become more representative, so too the "pool" of political appointees has tended to become more diverse and varied. Though the geographic distribution of Bush Jr.'s appointees tended, as expected, to favor his home state of Texas, much like prior presidents more than half are drawn from the D.C. area's think tanks, law firms and businesses (see Figure 4.2). Political appointees at the state and local levels, particularly as one moves closer to the grass roots, represent much more diversity in talent, training, income, and background. Generally, there is greater heterogeneity and better representation of social groups at lower governmental jurisdictions, though there is by no means a pure popular representation even there.[3]

While there are several prominent examples of political appointees whose faces reappear in government, usually at higher levels of bureaucracy when their party assumes office (Andrew Card, Donald Rumsfield, and Colin Powell crop up repeatedly in Republican administrations, and Donna Shalala, Alice Rivlin, and Warren Christopher in Democratic ones), most political appointees have limited backgrounds in government. Very few serve repeated spells in government; few work for more than one administration. Few survive election turnovers in the executive branch. Many simply do not want to stay more than a few years in office, nor can they, because of pressing outside professional or business commitments. Or, in Bush's senior advisor, Karen Hughes' case, a desire to return home to Texas in order to spend more time with her young family. Yet most are *drawn from and return to related fields of endeavor.* Western ranchers, businesspersons, and lawyers have tended to occupy the top slots at the Department of the Interior because of their prolonged involvement with western public lands; just as defense contractors, former military officers, and business executives have long been recruited to top political slots at DoD. And most return to these jobs afterwards. Thus different bureaucracies tend to draw their political appointees from different occupational-economic sectors of society as well as from different regions primarily because of these appointees' prior experience with the tasks and activities of the agency. An appropriate "track record" in the policy concerns of the agency, the correct party identification, and especially policy positions that are in accord with the chief executive's, are important qualifications for such appointments.

Their specific policy roles in bureaucracy can be conceived of as loose-jointed, concentric rings that emanate outward from the office of the elected chief executive—a president, governor, or mayor. The most powerful appointees are those who occupy leadership roles within the major Cabinet-rank departments, sometimes referred to at the federal level as the inner Cabinet. The inner Cabinet is composed of the secretaries of Defense, of State, and of the Office of Management and Budget, as well as senior noncareer or career ambassadors to major governments. These individuals are responsible for the operations of the largest public agencies (such as DoD) and subsequently have powerful policy agenda-setting functions (such as OMB). Similarly, inner Cabinets, made up of those closest to the governor or mayor and exercising major policy-organizational tasks, are found at state and local levels as well, though their titles differ. Inner Cabinet members at the federal level are often at the White House with the president or are representing their agencies before Congress. They are responsible for setting—and defending—the major policy priorities of the president and the agency they represent. They also exert the overall leadership within their particular organization, appoint numerous political personnel within the organization, and represent it before the media and special interest groups. Their most important function within government is to translate the campaign platforms and promises of the elected officials into administrative actions of major policy-administrative importance to the chief executive—the president, governor, or mayor. In short, they serve as linchpins between election-night rhetoric and actual institutional performance within their specific policy spheres.

Most elected chief executives are well aware of the importance of this group of men and women and give a good deal of consideration to their selection. (Senior political appointees also require confirmation by the Senate at the federal level and approval by legislatures of state and local governments and so chief executives consultations with and advice from key legislative interests prior to submitting their nomination is routine.) A successful track record in government or in large, complex organizations is a critical requirement. For example, Donna Shalala became secretary of Health and Human Services in the Clinton administration but only after having served as assistant secretary in President Carter's previous Democratic administration and afterwards having headed the California Institute of Technology. Paul O'Neill, secretary of Treasury in George W. Bush, Jr.'s Cabinet held prior posts in the Nixon and Ford administration. He later served as president of the ALCOA Corporation, America's largest aluminum company. Warren Christopher was appointed secretary of state by President

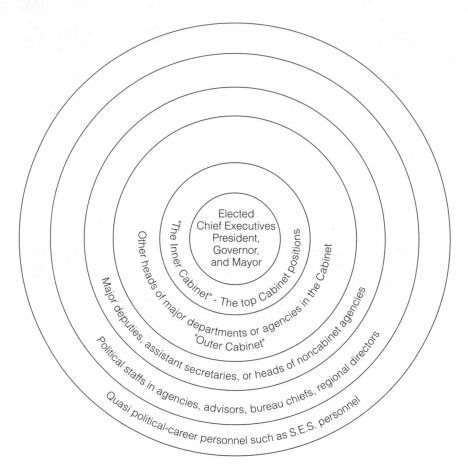

FIGURE 4.3   The five rings of political appointees in U.S. public bureaucracy

Clinton but had previously served in other Democratic administrations—deputy attorney (1967–1969) in the Johnson administration and deputy secretary of state (1977–1980) in the Carter administration. While their loyalty to the president and his program must be unquestionable, these appointees normally have not been highly visible or active in his previous political campaigns, aside from preparing briefing papers or holding ad hoc advisory roles. Knowledge of the job, its policy issues, ability to be "team players," and competence at running a major organization are generally preferred in order to make the president look good and to implement his programs within and throughout the bureaucracy. There also is a vital symbolic function; that is, political appointees must be representative of "a balanced" cross section of the coalition that supported the elected chief executive. In other words, the top appointees must be *seen* as a fair reflection of interests that backed the elected official to give legitimacy and authority to his or her exercise of power.

BY LOCHER FOR THE CHICAGO TRIBUNE

Elected chief executives rely heavily on political appointees to carry
out policies deemed vital for their administrations.

Source: *The Washington Post National Weekly*, August 22–September 2, 2001, p. 17.

The next ring, or the outer Cabinet, is composed of men and women who
see the president (or governor or mayor) less frequently but nevertheless hold
Cabinet rank (also normally requiring Senate or legislative confirmation). They
are frequently charged with running a major public agency such as the Department of Housing and Urban Development at the federal level or the Department of Corrections at the state level. They are a rung below the inner Cabinet
in *informal* power and status only, for their legal titles and prerogatives are normally much the same as those of their counterparts in the inner Cabinet. Indeed,
they may have many of the same responsibilities, such as directing a large department, providing its leadership, setting its policy agenda, defending it before
Congress, and so on. Because the work of their agencies is considered of less priority, they see the president less frequently, are involved in fewer of the major policy meetings, and are given, on the whole, less attention by the White House than
inner Cabinet members. This is not to say that they or their work is unimportant. What they do is simply of less, but sometimes only slightly less, urgency to
the success or failure of the administration. Generally, they do not decide major
war/peace or prosperity/depression issues. Hence, they are less visible to the
public eye, or for that matter, to the presidents, governors, or mayors.

The third level is generally termed the sub-Cabinet. It is composed of
deputy secretaries, assistant secretaries, and administrative heads of major non-
Cabinet agencies and bureaus. These individuals also occupy important policy-
making posts, and sometimes highly sensitive and critical ones, such as that of

deputy attorney general in the Department of Justice, who is normally responsible for the daily management of the department's activities, or of the assistant
secretary for International Security Affairs in the Department of Defense who
is charged with shaping broad strategic policies within DoD. These men and
women are generally more specialized in particular fields of expertise than the
inner or outer Cabinet members. While they may have had a variety of experiences and backgrounds in government, business, law, or the professions, their
training and work experiences tend to be more appropriate to the positions that
they occupy. They have also usually had considerable experience handling political issues related to these offices and are expected to take positions on these
issues in accordance with the president's overall priorities.

For example, Robert F. Burford, director of the Bureau of Land Management in the Reagan administration, before his appointment to this post had
been a long-time Colorado rancher and Republican speaker of the Colorado
House of Representatives. He had also been one of the leaders of the "sage
brush rebellion," fomented by a group of westerners who strongly backed President Reagan's election in 1980 and were vitally concerned with federal land
policies. And Dr. Everett Koop, surgeon general of the U.S. Public Health Service in the Reagan administration, was previously a practicing Philadelphia surgeon. He was also politically active in the national antiabortion campaign and
an early Reagan supporter. Likewise, George Bush, Jr., in 2001, appointed "seasoned political activists" like John Ashcroft for Attorney General to fill his top
policy-making posts, but like prior presidents he appointed only those in accordance with his policy goals. Dr. M. Jocelyn Elder, President Clinton's surgeon general of the United States, served Governor Clinton in Arkansas for five
years as the state's health director, where she fought for school-based health clin-
ics and for making contraceptives available for sexually active teenagers. Though
President Clinton made her one of his first political appointees after the 1992
election he fired her in 1994 when her policies "embarrassed" his administration. Likewise, George Bush, Jr., fired his team led by Paul O'Neill after 2002
mid-term election due to criticisms of Bush's handling of the economy. Appointees, in short, serve "only at the pleasure of the president" and are easily ex-
pendible if they no longer fulfill his purposes.

Given the increasing proliferation of special interest groups that watch
closely these sub-Cabinet appointments and their pronouncements (discussed
in Chapter 3), key sub-Cabinet officials, at least during the last few years, are often drawn from the ranks of special interest groups and return to these after government service. Democrats tend to draw their appointees from left-leaning
policy groups, while Republicans draw theirs from think tanks, legislative staffs,
and policy-advocate groups on the right-wing.

Yet some scholars, such as Thomas P. Murphy, Donald E. Nuechterlein, and
Ronald Stupak, have argued that the influence of this group of appointees over
the policy-making process has declined in recent years, because of its increase
in number.[4] For example, in 1924 the Department of the Interior's top-level
appointees included one departmental secretary, three administrative assistants,

and three assistant secretaries. By contrast, today this department has one secretary, several dozen on his immediate staff, one deputy secretary, six assistant secretaries, nine deputy assistant secretaries, and nineteen bureau directors or agency administrators. Though as a collective group, their prominence and power has on the whole increased in recent years; a modified Gresham's law operates here, that is, increasing numbers of political appointees at the sub–Cabinet level drive down their individual influence over policy decisions. Put simply: A call from an assistant secretary does not mean what it once did.

The fourth group of appointees encompasses a wide variety of advisors to the secretary and directors of agencies and bureaus. Like the previous level of appointees, this level has expanded enormously over the past three decades as secretaries brought in their own people to help run their departments. At the federal level these assorted political appointees do not require Senate confirmation, so for the most part their ranks have grown without legislative oversight and control. Few, however, are active politicians or were closely involved with the election campaign of the chief executive. Most are more directly identified with the professional or policy issues of the agencies where they work. Many have had personal ties or friendships with their immediate supervisors. They are generally reputed to be experts in the field of law, business, or education and may have actually been drawn from the ranks of the civil service. Some have known or worked with each other before or fought the opposition party together over the very sets of policy issues they are now actively administering and formulating.

Compared with appointees at other levels, these men and women are the most expert and specialized, and they are often more willing to push forward the interests of their particular agencies and resist political intrusions from others. And yet as Frederick Mosher has observed of these appointees: "Some are eminent figures in their fields, often principal representatives and defenders of the services which they superintend. Yet their stance differs from that of the members of the permanent services below them. They *can* be replaced or their situations can be made so uncomfortable as to induce them to resign or at least alter their behavior."[5] Their lack of tenure is the heavy stick that ensures their ultimate responsiveness to higher circles of appointees.

Finally, there is a large group of individuals in public bureaucracy today who occupy a limbo-land between quasi-political and nonpolitical territory. Their position at the federal level has been institutionalized through the creation of the Senior Executive Service (SES) in the 1978 Civil Service Reform Act.

SES developed a new category of upper-level administrators that is formed from supergrade officials in grades GS-16, 17, and 18 and in Executive Ranks IV and V, in which position assignments and pay are determined by political decision makers and yet are also protected by the civil service rules (career officials in SES have the option of retreating to GS-15 grades). The rationale for creating SES came mainly from argument that improved management in government could result from greater mobility of its top executives. Drawn from senior career ranks, it was argued that like in business, the president and top executives should be able to shift senior managers from one post to another more easily than the hide-bound civil service rules allowed prior to 1978. Further, as in the case of business, bonus incentives were provided for rewarding outstanding performances in SES. On the other hand, unsatisfactory performances could cause removal or replacement in SES. By law, the bulk of these individuals must be drawn from the ranks of the civil service, since at the most 10 percent of SES members (or 720 of the current 8,130 SES employees) can be political appointees. About 40 percent of SES positions are designated as "career reserved" because of their sensitive positions. Table 4.3 sums up the uniqueness, functions, and general characteristics of SES positions.

While the jury is still out on whether or not the introduction of SES has proven successful, it remains a *potentially* important tool for improving federal management and control. As one scholar notes:

> The framers of the 1978 CSRA believed that it was time to restore to executives more control over their personnel systems. If political executives were to be held accountable for accomplishing the missions of their organizations, they ought to have the authority to put together their own management teams to do the job. They also felt that political executives should have the management tools to be able to motivate their subordinate managers. The new flexibilities include the ability to assign either career or noncareer executives to most SES positions, authority to establish and fill SES positions by the agency head, and the authority to reassign SES members within an agency. . . . Agency heads can now create SES positions in their agencies and fill them as they see fit. . . . Agency heads can rearrange the whole top leadership in an agency, placing their chosen political appointees in whatever general position they choose, and moving career executives to positions chosen by the agency head. Agency heads can now put together their own management teams.[6]

On the state level, 12 states have created SES systems. Four did so prior to the 1978 CSRA: California (1963), Minnesota (1969), Wisconsin (1973), and Oregon (1977). After the creation of the federal level SES, several states adopted their own SES systems shortly afterwards: Connecticut (1979), Florida (1980), Iowa (1980), Michigan (1980), Washington (1980), and Pennsylvania (1981). Both Tennessee and New Jersey passed their SES legislation in 1986, and Massachusetts gave the governor statutory authority to set up a senior career management system, which has not yet been implemented. While the state-level SES systems, like the federal-level one, offer *potentially* enhanced career mobility, managerial control, and leadership flexibility, as Sherwood and Breyer suggest in their evaluation of state-level SES systems: "Little in the twenty-four-year history of executive personnel systems in the states suggests that they have come to occupy a highly significant role in the processes of governance."[7]

Table 4.3 The Federal Senior Executive Service

WHAT SES IS AND WHERE SES WORKS

Location of SES (in percentage)

Metropolitan area

Washington, DC	73
Other	27

Race/National Origin

Black	7
Hispanic	2
Asian/Pacific Islander	1
Native American	1
White	87
Not identified	1

Education

Bachelor's degree or less	31
Master's	35
Law degree[2]	16
Doctorate	18

Average length of federal government service	23 years
Average age	52 years

Type of appointment (percentage)

Career	89
Noncareer (political)	10

Department/Agency (percentage)

Agriculture	5
Commerce	5
Defense	17
Education	1
Energy	6
Environmental Protection Agency	4
General Services Administration	1
Health and Human Services	9
Housing and Urban Development	1
Interior	4
Justice	4
Labor	2
National Science Foundation	1
NASA	7
Nuclear Regulatory Commission	3
Office of Management and Budget	1
Commission	1
State	2
Transportation	5
Treasury	8
Veterans Affairs	4
Other	10

WHY THE SES IS UNIQUE

Government-wide personnel system

Rank-in-person

Decentralization of recruitment and training

Relaxed tenure, managerial flexibility

Responsiveness through political appointments to career jobs

Careerist opportunities through career appointments to political jobs

Pay-for-performance

Emphasis on general management

Mobility

Accountability through measurable performance goals and appraisals

(continued)

Table 4.3 (Continued)

WHAT SES DOES?

Policy Activity of SES	% SES Who Have Responsibility
Policy and program involvement	
Keep abreast of new issues and developments in my field	99.6
Choose among alternatives for achieving policy goals	99.0
Set priorities for my organization	99.0
Gather information	98.8
Initiate policy ideas	98.4
Recommend changes/improvements to regulations, policies or programs	97.5
Interpret and apply laws, regulations, and policies	96.6
Draft rules and regulations	81.5
Organizational liaison	
Meet with individuals from other departments and agencies	96.9
Explain merits of policies to supervisor	96.0
Explain merits of policies to individuals in other government agencies	87.4
Meet with interest group representatives	86.5
Meet with congressional staff	79.3
Testify before Congress on policy matters	75.9
Explain merits of policies to my department secretary	70.6
Explain merits of policies to OMB	62.1
Meet with members of Congress	57.2
Explain merits of policies to congressional committees	56.0
Explain merits of policies to White House staff	47.0
Budgeting	
Make budgetary decisions	91.6
Testify before OMB on budget matters	76.8
Testify before Congress on budget matters	75.3
Personnel	
Develop employee training policies	80.2
Develop employee recruitment policies	72.9
Develop employee promotion policies	72.7
Develop equal employment opportunity policies	70.4

SOURCE: *Public Administration Review,* Nov/Dec 2000, pp. 576–577.

Why the disappointing performance of state-level SES systems? According to Deborah D. Roberts, "State SES systems contain too many lofty and contradictory goals that cannot all be staisfied. These contradictions revolve around incentives, membership quandaries, and diversity among the important players"

- Give careerists real leadership as close and trusted advisers of top policy makers, yet also give political appointees (who may be strangers to the system and its capabilities) more power to make careerists more vulnerable to their wishes.

- Using performance-driven evaluations, increase rewards (which in reality turn out to be meager or nonexistent), but also increase SES members' risks of being reassigned, demoted, or penalized by political superiors.

- Be a select elite, yet a big enough class to act as a powerful motivator for those lower in the ranks aspiring to move up; also, defend elitism and excellence in a system geared to egalitarianism.

- Promise a highly mobile SES with transferable abilities, when most people have advanced through the ranks as either subject or technical specialists.

- Balance the mix between the careerist core and lateral entry by those with significant leadership and managerial talent, without degenerating into another patronage route.

- Identify, attract, retain, and enhance the skills of candidates without substantial commitments of time, training, or development; but expect results immediately.

- Convince many audiences—governors, appointed agency heads, legislators, personnelists, interest groups, potential candidates, and the rank-and-file civil service—of the merits without offending or damaging any of their separate interests.

Due to such challenging contradictions, according to Professor Roberts, existing state SES systems "are undergoing painful retrenchment and redirection, and few states appear willing to adopt new SES initiatives."[8]

To sum up the influence of the political appointee subsystem: First, these individuals occupy the highest, most prominent posts within public organizations. Thus, they serve as linchpins between campaign promises and bureaucratic performance. However, they are characterized overall as a very diverse, fragmented, and transitory group with little cohesiveness.

Second, their influence within bureaucracy depends upon the policy positions they hold, the length of their government service, their connections with top elected officials, their own personalities, their support from outside groups, their capacity to deal with immediate tasks at hand, and whether these tasks lend themselves to imminent solutions. Generally, as one moves up the hierarchy of political officials to the inner Cabinet, these individuals have the broadest backgrounds, and must deal with the broadest, most critical policy issues. They also exercise the widest, most influential policy roles inside public bureaucracy, if their tenure is long enough and their external support adequate to the performance of the tasks at hand. Here at the top the political winds blow the fiercest, the "turf battles" are the most intense, and the stakes are the highest.

Third, as one moves down the hierarchy of these political officials toward those of quasi-political status, greater degrees of specialization are found as well as more identification with the programmatic goals, tasks, and issues within the agencies they serve. They possess a narrower expertise and are more concerned with pushing narrower policy agendas, which often means they are less interested in and responsive to their top political chief's reelection priorities.

Fourth, sharp turf fights over policy issues therefore ensue frequently between these various levels of political appointees, largely because of the different perspectives built into their hierarchical roles. Here is where pitched policy battles frequently occur and are resolved. In the pecking order of appointees, those at or near the top push agendas that are broader and more responsive to the chief executive's agenda, while those lower down tend to be more programmatic and focused on the priorities and issues of the particular agencies in which they work.

Fifth, while the subsystem of political appointees is highly fragmented, appointees tend to cluster into networks in which those near the top have close personal ties, even long friendships, with the chief elected official (though not necessarily with each other, nor are they necessarily active in his political campaigns). Those on the lower rungs tend to be experts in particular fields with personal networks that run downward into the agency and outward into various external support groups associated with an agency's mission.

Sixth, what draws all appointees together and keeps them loyal and responsible, at least to some degree, to the elected official's policy agenda (and makes them a distinct bureaucratic subsystem) is the fact that they can be removed or transferred at any time by a president, governor, or mayor. Fear of losing a job can be a powerful incentive to stay in line with the top-level agenda, or at least to refrain from stating opposing views in public. Political history has demonstrated that publicizing opposition views or "going public" is highly dangerous to anyone's survival in this subsystem. The departures, of Walter Hickel in Nixon's administration, James Schlesinger in Ford's, Joseph Califano and Michael Blumenthal in Carter's, Alexander Haig and Martin Feldstein in Reagan's, or of Les Aspin and Jocelyn Elder in Clinton's administration are all reminders of the primary importance of loyalty to the boss at this level and of the hazards inherent in bucking the party line.

However, in this constantly shifting world of personnel and goals, as Norton Long pointed out, determining to whom one is loyal and what one should accomplish become difficult if not impossible tasks. This level in bureaucracy is an ambiguous world in which appearances frequently count more than on-the-job practices. Participants thus spend enormous amounts of time posturing and posing in order to appear to do the correct things for the right people and taking readings or soundings to find information about their own status and about the intentions of others. The closed door, the office nearest the boss's, an invitation to the right party, the frequency of meetings with the superior, and the seating arrangement at the conference table often signal more than the untrained eye can perceive or the written document explain. Hard-driving, ambitious men and women, even with considerable experience and exposure, become quickly frustrated and disillusioned with the confusion and pretense inherent in this subsystem, as autobiographies of recent incumbents testify. Policy activity at this level of bureaucracy is very much like the greased pole competition at the old-fashioned county fair, where few, if any, climb to the top and reach the prize. The way up is slippery, uncertain, and treacherous, often crowded with many other frenzied competitors. There are no sure rules for success. And the prize, once reached, is often temporary, of little value, and hardly worth all that fierce competition and furiously expended energy. Many leave disillusioned and despairing about what they have done or failed to do. Good luck rather than personal skills often decides outcomes.

Seventh, political appointees, despite the highly ambiguous world in which they operate, ultimately are central to the governing processes at all levels of government. They are critical, individually and collectively, in the words of presidential scholar James P. Pfiffner, to assist chief executives in "hitting the ground running." The Bobby Inman affair, in which the presidential nominee for secretary of defense declined the job just prior to what was thought "smooth sailing" through his Senate confirmation, due to what Inman claimed were "hostile press attacks" on his character and "family considerations," points up all too well the problems presidents face in recruiting able political appointees *and* the policy complications that can occur broadly for presidents when their political appointees are not promptly put into place. High job demands, family stress, extensive security checks, comparatively low pay (by contrast to other similarly responsible private-sector jobs), and detailed public and press scrutiny all combine to deter many from seeking such lines of work and to delay appointments. Indeed, as Figure 4.4 shows, Presidents Clinton, Bush, Sr., and Bush, Jr., have been slower than their predecessors in getting their own policy team in place, leading to early criticisms of their capacity to govern effectively.

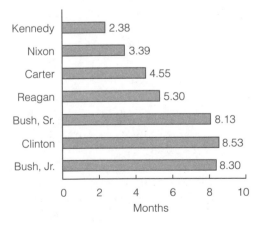

FIGURE 4.4 Average number of months from inauguration to confirmation for initial PAS appointees, by administration

Source: *Staffing a New Administration* (Washington, D.C.: The Brookings Institution, Nov. 2000), p. 13 and updated by data in *Washington Post National Weekly* (July 29–Aug. 4, 2002), p. 13.

THE PROFESSIONAL CAREERIST SUBSYSTEM:
PERMANENT CLUSTERS OF POWERFUL EXPERTS

Professor Samuel H. Beer has said that U.S. society is governed by "technocratic politics" in which specialists with in-depth training and experience in different fields of government have assumed the duty of charting the course of various public organizations. As Beer argues:

> I would remark how rarely additions to the public agenda have been initiated by the demands of voters or the advocacy of pressure groups or the platforms of political parties. On the contrary, in the fields of health, housing, urban renewal, transportation, welfare, education, poverty, and energy, it has been in very great measure people in government service or closely associated with it acting on the basis of their specialties and technical knowledge who first perceived the problem, conceived the program, initially urged it on the President and Congress, went on to help lobby it through to enactment, and then saw to its administration.[9]

Some scholars, including Zbigniew Brzezinski, have called the phenomenon "the technetronic age"; Don Price calls it "the scientific estate"; for Daniel Bell it is "the post-industrial age"; for Guy Benveniste, "the politics of expertise."[10] But whatever term is used to describe the role of experts within government, the professional strata, a subsystem below that of political appointees, is now recognized by many scholars as a significant influence over the activities of modern public organizations. As Frederick C. Mosher has perceptively written, "For better or worse—or better and worse—much of government is now in the hands of professionals (including scientists). The choice of these professionals, the determination of their skills, and the content of their work are now principally determined not by the general government agencies, but by their own professional elites, professional organizations and the institutions and facilities of higher education. It is unlikely the trend toward professionalization in or outside government will be reversed or even slowed."[11]

Professionalization in government influenced not only the domestic agenda, as Beer suggests, but also how we viewed our broad global responsibilities in the post–World War II era. According to Robert D. Kaplan:

> The global responsibilities thrust upon the United States after World War II led to the creation of area experts in government, academia, and think tanks. Their effect on policy and public opinion has been to splinter and compartmentalize what used to be geographic wholes. The academic and policy-making nomenklatura invented a new world based not on real borders so much as on the borders of their knowledge or lack thereof. As someone who has written extensively about Turkey and the Balkans, as well as the Middle East, I have seen how these areas constitute two entirely different subcultures of Washington society and workdom, with little or no cross-fertilization between the two.[12]

The development of professional control over the inner dynamics of U.S. bureaucracy came slowly and in piecemeal fashion, mostly in the twentieth century. Some agencies, such as DoJ, have since their inception been dominated by lawyers, but professionally trained lawyers with LL.B. degrees, steeped in learning, responsive to the American Bar Association's policy concerns, specialists in highly diverse elements of the law, did not appear at DoJ in any sizable numbers until the New Deal in the 1930s. Military officers held the top army posts from the time the War Department was established in 1789, but even throughout most of the nineteenth century officers were poorly trained and politically motivated amateurs with little or no technical competency (except for those trained as engineers at West Point).

The modern generalist-professional cadre of officers did not appear until after 1900, established largely through the reforms of Secretary of War Elihu Root, who created the Army General Staff, a unified personnel system, as well as a series of advanced professional educational institutions for military officers. The Rogers Act of 1924 instituted what we now know as the professional foreign service, but the dominance of quality foreign service professionals such as George Kennan and Charles Bohlen throughout key State Department slots did not emerge until after World War II.

Likewise, the professional control of state and local agencies in many regions began at roughly the turn of the century with the formation of small, fledgling professional associations such as the International Association of Chiefs of Police (1893), the International Association of Fire Chiefs (1893), the American Society of Municipal Engineers (1894), the Municipal Finance Officers Association (1906), the National Recreation Association (1906), the National Association of Public School Business Officials (1910), the National Organization for Public Health Nursing (1912), and the City Managers' Association (1914).

As Robert Wiebe observes of the process of grassroots professionalization in America:

> Social workers . . . acted first to dissociate themselves from philanthropy and establish themselves as a distinct field within the new social sciences. Beginning with local leagues in Boston and New York, they had formed the National Federation of Settlements by 1911 and soon after captured the old National Conference of Charities and Corrections, renaming it the National Conference of Social Work. Also early in the century, they moved from ad hoc classes of special training to complete professional schools within such universities as Chicago and Harvard. . . . So it went with architects, a variety of public and private administrators, and many more: definition, professional association, and specific academic training.[13]

The federal government also had an important hand in stimulating professionalism at the state and local levels. For example, again in the area of social work, Martha Derthick writes:

> Congress in 1939 gave the Social Security Board authority to set personnel standards, perhaps because it was sympathetic to some degree of professionalism in the performance of public administration (on the

assumption that it would lead to "efficiency") if not in the performance of social work. Even before this was done, the Board was demanding—on the basis of its authority to require efficient administration—that state plans include minimum standards for education, training, and experience (for local social workers).[14]

In many respects, at the local level and to a great extent at the federal level as well, professionalism was a means of battling "corruption as well as inefficiency," as Jeremy F. Plant and David S. Arnold point out: "Professionalism had to pervade the entire fabric of modern government," at least in the eyes of reformers who sought better government.[15] But, for the most part, until after World War II these professional groups were weak and ineffective voluntary associations exercising little control over the inner dynamics of local public bureaucracy. The postwar era, however, brought into grass-roots and higher-level government an influx of university-educated specialists with wide assortments of technical competence. The postwar era also brought about a new respect for and demand for these specialists to deal with a myriad of technical tasks from constructing highways, educating children, cleaning air and water, and administering complex regulatory machinery—often spawned by the professionals themselves—for certifying and controlling the application of skills inside and outside government. As Figure 4.5 indicates, today professional public official associations are extensive and varied, exercising hidden yet pervasive influence over government policy through certification, training, setting ethical standards, and playing policy advocacy roles within their specialized fields.

The story of the professionalization of U.S. bureaucracy is complex and has not been explained nor even understood fully by historians and political scientists. Yet the point is that there has been a silent revolution within U.S. government, as a result of which, as Samuel Beer and others observe, professionals decisively determine much of what government does or doesn't do. In some locales, the revolution toward grass-roots control of bureaucracy proceeded swiftly. Particularly in "clean reform states," such as California, professional groups have gained control of even the upper reaches of bureaucracy over the past several decades. In poorer, rural areas, such as Mississippi, trends in professional dominance have been slower, but even there they are occurring because of federal mandates and other laws that have aided the growth and dominance of professions and professionals. Wherever bureaucracy operates today, in the words of Corinne L. Gilb, these groups constitute "the hidden hierarchies of government."[16]

Professionals in government today, however, by no means make up a monolithic group or a homogeneous mass of experts; indeed, they differ considerably from one another. First, there are the *general professionals,* who practice their calling within *both* government and the private sector. They tend to exhibit all the trappings of what traditionally are viewed as the qualities of "classic" professionals, such as advanced training beyond the college level, high status as perceived by the general public, as well as a fairly clear-cut occupational specialty

Airport Operators Council, International
American Association of Airport Executives
American Association of Motor Vehicle Administrators
American Association of Port Authorities
American Association of State Highway and Transportation Officials
American College of Health Care Executives
American Library Association
American Planning Association/American Institute of Certified Planners
American Public Gas Association
American Public Health Association

American Public Power Association
American Public Transit Association
American Public Welfare Association
American Public Works Association
American Society for Public Administration
American Water Works Association
Association of State and Interstate Water Pollution Control Administrators
Building Officials and Code Administrators, International
Council of Governors' Policy Advisors (formerly Council of State Policy and Planning Agencies)
Council of State Community Affairs Agencies

Council of State Governments
Council of State Housing Agencies
Federation of Tax Administrators
Government Finance Officers Association
Government Refuse Collection and Disposal Association
Institute of Transportation Engineers
International Association of Assessing Officers
International Association of Auditorium Managers
International Association of Chiefs of Police
International Association of Fire Chiefs

International Bridge, Tunnel, and Turnpike Association
International City/County Management Association
International Conference of Building Officials
International Institute of Municipal Clerks
International Personnel Management Association
National Association of Attorneys General
National Association of Counties
National Association of Development Organizations
National Association of Housing and Redevelopment Officials
National Association of Regional Councils
National Association of Regulatory Utility Commissions
National Association of State Auditors, Comptrollers, and Treasurers
National Association of State Aviation Officials
National Association of State Budget Officers
National Association of State Development Agencies
National Association for State Information Systems
National Association of Towns and Townships
National Conference of State Legislatures
National Council for Urban Economic Development

(continued)

FIGURE 4.5   Major general/specialist, professional, public, and official associations (excludes elementary, secondary, and higher education as well as military)

National District Attorneys Association
National Governors' Association
National Institute of Governmental Purchasing
National Institute of Municipal Law Officers
National League of Cities
National Public Employees Labor Relations Association
National Recreation and Park Association
Public Risk Management Association
Southern Building Code Congress International
U.S. Conference of Mayors
Water Pollution Control Federation

FIGURE 4.5 *(Continued)*

Source: David S. Arnold and Jeremy F. Plant, *Public Official Associations and State and Local Government: A Bridge across One Hundred Years* (Fairfax, VA: George Mason University Press, 1994), pp. 10 and 11.

with lifetime career opportunities and adequate financial rewards (with sometimes huge opportunities in the private sector). General professionals occupy prominent posts in government and include physicians in local public hospitals or the National Institutes of Health; lawyers staffing DoJ or local district attorneys' and county counsels' offices; civil engineers in state highway departments or local public works offices; and accountants within the governmental affairs office or state auditing agencies. *Public professionals,* by contrast, are those whose sole employment is in government service, but whose characteristics are similar to those of the traditional general professional groups. Foreign service officers, public health officers, army, navy, air force and marine corps officers, urban planners, FBI agents, and city managers fall into this category. For various reasons *emerging professionals* have not obtained full-fledged professional status, pay, or career development opportunities as general or public professionals, but they have certainly been moving in that direction, as a fulfillment of their own "occupational ideal," for a number of years. Police officers, computer specialists, firemen, corrections officers, and environmental specialists are a few kinds of emerging professionals in the impressive array of specialists within public bureaucracy today. *Paraprofessionals* are among the newest groups of government workers; they are also striving for professional status and recognition. Paraprofessionals provide vital assistance to professionals in their work. They occupy the twilight zone between emerging professional groups and skilled workers in the public service. Paralegal assistants, various types of health and medical technicians, warrant officers in the military, and executive secretaries fall into this occupational group.

Whether or not individual professions fit into one or more of the above-mentioned typologies remains a moot question, but evidence supports the contention that most public organizations at every level of government today are controlled by one or more of these professional groups, which are most closely identified with that level's central missions, activities, and products. They make up what Burton J. Bledstein calls "the culture of professionalism,"[17] where the

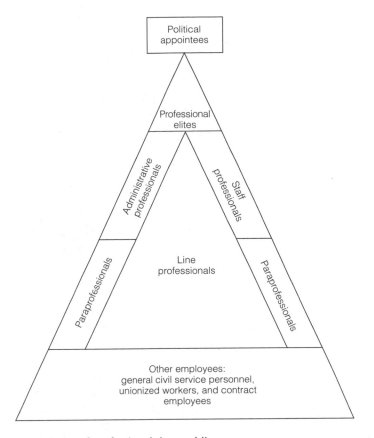

Political
appointees

Professional
elites

Administrative
professionals

Staff
professionals

Paraprofessionals

Line
professionals

Paraprofessionals

Other employees:
general civil service personnel,
unionized workers, and contract
employees

FIGURE 4.6   Varieties of professionals in a public agency

"regard for professional expertise compels people to believe the voices of authority unquestionably." If one could X-ray the insides of a typical public bureaucracy, one would see that the arrangement of professional dominance looks something like Figure 4.6.[18]

Note that directly under political appointees, *professional elites* comprise the core group of experts. These are the senior and most prestigious and respected members of the profession. They give not only internal direction to the profession but also to the entire agency by controlling the important positions and advancement to those positions, and by setting recruitment and entrance requirements as well as overall personnel policies and priorities for the organization. Rising to these posts is achieved only through long-term career investment in the field, attendance at the "right" schools for basic and advanced training in the field, and advancement through progressive levels of responsibility and prominence in areas closely identified with the central roles and responsibilities of the agency. Pilots in the air force, line officers in the navy, doctors in the U.S. Public Health Service, foresters in the U.S. Forest Service, senior staff lawyers at DoJ, and top-ranking educators in local school systems or in state departments of education as Table 4.4 highlights, tend to fill the elite slots within their respective agencies.

There are some exceptions to this pattern of elitist control. Some agencies with high turnover or a pattern of domination by political appointees (such as the Office of Personnel Management in recent years, those agencies run in a way similar to business corporations, such as TVA, and those dominated by public service unions, such as the U.S. Postal Service) exhibit little or no identifiable professional elites. It should also be added that elites in one agency are not necessarily transferable to another. A psychiatrist may be considered one of the elite at the National Institutes of Health but may well be a second-class citizen in a military hospital or in a local public health clinic in which MDs generally dominate the staff positions.

The pecking order of elites may indeed be multilayered within any public agency. A physician who is a general practitioner might be in charge of running a large Veterans Administration hospital, but a psychiatrist might head the mental health section of that same hospital because he or she is more specialized in that field. The psychiatrist holds an M.D. degree and can thus prescribe drugs, whereas the psychologist (who holds "only" a Ph.D.) who works for the psychiatrist in the same unit generally has less status because he or she lacks an M.D. degree and therefore cannot prescribe drugs. Occupying rungs under these elites may be other professional groups such as social workers, nurses, and medical technicians.

"Status" at times becomes an obsession with professionals. Knowing where one is or is not or how to advance "in the pecking order" of influence is important to most professionals. The registered nurse is considered an elite within that cluster of professionals. And not only is certification as an RN important to a nurse's elite status today, further certification within a very narrow specialized field within which she or he works, such as emergency room, orthopedic care, or surgery room practice, is also desirable. The continuous specialization of those who are already specialists within government is staggering. The professionals' rank order therefore moves on down the line of clusters of professional groups in a unit where length of education, type of educational certification, quality of schooling, degrees of responsibility, and status in the eyes of the community and of the profession itself are sources for determining who is or is not inside the nucleus of the particular professional elite.

The elites, in turn, within these various strata of professional clusters provide key leadership as well as set the work standards, the qualifications for entrance and advancement, and the overall values for the profession. Much of the critical tensions and conflicts between clusters of professional elites are over policy questions and control of turf—between doctors and nurses in hospitals or between air force, army, navy, and marine corps top-ranking officers within DoD. Much of this conflict is hidden from public view. Rarely does it become public, because it can most often be settled between the competing parties or by political superiors. But at times internal dissent can become so strained that work production slows and the mission of the unit is even jeopardized.

Table 4.4 Types of Professions and Their Elites in Several Public Organizations

Public Organization	Key Profession	Professional Elite
National Level		
State Department	Foreign Service Officers	Senior FSO 1 and 2 level career ambassadors and staff
Army, Air Force, Navy, and Marines	Career Officers in Armed Service	General or flag rank officers from combat arms in senior policy line positions
Justice Department	Lawyers	Senior careerists in key litigating divisions
Forest Service	Foresters	Career forester in highest policy and line posts
National Institutes of Health	Scientists	"Name" scientists heading research projects
Federal Reserve Board	Economists	Prestigious economists in key analytical or policy units
Local and State Levels		
Auditing or Accounting Agencies	Accountants	CPAs who are in charge of major auditing or accounting divisions or units
Public Hospitals	Doctors	Senior MDs directing major units or depts.
Highway and Public Works Agencies	Engineers	Civil engineers with seniority in the agency
Elementary and Secondary School Systems	Teachers	Principals, asst. superintendents, or superintendents
City and Town Government Administrations	City Managers, Chief Administrators	Senior career managers of major cities
Welfare Services	Social Workers	Ranking career social workers in top level agency posts

Line professionals, who fall just below the level of the senior elites, actually carry out the day-to-day functions of the public agency. Whereas a few dozen three- and four-star generals compose the army's top professional elite, more than 200,000 army officers from second lieutenants to generals direct much of the real work of the army in a wide variety of combat and noncombat jobs. Some, given their West Point training and combat duties in the infantry, armor, or artillery (combat sections that are considered "ideal" rungs in the ladder to the level of the elite) may become part of the professional elite; others in the line may have neither the interest, nor the proper backgrounds, nor good luck to attain those high-level assignments. The line officers are essentially the "doing" and "implementing" functionaries of bureaucracy and are most directly associated with the central missions of an agency.

Most public professions, such as the foreign service, have no "West Points" to train recruits in "the ideal" of an agency's mission. Foreign Service Officers (FSOs) instead come from a wide assortment of civilian backgrounds—economics, law, political science, and so on—but FSOs tend to favor a broad liberal arts, Ivy League background because of internationalist traditions and diplomatic breadth of knowledge required in line posts. Being assigned as political representatives abroad remains today the central mission of State Department employees. Diplomacy is the key function at the State Department, but FSOs can serve as staff or administrative professionals when they assume narrow special roles within the department.

Staff professionals in public agencies include a wide assortment of specialists and technical assistants who have unique and specialized expertise that may not be directly connected with the central tasks of the agency but are nonetheless critical to carrying out its assigned functions. Today almost every public bureaucracy employs a wide array of these individuals. In such diverse public organizations as the General Accounting Office at the federal level, where accountants staff the elite and the line jobs, or at a state highway office, where engineers are generally in charge, or a local social work agency, where social workers are the principal professionals, these and sundry staff professionals such as lawyers, computer specialists, public relations experts, and legislative relations officers, cluster around their headquarters' operations and are essential to fulfilling the agency's missions. They assume the critical advisory roles within an agency and in some government offices frequently assume large and powerful policy-making roles, even though they are not directly in either the line or the elite ranks. In every federal department, the legal counsels, for example, not only can command high salaries, large staffs, exemptions from civil service hiring rules, and the ear of the top brass in the agency, but also frequently exercise enormous yet quiet influence over central policies of an agency through knowledge and expertise in the law. The top political and professional cadre yield often to such legal policy advice on technical matters because few insiders can supply this knowledge (alternatively the advice can be purchased at high cost from outside law firms). One only need attend a city council or county board of supervisors' meeting to watch the frequency with which elected members turn to legal counsel for assistance or to view federal organization charts to discover the strategic positions legal counsels occupy within most departments.

Administrative professionals comprise an assortment of budget officials; program officers; planning personnel; and finance, purchasing, auditing, and supply officials found in every public organization (the G-1 through G-5 jobs in the U.S. military). These men and women are critical to the activities of the agency because they essentially serve as "the directing brain" of the organization ("the directing brain" is Elihu Root's name for this group in his 1902 proposal for the creation of a general staff in the U.S. Army, which was a pattern copied by other public agencies and business corporations).

In some agencies these administrative staffs are quite large; for example, the Department of Health and Human Services employs several thousand individuals in this category. But in many places the staffs are quite small, as in small towns where a city manager may perform all these administrative support tasks. In larger organizations some of these slots are temporarily held by line professionals, but many are filled by permanent careerists from emerging professional groups, such as budgeting, personnel, and purchasing specialists. While these individuals may not as yet rank as full-fledged professionals, they are increasingly taking on all the trappings of professionals, having their own associations, journals, "ideal career tracks," and educational requirements. Some even command higher salaries and status than their professional superiors. Municipal budget officers, for example, today are sometimes paid higher salaries than their bosses, city managers, or chief administrative officers, because of their critical budget and finance expertise in municipal decision-making processes.

In the uncertain environment within which agencies must operate, staff professionals must be adaptive and inventive in coping with the changing needs of their agencies. Much of their work is simply "fire-fighting" in order to maintain their structure amid turbulence, but much also is directed at thinking about the future of the organization, even if this planning is only incrementally achieved through short-term budgets, ad hoc personnel recruitment and selection, and partial programmatic design or redesign.

Finally, paraprofessionals make up another group increasingly seen within public agencies. These people receive substantially lower remunerative rewards for their work, although many units of government simply could not perform their assigned tasks without them. Many of these "paras" aspire to becoming full-fledged professionals and use the experience as apprenticeship training. Others see this line of work as a rewarding lifetime career and seek no higher positions. From the standpoint of government, however, these workers are taking on increasing responsibility in various offices because of the rising costs of hiring fully qualified professionals. In other words, using "paras" is an effective governmental strategy for keeping down rapidly escalating personnel costs. In many cases "paras" perform the work as well as, if not better than, their highly paid counterparts. In this respect, their primary roles inside public organizations may well be an important economic function.

On the whole, what can be said about the influence of all the professional subsystems upon the activities and outputs of public bureaucratic institutions?

First and foremost, professionals are essential to the performance of the central missions of virtually every public agency. They define its mission, decide how it should be accomplished and who should accomplish it, as well as when it should be accomplished and where. As noted by Professor Beer, professionals in an age of "technocratic politics" play major roles from the conceptualization of a policy through to its implementation.

Second, by comparison with top-level political appointees, professionals by and large have longevity within agencies, thus giving them an enormous edge in the policy-making processes. They simply outlast their rival superiors. A classic example is the TFX decision. In the mid-1960s, Defense Secretary Robert McNamara, over violent objections by the individual services, rammed through approval for a joint-service tactical fighter aircraft, the TFX, which could be utilized by the combined commands of the air force and navy. However, within

2 months of McNamara leaving DoD, on February 28, 1968, TFX died quietly as the navy and air force each went ahead and developed its own separate tactical fighter. Ultimately, the separate service professionals had *their* way over that of the political appointee (and McNamara was probably one of the most powerful of all defense secretaries).

Third, professionals are not a single, unified group. They are part of a well-established pecking order, from elites down to "paras," that is based on education, skills, seniority, levels of responsibility, and general competence and experience. Each level of professional brings different capabilities, policy roles, and political influences to the shaping of agency outputs. Elites occupy the highest level of policy-making roles; line professionals shape actions mainly through implementation practices; staff professionals fill advisory roles; administrative professionals prepare and plan tasks; and paraprofessionals carry out lower-level and lower-cost work. Each, therefore, is essential to the performance of the bureaucratic process. As a whole, though, professionals shape government agencies by controlling recruitment, selection, and other personnel actions as well as the overall organizational structure within many agencies.

Fourth, continuing political strength and popular support of professionals ultimately rest upon their recognized expertise and competence as well as on their ability to exercise these skills in a regular, uniform manner in the public interest. The widespread popularity of city-manager government rests fundamentally on its ability to apply systematic expertise to urban issues at the local level. Since expertise is professionals' stock in trade and is a source of authority and of legitimacy within government, a great deal of their efforts are directed at higher education and improving professionals' reputation for competence and application of knowledge. Professionals look to institutions of higher learning to sustain and enrich their knowledge base through training programs that give the professionals their credentials, and nurture the fundamental ethos and values of the profession. If political appointees draw support from their elected chiefs, professionals in government conversely derive their legitimacy from expertise acquired through higher education. The educational content as well as its application to pressing public problems influence the long-term priorities and fundamental value of professions. Hence, professions pay enormous attention to the shaping of professional education programs, examinations, accreditation, and licensing processes that help to determine the nature and content of professional work, as well as the knowledge and skill it requires. In the words of Ralph Hummel, "Professional associations are the externalizers of the superego in their own right; they constitute the conscience for the individual professionals who go astray and exercise the power of punishment."[19]

Fifth, professionals shape public policies not only by contributing a substantial share of the public workforce and its top leadership cadre but also by moving upward and outward beyond the contours of their roles within agencies. As noted in the discussion of political appointees, they frequently assume temporary assignments at this level. Half the Cabinet in both the Johnson and Carter administrations was made up of former professors and of "in-and-outers" from various professional callings. As Table 4.2 shows, roughly one-quarter of both

President Bush Sr.'s and President Clinton's political appointees held Ph.D.s. Similarly, the influence of professionals moves increasingly outward into legislative staff assignments or related nonprofit or business firms that directly and indirectly influence the course of bureaucratic policies. For example, retired military officers have for many years moved into prominent defense contracting firms with influential ties to the Pentagon. Professional links, formal and informal, with a wide assortment of "think tanks" and universities are critical sources for developing, shaping, and implementing public policies in most fields.

Finally, the most serious tensions and conflicts within public organizations are generally hidden from view, since they arise mainly from policy disputes *between* clusters of key professionals as much as from disputes between professional elites and political superiors. Many top political appointees today look highly professional, indeed *are drawn* from professional cadres, thus the tensions between political appointees and careerists are frequently not as sharp and long term compared to those *between* professional groups. Fights between the army, navy, and air force over defense appropriations and priorities are a permanent part of the Washington landscape, but it is within these professional service battles that defense policies for DoD develop. Likewise, the typical controversies that occur at the grass roots between police and firefighters over annual budget appropriations, length of work day, and salary increases figure equally prominently in determining the directions of local public safety policies.

THE GENERAL CIVIL SERVICE SUBSYSTEM: LADDERS OF BUREAUCRATIC SPECIALISTS, GENERALISTS, AND WHITE COLLAR WORKERS

The classic professional career subsystem is characterized by long-range progressive career planning, a clear-cut occupational field of expertise, rank inherent in the individual, separate, self-governing personnel systems controlled by the professional elite, higher educational requirements, and requirement of credentials as prerequisites for entrance into lifetime careers with opportunities for increasing responsibility and financial rewards.

While bits and pieces of the "ideal professional model" are incorporated gradually into the general civil service, the bulk of government personnel are members of civil service and do not share in the professional model. Civil service is founded on the merit system, whereby positions are assigned on the basis of open, competitive examinations (written and/or oral) and candidates are evaluated and ranked in relationship to particular task requirements of a specific job. Generally, selection is made from among the top three scorers. Unlike the professional subsystem, civil service has no progressive job planning or control by elites but has, rather, a laissez-faire approach in which each individual seeks out and designs his or her own path within the system. Advanced training may or may not be essential. Rank is inherent in the job, not the person. Meeting

Personnel Analyst I
$19,407–$28,674

Definition
Under close and instructional supervision, to perform a variety of technical duties in one or more phases of the personnel program; and to do related work as required.

Typical Tasks
Conducts on-the-job position audits to determine level and kinds of duties and responsibilities, makes analyses of information obtained, and recommends allocation of positions to classes as a result of analyses, assists in conducting wage surveys by compiling and recording data supplies on questionnaires and preparing simple analyses of data; assists in developing training materials by assembling resource material; preparing outlines of information to be covered, and researching material for data or information to be used; receives, reviews for accuracy, and conformity, with appropriate rules and regulations, and recommends approval of personnel action forms submitted by departments to reflect hirings, dismissals, transfers, promotions, reclassifications, and other personnel changes, assists in the positive recruitment program by interviewing applicants to determine interests, aptitudes, and qualifications, advising applicants of job opportunities to specific departments for interviews with operating officials, and works with departments in locating applicants for specific job openings; assists in the construction of examinations and administering examinations to applicants, assists in gathering data for use in developing or revising fringe benefit programs.

Employment Standards
Graduation from a 4-year college or university

Upon completion of the training program, employees must be promoted, transferred or dismissed.

Knowledge of the principles of public personnel administration; knowledge of statistical methods; ability to prepare graphs, diagrams, and organization charts; ability to interview effectively; ability to analyze data and reach sound conclusions; ability to develop and maintain effective relationships with officials and other employees.

FIGURE 4.7   Within each classified grade level the salaries, duties, and employment standards are clearly outlined according to civil service rules.

Source: George Mason University Personnel Office.

the specific task requirements of the job as spelled out in Figure 4.7, for example, is what counts most in landing a slot in civil service. Status, in turn, is derived from the specific job. A GS-9 civil servant, for instance, is a GS-9 because he or she holds that slot. If the employee leaves it, he or she is no longer a GS-9, unlike, for example, a profession careerist such as an air force colonel, who is a colonel wherever he or she serves. In the professional subsystem, conversely, rank inheres in the person, not the job.

In the words of O. Glenn Stahl, perhaps the foremost authority on this subject, the general civil service, at least in its ideal format, is "a personnel system in which comparative merit or achievement governs each individual's selection and progress in the service and in which the conditions and rewards of performance contribute to the competency and continuity of the service."[20] Of course, the merit ideal is not always achieved in practice, but it does serve as the basic driving ideological idea behind this subsystem.

The civil service subsystem was grafted onto U.S. bureaucracy somewhat haphazardly almost a century after the creation of the Republic. Even today its "fit" into government seems somewhat awkward and unsure. For the most part, this uncertainty about its place in U.S. public bureaucracy is caused by, as many scholars have noted, the growth of the general civil service out of a reaction to the excesses of the nineteenth-century spoils system, in which employment in public service was based largely, though not entirely, upon party loyalty and political patronage. In other words, the modern civil service was built on a negative moral reaction to what was perceived as "evil" rather than on a positive and deliberate design.

The story of its growth is long and complex. To sum it up, in the late 1860s and throughout the 1870s a small band of reformers waged aggressive moral and political campaigns on behalf of civil service reform and against incompetence, graft, favoritism, and partisanship within the public service. Merit, they argued, should be the basis of appointment. Substantially modeled on the English civil service system, which had been in operation for nearly a half-century but was adapted to special pragmatic U.S. needs and concerns, the Civil Service Act (Pendleton Act) was enacted in 1883 mainly as a national reaction to the shooting of President James Garfield by a political supporter who had been refused a small patronage post.[21]

Pendleton became the classic model for "good personnel practices" throughout the nation. Extended gradually through executive order to cover increasing percentages of federal workers, it was also copied almost word for word by numerous states and localities (see Figure 4.8 for the most recent authoritative definition of "merit"). Localities borrowed from it their basic structural arrangements and concepts of merit processes, such as notions of a nonpartisan commission appointed by the chief executive to oversee the system, requirements for open, competitive examinations, probationary period prior to tenure, strict provision against political interference within civil service activities, classification of positions, and equal pay for equal work.

On the state level, New York passed a civil service law the same year as the federal government, and Massachusetts passed one the following year. Much of the civil service movement came in fits and starts. For example, Connecticut passed a civil service law in 1912, then weakened it, and finally repealed it in 1921, only to readopt a stronger civil service act in 1937. Some states, like Texas, never adopted a civil service system, and others like Virginia, recently abandoned the system entirely. Municipalities likewise moved to developed civil service systems, and most large cities by 1940 had some kind of merit system in place. Counties, though, have remained more backward; relatively few have comprehensive merit systems in place.

The impetus for adoption of state/local merit systems came from essentially three forces. One was local and state reform groups that saw "merit" as a method of improving economy and efficiency in government and ridding government of corrupt political machines; another was the federal government, which played a major role in the adoption of grass-roots civil service systems. The Social Security Act of 1935 and its 1940 amendments required state and local government employees administering health, welfare, and employment programs funded by the federal government to be covered by merit systems. The Intergovernmental Personnel Act (IPA) of 1970 further spurred local merit system

The most authoritative statement of the meaning of "merit" is found in the Civil Service Reform Act of 1978.

1. Recruitment should be from qualified individuals from appropriate sources in an endeavor to achieve a work force from all segments of society, and selection and advancement should be determined solely on the basis of relative ability, knowledge and skills, after fair and open competition that assures that all receive equal opportunity.
2. All employees and applicants for employment should receive fair and equitable treatment in all aspects of personnel management without regard to political affiliation, race, color, religion, national origin, sex, marital status, age, or handicapping conditions, and with proper regard for their privacy and constitutional rights.
3. Equal pay should be provided for work of equal value, with appropriate consideration of both national and local rates paid by employers in the private sector, and appropriate incentives and recognition should be provided for excellence in performance.
4. All employees should maintain high standards of integrity, conduct, and concern for the public interest.
5. The federal work force should be used efficiently and effectively.
6. Employees should be retained on the adequacy of their performance, inadequate performance should be corrected, and employees should be separated who cannot or will not improve their performance to meet required standards.
7. Employees should be provided effective education and training in cases in which such education and training would result in better organizational and individual performance.
8. Employees should be *(a.)* protected against arbitrary action, personal favoritism, or coercion for partisan political purposes, and *(b.)* prohibited from using their official authority or influence for the purpose of interfering with or affecting the result of an election or a nomination for election.
9. Employees should be protected against reprisal for the lawful disclosure of information that the employee reasonably believes evidences *(a.)* a violation of any law, rule, or regulation, or *(b.)* mismanagement, a gross waste of funds, an abuse of authority, or a substantial and specific danger to public health and safety.

FIGURE 4.8   Merit principles

Source: P.L. 95–454, Oct. 13, 1978, Civil Service Reform Act of 1978, Title I.

development through its various programs to upgrade public personnel systems and employee skills. Finally, Supreme Court decisions played a major role, especially in limiting patronage systems. In such cases as *Elrod v. Burns* (1976) and *Branti v. Finkel* (1980), the Court struck down patronage practices involving the firing of nonpolicy-making, nonconfidential employees.

The federal civil service workforce has stayed fairly constant in size over the past 30 years, but the local and state workforce has grown, nearly tripling during the same period (see Figure 4.9). In fact, the federal share of the public workforce fell from 27.7 percent of the total in 1961 to 15 percent in 2002. Also, the distribution of the federal workforce shows certain regional biases; a higher percentage (32 percent) is located in the South, compared to 17 percent of the total civilian workforce.

Today, 91 percent of the federal civilian workforce, or approximately 2.7 million workers, are covered under civil service personnel rules. While several structural and procedural adaptations over time have been added, such as the Civil Service Reform Act of 1978, its essential concepts of "merit," "Open, competitive examinations," and "equal pay for equal work" remain intact. Patricia W. Ingraham and David H. Rosenbloom summed up the current status

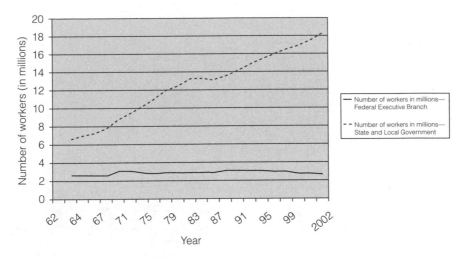

FIGURE 4.9 Government employment in millions, 1962–2002

of "merit" on the federal level: "While there continues to be strong support for the fundamental principles of merit, dissatisfaction with and confusion about the current system is high." They cited the complexity of regulations, the lack of training and trust of agency personnel dealing with civil service provisions, the absence of a clear definition of "merit" or of guidance for achieving a quality workforce as critical problems.[22] At the local level 36 states have comprehensive merit systems, while most others have either fragmentary or partial systems. All cities with populations of over 250,000 operate with comprehensive merit systems as well as 90 percent of those with more than 25,000 people. However, as Jay Shafritz has observed, "All statistics concerning merits systems' coverage are inherently deceptive."[23] For the most part this is because of the wide discrepancies between legal mandates and actual operations of the civil service in various locales.

Even though a considerable diversity in civil service laws is found across the United States, in those areas of the public service covered by its practices, scholars have discovered several common characteristics: First, the U.S. civil service is largely representative of the general population. Repeated studies have indicated that civil servants unlike political appointees or upper-level professionals— are broadly reflective of the American people's education, income, social status, age, and geographic backgrounds. Though these representational attributes appear in the aggregate—that is, when the entire public service is viewed statistically— they tend to break down in the various particular units or levels of government. Women are predominant in the bottom ranks as well as in certain fields such as nursing and teaching but are small minorities in police, fire, or other traditionally male occupational roles. Blacks and other minorities have made impressive gains in recent years in all areas of the public service, but the upper ranks still tend to be heavily representative of white males. In the higher ranks, as Kenneth J. Meier points out, greater advanced educational degrees and professional backgrounds are apparent.[24] The fathers of one-half of the higher federal civil service workers were professionals or businessmen, while only 14 percent of Americans in the general population reflected this characteristic; this unrepresentativeness is also apparent in the higher ranks of business and professional fields outside of government.

The compositions of the workforces of individual agencies look particularly unreflective of the general population. The Bureau of Land Management in the Interior Department and the Bureau of Alcohol, Tobacco, and Firearms within Treasury, and state and county agricultural departments tend to be composed overwhelmingly of males drawn from rural, agricultural, and land-grant colleges. Many enjoy hunting, fishing, and outdoor hobbies. Few are liberal arts graduates of large, urban institutions; most were trained in various narrow technical specialities pertaining to their fields. By contrast, civilians at the Departments of Justice and Defense are drawn largely from urban, eastern, and ivy league colleges.

Even within departments, sharp differences in backgrounds can be discovered. As Kenneth Smith observed, within the State Department, Foreign Service Officers still are drawn heavily from upper-class, eastern, prestigious universities and have a "generalist" liberal arts orientation, while those who work for the Agency for International Development tend to be drawn from less prestigious schools and socioeconomic backgrounds and have a wider diversity of occupational specializations and geographic backgrounds.[25] In other words, the personnel of AID is more heterogeneous, "middle class," and specialized than State's. In large part, these socioeconomic differences are caused by the fundamentally different needs of the agency itself. State's task demands are diverse and the FSOs' generalist backgrounds fit their representational duties abroad. On the other hand, the function of AID is mainly to provide specialized technical expertise to third-world nations. Hence more heterogeneous sorts of specialists predominate within that agency.

Anyone who has worked in government or seen it from the inside knows quite well that moving from agency to agency—even within the same department—can be like traveling into another country with sharply different customs, language, traditions, practices, rituals, and backgrounds. Each agency is unique. Understanding the peculiarities of each territory requires the skill of an anthropologist; at the very least it takes time to appreciate the unique qualities of the organizational culture, adjust to the people, and acclimate to the peculiar flora and fauna of the landscape.

Members of the general civil service subsystem generally lack the cohesiveness and unity found among professionals. Marver Bernstein notes that "there are more differences among career jobs than there are between a career job and that of the immediate political boss, an assistant secretary."[26] Today there are more than 900 occupational titles in the federal civil service with 30 different pay systems and a wide variation of occupational specialities in state and local bureaucracies. States and localities reflect even more diversity. For example,

South Dakota lists 510 occupational specialities versus 7,300 in New York. The diversity of work leads to few similarities among the personnel of a particular agency beyond the statement that describes their work.

When asked what she or he does, the typical bureaucrat will say, "I work at the Office of Education" or "I'm with the County Sheriff's Department." Few are likely to see themselves in broader terms and to say, "I'm a bureaucrat" or "I work for the civil service." Whether because of the pejorative connotations attached to government work or the more personal attachment to a particular assigned task, most bureaucrats lack common ties with government as a whole or with the broad *public orientation* of their work. This phenomenon no doubt exists in the private sector as well, where few business people see themselves as dedicated to the free market, but rather perceive themselves as real estate agents, autobody repairmen, or retail sales clerks. Most are like civil servants, who identify with the agency or skill at which they work or with the people with whom they work. The grand design of the organization or the broad purposes of their occupation generally elude their interests or understanding.

This lack of common ties to the broad aspects and purposes of government may in large part be caused by the general lack of mobility within the civil service. In theory, the civil service subsystem provides for open, competitive exams that permit advancement into every level or part of government (though restricted to particular federal, state, or local jurisdictions). In practice, however, most civil servants spend their working lives within one agency. Eugene B. MacGregor, Jr., who studied the mobility of civil servants at the GS-14 level and above, discovered an average of 17 to 25 years of service in the same agency or department.[27] Civil servants' depth of policy understanding, long-term views of issues, and particular expertise in an agency is therefore unmatched by comparison with those of transitory political appointees, who last in a post a mere 22 months at the federal level. Their longevity in an agency, expertise, sheer numbers, and longer time perspectives also make civil servants the core of modern bureaucracy. The first Hoover Commission Report (1949) put it well:

> It is the function of . . . careerists . . . who must serve whatever responsible officials are in office, to provide the reservoir of knowledge, managerial competence based upon experience, and understanding of the peculiarities of government administration. It is their job to keep the Government operating as effectively as possible at all times. They are essential to maintain the . . . administration. They can put political executives in touch with the large background behind most important issues, and help them to understand the probable consequences of alternative courses of action.[28]

While there was a series of noticeable examples of political appointees from the Nixon, Carter, and Reagan administrations who disregarded this "pool of expertise," nonetheless, civil servants perform most of the work in government and provide much of its leadership. In the words of Hoover, the civil service is the great reservoir of "knowledge, managerial competence, . . . and understanding."

So far, this discussion has pointed up several salient features of the civil service subsystem—its representational attributes as a whole, yet its uniquely unrepresentative elements in agencies or levels within the hierarchy: its lack of cohesiveness; its absence of mobility; its emphasis on rank inherent in the job; its diversity of jobs; the long-term career perspectives of its members; and its function as "the reservoir" of government expertise. Given these attributes, it is especially difficult to generalize about its influence on "bureaucratic outputs." As one veteran of government service says, "Civil servants don't really have mutual bonds or ties. There's nothing in particular in common except that these are people who know all the angles about how government works."[29]

Such seasoned cynicism, however, may obscure some of this subsystem's fundamental influences on bureaucratic activities. For one thing, as has already been emphasized, civil servants generally take the longer view of issues, problems, events, and actions, at least by comparison with political appointees (though they share this attribute with professional careerists). Their tenured positions make them somewhat more immune to the need for "quick fixes" or "instant results," compared to their politically driven bosses, who often see no further than the next election: For the most part, permanent bureaucrats realize that much that passes for "instant success" is ephemeral and that any real achievements in government come only in the long haul, after much struggle and persistence. Their view of what constitutes real, enduring change is therefore fundamentally different from the view of political appointees and leads to a much more realistic, conservative approach based upon recognition of the worth of incrementalism; namely, that small, steps taken over a long period of time will lead to permanent, solid achievements. This strategy of gradualism can be the source of exasperation and deep conflicts between civil servants and endless successions of political appointees, who normally want government to accomplish this or that task immediately, even yesterday. In particular, appointees in recent administrations who are fired up to make speedy changes and who have little exposure to the realities of government find this philosophy of incrementalism frustrating. It quickly becomes the butt of their jokes about those "damn bureaucrats." These negative references symbolize the radically different time zones within which each subsystem operates. Their different "internal clocks" influence the basically different approaches to handling issues. Though most important, as Tables 4.5 and 4.6 indicate, careerists are recognized by political appointees and recognize themselves that it is their expertise that makes them invaluable. Indeed their very specialized skills and institutional memory gives them incredible power within agencies and over policy agendas compared to "in-and-outer" appointees.

Unlike political appointees, civil servants are restrained by the Hatch Act, and various "little Hatch Acts" that operate on state and local levels, from going public with their political opinions or policy views. Occasionally it may happen that dissent leaks out in the press, but active campaigning is expressly forbidden by law. Hence, civil servants generally must be discreet and work behind the scenes in dealing with the development, formulation, and implementation of policy questions. They realize that a head–on frontal assault on policy issues

Table 4.5 Skills of Career Civil Servants Considered by Political Appointees "Helpful" or "Very Helpful"

	Career Executives "Helpful" or "Very Helpful"
Mastering substantive details	81%
Day-to-day management tasks	80
Technical analysis	80
Liaison with the bureaucracy	76
Liaison with Congress	42
Anticipating political problems	34

SOURCE: James P. Pfiffner, *The Strategic Presidency* (Lawrence, KS: University Press of Kansas, 1996), p. 83.

Table 4.6 Skills Career Civil Servants Themselves Considered Very Important for Success, at Current Job[a]

PERCENT	GOVERNMENT			Private Sector	Nonprofit Sector
Skill	Federal	State	Local	Private Sector	Nonprofit Sector
Maintaining ethical standards	81	75	84	81	89
Leading others	70	62	75	75	76
Managing conflict	52	54	67	64	66
Managing information and communication technology	57	54	67	64	66
Influencing policymakers	56	54	55	57	54
Managing innovation and change	52	53	55	57	57
Doing policy analysis	64	69	61	41	55
Budgeting and public finance	56	54	64	45	46
Managing a diverse work force	50	39	43	40	42
Analyzing and influencing public opinion	36	34	35	35	42
Raising money and generating extra revenue	17	21	19	34	51
Managing media relations	25	23	29	27	31
Writing regulations and legislation	37	35	23	22	22

a. $N = 117$ for federal, 167 for state, and 108 for local government; $N = 275$ for the private sector; $N = 166$ for the nonprofit sector.

SOURCE: Paul C. Light, *The New Public Service* (Washington, D.C.: The Brookings Institution, 1999), p. 110. Reprinted by permission of the Brookings Institution.

will only get them into needless political controversy. Experience over the years has taught them that those sorts of political firestorms are to be avoided at all costs; they waste time and energy and lead to few tangible results. As a result, on the whole they favor quiet discretion in handling problems. In the words of Louis Brownlow, they have "a passion for anonymity" (the famous title of the second volume of his autobiography). As with soldiers at the front, a "heads-down" attitude prevails most of the time.

This cautious posture comes not merely from pragmatism in effecting pro-grammatic change but also from fear about long-term personal survival. In a world of endlessly shifting political appointees, the civil servant, at least in the top ranks, knows quite well that job security depends on his or her not being too closely allied with any one political party, else he or she become "politically tainted" and shunned by the next group taking office. The desire to stay neutral from the political appointee subsystem and to work quietly from the inside, at least for most top-level civil servants, springs from a very fundamental interest in long-term survival.

Unlike the professional careerist, on the other hand, the general civil servant operates *without* the control of a professional elite and without an extensive mu-tual support network of peers with status in the subsystem ("the ring knock-ers," in West Point parlance). In the civil service subsystem, every employee charts his or her own way through the bureaucracy. The hazards are many and the minefields often hard to locate. Thus much of their time is spent network-ing outward and downward into the bureaucracy, building personal bridges and personal friendships inside and outside agencies in order to develop the myriad horizontal and vertical contacts that are necessary for gaining information, ac-curately assessing the landscape, and making alliances in this hazardous, uncer-tain, and often lonely bureaucratic world.

Such contacts are essential for creating the mutual support groups necessary for personal advancement and for making policy impacts in a world without clearly defined professional career ladders or professional elite controls over inter-nal personnel systems and programmatic policy-making machinery. In this con-fused, fragmented, and shifting institutionalized world, networks of "friends" are valued not merely as potential sources of information, policy alliances, and assis-tance to later career advancement but also as social support groups—"shoulders to cry on" or "good partying company"—perhaps fulfilling the most elemental human need of communal companionship. In turn, these clusters of civil servants influence public policies through the social networks they have established over long periods, running in strange and uncharted pathways that run through an agency and outside into other unlikely agencies and even beyond government where information is swapped informally and ideas are traded within social con-texts. When presidents complain about government leaking like a sieve, this is why. The informal group, as Elton Mayo and the Hawthorne researchers discovered long ago, operates with a similar potency in government and in business settings, though it is well hidden inside the civil service.

As opposed to group motivation, individual motivation to work for gov-ernment is varied and highly complex. As Gregory B. Lewis and Sue A. Frank, both Georgia State University faculty members, emphasize however, in a recent empirical study of federal civil servants in "Who Wants to Work for Govern-ment?" some generalizations can be made:

> Contrary to our perception that the private sector pays better than
> government, we found that the more strongly respondents valued high
> income, the more likely they were to prefer government employment. . . . On

the other hand, those who place more importance on high income were less likely to actually work for government . . . suggesting that government salaries do not hold workers who place a special emphasis on high pay.

Consistent with most previous research, those who strongly valued job security were more likely to want to work for government. . . .

Those who placed a higher priority on helping others and being useful to society were slightly more likely to choose government service, though the impact was weaker than the literature suggest. . . . It was somewhat stronger for high income but weaker than job security.

Those whose party affiliation suggested pro-government attitudes were more likely than others to prefer but not have government jobs. Democrats were also significantly more likely than comparable non-Democrats to prefer government work . . . with the effect again about as strong as that for job security. Party affiliation was not significantly related to actually having a government job. . . .

As expected, better-educated Americans were more likely than others to work for government—largely because most teaching jobs are in the public sector—but they appeared less likely than others to prefer government jobs.

. . . "protected groups" (women, minorities, and veterans) appeared more likely than others to choose public employment. . . . In terms of actual employment, women were no more likely than men to hold government jobs. . . . Minorities were nearly twice as likely as whites to want government jobs . . . although they were no more likely to have them. . . . Veterans were substantially more likely than nonveterans to want and hold government jobs. . . .

People who had a parent working for government were more likely than others to have government jobs, but not to prefer civil service.

Younger people were less likely both to want and to have government jobs.[30]

The *formal* structure of civil service makes a significant impact on what motivates government employees, as well as the sort of work they do. Civil service structure remains perhaps "the bottom line" in determining the type, intensity, role, and variety of bureaucratic outputs performed by any individual civil service employee. Federal civil service, like state and local civil service (though they frequently use different titles), is based upon the classified General Schedule (GS) for all personnel—clerical, administrative, and managerial. The General Service schedule ranges from grades GS-1 through GS-15. Each grade indicates the level of responsibility required in a job. Further, within each grade level are steps 1 through 10, which indicate seniority or time-in-grade. On the basis of these categories, salaries are assigned based upon the concept of equal pay for equal work. Generally, the lower four grades are composed of nonpolicy personnel, who perform the more menial tasks in government. These are custodians, typists, clerks, and aides. Grades GS-5 through GS-9 are generally considered professional entry levels for college graduates—GS-5 for typical entrants and GS-7 and GS-9 for those with exceptional test scores and/or master's degrees. GS-6, 8, and 10 are grades normally reserved for executive secretaries and high-level clerical personnel. GS-11 through 13 designate middle managers in the government service with responsibilities for minor offices and units of government or important staff responsibilities. The GS-14 and 15 slots are reserved for those with high-policy making and/or management duties. They are just below the executive senior service groups, SES (described earlier in this chapter), which are composed of the highest-level cadre of government executives.

Generally, then, the higher the GS rating, the more responsibilities and influence the civil servant has. Thus the realities of the policy-making apparatus within the civil service subsystem is circumscribed at least to some degree by the formalistic assignment of GS job classes, with those at the higher levels having significantly greater expertise, seniority, more responsible policy assignments, and significantly broader inputs than those on the bottom GS rungs by virtue of the offices they hold.

What challenges are facing the civil service subsystem as a whole? Three significant task force reports examined civil service performance and made numerous recommendations for reform: *Civil Service 2000,*[31] prepared by the Hudson Institute on the federal public service; also at the federal level, *Leadership for America,*[32] a privately sponsored review, called "The Volcker Commission" in honor of its chair, former Federal Reserve chairman Paul A. Volcker; and at the state and local levels, *Hard Truths/Tough Choices,*[33] a "Winter Commission" report, named for its chair, former Governor William F. Winter. These studies drew upon some of the most talented expertise from a wide cross section of business, nonprofit, and government to analyze many of the present problems facing America's public service. Collectively, they offered numerous suggestions for improvement. While these reports are too lengthy and complicated to be summarized in any concise way, overall they found no simple solutions for reforming civil service subsystems, but each one stressed important issues needing attention:

1. *Poor public image:* The Volcker Commission placed the first priority on dealing with the poor public image of the federal civil service. The report repeatedly cited data and examples of the low esteem that Americans had for public service. These negative perceptions led, in the Commission's thinking, to a general distrust of government and to its broader incapacity to function effectively and recruit capable candidates to serve in government. The Commission surveyed, for example, 403 of the "best and brightest" college graduates who accepted employment and found only 16 percent chose positions in government (and half of those who selected public employment were graduates of public administration programs). Big businesses, small businesses, and academic institutions were preferred by a wide margin, leading to the conclusion that "the public service cannot compete for top graduates." Thus, this report laid stress upon targeting the recruitment of a better pool of candidates.

2. *Competence crisis:* Similarly, the Hudson Institute study's key findings and recommendations centered upon the "competency crisis" facing the federal

The American Society for Public Administration (ASPA) exists to advance the science, processes, and art of public administration. The Society affirms its responsibility to develop the spirit of professionalism within its membership, and to increase public awareness of ethical principles in public service by its example. To this end, we, the members of the Society, commit ourselves to the following principles:

I SERVE THE PUBLIC INTEREST

Serve the public, beyond serving oneself.
ASPA members are committed to:

1. Exercise discretionary authority to promote the public interest.
2. Oppose all forms of discrimination and harassment, and promote affirmative action.
3. Recognize and support the public's right to know the public's business.
4. Involve citizens in policy decision-making.
5. Exercise compassion, benevolence, fairness, and optimism.
6. Respond to the public in ways that are complete, clear, and easy to understand.
7. Assist citizens in their dealings with government.
8. Be prepared to make decisions that may not be popular.

II RESPECT THE CONSTITUTION AND THE LAW

Respect, support, and study government constitutions and laws that define responsibilities of public agencies, employees, and all citizens.
ASPA members are committed to:

1. Understand and apply legislation and regulations relevant to their professional role.
2. Work to improve and change laws and policies that are counter-productive or obsolete.
3. Eliminate unlawful discrimination.
4. Prevent all forms of mismanagement of public funds by establishing and maintaining strong fiscal and management controls, and by supporting audits and investigative activities.
5. Respect and protect privileged information.
6. Encourage and facilitate legitimate dissent activities in government and protect the whistleblowing rights of public employees.
7. Promote constitutional principles of equality, fairness, representativeness, responsiveness, and due process in protecting citizens' rights.

III DEMONSTRATE PERSONAL INTEGRITY

Demonstrate the highest standards in all activities to inspire public confidence and trust in public service.
ASPA members are committed to:

1. Maintain truthfulness and honesty and to not compromise them for advancement, honor, or personal gain.
2. Ensure that others receive credit for their work and contributions.
3. Zealously guard against conflict of interest or its appearance: e.g., nepotism, improper outside employment, misuse of public resources, or the acceptance of gifts.
4. Respect superiors, subordinates, colleagues, and the public.
5. Take responsibility for their own errors.
6. Conduct official acts without partisanship.

IV PROMOTE ETHICAL ORGANIZATIONS

Strengthen organizational capabilities to apply ethics, efficiency, and effectiveness in serving the public.
ASPA members are committed to:

1. Enhance organizational capacity for open communication, creativity, and dedication.
2. Subordinate institutional loyalties to the public good.

(continued)

FIGURE 4.10 Code of ethics

Source: The American Society for Public Administration. Reprinted by permission.

3. Establish procedures that promote ethical behavior and hold individuals and organizations accountable for their conduct.
4. Provide organization members with an administrative means for dissent, assurance of due process and safeguards against reprisal.
5. Promote merit principles that protect against arbitrary and capricious actions.
6. Promote organizational accountability through appropriate controls and procedures.
7. Encourage organizations to adopt, distribute, and periodically review a code of ethics as a living document.

V STRIVE FOR PROFESSIONAL EXCELLENCE

Strengthen individual capabilities and encourage the professional development of others. ASPA members are committed to:

1. Provide support and encouragement to upgrade competence.
2. Accept as a personal duty the responsibility to keep up to date on emerging issues and potential problems.
3. Encourage others, throughout their careers, to participate in professional activities and associations.
4. Allocate time to meet with students and provide a bridge between classroom studies and the realities of public service.

FIGURE 4.10 (*Continued*)

Source: The American Society for Public Administration. Reprinted by permission.

public service. *Civil Service 2000* argued that there was a rising need for "a highly educated-skilled work force," yet attracting these workers "will become much more difficult." Recruitment is a problem, especially in high-wage locales such as New York City and in those top civil service grades, above GS-9 in which "the gap between top federal personnel civil service salaries and comparable private salaries was an average of 24 percent."

3. *Removing barriers to a high performance workforce:* On the state and local levels, the Winter Commission Report, by contrast, focused on the problems of "the highly fragmented local structures that impeded executive leadership and performance of the grassroots civil service systems." At the outset of the Winter Report, the priority was seen to:

Give leaders the authority to act. Put them in charge of lean, responsive agencies. Hire and nurture knowledgeable, motivated employees and give them the freedom to innovate in accomplishing the agencies' missions. Engage citizens in the business of government, while at the same time encouraging them to be partners in problem-solving.

The report emphasized that achieving such reforms will "hardly be painless or easy. Reforms may require constitutional amendments, new legislations, changes in rules and regulations, and restructuring many agencies and departments. Accomplishment of many of the changes may require political leaders and civic groups to mount aggressive campaigns."

THE UNIONIZED SUBSYSTEM: CADRES OF
WORKERS INSIDE BUREAUCRACY

Most texts on government or bureaucracy ignore an important policy-making subsystem of public agencies that over the past three decades has grown rapidly into one of the most potent forces determining the internal directions and external outputs of bureaucracy: namely, unionized public service workers. As David Stanley observes, "A whole new ballgame has started since unions in the public sector have begun to operate."[34] Like the aforementioned subsystems, unionization has increasingly gained its own share of power and a role in shaping the inner dynamics of public bureaucracy—that is, its rules, regulations, operating procedures, and structural relationships. Unions also exercise external controls over bureaucratic performance and influence upon society—that is, its productivity, enforcement practices, political relationships, and policy agendas.

The formal institutional structure of public sector collective bargaining is essentially derived from the private sector, as Joel Douglas writes: "The present Public Service Labor Relations (PSLR) . . . legislative and legal framework is based on an adversarial relationship rooted in the National Labor Relations Act (NLRA) and is structured on private sector principles. These include narrow unit determination requirements, bargaining agent election procedures, exclusive union representation, a series of unfair labor and employment practices, and a decentralized bargaining structure. Reliance on the private sector model was successful in developing the (PSLR) legal framework in which employees, subject to restrictions, most notably the antistrike ban, negotiate with government the terms and conditions of employment. Although the private and public sectors contain many similarities, a distinct difference is noted in the public sector, since the government is both employer and regulator at the bargaining table. Other differences include the private sector's reliance on market forces, distributive bargaining and the use of strikes and lockouts."[35]

Much like the professional careerist and civil service subsystems, the union subsystem was not a planned innovation. It just grew inside government, evolving particularly rapidly since the 1960s. As Frederick C. Mosher remarked, "the founders of the civil service did not bargain on collective bargaining."[36] If the Pendleton Act was the landmark piece of legislation creating the civil service, the explosion of union involvement within bureaucracy did not begin in earnest until John F. Kennedy signed Executive Orders 10987 and 10988 in 1962. These two orders for the first time gave unions the right to bargain collectively with federal management representatives on a limited range of items. They stimulated similar measures in numerous states and localities throughout the 1960s and 1970s. And while the unionization movement in government has slowed perceptibly during the 1980s because of cutbacks and the weakening of unions generally, the collective bargaining processes now in place are based largely upon legislation of the 1960s and 1970s and are accepted institutional practices within many jurisdictions throughout the United States.

Though the phenomenon of significant union influence over the activities of public bureaucracy is relatively new, some deep pockets of union activity date from the turn of the century. Indeed, in 1912 the Lloyd-La Follette Act gave federal workers the right to unionize, and for a number of years several large unions represented most of the U.S. postal employees, as well as employees in certain fields of civilian defense and in several government corporations such as the Tennessee Valley Authority. States and localities with large urban and industrial populations, which had traditionally strong private sector unions, also saw unionization in limited areas of their public bureaucracies, such as in New York, Michigan, and California. Yet these public service unions were for the most part economically weak, poorly organized, and had few legal rights to bargain collectively with representatives from the agency's management.

Why did the 1960s usher in a new era of union influence inside government? The historical reasons are still not clear. Certainly the election of John F. Kennedy in 1960 was a critical factor. Throughout Kennedy's campaign he pledged union recognition and collective bargaining at the federal level. Shortly after his election, he appointed a task force headed by Arthur Goldberg to make recommendations on how to handle union-management relations within government. In turn, this task force study led to the two executive orders just cited. But other factors were also at work behind the scenes. Statistics show that private sector unionization reached its high point in 1955 with one-fourth of the national workforce belonging to unions. This percentage of national union membership has been declining gradually ever since (now standing at 13.5 percent, refer to Table 4.7). With the "drying up," so to speak, of the private sector, major union leaders as early as the 1950s recognized that the public service was the last major untapped pool of nonunionized workers, and so they pressed their demands on Kennedy and subsequent administrations for the extension of union rights and prerogatives within this governmental sector. Particularly through the aggressive leadership of individuals such as the late Jerry Wurf, who for many years headed the American Federation of State, County, and Municipal Employees (AFSCME), and others, numerous public servants at the grass roots were brought into the rank and file. AFSCME and other groups were instrumental in lobbying state legislatures for the right to organize and bargain collectively with state and local jurisdictions on behalf of public workers. Virtually all states permit some form of collective bargaining, yet today 22 states prohibit collective bargaining and public employees joining unions, and forbid recognition of unions in government.

Much of the union intrusion into the ranks of bureaucracy resulted from a more tolerant, even perhaps permissive, public attitude toward unions in government. By the 1960s unions were no longer considered entirely "evil" and antithetical to the public interest. No doubt, very real economic forces were at work as well. The promises of higher paychecks, shorter work weeks, and better working conditions lured many government workers, principally blue collar employees but increasing numbers of white collar employees as well, into public service unions. Certainly the postal strike of 1970 and the New York City transit strike of 1966—two early key disputes—stimulated

Table 4.7 Union Membership in the Public and Private Sectors (in percentages) 1962–1994

Year	Federal*	State and Local**	Private
1962[a]	26.9	9.8	25.1
1970[a]	39.6	16.6	24.3
1976[a]	41.5	20.6	23.3
1982[a]	37.2	18.6	22.3
1986[b]	30.9	33.5	15.6
1987[b]	28.1	31.9	15.2
1988[b]	31.2	34.7	14.6
1989[b]	35.9	34.3	14.2
1990[b]	36.1	34.6	14.2
1994	38.7	37.5	10.9
2000	37.2	35.4	13.5

*Includes postal service

**Excludes education

SOURCES: a. Adapted from Troy and Sheflin, 1984, p. 22 b. Tabulated from the Correlation Survey (CPS), U.S. Bureau of the Census.

union membership. Finally, union growth was fostered by legislation such as the Civil Service Reform Act of 1978, which formalized union–management collective bargaining procedures by federal statute. Likewise, on the local level, in New York State, representatives of the Civil Service Employees Association had been meeting with management representatives since the early 1900s, but the Taylor Law was established by statute's formal collective bargaining arrangement for state and union representatives in 1967. In a few states, such as Massachusetts, union membership became a requirement for attaining a public job. In order for workers to have a job and a voice that would represent them at the bargaining table and involve them in the determination of their agency's activities, they joined public employee unions (see Figure 4.11 as a sample union agreement with a public agency).

Whatever the causes of growth—and there are undoubtedly many—in contrast to the private sector, a sporadic but continuous climb in union strength has been apparent within public organizations. Today 37.2 percent of all federal civilian employees belong to unions (not including the 600,000 postal workers, 90 percent of whom are unionized); 35.4 percent of state and local workers are union members (see Table 4.7). Levels of unionization, however, range significantly from agency to agency and locale to locale. Thus, in practice the political clout of union members inside bureaucracy varies considerably. The postal service, made up largely of blue collar workers, is almost entirely unionized, whereas the employees of the Federal Reserve Board and the State Department are mainly white collar professionals, largely (though not altogether) untouched by unions. Urban industrial states and large metropolitan communites are heavily unionized, and public unions play major policy-making roles within their various public bureaucracies. On the other hand,

Excerpts from "Agreement between The Board of Education of the City School District of the City of New York and United Federation of Teachers-Local 2 American Federation of Teachers—covering Teachers":

—Article 1: Union Recognitions—"The Board recognizes the Union as the exclusive bargaining representative of all those assigned as teachers. . .

—Article 2: Fair Practices—a) Non-discrimination policy of Board and Union. b) "The Board agrees that it will not require any teacher to complete an oath or affirmation of loyalty. . .

—Article 3: Salaries and Benefits—a) . . . A person holding a BA with no experience receives approximately \$14,500 annual salary; a person holding an MA plus 30 credits and 15 years of experience receives approximately \$31,000 annual salary. b) Extra pay for additional college credits, industrial experience, nursing experience, special ed. c) Choice of Health Plan with shared payment.

—Article 4: Pension and Retirement program—a) For the first 20 years of service, a retirement allowance equal to 1/2 the salary of the final year; further work years add to that; retirement at age 55. b) Disability and death benefits.

—Article 6: Hours—a) School day is 6 hours and 20 minutes and such additional time as the by laws provide. b) Work Year begins the Wednesday after Labor Day and does not exceed the last weekday in June.

—Article 7: Working Conditions in Schools—a) Number of teaching periods. b) Number of students. c) Coverage of classes substitutes. d) Relief from non-teaching chores. e) Not responsible for maintaining or repairing equipment.

—Article 8: Statement of Policy—a) A programming preference for the following year is submitted by the teacher 60 days before the end of the school year; 10 days before the end of the school year teachers are notified of their assignments for the following year. b) Every teacher should have one unassigned period each day.

—Article 9: Procedure for Handling Special Behavior Problems—The child is referred to the principal. If the principal cannot solve the problem and the situation continues, the teacher may appeal to the assistant superintendent.

—Article 10: Safety—a) Legal Services are offered in cases of assault. b) The principal has the responsibility for the School Safety Plan.

—Article 16: Leaves—a) Sick Leave is granted at a rate of one hour for every 20 hours of work, up to 200 days. b) A sabbatical leave granted for one year at 70% pay, after 14 years of service.

—Article 17: Layoff Policy—'The teacher with the latest date of appointment will be the first to be excessed.' Teachers shall be assigned to appropriate vacancies.

—Article 18: Transfers—a) Teachers must list six choices; transfers are based on district need, seniority, etc. b) Hardship transfers are considered after three years of service.

—Article 19: Union Activities, Privileges and Responsibilities—a) 'No teacher shall engage in Union activities during time he is assigned to teaching or other duties.' b) Special times are allotted for union activities. c) Every school will have a bulletin board for Union business.

—Article 21: Due Process and Review procedures—a) Explanation of teacher files. b) A teacher summoned for disciplinary action has the right to be accompanied by a union representative.

—Article 22: Grievance Procedure—Step 1 is at the school level; Step 2 case brought before the assistant superintendent; Step 3 case brought before the Chancellor; Step 4 Union submission to arbitration.

—Article 23: Special Complaints—In the case of 'harassing conduct, acts of intimidation' directed against the employee in the grievance process a special Fact Finder will report to the City School Board for a determination.

—Article 25: No Strike Pledge.

FIGURE 4.11 Sample outline of an agreement between a public employee union and a government agency

Source: City School District of New York.

rural, poorer, and less-industrialized regions contain fewer union members, who therefore have less policy involvement in their regions of the public sector. Some functional state/local activities, such as education, transportation, and refuse collection, show a much higher level of union activity than other fields.

Today there are three prominent and powerful public service unions (and numerous lesser ones) that speak for many, though certainly not all, public employees: the American Federation of State, County, and Municipal Employees, the American Federation of Government Employees (AFGE), and the American Federation of Teachers (AFT). The National Education Association is technically *not* a union but rather a professional association of primary and secondary schoolteachers, yet it looks and acts like a union, often aggressively representing its rank and file in collective-bargaining negotiations in various school districts across the country. NEA became especially active within the Democratic party, substantially assisting President Jimmy Carter's election in 1976 and his bid for reelection in 1980. AFSCME, AFT, and AFGE have grown rapidly in power and prominence within the AFL-CIO labor council over the last decade, extending their activism well beyond traditional union concerns into national political circles of the Democratic party by aiding the party financially as well as through considerable campaign manpower. Public service unions are active at the state and local levels as well, particularly where there are large concentrations of public workers (such as in state or county capitals) and strong Democratic party organizations.

However, the actual conduct of negotiations between unions and management within government—the principal source of union inputs into bureaucracy—remains a highly decentralized process, with local representatives of public employee unions conducting agency-by-agency or local jurisdiction-by-jurisdiction negotiated agreements (see Figure 4.12). In other words, while the public employee unions have grown into the "big three" (or four, depending on how one counts NEA), no one person or group speaks for "the entire management side" of government. Separate bargains must be made with roughly 80,000 governmental jurisdictions in the United States and with many more "suborganizational" units within these separate governments that recognize the union right of negotiation. Not only is the process decentralized, but who actually speaks for the employers or management is also a highly complex and unsettled issue in many areas. Some governments use the civil service as spokescommission for management (Office of Personnel Management at the federal level); others have teams of top-level executives from *both* legislature and bureaucracy that speak for management. Highly diverse institutional arrangements for representation and the conducting of the actual negotiations are found across the United States, largely because the process still remains somewhat new, experimental, and undeveloped.

Equally unsettled is the scope of the bargaining that is allowed. In most jurisdictions, wages and hours—the two principal bargaining concerns in private industry—are legislatively determined and beyond the scope of public sector negotiations. These negotiations, therefore, mostly center on working conditions, grievance procedures, and other less major subjects. But even here, working conditions, grievance-procedures, and "fringes" are often precisely

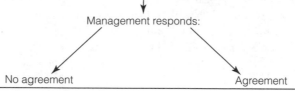

The actual conduct of union negotiations is a highly decentralized process governed by specific federal, state, or local laws, but generally, specific steps involve: As contract nears end union representatives initiate process by outlining demand for new contract.

Management responds:

No agreement	Agreement
If no agreement is reached, then the parties may turn to: 1) Fact-Finding—An independent third party is appointed to investigate and lay out the facts of the situation for both parties to review 2) Mediation—A third party is agreed upon to mediate the dispute 3) Arbitration—A third party is asked to hear and review the case; the verdict will be binding on both sides 4) Deadlock, work stoppage, strike	If management agrees, contract is concluded with union and then ratified by the required political body, that is, the city council, school board.

FIGURE 4.12 Union negotiations

prescribed by legislation, leaving little room for negotiations, even over these seemingly mundane matters. Further, laws on the books often stack the deck in management's favor. For example, according to the 1978 Civil Service Reform Act (CSR), management officials are authorized "to determine the mission, budget, organization, number of employees, and internal security practices of an agency . . . to hire, assign, direct, lay off and retain employees . . . or to suspend, remove, reduce in grade or pay, or take other disciplinary action."[37] In short, the CSR's tilt clearly favors management prerogatives over union rights, although through court decisions and legislative amendments unions have chipped away at these restrictions.

Another important, unique condition of the union subsystem in government involved the limited means for enforcing its demands at the bargaining table. The ban on strikes by public employees in most sectors of government basically limits their power. The basic weapon used by private sector unions to enforce their demands in negotiations is illegal at the federal and many state and local settings, though thirteen states allow some or all public employees the right to strike (see Table 4.8). As Theodore Kheel writes, "The strike enables employees through their representatives to participate in the decisions setting wages, hours, and working conditions. In the absence of the right to strike, an alternative system of determination is required when negotiating parties reach an impasse."[38] However, no such technique has yet been found for breaking public sector impasses. In reality, however, whether or not public employees are legally permitted to strike, strikes do occur in the public sector; sometimes they

Table 4.8 State and Local Government Employees with the Right to Strike

State	Employees Covered
Alaska	All public employees except for police and firefighters
California	All but police and firefighters, *providing* a court or California PERB does not rule that striking is illegal[a]
Hawaii	All public employees
Idaho	Firefighters and teachers
Illinois	All public employees except for police, firefighters, and paramedics
Minnesota	All public employees except for police and firefighters
Montana	All public employees
Ohio	All public employees except for police and firefighters
Oregon	All public employees except for police, firefighters, and correctional officers
Pennsylvania	All public employees except for police, firefighters, prison guards, guards at mental hospitals, and court employees
Rhode Island	All public employees
Vermont	All public employees except for correctional officers, court employees, and state employees
Wisconsin	All public employees except for police, firefighters, and state employees

Note: a. The California State Supreme Court, in *County Sanitation District v. L. A., County Employees Association* (699 P. 2d 835, 1985), said that unless expressly prohibited by statute—or case law—striking by public employees is not illegal. Firefighters are prohibited by statutory law, police by case law.

SOURCE: Adapted from Kearney, 1992. Updated by *Labor Relations Reporter,* 1989–1990.

are called "the blue flu" or "sick-outs," or they are actual walk-outs, such as the air traffic controllers' strike in 1981, which met with varying degrees of success and failure. In the extreme case, the air traffic controllers, who went on strike over pay and fringe benefits, lost their jobs and their union as well. The union was fined and decertified, and its leaders were jailed for a short period. At the other extreme, some public workers who have walked off their jobs not only got them back but were well rewarded for them to the point of almost bank-rupting the community. Such was the case in the New York City transit strike in 1966, which was quickly settled by Mayor Lindsey with wage hikes and fringe benefits well beyond what the city could afford in the long run.

If strikes are allowed in only a few jurisdictions as are picketing, compulsory arbitration, and a whole range of typical weapons used by private sector unions to enforce their demands, this does not mean that labor is powerless in the pub-lic sector. As Wellington and Winter point out, labor's real leverage is through the use of "institutional power of public employee unions in a way that would leave competitive groups in the political process at a permanent and substantial disadvantage."[39] To be more precise, public unions know very well how to play the inside political game. During negotiations they regularly make "end runs" around management to outside supporters, such as sympathetic legislators on city councils, in state assemblies, or in Congress. These potent friends of public unions frequently enable them to cut deals and achieve their priorities through the "back door" thus undercutting, so to speak, management's position or potentially dividing it so badly that its official bargaining position crumbles.

How then can the union subsystem's influence over policy outputs in bureaucracy be summarized vis-à-vis the other previously mentioned bureaucratic subsystems?

The first and perhaps the most significant aspect of union involvement with what happens inside U.S. bureaucracy is its variety. Some unions strive for nothing less than complete control from top to bottom of public bureaucracy. They want the options to select a public agency's top-ranking political cadre; to determine its internal structural arrangements, procedures, and rules as well as its methods of promotion, hiring, and firing; to specify its relations with other external groups; and most of all to call the shots as to what the agency will or will not do for the public. In general, those agencies are characterized by weak political executive oversight, an absence of a controlling professional elite, a strongly unionized rank and file, a degree of institutional autonomy, and traditions of union assertiveness, such as in the federal postal system and in large "weak-mayor" cities such as New York and San Francisco, where public service unions exert powerful long-term influence. At the other extreme, public sector unions are dormant or ineffective in right-to-work states, where public sector unions are outlawed entirely, and in agencies in the tight grip of professionals (strong city manager communities or the military) or under strong, united antiunion political executive leadership (similar to what the air traffic controllers faced in 1981 under the Reagan administration, particularly from former Secretary of Transportation Drew Lewis). Most situations in which unions operate, though, are at neither extreme, and so unions end up jockeying with other internal bureaucratic subsystems—political appointees, professionals, and civil servants—for varying degrees of autonomy and control over bureaucratic policies and outputs.

Second, the growth and intrusion of unions within bureaucracy have added new levels of complexities and complications to an already complex bureaucratic world. The procedures, rules, and requirements for labor management practices at the federal level fill 23 pages of the Civil Service Reform Act of 1978, which set up new units of bureaucracy, such as the National Labor Relations Board, to administer and oversee these operations. New varieties of specialists, such as mediators, contract specialists, labor-management training instructors, and the like, are now needed to implement these tangled legalistic processes. Whether such complexification of government has slowed down its institutional outputs or made it more productive is unclear and unmeasured, but it is apparent in many instances that new personnel and attendant rules and procedures have been added to administer this new subsystem and that relationships between labor and management have therefore become more formal and legalistic. Ironically, the union subsystem has stimulated a new growth of job specialties such as labor-management experts in the professional career subsystem within government, hence furthering professionalization within bureaucracy's ranks.

Third, in cases where the union subsystem has matured fully within public bureaucracies but has not become the dominant subsystem, it has brought about bipartisan management practices. Collective bargaining forces management to sit down at regular intervals with union representatives to discuss grievances, working conditions, and other matters of concern to both parties. In other words, unions and their memberships have an increasing formal role and stake in the management processes of public agencies, whereas before employees had no formalized role (though certainly their informal influence was and always has been considerable). While the range of what is permissible for negotiations remains sharply limited in most cases, the collective process does circumscribe the previously unbounded prerogatives of management and offers workers some formal, regular channel for making inputs into workplace governance.

Fourth, in many cases public service unions have won positive reforms that have long been advocated by public administration specialists to enhance, on the whole, the cause of "good government," such as better wages, working conditions, training programs and staffing levels, and organizational reforms promoting institutional productivity. Most union concerns, in other words, focus on internal issues rather than on external policies, but with important indirect spinoffs for bureaucratic policy outputs that are sometimes distinctly economic in nature. Certainly there have been union demands and victories notable for their fiscal excess, for example, San Francisco streetsweepers, who are notorious because they earn excessive salaries annually, and New York City transit workers, who have earned fringes and early retirement packages purchased at the price of the city's fiscal solvency. But these instances generally are rare and confined to locales where unions clearly dominate local politics (an increasingly rare phenomenon today, even in big cities). The specific effects of public service unions on U.S. bureaucracies in reality are thus highly varied patterns—neither totally negative nor wholly positive but falling somewhere in between, depending on the particular agency, the strength of its public employee unions, the leadership of their top-ranking members, and the politics of the locale within which a bureaucracy operates. Much depends on the many factors composing the external environment discussed in Chapter 3: the level and degree of socioeconomic support and the political configurations and institutional patterns within which public service unions find supporters or allies for their goals. Public agencies, depending on their political environs, can either be "pushed to the extreme" by unions, or union demands can be tempered by the surrounding socioeconomic realities and interest group interplay.

Fifth, the rise of union influence within public bureaucracy has brought about internal tensions among the ranks of white-collar professionals, a group generally hostile to unionization. Where professionalization is strongest and most pervasive, say among the military and state department employees at the federal level, generally public employees unions can make little or no impact(s), or are a key source of conflict and competition over organizational resources and policy making.

Finally, the real loser with the advent of public service unions into the internal dynamics of bureaucratic policy making has probably been the underlying philosophy and practices of the century-old civil service subsystem.

Concepts such as merit selection, open competitive exams, nonpartisan civil service boards, and "color blind" promotions based upon individual competence have yielded in many localities to union emphasis upon seniority, "closed shop" union membership, and neutral third-party mediation of disputes by those outside civil service. Indeed, in many instances the old neutral civil service commission has been replaced by partisan, political oversight agencies such as the Office of Personnel Management at the federal level. This is not to argue that the civil service subsystem will soon fade into a distant memory and its controlling procedures, rules, and personnel become history. To the contrary, it is alive and well today in many bureaucratic institutions, but it certainly has changed, or given ground to the influx of unionization over the last four decades inside the public service.

In several cases as well, due to the fiscal constraints of recent years, we have witnessed considerable union cooperation with civil service managers for the self-interest of each party.[40] Carolyn Ban and Norma Riccucci concluded about recent trends in local public service unionization:

> ... while labor and management must—at least in theory—be seen as adversaries (to promote credibility among the rank and file), a good deal of cooperation is taking place either formally or behind the scenes. Indeed, formal cooperation measures have become more common, particularly in the wake of fiscal crises. Although such issues as wages may not feasibly lend themselves to cooperation, a number of states and localities have reported successes with joint ventures offer a host of issues. It seems that, in jurisdictions that have collective bargaining, the support and participation of labor is key if state and local governments seek to make effective changes in civil service systems, since unions and the employees they represent perceive these systems as protections against management abuses.[41]

CONTRACT EMPLOYMENT: THE NEWEST, FASTEST-GROWING BUREAUCRATIC SUBSYSTEM

At the federal, state, and local levels, public agencies up to roughly 1950 did most, if not all, of the tasks assigned to them in-house, using their own personnel and resources and the facilities allocated by legislatures and political executives. Hence much of the theory of bureaucracy, as well as the managerial approaches to public enterprise put forward by public administration experts and scholars, were based upon assumptions, increasingly erroneous, that bureaucracies controlled their own operations, did their assigned work inside, with neat, clear lines of managerial control running from top political executives down to the workers who actually carried out the agency's assigned missions.

The reality of internal bureaucratic life today, however, is far different. The federal budget tells this different story about how government agencies actually

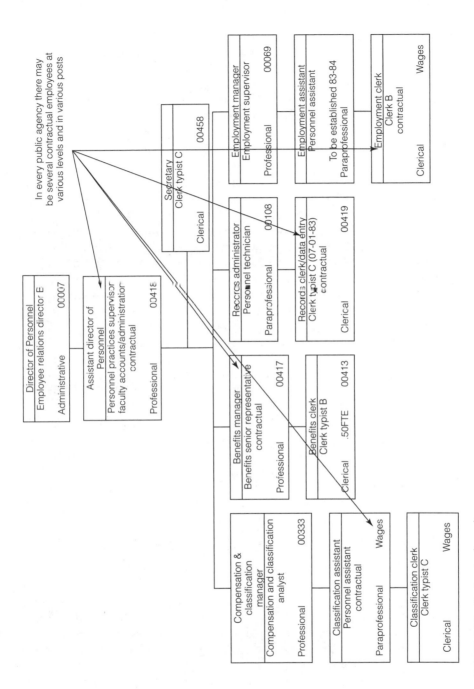

In every public agency there may be several contractual employees at various levels and in various posts

FIGURE 4.13 Contractual employees

Source: Commonwealth of Virginia.

function in percentages of expenditures. Roughly 14 percent of the national budget goes for its own internal personnel services and benefits (excluding pensions). This means that only slightly more than one-eighth of the total federal budget is spent on directing activities that the government performs itself, such as law enforcement, food and drug regulation, forestry service, air traffic control, and so on. However, the category of "other contractual services" indicates the roughly 16 percent of the total annual operating budget that is spent for sundry activities performed by others who are contracted to render services from *outside* the federal bureaucracy.

In other words, close to 60 percent of the total obligation for goods and services produced by the federal government is contracted out (excluding funds for grants-in-aid to states and localities, direct transfer payments to individuals, debt servicing, and so on). The percentages run much higher for some agencies, such as NASA and the Department of Energy, which have traditionally contracted out much of their work. The development of most major weapons systems is contracted out to private businesses, as is the construction of large capital projects such as dams, roads, bridges, and sewer systems. Three-fourths of research and development funding at the federal level is contracted out to universities, think tanks, consultants, and private industry.

At the state and local levels there are no comparable figures on the levels of contracting-out by governmental bureaucracy, though they probably mirror the federal pattern, with some communities going to extremes, such as Lakewood, California (Figure 4.14, originators of the Lakewood Plan), which contracts out all its municipal functions, including police protection. City Hall consists of little more than a city manager and a secretary, who principally act as contract-managers for the city council. While most localities do not go to the extreme degree of contracting for municipal services, many do draw upon private vendors and business enterprises in many ways for the construction of capital projects as well as for a variety of ongoing services, such as data collection, medical facilities, computer services, refuse disposal, as well as for accounting, auditing, and payroll functions. Today, as Figure 4.13 points out, most government agencies house varying mixes of full-time employees and temporary or long-term contract employees working side by side (refer to Figure 4.13). The regular public employees and contractual employees are often difficult to differentiate from one another. For example, 15 Massachusetts state agencies budgeted over $750 million or about 7 percent of the state budget to purchase, from over 1,200 contractors, a wide range of social services, including alcoholism treatment, family crisis intervention, English as a second language, and daycare, in addition to 200 other services—with many of the private contractors working alongside of public employees.

The story of the rise of contract labor inside bureaucracy is a complicated one. As was pointed out in Chapter 2, early in the history of the U.S. government, mail delivery and canal projects were contracted out. However, until roughly 50 years ago, the use and application of contractual arrangements were drastically limited in most public agencies. All this changed, as Chapter 2 explained, with the hot and cold war demands of the postwar era, when govern-

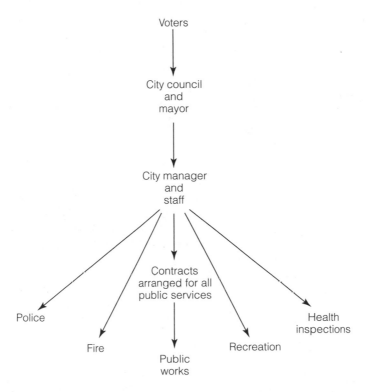

FIGURE 4.14   Some public organizations go to the extreme and contract-out all or most of their work, as in Lakewood, California.

ment increasingly needed highly skilled scientific and engineering talent from universities, private enterprises, and consulting firms to conceptualize, build, and implement numerous weapons programs. The Rand Corporation and the National Science Foundation after World War II were created by the federal government to draw upon outside scientific personnel for accomplishing essentially in-house missions of DoD, without formally employing these civil servants.

The growth of contracting-out for government services since then has been unprecedented in size, scope, and intensity (see Table 4.9). Government has been driven into contracting willy-nilly in so many fields because it has been asked to perform greater numbers of tasks of ever-greater complexity within shorter time frames, tasks for which it has neither the expertise nor the capacity to acquire it on a short-term basis. At the state and local levels, contractual employment accelerated in the past three decades as a device for accomplishing programmatic goals while avoiding rising costs of hiring permanent civil servants (today a permanent civil servant costs government roughly twice the worker's *actual* salary, largely because of "hidden fringes" such as retirement programs and health and other benefit packages). Contracting-out is also a method of doing complex work in which the federal government, states, and localities

Table 4.9 The Wide Range of Contracted-Out Municipal Services

adoption service

air pollution abatement

ambulance service

animal control

assessing

auditorium and convention center management

bridge construction and maintenance

building demolition

building and mechanical inspection

bus shelters

cafeteria operation

catch-basin cleaning

cemetery operation

child protection

civil defense communications

communications maintenance

crime laboratory

custodial services for buildings and grounds

data processing

day care

election administration

electrical inspection

electric power

elevator inspection

engineering services

family counseling

fire communications

fire prevention

fire service

foster-home care

guard service

homemaker service

hospital managment

housing

hydrant repair

industrial development

institutional care for the disabled and retarded

irrigation

jail and detention

juvenile delinquency programs

keypunching

laundry service

lawn maintenance

leaf collection

legal aid

legal services

library operation

licensing

management consulting

mapping

mental health service

microfilming

mosquito control

noise abatement

nursing services

park maintenance

parking lots

parking meter collections and maintenance

parking ticket processing

patrol service

payroll processing

personnel services

planning

plumbing

police communications

public health service

public relations

records maintenance

recreation facilities

rehabilitation of addicts and alcoholics

rehabilitation of buildings

school buses

secretarial and clerical work

sewage treatment

sewer maintenance

snow removal

soil conservation

solid-waste collection

solid-waste disposal

street constuction

street lighting

street maintenance

street sweeping

(continued)

Table 4.9 *Continued*

tax collection	urban renewal
test scoring	utility billing
towing of illegally parked autos	vehicle maintenance
traffic control	voter registration
traffic markings	water-meter maintenance
traffic sign and signal maintenance	water pollution abatement
training of municipal employees	water supply
transit management	weed abatement
treasury functions	welfare
tree planting, pruning, removal, and stump removal	zoning and subdivision control

have little expertise. But it has broad implications, for as Clarence Danhof, a prominent authority in this field, has written:

> The contractual system is . . . more than a device to get work done for a government agency. An agency's program is built upon contributions from many sources, public and private. There are numerous channels through which interested and knowledgeable groups may suggest courses of action to accomplish broadly defined objectives. A formal contract is merely a step in a process of interaction between private and public groups with an interest in a scientific or technical area. In this process the government agency assumes responsibility for preparing programs and seeing them through the normal authorization and budgeting routines. It also chooses from among the proposals made to it those which it will include as contractual projects in its approved programs. In both the formulation and the execution of its program the agency is heavily, and sometimes wholly, dependent upon the initiative of outside institutions in developing the expertise necessary to prepare the proposals and do the work.[42]

As Danhof correctly suggests, contractual relationships become extremely complex interactions between the purveyors of goods and services and public agencies, and as such they evidence a staggering array of formalized relationships, informal behavior, and complex ethical and institutional problems. However, the important point is that, as Bruce L. R. Smith has stated, the contracting phenomenon is "one of the most striking features of America's postwar public organizations."[43] The contractual subsystem has grown haphazardly and largely out of the public view. The implications of increasing reliance upon "outsiders" to perform the inside work of public bureaucracies are still not fully understood nor appreciated, even by experts in political science, public administration, and government, and certainly not by the general public or by most public officials.

According to Susan R. Bernstein, for those within its ranks, the "game metaphor" best characterizes how the contractual subsystem works:

> Managers find contracted services "crazy"; the game metaphor keeps them from succumbing to "craziness." The paradoxical nature of contracted

EXECUTIVE OFFICE OF THE PRESIDENT
Office of Management and Budget
Washington, D.C. 20503

March 29, 1979

Circular No. A–76
Revised

TO THE HEADS OF EXECUTIVE DEPARTMENTS
AND ESTABLISHMENTS

Subject: Policies for Acquiring Commercial or Industrial Products and Services
        Needed by the Government

1. *Purpose.* This Circular establishes the policies and procedures used to determine whether needed commercial or industrial type work should be done by contract with private sources or in-house using Government facilities and personnel. This Circular replaces OMB Circular No. A–76, dated August 30, 1967, and all subsequent amendments.

2. *Background.* In a democratic free enterprise economic system, the Government should not compete with its citizens. The private enterprise system, characterized by individual freedom and initiative, is the primary source of national economic strength. In recognition of this principle, it has been and continues to be the general policy of the Government to rely on competitive private enterprise to supply the products and services it needs.

This policy has been expressed in Bureau of the Budget Bulletins issued in 1955, 1957, and 1960. In 1966, Circular No. A–76 was issued and, for the first time, prescribed the policy and implementing guidelines in a permanent directive. The Circular was revised in 1967, by Transmittal Memorandum No. 1, to clarify some provisions and to lessen the burden of work by the agencies in implementation. Transmittal Memorandum No. 2 was issued in 1976, providing additional guidance on cost comparisons and prescribing standard cost factors for Federal employee retirement and insurance benefits.

In 1977, a comprehensive review of the Circular and its implementation was initiated. Transmittal Memorandum No. 3 was issued on June 13, 1977, announcing the review and temporarily reducing the Government retirement cost factor. This revision is the result of that review and careful consideration of comments from all interested parties.

3. *Responsibility.* Each agency head has the responsibility to ensure that the provisions of this Circular are followed. This Circular provides administrative direction to heads of agencies and does not establish, and shall not be construed to create, any substantive or procedural basis for any person to challenge any agency action or inaction on the basis that such action was not in accordance with this Circular.

FIGURE 4.15 At the federal level, OMB circular no. A-76 has been particularly instrumental in expanding the use of contracting-out public services.

services makes the metaphor compelling. Managers talk of being very serious about what they do, but of not taking contract compliance too seriously. . . . Repeatedly, managers describe situations in which aspects of the management of contracted services conflict with reality. In accepting these paradoxes, managers perceive their task as a game. This perception enables them to understand, get control of, and keep in perspective contracted services.[44]

Some effects on public agencies and their outputs are fairly obvious. First, the growth of the contractual subsystem makes it increasingly hard to tell where government bureaucracy begins and ends. Is the permanent public agency that relies on the expertise of a single outside contractor *really* independent of that outside private enterprise? Or is the private contractor who relies on a public bureaucracy for all or most of his annual income *really* private, and not merely an extension of a public bureaucracy? Increasingly, the worlds separating government agencies and private sector businesses, universities, and consulting firms are dissolving into an area where boundaries overlap or are unclear and difficult to define.

What is clear, however, is that these "outside" groups perform much of the bureaucratic work of government. If their personnel were counted as government employees, the size of government bureaucracy would probably be twice as large as it is. Contracting-out, then, enables politicians to gain services as well as jobs for their constituents *and then* claim that they have "kept the lid on government personnel costs." Such a claim is clearly untrue and leads to further confusion—and deception—about the realities of the size and scope of government.

Second, some sectors of government have clearly become "captives" of their contractors. The purveyors of many large DoD weapons systems, such as Boeing, not only design and develop these multibillion dollar, multiyear systems but by proposing new weapons systems are also actively involved in establishing DoD and individual service priorities, budget requirements, personnel needs, and even the broad global strategic priorities of U.S. defense policy. And once the weapons are sold, these firms become the sole-source suppliers virtually dictating the costs—often overrun by huge amounts—to the contracting agency. Top executives move back and forth with ease between these firms and top policy-making posts within DoD. Harold Brown (DoD Secretary under President Carter), William C. Foster (Brown's research and development specialist), Caspar Weinberger (DoD Secretary under President Reagan), John Lehmann (Weinberger's Secretary of the Navy), and William J. Perry (President Clinton's Secretary of Defense) are all products of the contract world surrounding DoD. This is not meant to suggest that these individuals or others who serve "in-and out" at high DoD policy-making levels have acted unethically or dishonestly; it simply means that their backgrounds and skills are utilized in *both* government and business at various managerial and staff levels and that they therefore significantly influence policies and administration in *both* sectors.

Another effect of the increasing rise and reliance upon the contractual subsystem within public bureaucracy is that there is less and less use for traditional bureaucratic techniques, such as standard in-house top-down rules, for direction and control of personnel and resources. More emphasis is now placed upon contract negotiations, formal agreements, legal sanctions, economic rewards, and penalties for inducing compliance by contractors, and auditing and management information systems for "tracking" completion dates. All these procedures are essential for quality control and to make the contractors and subcontractors perform their services according to schedule. Bureaucrats at every level increasingly find themselves becoming contract managers as opposed to fulfilling their traditional line management roles directly supervising "in-house" civil servants. As Table 4.10 underscores, especially as the complexity of contracting increases (i.e., length of time, number of contractors, size of budget, and so on), the roles and responsibilities of government contract administrators expand significantly.

Also, as suggested before, with the growing numbers of public personnel "off the books" because of their nontenured status, the traditional sorts of personnel work rules, personnel oversight controls, and procedures governing employee behavior have diminished in importance. Thus the problems of imposing public accountability on contract workers grow as the numbers of contract agents and subcontractors grow. Proper policy performance and implementation in regard to legality, honesty, competence, correctness of action, and effective completion of projects become increasingly difficult to ensure as the number of private businesses, universities, and others who perform the work of public agencies increases. Recent leaks of highly sensitive national security information by contractual employees and the massive fraud cases of subcontractors working on various defense projects illustrate these enormous problems of public accountability and oversight. Indeed, *should* bureaucracy impose its public standards of accountability on such "private" groups and citizens? The difficult and uncharted ethical dimensions of such problems loom large.

Finally, as the pressures of the contractual subsystem force new commitments and expenditures of public funds years ahead of time, contractual arrangements become legally and politically "untouchable." As many scholars and budget experts now observe, not only is the federal budget "uncontrollable," but also no one really knows how much of a share is really being spent annually, largely because of the pressures of the growing contractual subsystem. Many contractors simply operate beyond control of the budget process—off the books and out of sight—developing independent accounting, auditing, and budgeting systems along with separate personnel rules, regulations, and procedures that are well beyond present-day public scrutiny and oversight mechanisms.

SUMMARY OF KEY POINTS

If public bureaucracy is the core system of U.S. government today, certainly the core of that core is composed of critical groups within bureaucracy. Bureaucracy's inner dynamics, or, in the words of Aristotle, its "real constitution," are made up of five subsystems, each in its own way determining what happens to bureaucratic activities in government. These subsystems decide what public agencies can and cannot do, and how and when they will perform tasks. The "balance" or "imbalance" of these groups within every agency is fundamental to its character, policies, and performance. The three basic patterns of distribution of these internal subsystems' power and authority within public bureaucracies are depicted by Figure 4.16.

In an agency dominated by political appointees, as in the case of the local county commission, short-term goals, interest in broad political issues, responsiveness to the general electorate or to special pressure groups, and attention to the immediate requirements of the elected chief official become paramount. An

Dominance of an agency
by one subsystem

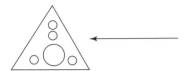

One is dominant over others and hence
controls virtually all agency actions; e.g.,
lawyers at the Department of Justice or
medical professionals at the National
Institutes of Health create a stable long-term
powerful source for agency direction.

Dominance of an agency
by two or three subsystems

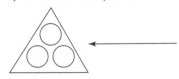

No one group gains control, but two or three
powerful subsystems compete for influence
in an agency, creating a stalemate or shared
power with healthy checks and balances
between competing groups, e.g., army, navy, and
air force professionals within the DoD can offer
a stability or instability due to rivalry within an
agency.

No subsystem dominant
within the agency

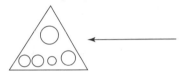

No group or groups dominate, but rather
several roughly equal subsystems share
power and authority through often temporary
shifting arrangements, e.g., the Agency for
International Development, thus creating
often weak and unstable agencies.

FIGURE 4.16   Three basic patterns of distribution of subsystem power and authority
within public bureaucracies

agency dominated by professional careerists, on the other hand, tends to be more
removed from the public, views the world in much longer time frames, and is
motivated by professional norms, goals, and criteria for action. Status, credentials,
rank-in-person, narrow expertise career ladders, and control over careers by professional elites—all are deemed critical within such a public bureaucracy. Thus
these agencies can become more remote, more isolated, even unresponsive and
conservative vis-à-vis immediate public pressures, which inspires both *criticism*
and *respect* for the professions and is the root of their popular support as well as
of hostility toward them. It is the basis of both their constitutional legitimacy as
well as their institutional difficulties within government.

The civil service subsystem operates without distinct career ladders or professional elite controls. Rank is gained from the job. Less status and credential-
ism is evident. Hence, this subsystem is much more laissez-faire. It is a more
"open" subsystem that comprises a broad range of specialists and generalists.
Like professional careerists, these tend to share the attributes of longer time perspectives and to be conservative and gradualist in dealing with issues. But, unlike professional careerists, they also tend to look less to their immediate peers
or to the values and knowledge of higher educational institutions for direction
and more to individualized networks of like-minded friends up and down the
bureaucracy for support and alliances.

Table 4.10 As Complexity of Contracting-Out Public Services Increases, the Roles and Responsibilities of Government Contract Administrators Expand Significantly

Low Complexity	Mid-Level Complexity	High Complexity
Contractor has maximum discretion to choose service delivery means.	RFP describes services and scope of work in more detail.	Public-private partnership should be created, requiring all participants to be considered as equals.
No equipment or personnel restrictions specified.	SOW may specify equipment and restrict personnel.	RFP provides general goals and results, inviting bidders to specify service delivery means.
No description of service delivery means in the bidder response.	Contractor discretion to choose service delivery means is limited.	Competitive negotiations are expected.
CA knowledge about service delivery means can be minimal.	CA will have sufficient understanding of service delivery means.	Long-term commitments are expected more frequently.
CA activities are minimal, using sampling or management by exception approach.	CA must check that milestones are met and deliverables are of appropriate quality.	CA staff need to work as a team, involved in all aspects of contract management.
Contract negotiations are minimal.	Performance measures are needed to ensure contract performance.	CA and contractor will jointly choose specific service delivery means, expecting that these may change over the life of the partnership.
No change orders are needed.	Conflict-resolution skills are more necessary.	Education and training of CA is a continual process.
	Need for service may change over life of contract, leading to change orders.	

SOURCE: Wendell C. Lawther, *Contracting for the 21st Century* (Arlington, VA: The Pricewaterhouse Cooper Endowment, Jan. 2002), p. 31.

Terms: CA = Contract Administrator; RFP = Requests for Proposal; SOW = Statement of Work.

The union subsystem, by contrast, is made up of mainly blue collar workers and increasing percentages of white collar employees, such as teachers, who look to their particular unions to represent their interests in periodic contract negotiations with government representatives. The subsystem's impacts upon bureaucratic operations range from wholesale takeovers to limited or no involvement with bureaucratic policy outputs. But, on the whole, the union subsystem has added new dimensions of complexification, bipartisanship, and formalistic worker-management relationships inside government organizations. Seniority, not merit, governs appointments and promotions.

Finally, the contractual subsystem is rapidly blurring distinctions between public and private organizations by introducing a crazy quilt of private workers within public agencies and public bureaucratic involvement deep within private sector, profit-oriented, and nonprofit firms. Where its processes dominate an agency, as in DoD weapons acquisitions, an agency may well become entirely a "captive" of its business suppliers.

Table 4.11 Summary of Key Aspects of Five Subsystems

	Political Appointees	Professional Careerists	Civil Service	Union Workers	Contract Employment
Position Inside System	Occupy top levels of system	Mid to upper levels	Throughout government	Blue collar, increasing white collar workers	Activities vary significantly by agency
Purposes and Goals	Provide top level policy direction	Key policy, management, expert roles	Generalists and specialists doing many jobs	Largely nonprofessional and paraprofessional work	Hired for fulfilling specific technical and general tasks within a limited time
Time Frames	Short term	Long term	Long term	Short/medium/long term	Mostly short term
Sources of Recruitment	Largely upper class	Largely middle class	Largely middle class	Largely blue collar	Largely from major corporations or small businesses or universities
Ladders for Promotion	Tend to be "in and outers"	Clearly defined hierarchy	Less clearly defined than careerists due to "rank in job"	Seniority system	Open competitive bidding for employment
Dominant Motivations Adhered to	Political responsiveness	Professional norms and values	Mixed motives	Based upon union contracts	Profit motives—"the bottom line"
General Responsiveness to Public or Special Interests	Can be high to public and/or special interests	Generally low responsiveness to both	Mixed	Mixed	Oriented to mainly private business
Major Dilemmas Posed for Government	Lack of expertise and short tenure	Conservatism, monopoly on expertise and long tenure	Slow responsiveness due to emphasis on gradualism and fragmented oversight	Desire to "work to rules" in contract and seniority emphasis	Pressures of the "bottom line" subverting "the public interest"

(continued)

Table 4.11 *Continued*

	Political Appointees	Professional Careerists	Civil Service	Union Workers	Contract Employment
Example of Agency Dominated by This Group and Impacts on Agency's Policies, Structure, and Character	U.S. Attorney's Office in Dept. of Justice—staffed by political appointees and highly responsive to local interests with limited control from above at D. J.—thus decentralized, highly political, and uneven program operations	U.S. Marine Corps—highly skilled at performance of limited military roles; centralized, hierarchical, expert and mission-oriented	Veterans Administration—large, complex, varied workforce, linked to VA groups and legislative allies, with autonomy from Pres. oversight	U.S. Postal Service—Activities based upon negotiated contracts and support from unions, bilateral decisions between union and management	NASA—highly technical, complex space activities draw upon services from many large contractors, who shape agency goals, priorities, political support, budget organization, etc.

Table 4.12 Summary of Key Historic Dates in the Development of Five Subsystems

Political Appointees	Career Professionals	Civil Service	Union Workers	Contract Employees
1789 First Cabinet secretaries, key aides, ambassadors appointed by President Washington	1802 West Point established as first public professional training school in U.S.	1871 First civil service law passed as a rider by Congress and then dies for lack of appropriations	1857 National Teachers Assoc. formed	1860 Act of Congress establishes "open competitive bidding"
1829 President Jackson introduces "spoils system"	1902 General Staff and Army War College created for advanced professional planning and training	1879 Dorman Eaton writes *Civil Service in Great Britain* and founds the National Civil Service Reform League	1912 Lloyd-La Follette Act gives federal workers right to join unions	1940 "Cost-plus-fixed fee" contracts approved
1936 Brownlow Report advocates civil service should be an "arm of the presidency" (rather than a neutral position)	1908 First city manager hired in Stanton, Ohio	1883 Civil Service Act enacted	1959 Wisconsin passes first law allowing local collective bargaining	1940–45 Manhattan Project creates atomic bomb and establishes prototype of large-scale postwar government contracting with businesses and universities
1952 Schedule C positions introduced	1914 Professional assoc. of city managers begun	1906–8 NY Bureau of Municipal Research develops first efficiency ratings and position classifications	1962 Pres. Kennedy signs Executive Orders 10987 and 10988 permitting federal collective bargaining	1948 RAND Corporation created as first government "think tank"
1955 Second Hoover Report advocates a senior executive service	1922 GAO created as first professional staff for Congress	1912 Chicago adopts the first personnel classification system	1966 New York City transit strike	1948 NIH develops first large scale "domestic" contracting-out
1963 California is first state to create an SES system	1924 Rogers Act creates the foreign service	1916 The Model City Charter advocates local civil service systems	1967 New York enacts the Taylor Law formalizing union-management relationships	1950 NSF established
	1936 Brownlow Report recommends increasing professional staff for president		1969 Federal Labor Relations Council created	

(continued)

Table 4.12 *Continued*

Political Appointees	Career Professionals	Civil Service	Union Workers	Contract Employees
1978 Civil Service Reform Act creates SES and OPM as management arm of the White House	1939 Reorganization Act creates BoB as staff arm of president	1923 Classification Act adopted	1978 Civil Service Reform Act gives first statutory approval to labor-management collective bargaining on federal level	1961 BoB Circular A-49 approved use of management and operating contracts
1990 Supreme Court decision *Rutan v. Republican Party of Illinois* limits uses of local patronage	1939 ASPA created	1939/40 Hatch Acts approved	1981 Air traffic controllers strike	1967 BoB circular A-76 (revised in 1976, 1979, 1981) governs federal contracting policies
	1955 Federal Service Entrance Exam established (later changed to PACE)	1940 Social Security Act Amendment requires states to establish merit systems to receive federal funds		
	1969 FEI established	1944 Veteran Preference Act approved		
	1970 Intergovernmental Personnel Act passed	1978 Civil Service Reform Act		
	1978 Civil Service Reform Act creates more training and research opportunities for public service	1993 Hatch Act Amendments		

Most bureaucracies in the public sector are, however, dominated not by any one subsystem but by several; indeed, all these subsystems normally are found within their structures. Hence, policy outcomes frequently result from their jockeying for position, influence, and power over public bureaucratic actions. Conflicts between various subsystems are common. Sometimes the competition for power and control over the policy-making apparatus can become quite severe and intense, as in conflicts between professionals and political appointees, or among professional elites, or between union and management representatives. This can result in *either* healthy competition *or* a stalemate. More often than not it also is well hidden from public view and surfaces in the press only rarely. Finally, in some agencies *no* subsystem dominates but rather several roughly equal subsystems share power and authority through often temporary, unstable, and shifting arrangements. In many cases, this situation can, in turn, create weak, fragmented, and unstable agencies that can accomplish little or nothing. How government agencies accomplish their tasks and responsibilities will be the subject of the next chapter.

KEY TERMS

political appointees

sub-Cabinet officials

general professionals

public professionals

SES

"inner" versus "outer" Cabinet

Pendleton Act

GS rating

rank "in person" versus "in job"

Kennedy's Executive Orders 10988 and 10987

public service unions

contract employment

line versus staff personnel

REVIEW MATERIAL

Review Questions

1. What are the five major subsystems in public agencies that decisively influence bureaucratic policy? Briefly describe the characteristics of each one.

2. Where are political appointees situated in the bureaucracy and what functions do these individuals serve in U.S. government? Can you name a few current political appointees in government?

3. What are the essential differences between the professional careerist subsystem and the general civil service subsystem? What are the

sources of each one's influence and authority?

4. How do general professionals, public service professionals, emerging professionals, and paraprofessionals differ from each other? Can you offer specific examples of each type of professional group in government?

5. Why has the contractual subsystems grown so rapidly within public bureaucracy in recent decades? Why is it now important to setting public policies?

Class Debate: Pro/Con

Resolved that the increase of the size and influence political appointees over the last three decades or so at the federal level significantly reduces government's efficiency and effectiveness to carry out its assigned roles.

Student Homework Exercise

Select a state or local public agency and identify the types of internal personnel subsystems operating within that agency, especially their size, function(s), location, recent changes in composition, influence over policy making, as well as their general power that they exercise within that organization. Then compare and contrast your agency's internal subsystems with others which have been studied by the class—do they look and operate similarly? Or, are they different? Why or why not?

Case Analysis

Read "The Blast in Centralia No. 5" in any edition of Richard Stillman's *Public Administration: Concepts and Cases.* Examine how the separation (or its lack thereof) between political appointees and tenured civil servants influenced the outcome of this case study. If there had been a clearly explicit division of those two types of personnel, could the mine disaster have been prevented? If so, how? Or, if not, why not? Ideally where should a line dividing the two have been placed? How can it be determined? And what criteria did you use for selecting where that dividing line should be?

NOTES

1. Hugh Heclo, *A Government of Strangers* (Washington, DC: Brookings Institution, 1977), p. 103.

2. These characteristics of political appointees have been true for some time. See David T. Stanley, Dean E. Mann, and Jameson W. Doig, *Men Who Govern* (Washington, DC: Brookings Institution, 1967).

3. For data on the backgrounds of city managers that tend to show a high degree of heterogeneity, read Richard J. Stillman II, "Local Public Management in Transition," *The Municipal Year Book 1982* (Washington, DC: International City Management Assoc., 1982), pp. 161–73.

4. Thomas P. Murphy, Donald E. Nuechterlein, and Ronald Stupak, *Inside Bureaucracy: The View from the Assistant Secretary's Desk* (Boulder: Westview Press, 1978).

5. Frederick C. Mosher, *Democracy and the Public Service,* 2d ed. (New York: Oxford University Press, 1982), p. 183.

6. James P. Pfiffner, *The Strategic Presidency: Hitting the Ground Running* (Chicago, IL: Dorsey Press, 1988), p. 105.

7. Frank P. Sherwood and L. J. Breyer, "Executive Personnel Systems in States," *Public Administration Review* 47 (Sept./Oct. 1987): 410f.

8. Deborah D. Roberts, "The Governor as Leader: Strengthening Public Service Through Executive Leadership," in Frank J. Thompson (ed.), *Revitalizing State and Local Public Service: Strengthening*

Performance, Accountability, and Citizen Confidence (San Francisco, CA: Jossey-Bass, 1993), pp. 51–52.

9. See Samuel H. Beer's presidential address before the American Political Science Association, "Federalism, Nationalism and Democracy in America," American Political Science Review, 72(1) (March 1978).

10. Zbigniew Brzezinski, *Between Two Ages: America's Role in the Technetronic Era* (New York: Viking, 1970); Don Price, *The Scientific Estate* (Cambridge: Harvard University Press, 1965); Daniel Bell, "Notes on the Post-Industrial Society," *Public Interest,* 6 (Winter 1967): 24–35; and Guy Benveniste, *The Politics of Expertise,* 2d ed. (San Francisco: Jossey-Bass, 1983).

11. Mosher, *Democracy,* p. 142.

12. Robert D. Kaplan, "There Is No 'Middle East,' " *New York Times Magazine,* Feb. 20, 1994, pp. 42–43.

13. Robert Wiebe, *The Search for Order: 1877–1920* (New York: Hill and Wang, 1967), pp. 120–21.

14. Martha Derthick, *The Influence of Federal Grants: Public Assistance in Massachusetts* (Cambridge, MA: Harvard University Press, 1970), p. 159.

15. David S. Arnold and Jeremy F. Plant, *Public Official Associations and State and Local Government: A Bridge across One Hundred Years* (Fairfax, VA: George Mason University Press, 1994), p. 59.

16. Corinne L. Gilb, *Hidden Hierarchies: The Professions and Government* (New York: Harper and Row, 1966).

17. Burton J. Bledstein, *The Culture of Professionalism* (New York: Norton, 1976), p. x.

18. Much of the following discussion is drawn from the research on professions in government contained in Frederick C. Mosher and Richard J. Stillman II, *Professions in Government* (New Brunswick, NJ: Transaction Books, 1982).

19. Ralph P. Hummel, *The Bureaucratic Experience: A Critique of Life in the Modern Organization,* 4th ed. (New York: St. Martin's Press, 1994), p. 118.

20. O. Glenn Stahl, *Public Personnel Administration,* 7th ed. (New York: Harper and Row, 1976), p. 42.

21. The best account of the development of civil service remains Paul P. Van Riper's *History of the United States Civil Service* (Evanston, IL: Row Peterson, 1958).

22. Patricia W. Ingraham and Donald F. Kettl, *Agenda for Excellence: Public Service in America* (Chatham, NY: Chatham House, 1993).

23. Jay M. Shafritz, *Public Personnel Management* (New York: Praeger, 1975), p. 33.

24. Kenneth J. Meier, "Representative Bureaucracy," *American Political Science Review* (1975), pp. 535–53.

25. Unpublished data prepared by Kenneth Smith, DPA, George Mason University, Fairfax, VA.

26. Marver Bernstein, *The Job of the Federal Executive* (Washington, DC: Brookings Institution, 1958), p. 49.

27. Eugene B. MacGregor, "Politics and Career Mobility of Civil Servants," *American Political Science Review,* 68 (1974): 24.

28. *Task Force Report on Personnel and Civil Service: The Organization of the Executive Branch of the Government,* First Hoover Commission Report, pp. 1–2.

29. As cited in Heclo, *Government,* p. 142.

30. Gregory B. Lewis and Sue A. Frank, "Who Wants to Work for Government?" *Public Administration Review,* 62 (July/Aug. 2002), pp. 398–400.

31. The Hudson Institute, *Civil Service 2000* (Washington, DC: U.S. Office of Personnel Management, 1988).

32. Paul A. Volcker, chair, *Leadership for America: Rebuilding the Public Service* (Lexington, MA: Lexington Books, 1990).

33. William A. Winter, chair, *Hard Truths, Tough Choices: Agenda for State and Local Reform,* Winter Commission Report, 1993.

34. David T. Stanley, *Managing Local Government under Union Pressure* (Washington, DC: Brookings Institution, 1972), p. 136.

35. Joel M. Douglas, "Public Sector Collective Bargaining in the 1900s," in Frederick S. Lane (ed.), *Current Issues in Public Administration,* 5th ed. (New York: St. Martin's Press, 1994), p. 261.

36. Frederick C. Mosher, *Democracy and the Public Service* (New York: Oxford University Press, 1968), p. 178.

37. PL 95-45, October 13, 1978, Section 7106.

38. As quoted in Harry H. Wellington and Ralph K. Winter, Jr., *The Union and the Cities* (Washington, DC: Brookings Institution, 1971), p. 30.

39. Ibid.

40. As Joel M. Douglas concludes, "Bilateralism has replaced unilateralism in the decision-making processes." Douglas, "Public Sector Collective Bargaining in the 1990s," pp. 271–72.

41. Carolyn Ban and Norma Riccucci, "Personal Systems and Labor Relations: Steps toward a Quiet Revitalization," in Frank J. Thompson (ed.), *Revitalizing State and Local Public Service: Strengthening Performance, Accountability, and Citizen Confidence* (San Francisco, CA: Jossey-Bass, 1993), p. 80.

42. William Danhof, *Government Contracting* (Washington, DC: Brookings Institution, 1968).

43. Bruce L. R. Smith, "The Future of the Not-for-Profit Corporation," *Public Interest* (Summer 1967), p. 77.

44. Susan R. Bernstein, *Managing Contracted Services in the Nonprofit Agency: Administrative, Ethical, and Political Issues* (Philadelphia, PA: Temple University Press, 1991), p. 22.

FURTHER READING

A number of excellent books deal with the origins, growth, and operations of the various types of bureaucratic subsystems discussed in this chapter. The best account of the rise of the U.S. Civil Service remains Paul Van Riper's *History of the U.S. Civil Service* (1958). For a history of the European civil service, read Brian Chapman's *The Profession of Government* (1959). For accounts of professionalism in the civil service, read C. L. Gibb, *Hidden Hierarchies* (1966), Don Price, *Scientific Estate* (1965), Frederick C. Mosher, *Democracy and the Public Service,* 2d ed. (1982), and Eliot Friedson, *Professionalism Reborn* (1994). Studies advocating reforms in the civil service systems, such as the Volcker Commission Report, *Leadership for America* (1990), The Hudson Institute, *Civil Service 2000* (1988), and Frank J. Thompson (ed.), *Revitalizing State and Local Government: Strengthening Performance, Accountability, and Citizen Confidence* (1993), are some of the best guides to civil service problems. For an account of the interplay between political appointees, professionals, and civil servants, read Frank J. Thompson, *Personnel Policy in the City* (1975), Hugh Heclo, *A Government of Strangers* (1977), James P. Pfiffner, *The Strategic Presidency* (1988), Robert F. Durant, *The Administrative Presidency Revisited* (1992), and Mark Huddleston and William Boyer, *The Higher Civil Service in the United States* (1996). Three books dealing with political appointees include John W. Macy, Bruce Adams, J. Jackson Walter (eds.), *America's Unelected Government: Appointing the President's Team* (1983), G. Calvin MacKenzie, *The Politics of Presidential Appointments* (1981), and by the same author, *The In and Outers* (1987). Excellent reviews of the impact of the 1978 Civil Service Reform Act are found in Patricia W. Ingraham and Carolyn Davis, *Legislating Bureaucratic Change* (1984), and Patricia W. Ingraham and David

H. Rosenbloom (ed.), *The Promise and Paradox of Civil Service Reform* (1993). For the current operation of SES that was created by CSRA 1978, see OPM, *The Status of the Senior Executive Service* (1991), the Merit Protection Board, *The Senior Executive Service—Views of Former Federal Executives* (1989), and the thoughtful essay by Norton Long, "SES and the Public Interest," *Public Administration Review* (May/June 1981). For a helpful overview of the civil service today, review Patricia W. Ingraham and David H. Rosenbloom, *Agenda for Excellence* (1992); Carolyn Ban and Norma Riccucci, *Public Personnel Management* (1991); Paul Light, *The New Public Service* (1999); and by the same author, *The True Size of Government* (1999).

For useful perspectives on professional career systems, see Frederick C. Mosher and Richard J. Stillman II (eds.), *Professions in Government* (1982). For more current aspects of professionalism, see James A. Smith, *The Idea Brokers* (1991), and David S. Arnold and Jeremy F. Plant, *Public Official Associations and State and Local Government: A Bridge Across One Hundred Years* (1994).

For perhaps the best current studies of where we are today involving the problems of unions and the public service, read Joel M. Douglas's three essays: "Collective Bargaining and Public Sector Supervisors: A Trend Towards Exclusion?" *Public Administration Review* (Nov./Dec. 1987); "State Civil Service and Collective Bargaining Systems in Conflict," *Public Administration Review* (March/April, 1992); plus "Public Sector Labor Relations in the 21st Century: New Approaches, New Strategies," in Carolyn C. Ban and N. Riccucci (eds.), *Public Personnel Management* (1991), as well as A. Lawrence Chickering (ed.), *Public Employee Unions* (1977) and David T. Stanley, *Managing Local Government under Union Pressure* (1972). Though Clarence H. Danhof's *Government Contracting* (1968) is somewhat dated, it is still useful for its history. Various books offer useful insights into portions of the contract subsystem: Harold Orlans (ed.), *Nonprofit Organizations* (1980); Ruth Hoogland De Hoog, *Partners in Public Service* (1986); John Donphue, *The Privatization Decision* (1989); John Donahue, *The Privatization Decision* (1989); Donald Kettl, *Sharing Power* (1993); James F. Nagle, *A History of Government Contracting* (1992); Wendell Lawther, *Contracting for the 21st Century* (2002); and Phillip Cooper, *Governing by Contract* (2003). Daniel Jimenez, *A Study in Contracting Problems between Government Agencies and Non-Profit Organizations in California* (1981); Susan R. Bernstein, *Managing Contracted Services in a Nonprofit Agency* (1991); John Cibinic and Ralph Nash, *Administration of Government Contracts,* 3rd ed. (1995); and Ralph Nash, *Formation of Government Contracts* (1998).

One should not overlook several good agency studies that analyze aspects of this issue such as John T. Tierney, *The U.S. Postal Service* (1988); Donald F. Kettl, *Leadership at the Fed* (1986); Theodore R. Marmor, *The Politics of Medicare,* 2nd ed. (2000); Jerry Mitchell, *The American Experiment with Government Corporations* (1999); and Paul C. Light, *Monitoring Government* (1993). Also helpful on this topic are firsthand "insider" views, including Alexander Haig, *Caveat* (1984), Joseph Califano, *Governing America* (1981), Elliot Richardson, *The Creative Balance* (1976), Ben W. Heineman and Curtis A. Hessler, *Memorandum for the President* (1980), Thomas P. Murphy, Donald E. Nuechterlein, and Ronald J. Stupak,

Inside the Bureaucracy (1978), Deborah Shapely, *Promise and Power* (1993), General Wesley Clark, *Waging Modern War* (2001), David Kessler, *A Question of Intent* (2001), Bob Woodward, *Masstro* (2000), as well as the several leadership profiles found in Jameson W. Doig and Erwin C. Hargrove (eds.), *Leadership and Innovation* (1990) and Norma Riccucci, *Unsung Heroes* (1995).

WEB SITES

http://douglass.speech.nwu.edu/fran_a87.htm: Benjamin Franklin, "Dangers of a Salaried Bureaucracy"

http://www.ypa.org/: Young Politicians of America

http://www.afge.org/Index.cfm: American Federation of Government Employees

http://www.lib.umich.edu/govdocs/jfkeo/eo/10987.htm: Kennedy Executive Order 10987

http://www.lib.umich.edu/govdocs/jfkeo/eo/10988.htm: Kennedy Executive Order 10988

5

■

Outputs of the
American Bureaucracy

L
ack of cooperation between the FBI and CIA misses early warning of 9/11 terrorist attack on the United States.

The Security Exchange Commission is called a "toothless tiger" for failing to regulate Enron, Worldcom, Global Crossing, and other businesses that "cooked the books."

In Boston, a twenty-three-year-old woman is brutally killed by a former boyfriend whom the police and district attorney knew was "a repeat offender" but failed to "lock up."

Eighteen U.S. Army Rangers are killed "in a fire fight" in Somalia (East Africa) due to a communication failure of the top command.

A contractor's flaw in casting the mirror for the Hubble Space Telescope causes blurred images from space and widespread criticism of NASA's management of a 20 year, billion dollar project.

A local welfare social worker with a case load of over one thousand children, half of whom are in poverty, is fired after the press reveals one of her cases, a family of eighteen children, is found starving in a rat-infested "crack house."

A miscalculation of a Medicaid payment provision by a mid-level Department of Health and Human Services bureaucrat costs U.S. taxpayers over $2 billion.

An aging bridge collapses, killing six people, and a state inspector is blamed for negligence.

Terrorist Osama bin Laden slips out of Afghanistan under intensive air/ground assaults by coalition forces.

News accounts such as these repeatedly highlight bureaucratic failures. Bureaucrats are regularly "roasted in the press" for what appears to be blatant neglect of their assigned work; few are applauded for their successes. This chapter focuses on how bureaucracies and bureaucrats get their jobs accomplished—or why they fail to do so.

Police catch crooks, firefighters put out fires, social workers help the needy, the military defends the nation. No public organization is created, funded, and sustained for very long without some prescribed legal purpose to fulfill for the public. Whether it performs its mandated missions well, or even at all, is another matter. Many perform their goals in cooperation with other public, private, or nonprofit units. Many agencies fall far short of performing their explicit goals. Many of bureaucracy's actual goals are not even explicitly defined. Yet, to whatever degree bureaucratic goals are publicly stated or in practice imprecisely defined, government agencies are ultimately purposeful entities, that is, they are made up of people who are organized around the execution of some task or activity to be accomplished for someone, some interest group, or the public at large.

Legislators give much time and attention to framing these agency missions in enabling legislation as well as to continuously overseeing bureaucratic activities through budgetary approval, personnel authorization, and so on. Agency administrators, from first-line supervisors to top-level leadership, are actively involved in ongoing processes that clarify, modify, revise, and achieve various organizational goals. And certainly government workers are on the firing line, making whatever happens in any organization actually happen. Much of public organizational life therefore centers around the struggle over deciding what should be done and then carrying out that task or tasks within specific time frames and budgetary limits and despite tedious, tangled hierarchies, procedural routines, and numerous other complexities.

Ironically, though, when a governmental employee is asked, "Precisely what work does your agency perform for society?" the response is frequently ambiguous. The reply may be, "Legally we are responsible for undertaking this or that job, but let me tell you there is a lot more we do (or a lot less)." In other words, questions about precisely what public bureaucracy does normally lead to less-than-precise statements, even embarrassment or qualifications, and few clear-cut answers.

Part of the reason for this inconclusiveness was cited in Chapter 3. Most public agencies have more than one purpose. Some agency missions are vague or ill defined in the enabling legislation. It may be of very little value to consult the law books to determine what activities a public organization performs (or fails to perform). The 1789 enabling legislation that created the State Department (first called a Department of Foreign Affairs) said that the department

> shall perform and execute such duties as shall from time to time be
> enjoined on or entrusted . . . by the President of the United States,
> agreeable to the Constitution, relative to correspondences, commissions or
> instructions to or with public ministers or consuls, from the United States,
> or to negotiations with public ministers from foreign states or princes, or
> to memorials or other applications from foreign public ministers or other
> foreigners, or to such other matters respecting foreign affairs, as the
> President of the United States shall assign said department.[1]

Such an open-ended statement of purposes hardly gives even a glimmer of insight into the complex, multifunctional roles of the current State Department, many of which were outlined in Chapter 2. Like topsy, most of State's missions just grew.

Further, such lack of clarity in defining the purposes and goals of public organizations may be due to various groups—administrators, legislators, and citizens—wanting it that way for many reasons. Vague purposes often give administrators more flexibility in deciding on issues or managing programs. Legislators creating a new department may not themselves be very sure of the future duties it might someday acquire or of how they will be developed. Some fields, such as national security, require a degree of secrecy, hence its goals are unspecified. Certainly the CIA's charter as contained in the National Security Act of 1947 (with 1949 amendments) articulates its functions in the broadest, haziest language: "advise the National Security Council"; "make recommendations to the National Security Council"; "correlate and evaluate intelligence relating to the national security"; "provide for the appropriate dissemination of such intelligence within the Government"; and "perform for the benefit of the existing intelligence agencies, such additional services of common concern as the National Security Council determines."[2]

Imprecise objectives may in reality stem also from the inability of even the most gifted minds to comprehend all the ramifications of governmental actions. The Federal Reserve Board's responsibility for changing the discount rates periodically in order to "fine tune the economy" now have so many ripple effects on the country's and the world's economies that its actions become deeply intertwined with a broad variety of public purposes (stated and unstated). Disentangling the *actual* objectives of this agency's actions as the country's central banker from *symbolic* ones can be difficult indeed. Stated purposes, in other words, may sometimes have nothing to do with the actual purposes of organizational actions, *and* the agency itself may not even know the difference.

Given all the complexity in fathoming the purposes of public organizations, this chapter will study such questions as: first, how can we conceptualize bureaucratic outputs? Second, how are these outputs then produced or *not* produced by public agencies? Finally, what, therefore, is a realistic way by which to comprehend overall the output processes of public organizations? Or, what is a valid model of the output process?

THE VARIETIES OF BUREAUCRATIC
OUTPUTS IN GOVERNMENT

At the outset of this book, the peculiar federal structure of American Government within which bureaucracies operate was outlined. Each "layer of government" as stressed in Chapters 1 and 2, tends to have specialized functions or tasks it performs through a variety of public agencies (see Table 5.1). Furthermore, Chapter 4 examined the interdynamics of public bureaucracies and observed that they revolve primarily around the interplay of five key subsystems: political ap-

Table 5.1 The Primary Functions Performed by Level of Government (Based on Major Governmental Expenditures)

Federal	State	Local (City, Special District, and County)
Defense	Public welfare	Police
Postal services	Highways	Fire
Retirement	Higher education	Libraries
Veterans affairs	Corrections	Elementary/high school
Natural resource management	Inspection services	Parks and recreation
Health and human services	Regulatory functions for state/local levels	Water and sewage
Foreign affairs		Housing
Space and scientific research		Hospitals
National regulatory functions		

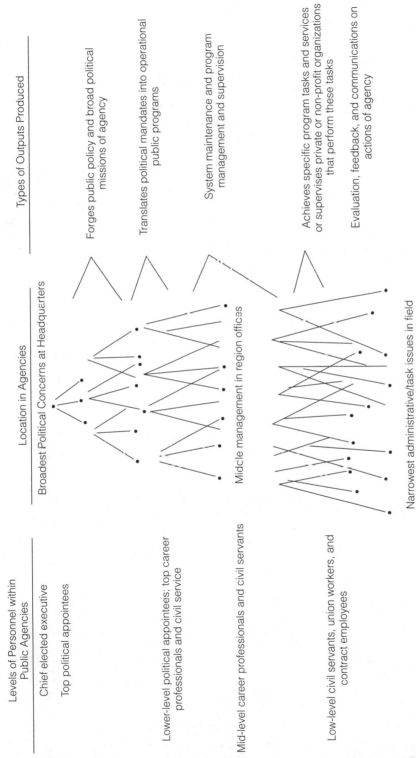

FIGURE 5.1 The varieties of public agency outputs

pointees, professional careerists, general civil servants, union workers, and contract employees. Depending on its place in the bureaucratic hierarchy, each group plays an important role in shaping bureaucratic outputs and produces a unique type of "service," "product," or "result."

As Figure 5.2 indicates, elected and appointed political officials occupy the very highest echelons of public bureaucracy. These political leaders as well as their Cabinet and sub-Cabinet officials formulate the overall political missions of agencies and forge public policy for these programs. As Chapters 3 and 4 underscored, these political officials often work closely with the legislature, their committee staffs, the courts, other executive offices, and important interest groups outside government in developing policy goals through such means as initiating legislation, framing budgets, issuing political recommendations, informing the public by press releases and speeches, and devising new programs or revisions of old ones. What should U.S. policy be toward South Africa? Should the United States design a new terrorist defense system? Can the present state highway system meet future transportation needs? These and other large questions occupy much of the time and attention of appointed officials. In a word, these officials produce outputs that *formulate policy directions and public goals for their agencies.*

The next level, occupied by lower-level political appointees, top career professionals, and civil servants, is also involved with the policy-making process but

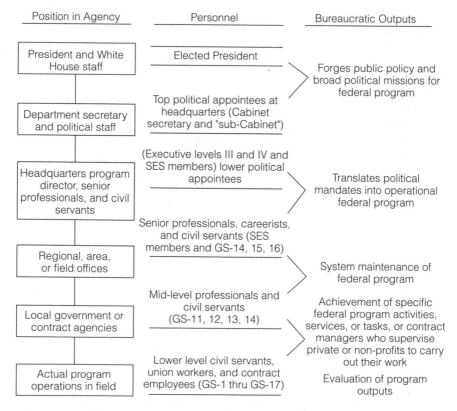

FIGURE 5.2 In typical federal programs, outputs vary by bureaucratic levels.

in a different way. The expertise at this level is generally narrower and more focused on *translating the broad policy mandates into operational programs*. This expertise is sought and valued by elected officials because it can turn large and often vague political promises into functioning programs within agencies. When a president launches a space shuttle program, or a governor promises to upgrade the quality of education in public schools, or a mayor announces a new drug treatment program, it is often the "pros" inside government (top scientists/engineers at NASA, education specialists within a state, or public health officials in a city) that the political officials ask to design and initiate such new policy directions. Again, this "translation function" is not accomplished by these individuals alone; rather they act in cooperation with various other parties, for example, clients to be served, political officials who initiated the idea, as well as a variety of individuals inside and outside government.

The middle levels of the civil service and professional career cadre, the next tier down, are largely concerned with still another product of public bureaucracy, namely, *system maintenance*. By exercising various skills of management, supervision, control, and personnel and fiscal oversight, they see to it that the system runs as designed. These men and women are the managers and supervisors who ensure the social security checks are processed in a timely manner and that air quality standards are monitored and enforced according to the law and that local firefighters are prepared to fight fires. These administrative tasks involving system maintenance cover a wide array of activities, including collecting and analyzing data, issuing reports and orders, enforcing orders, developing policy alternatives for superiors, budgeting funds, awarding contracts, hiring personnel, and negotiating with citizens' and interest groups and other units of government.

Lower levels of the civil service, union members, and contract employees in field offices or at the bottom of bureaucratic units, are largely concerned with *actual program implementation and service delivery*. Here is where the rubber meets the road, so to speak—the city police direct traffic, teachers instruct students, the IRS agent audits a taxpayer's Form 1040, and a postal worker delivers the mail. These men and women actually do the work of the agency or department. However, as Chapter 4 pointed out, the rapid growth of contract employment in government in recent years had made it increasingly difficult to tell who *really* performs government services. Not all the work of government today is done by government employees in-house. Many private sector firms and non-profit organizations work as largely "contract agencies" for the government.

All these groups share in still another important output of public bureaucracy, namely, *evaluation of the entire process*. Communications, or positive and negative feedback, from all elements of any public agency can serve to shape and reshape policy agendas and political directions. Sometimes the evaluation is quite complex, formalized, and specialized, where evaluation reports are prepared by large bureaucratic staffs "in-house" or contracted to firms outside of government. More than 70 units of the federal government, such as Inspector General offices in the various agencies or the Office of Management and Budget in the White House alone, are involved in producing these evaluations. At other times, the evaluation may simply be word-of-mouth gossip passed along from the bottom ranks of the agency or from the outside to its top levels. Both formalized and informal communications can have significant effects upon agency actions. Figure 5.2 points out these five bureaucratic outputs in a typical federal program.

But how are these various outputs *actually* produced by public agencies? How does public bureaucracy *really* make things happen? First, let us examine four "generic" ways of achieving bureaucratic outputs, including their shortcomings. Then let us look at an alternative, more realistic model to explain this process.

MAKING BUREAUCRATIC OUTPUTS HAPPEN

Woodrow Wilson's famous observation may be pertinent here. In 1887 he perceptively observed in the first essay ever written by an American on U.S. public administration that "it is getting harder to run a constitution than to frame one."[3] Wilson's insight is even more true—and critical—today, for it is comparatively easy to frame laws and devise policies pertaining to what an agency *ought to do* (constitution-making) in contrast to seeing to it that programs are *carried out* in a wise, efficient, and timely manner (constitution-running). What Wilson was arguing for was a science of administration to assist in the development of the accomplishing side of government—its performance of public activities. Grover Starling has called it "all those activities involved in carrying out the policies of elected officials and some activities associated with the development of those policies . . . in short, all that comes after the last campaign promise and election night cheer."[4]

With the growth of government and its increasing breadth of activities, these performance problems have become immensely more complicated *and* central to the government as a whole as well as to that of individual agencies. Indeed, the subject of implementation of government actions and programs has grown into a major preoccupation (perhaps "cottage industry" is the more correct term) of public administration experts and policy specialists. How should bureaucratic operations be carried out? Efficiently? Economically? Promptly? Fairly? Honestly? And in the public interest? Such questions have occupied the attention of a vast number of theorists, and their responses range from Frederick W. Taylor's scientific management principles to Peter Drucker's management by objectives concept to W. Edwards Deming's principles of TQM to Osborne and Gaebler's reinventing government concept.

Perhaps the classic formulation of "good" practices for accomplishing the basic purposes of government is found in *Papers on the Science of Administration* by Luther Gulick and L. Urwick (1937). These authors envisioned "the best" execution of public programs by means of the acronym POSDCORB, standing for a series of executive functions that presumably should be done in the following order:

Planning: goal-setting techniques/methods applied by executives as a means for preparing future courses of organizational action

Organizing: arranging the organizational structure and processes in an appropriate manner essential to achieving these ends

Staffing: recruiting and hiring personnel to carry out the essential agency work

Directing: supervising the actual processes of doing the assignments

Coordinating: integrating the various detailed elements of these tasks in cooperation with other units and people in government

Reporting: tracking and communicating the progress of the work within the organization

Budgeting: fiscal and financial activities necessary to economically support the completion of these programs, services, or activities.[5]

Various additions, changes, amendments, and refinements to the Gulick–Urwick sequence have been made over the years by other noted management authorities, such as Bertram Gross in his fivefold approach to producing organizational outputs:

Decision making: defining the problems, setting out alternative courses of action, and choosing the best one

Communicating: getting out the information about the decision in oral and written form to those involved in its implementation and monitoring feedback and responses

Planning: developing purposeful actions toward the organizational future and correcting and adjusting these plans as they progress

Activating: through persuasion, pressure, controls, and so on, getting specific action from the organization, its subunits, and its members

Evaluating: readjusting, correcting, and revising plans for the future and adjusting changes in the outputs, both qualitatively and quantitatively, as may be required for organizational survival and growth.[6]

In the late 1970s, Graham Allison attempted to synthesize these varied lists of "good" practices into one "grand" functional listing of eight generic processes:

Strategy

1. *Establishing objectives and priorities* for the organization (on the basis of forecasts of the external environment and the organization's capacities).

2. *Devising operational plans* to achieve these objectives.

Managing Internal Components

3. *Organizing and staffing:* In organizing, the manager establishes structure (units and positions with assigned authority and responsibilities) and procedures (for coordinating activity and taking action); in staffing he or she tries to fit the right persons in the key jobs.

4. *Directing personnel and the personnel management system:* The capacity of the organization is embodied primarily in its members and their skills and knowledge; the personnel management system recruits, selects, socializes, trains, rewards and punishes; the organization's human capital, which constitutes the organization's capacity to act to achieve its goals and to respond to specific directions from management.

5. *Controlling performance:* Various management information systems—including operating capital budgets, accounts, reports, statistical systems, performance appraisals, and product evaluation—assist management in making decisions and in measuring progress toward objectives.

Managing External Constituencies

6. *Dealing with external units* of the organization subject to some common authority; most general managers must deal with general managers of other units within the larger organization—above, laterally, and below—to achieve that unit's objectives.

7. *Dealing with independent organizations:* Agencies from other branches or levels of government, interest groups, and private enterprises that can affect the organization's ability to achieve its objectives.

8. *Dealing with the press and public,* whose action or approval or acquiescence is required.[7]

In the 1990s, by contrast, Michael Barzelay, with the collaboration of Babak J. Armajani, proposed a "customer-driven model" in their book, *Breaking Through Bureaucracy:*

- A customer-driven agency focus on customer needs and perspectives.
- A customer-driven agency enables the whole organization to function as a team.
- A customer-driven agency defines itself by the results it achieves for its customers.
- A customer-driven agency creates net value over cost.
- A customer-driven agency modifies its operations in response to changing demands for its services.
- A customer-driven agency competes for business.
- A customer-driven agency builds choice into its operating systems when doing so serves a purpose.
- A customer-driven agency builds in two-way communication with its customer in order to access and revise its operating strategy.
- A customer-driven agency empowers front-line employees to make judgments about how to improve customer service and value.[8]

PROBLEMS WITH GENERIC OUTPUT MODELS
FOR UNDERSTANDING HOW BUREAUCRATIC
PURPOSES ARE ACHIEVED

The aforementioned lists of the "best" management practices by Gulick–Urwick, Gross, Allison, Barzelay, Armajani and others as summed up in Table 5.2, are drawn heavily from "generic management" thinking or the notion that "good"

Table 5.2 The Changing Twentieth-Century Generic Management Models

Time	Management Model	Key Theorists	Values Emphasized in Making Outputs Happen
1900s	Scientific Management	Frederick Talor	Workplace efficiency and economy
1920s	Human Relations Movement	Elton Mayo	Workplace human relationships for cooperation and productivity
1930s	POSDCORB	Luther Gulick	Overall general management effectiveness
1950s	Systems Theory	Peter Drucker and Bertram Gross	Large-scale systems approaches for overall effectiveness
1960s	Organizational Development	Chris Argris, Rensis Likert, Douglas McGregor, and Frederick Herzberg	Human development for organization achievement
1970s	Political-Strategic Models	Graham Allison	Political strategizing and planning contingency
1980s	Total Quality Management (TQM)	Edward Deming	Product-quality focus (i.e., both quality *in fact* and quality *in customer perception*)
1990s	Reinventing Government Ideas	David Osborne and Ted Gaebler	Customer satisfaction focus

management is "good" wherever it is practiced—in business, nonprofit organizations, or government. Thus most tend to focus on "system maintenance" or "implementation" aspects of bureaucratic work and overlook other critical aspects of bureaucratic output realities such as political power and constitutional limitations.

Such a point of view is not so much wrong as it is simply incomplete when it attempts to explain accurately the carrying out of programs and policies by public agencies. As the late Columbia University political scientist Wallace Sayre so aptly remarked, "Public and private management are fundamentally alike in all unimportant respects."[9] Or, as Paul Appleby put it, "Government is different."[10] Appleby might have added that the process of making public outputs happen is a lot different (in organizational structure, activities, purposes, and internal components) from the process of making private outputs happen. Several unique attributes make government agencies fundamentally *dissimilar* to business or other organizations.

Lack of a Bottom Line

Often (though not always) businesses operate with one clear priority, making a profit. Some, of course, do better than others at achieving this goal, but at least businesses *have a single goal*—profit making. Or, another way of putting it is that business has a single goal but multiple objectives, whereas government has multiple goals *and* multiple objectives. As Chapters 2 and 3 emphasized, few public organizations operate with such clear, singular objectives. Most pursue multiple goals and objectives to which simple quantitative measures regarding their outputs for society are frequently, though certainly not always, difficult to apply. Who can really tell whether a new ruling of the Nuclear Regulatory Commission (NRC) is appropriate and fair? Whether it is cost-efficient? Equitable? Whether it will impose undue burdens or additional costs to nuclear industry? Or whether it will prevent some future technological mishap such as that at Three Mile Island? How can one assess those "preventive" costs and benefits for society as a whole? The NRC, like most public agencies, is constantly juggling *many, even competing, bottom lines*—social, political, economic, technological—and there are often no simple, quantitative ways of judging the worth of its actions. Often, public units have "symbolic" goals. A large standing defense force may "symbolize" a nation's will to fight and hence deter a potential enemy from aggressive actions. How can one measure the "price" of maintaining the peace?

Diversity of Institutional Arrangements

As Chapter 2 outlined, there is a wide array of public organizations in the United States. Some, such as the Defense Department, are larger than any business firm. Some, such as the small town with only one full-time employee, a village clerk of the council, to keep the doors of the city hall open and to pay the bills, are "mom and pop" operations. Some are organized like businesses, such as the more than one hundred government corporations operating on the national level or the 30,000 special district units rendering a multitude of special services on county and municipal levels. As a result of such institutional diversity, these public entities are enormously varied in their institutional and managerial infrastructure. Some utilize highly sophisticated technology, advanced professionalized managerial expertise, and quantitative measures in shaping, directing, and controlling their outputs that rival those at General Motors. Many do not use much more than pencil, paper, table, chair, and telephone to fulfill their assignments, simply because they have neither the need nor the finances to develop any high degree of managerial sophistication.

Fragmentation of Public Organizations
and Their Authority

Business enterprises usually operate with one person ultimately in charge of seeing to it that things get done. But as Chapter 3 stressed, the U.S. Constitution created a political environment within which every public bureaucracy must operate, thus fragmenting authority in several ways, breaking it up horizontally through a federal design and vertically through a division of power among separate, coequal branches of government. As a result of this scatterization of authority (intended by the founders to "preserve individual liberties"), executives inside every public agency must work with, in, and through many other units and levels of government such as courts, Congress, and so on in order to accomplish their assignments. It is this quality that has led Harvard professor Richard Neustadt to comment that the U.S. government is one of "separated institutions sharing powers." Government administrators must constantly work with others beyond the boundaries of their own organizations in joint cooperative endeavors to reach collective decisions and achieve results for the public at large.

Public Agencies Operate in Goldfish
Bowls with Varied Popular Support

To complicate matters further, all these activities have to be done in the open with full public disclosure and accountability to legislature, media, and other oversight units such as independent auditors, subcommittees, hearings, and inspectors general. Furthermore, legal requirements for open, regular public hearings require government openness and transparency. What is done in the business firm's boardroom by contrast can be decided largely in secret and without the same degree of public scrutiny. Few public agencies enjoy that luxury or autonomy from such oversight today. The 1974 Freedom of Information Act at the federal level and "sunshine" laws enacted in the 1970s years at the local level give the public press wide access to agencies' internal activities. Even the Central Intelligence Agency and Federal Bureau of Investigation have opened up their files and internal processes in unprecedented ways during the last decade. Both employ large full-time public relations offices to handle such external public "interface." Managers in every public agency know full well that what they say or do may hit the newspaper's front page tomorrow or local television news

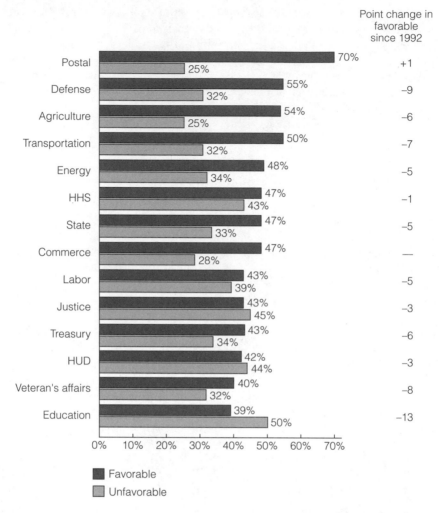

FIGURE 5.3   Diversity of federal departments' popular support: favorable versus unfavorable

Source: Roper Reports, Aug. 2002, pp. 93–95. Reprinted by permission of Roper ASW, an NOP World Company.

tonight. Most learn to act accordingly and to gauge their actions in light of the possible glare of public opinion. Figure 5.3 shows the wide variation of public support for federal agencies. Some have strong backing, while others do not.

Mandated Government Programs
and Entitlements Restrictions

Business firms respond to changes in the particular markets they serve—autos, steel, housing, and so on. However, as Chapter 3 stressed, public bureaucracies respond to broad socioeconomic trends within society in very immediate, often au-

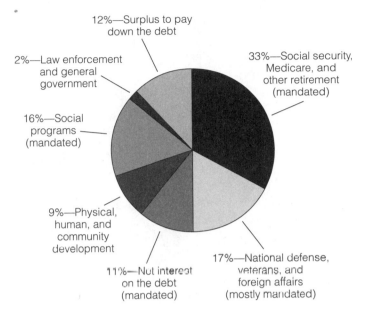

FIGURE 5.4   Where the federal government spends its money

Source: Internal Revenue Dept., Form 1040, 2001 (back cover).

tomatic ways—a rise in the unemployment rate may mean an immediate increase in workload for a local welfare agency or state unemployment office. Mandated public programs like these mean public agencies in these situations have little choice *but* to respond *as charged by law.* Large corporations may often, on the other hand, be entirely oblivious to changing local socioeconomic conditions and voter demands. A local Ford Motors auto plant, WalMart store, or General Electric assembly plant may function in a community regardless of changing voter preferences or local socioeconomic patterns of life. Regional recession or prosperity may or may not have much to do with a multinational firm's decision to locate in a certain region. Further, private firms can and often do run their affairs without reference to local popular pressures, legislative concerns, and special interests (though, again, some do not). When one observes government outlays of money, one sees the bulk of funds going to "mandated" programs or entitlements that give little flexibility for government choices (see Figures 5.4 and 5.5).

Complexity, Rigidity, and Diversity
of Internal Subsystems

Chapter 4 of this book outlined the five competing subsystems that operate within most public organizations and that decisively shape bureaucratic policy and programmatic outputs. Each of these internal bureaucratic subsystems reflects an incredible degree of complexity, diversity, and rigidity. Unlike the private entrepreneur, who can for the most part hire and fire his employees at will,

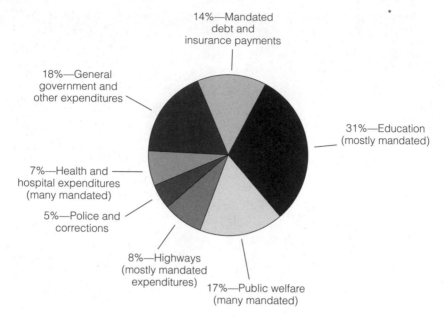

FIGURE 5.5 Where state governments spend their monies.

Source: *Public Management: OECD Country Profiles, 2002.*

government managers in professional, union, and civil service subsystems are bound by an enormous quantity of detailed rules, procedures, and laws governing recruitment, selection, and promotion of personnel. No public manager can willy-nilly get rid of the professional, union, and civil servant staff he or she inherits in an agency and hire entirely new personnel. Unlike managers of private firms, public managers have limited authority over personnel. This is also true for budgetary and most procedural routines inside government. Even political appointees, the most responsive group to elective officials, must meet basic financial disclosure rules and sometimes undergo security background checks in order to receive their appointments that, in turn, discourage and limit some applicants.

Differing Time Perspective of Each Subsystem

Whereas businesses and nonprofit organizations can and frequently do plan 5, 10, even 20 years ahead, as Chapter 4 pointed out, each of the five competing subsystems that operate inside public bureaucracies operate with their own time frame or "internal clock." The political appointees know that their time in office is limited to approximately 22 months on an average, and so they must act accordingly in selecting and effecting short-term changes. The sights of the professional careerists and civil servants, in contrast, are mostly on the long term, and their activities are paced accordingly. The contract system's personnel look toward the built-in time frame involving the duration and completion of the specific project dates they are "contracted" to complete for government.

Failure to perform their assigned tasks is a frequent source of much public criticism, as NASA discovered when its Mars Observer suddenly quit functioning.

By Auth for *The Philadelphia Inquirer,* by permission of Universal Press Syndicate.

Growth of the Contractual Subsystem Brings a Special Complexity to Public Management

As outlined in Chapter 4, the proliferation of the contractual subsystem in government over the past few decades is fundamentally changing the jobs of public managers in areas of service delivery and program implementation. More and more government managers no longer are responsible for overseeing tasks performed in-house, but rather the work of bureaucracy is increasingly performed through contracting-out for services by long chains of nonprofit and not-for-profit vendors. The "pluses" of contracting are threefold: (1) it reduces costs, (2) outside expertise can be obtained, and (3) "red tape" in government can be avoided. But there are also many problems with contracting-out public services. Contracting drastically shifts traditional tasks and responsibilities of public managers from managing line operations in-house to out-of-house demands of contract negotiations, contract management, oversight, auditing contractor performance, and so on. Complex ethical and accountability issues are furthermore involved that have little or no counterpart in private sector management practices. Specifically, there are numerous problems in:

1. Selecting good contractors
2. Setting forth clearly the tasks to be performed
3. Insuring their compliance to contracts

4. Imposing sanctions for "noncompliance"

5. Dealing with corruption resulting from government contracts where there is limited or no oversight of contractors

Overpromising, Underfunding, and Understaffing

Still another critical problem facing public bureaucracies today, unlike their private counterparts, is frequently the wide gap between what is often promised by elected officials on the campaign trail and what can reasonably and effectively be delivered by government agencies. James W. Fesler and Donald F. Kettl note, "Resources, both in money and in skilled people, are often inadequate for implementing the ambitious programs created by legislatures."[11] In their zeal for getting elected, or reelected, the incentives are high for candidates to overpromise program "payoffs" to voters; once in office they set up "underfunded" and "poorly staffed" agencies to carry out the promised activities. Then, in the next election, they blame "those damn bureaucrats" if the original programs fail or do not succeed as promised. Too-high aspirations, raised at the outset by often well-meaning politicians, combined with inadequate programmatic resources combined to make the perfect setup for bureaucratic failure. In the words of Elliott Richardson, "All too often, new legislation merely publicizes a need without creating either the means or the resources for meeting it. The readiest answer to the constituent's question, 'What have you done for me lately?' is 'I sponsored a bill.'"[12]

Constitutional Limits on Methods and Means of Service

Public agencies do not have the flexibility in targeting and responding to the needs and demands of their audiences that businesses do. Rather, they must serve the public equally, fairly, and according to standards set forth in the U.S. Constitution, such as requirements for due process and equity and observance of the laws created by Congress. The U.S. Postal Service *must by law* treat all citizens fairly and equally, but a private business, Federal Express, for example, can decide who, how, and where it offers its mail services. Fundamental constitutional values create radically different criteria for administrative action in the public sector than for that in the private sector. Concerns about equity, for instance, often, though not always, must outweigh considerations of efficiency in determining managerial choices for public agencies. For example, public schools *must* by law admit every child of school age (even illegal aliens), whereas private schools can base their selection of students on ability to pay, religion, sex, and mental or physical abilities. The comparative openness of public institutions, while making them considerably more heterogeneous and democratic, imposes special burdens, demands, and problems upon those responsible for making them operate.

And here perhaps is the most basic difference between private and public management practices, which Justice Louis Brandeis pointed out long ago, namely, that the goal of government is "not to promote efficiency but to preclude the exercise of arbitrary power."[13] This basic point had already been made by James Madison in his arguments for the checks and balances of the U.S. Constitution. In "The Federalist Papers, 51," he wrote: "The great security against a gradual concentration of several powers in the same branch, consists in giving those who administer each branch the constitutional means and personal motives to resist encroachment of the others. Ambition must be made to counteract ambition."[14]

The founders' tough-minded realism regarding human nature thus built into U.S. government—and especially into its public bureaucracy—a variety of internal and external checks on the activities of its officials that decisively constrains the myriad activities of public administrators at all levels today. The Constitution through its scatteration of authority and built-in system of intricate checks and balances (i.e., through concepts of separation of powers, federalism, due process, guarantees of individual rights, and so on) works to set up every possible institutional provision to *prevent* swift, decisive managerial action. Protection of individual liberty rather than promotion of effective management was truly the founders' "bottom line." *And* by and large it remains today as they conceived it in 1787 with an accent upon protecting individual liberty, not promoting organizational efficiency and effectiveness A remarkable success story *but* one that creates huge problems for modern public management to run government bureaucracies.

GAMESMANSHIP: THE REALITY OF MAKING
BUREAUCRATIC OUTPUTS HAPPEN

If public agencies are created to accomplish certain tasks, but if the various generic models do not explain very well *how* these tasks are accomplished, what approach does? What best explains how bureaucratic activities are really performed in government? If U.S. public bureaucracies operate within a fluid, loose-jointed environment, surrounded by continually shifting socioeconomic forces and polycentric power structures, if they are assigned multiple, often unclear missions by legislatures, if, further, they are designed with severe constitutional limits that constrain actions, and if they are made up of competing, highly rigid, internal subsystems that prevent much managerial flexibility, how are outputs achieved in practice, given all these unique features? Indeed, how can *anything* be accomplished, given all these constraints?

While there are numerous approaches to understanding this process, as Richard E. Neustadt has observed, the hard reality of bureaucratic life is that administrative actions involving implementation of programs and policies are "a great game, much like collective bargaining, in which each seeks to profit from the other's needs and fears. It is a game played catch-as-catch-can, case by case. And everybody knows the game, observers and participants alike."[15]

Viewing the operations of bureaucracy as essentially gamesmanship may make it seem that the work of government is not very serious or purposeful, but as Laurence Lynn has written, "Public management . . . is neither all substance nor all process; it is a complex blend worked out over time in concert with others with whom one shares power and interests."[16] Lynn continues, "Thus the game metaphor can have immense practical value to executives attempting to orient themselves to new issues and circumstances involving uncertainty, ambiguity, and conflict."[17]

Gamesmanship in accomplishing bureaucratic tasks runs the gamut from conceptualizing the job to be performed to actually implementing the means of accomplishing it. It begins at the time an individual or group advocates a change in the status quo and ends when the discourse ceases and the services or tasks are finished. Gamesmanship activities can involve purposeful actions by managers with all the groups and units of government *outside* its formal boundaries as well as with internal subsystems within bureaucratic entities. What differentiates gamesmanship in government is often the level at which it is played: high, middle, or low. At each of these three levels public managers strive to obtain different sets of goals using different strategies; the gamesmanship at each level, too, involves different stakes.

High-Stakes Games

Focused on bringing about big, decisive public outcomes, high-stakes games influence the basic purposes and roles of government. These outcomes bring major impacts to the community or nation as a whole. At the federal level, high-stakes questions involve the type of problems that the Department of Health and Human Services confronts over whether or not to fund abortions or the Defense Department faces in deciding whether or not to place troops in the Middle East or Latin America. At the local level, some high-stakes games are: Should a city create a voucher system for schools or a new master plan for the year 2020? Should the state government develop a comprehensive system of higher education? Such issues involve the most fundamental questions of society as well as shape the future directions of governmental programs to fulfill critical public needs.

This level of gamesmanship in government normally involves only the top-level political appointees, senior professional careerists, and civil servants. These high-ranking officials play these broad policy games well beyond the confines of their particular agencies, working and interacting with various elected officials, legislative committees, media representatives, pressure groups, and even the judiciary. High-stakes games involve the broadest possible strategies for mobilizing external support from various interest groups, jockeying with and outsmarting the opposition, gaining the backing of public opinion, and obtaining political influence and policy objectives through various agencies and branches of government. Many of the high-stakes strategies utilized at this level of "gaming" involve the broadest aspects of persuading, trading favors, arm-twisting, negotiating, and even issuing threats aimed at effecting purposeful change at the highest policy levels of government.

Middle-Stakes Games

At this level, games involve accomplishing more concrete, narrower bureau-cratic goals: Should an agency act or not act in a specific manner, spend or not spend monies in particular ways, change or not change the methods by which it renders services. At the state level, middle-stakes games translate into such choices as: Should a new welfare program be devised to aid the elderly? Or, at the municipal level, should the park authority charge tennis players for using the lighted tennis courts at night? At the federal level these games might include the question of whether more extensive background checks and longer waiting pe-riods should be required on handgun purchases.

In the words of the late Columbia University sociologist C. Wright Mills, "American policies, as discussed and voted and campaigned for, have largely to do with these middle levels and often only with them. Most political news is news and gossip about middle level issues and conflicts."[18]

Every bureaucratic subsystem inside government organizations shape these issues—from top level political appointees to low-level unionized workers—not to mention the myriad external political and institutional forces surrounding every agency, such as the media, interest groups, the courts, and legislative bod-ies. Since the stakes are normally narrower, more expertise is required to "play" effectively at this level; and the "play" is not always carried out in full public view.

A good deal happens "sub rosa" in middle-stakes games, where personnel of more technical experience debate and resolve problems before they gain wide public attention. Middle-stakes games generally require more long-term famil-iarity with the political, social, and economic environs of the public organiza-tion. Also mid-level gamesmanship generally is played out within the fine points of legislative drafting, program implementation, or over budgetary appropria-tions. There is less need to "play at" or "play to" a national audience and the larger public opinion. More managerial attention is directed at narrower ranges of bargaining, persuading, maneuvering, horse-trading, and swapping-off be-tween particular key players who can influence decisively the outcomes of these middle-stakes games.

Low-Stakes Games

These games focus on the implementation and execution of public programs and policies and thus involve almost entirely the lower echelons of bureaucracy—professional careerists, general civil servants, union workers, and contractual em-ployees. Low-stakes games concern "the workers in the vineyards of bureaucracy." This is not to say that these low-stakes games cannot create *big* headaches for top-level managers. At times the minor obstacles involved in low-stakes gamesman-ship can mushroom into controversies of major significance throughout all of government. But most of the time low-stakes games are played out of the narrow confines of bureaucratic expertise and within the corridors of an intraagency or interagency arena. They concern issues like how the specific job should get done, when, how much effort should be made, and who is in charge—in other words, issues that come up *after* the program is in place and work begins.

Within a county government, a low-stakes game might involve the question of how to get rid of a problem employee who is slowing up road maintenance or snow removal schedules. At the state level it may involve a programmatic issue of a state revenue collection agency, such as what information should be added on the state income tax form to ensure higher compliance rates. At the federal level the Agency for International Development may wrestle with a low-stakes issue such as the construction dates for a new hydro-electric project in a third-world nation that is funded and administered largely through AID sources. Such questions normally involve the operational aspects of carrying out the missions of a government agency. In low-stakes games larger policy choices and questions of program development and appropriations have already been settled. The disputes and conflicts that can and frequently do arise are usually internal problems involved with putting the program into action. Gamesmanship at this level is normally confined to a very narrow range of specialists—technical, scientific, and staff experts within the programmatic area—and these disputes are mostly, if not entirely, hidden from public view.

Participating at this game level usually requires long involvement with the particular agency and field of policy as well as a thorough understanding of the technical language and detailed operating substance of the particular program and its policies. Here, fewer issues of "pure politics" are involved (i.e., the typical broad political questions that Harold Lasswell described as "who gets what, when, how"), and more technical bureaucratic expertise or, what Samuel Beer called "techno-politics," is valued (i.e., traditional sorts of public administration concerns over matters of efficiency, economy, and effectiveness—the three E's). Given the types of issues involved in low-stakes games, it may be surprising to note that, as Francis E. Rourke has observed, "The sustained attention which bureaucrats can devote to specific problems gives them a decided advantage in framing such decisions over political officials who deal with a wide variety of problems and confront each issue of public policy only at sporadic intervals."[19]

While these are called low-stakes games, no top policy maker can safely assume they will remain lowly or out of sight. A simple problem of inadequate snow removal by a local public works department on a night of a big snowstorm could explode suddenly into a massive public controversy and "bad press" for top-level political executives. Indeed mayors have lost elections on their one "low game" mistake of *not* getting snow plows moving fast enough! In other words, low-stakes implementation questions can become high-stakes games of survival for the top echelons in public agencies. Thus, distinguishing the features between high- and low-level games can sometimes be quite difficult. They can overlap one another's turf and are not all that clear-cut in practice.

At times, also out of necessity, top-level executives must get involved in low-stakes games and, conversely, low-level bureaucrats can suddenly find themselves in the midst of high-stakes controversies. Both situations are awkward and rarely work out very well. When President Carter got involved in the specific details of scaling back western irrigation projects—or allocating tennis court times at the White House—he found himself entering a firestorm that was best left to the specific policy analysts and policy makers in this field. Conversely, when bureaucrats far down inside the bureaucracy try to establish broad policy agendas, they frequently do not have the breadth of policy vision nor the political capacity to carry them through. Many of the difficulties, for instance, that arose in establishing Zero Based Budgeting in the Carter administration or Program Planning Budgeting Systems in the Johnson administration resulted precisely from the fact that instituting both new types of budgetary systems required that fairly low-level budget specialists decide upon major policy choices. These choices frequently involved middle- or high-stakes games, well beyond the competence or capacity of these personnel to resolve.

As Laurence Lynn sees it, bureaucrats must be game players. "Game playing is the nature of their job."[20] Indeed, they may have little choice concerning which games they play, with what objectives, or even with what intensity. But deciding which game to play, if they do have a choice, may be their most critical problem. Given the limitations on time and resources, unlimited gamesmanship is impossible, so selecting what level to play at and what resources to utilize is critical for shaping bureaucratic outputs. *Internal* and *external resources* are two varieties of resources that can be summoned by bureaucrats to play these various levels of games. These resources are used to gain organizational cohesion and cooperative action for producing bureaucratic outputs.

INTERNAL RESOURCES FOR GAINING ORGANIZATIONAL COHESION AND COOPERATIVE ACTION

As already emphasized in this chapter, the constitutional framework within which every public organization must operate was not created to promote cohesion, unity, or purposeful, efficient actions on the part of government agencies. The founding fathers built into the system every conceivable device to do precisely the reverse, to promote division, disharmony, disarray, and disunity. Public organizations are constantly being pulled and tugged apart from the outside by media, pressure groups, and legislative oversight and from the inside by various competing organizational subunits and personnel subsystems. Government agencies swim with a vortex of fragmenting pressures that threaten programmatic integrity, organizational alignments, personnel allegiances, and even the survival of the basic organization itself—what Herbert Simon, Donald Smithburg, and Victor Thompson call "the struggle for organizational survival."[21] Gaining organizational unity and cooperative action and surviving at the same time are therefore a challenging, ongoing, full-time process (and preoccupation) within bureaucracy. In playing at their various levels of gamesmanship, however, bureaucrats can summon four basic types of resources from within their agencies to achieve programmatic direction, cohesiveness, and cooperation—and survival. Their ability to use these internal resources determines how the overall organization performs and what outputs a bureaucracy can or cannot achieve (which, in turn, affects their own advancement and prestige).

Legal Resources

Used to create the agency in the first place, legal resources define its missions and its powers, and provide its independence from other units. These resources are provided for in the basic enabling legislation and in amendments to these laws and statutes. Legal resources can be highly potent vehicles for exercising control over bureaucratic activities and outputs. J. Edgar Hoover provides the classic illustration of their use. He saw to it that the FBI was granted legal authority to create a highly professionalized personnel system that operated independently of the civil service system, thereby giving the director vast discretionary powers over hiring, firing, and promotion of personnel. Even though the FBI operated within the Justice Department under the attorney general, Hoover made certain that the statutes governing the FBI gave the director a considerable degree of independence from both Justice and the attorney general. He saw to it that the statutes governing the FBI's central missions excluded involvement in law enforcement fields that were difficult, such as drug enforcement and "white-collar crime," and included those that only made the bureau statistically look good, such as recovering stolen autos and capturing bank robbers. Further, Hoover worked hard throughout his nearly 50-year career as head of the FBI to ensure that administrative oversight of his agency was always delegated to "friendly" subcommittees in Congress and then did everything possible to curry the favor and support of these congressional figures. Moreover, he attained the authority to create a vast, effective intelligence-gathering and information network that kept his friends "friendly" and his enemies at bay. In short, few individuals in government have ever exceeded Hoover in his ability to craft legal resources that benefited his own agency. The concrete results gave the FBI legal autonomy, the responsiveness of professional careerists, high funding, achievable agency missions, overall organizational unity, and long-term "friendly" congressional oversight (as well as autonomy from attorneys general and even presidents). These factors made the bureau a highly cohesive, potent instrument for implementing programs and policies it decided to undertake. Though by the late 1960s and early 1970s, just prior to Hoover's death, his grasp upon effective control of the bureau's enforcement programs and policies had waned significantly.

Though nowadays possibly the most powerful legal resources possessed by public bureaucracy is its rule-making capacity. Administrative law and rule-making procedures established at the federal level by the 1946 Administrative Procedures Act give public administrators, not judges, enormous capacity to set rules and regulations that impact significantly broad economic and social spheres as well as other levels of government. Table 5.3 sums up the current size of federal regulations, their costs and impacts throughout American society as a whole during the last decade. Though as Tables 5.3 and 5.4 stress, some federal agencies promulgate more administrative rules than others, the five top producers being the Department of Transportation, Department of Treasury, Department of Interior, Environmental Protection Agency, and the Department of Commerce. However, the influence and impacts of administrative rule making

Table 5.3   Federal Regulations, Their Costs and Impacts

	2001	1-Year Change	5-Year Change (97–01)	10-Year Change (92–01)
Total regulatory costs	$854 billion	NA	NA	NA
Agency enforcement budgets (real $)	$21 billion	9.4%	19.5%	28.2%
Net *Federal Register* pages	64,431	−13.2%	0%	13%
Federal Register pages devoted to final rules	19,643	−19.8%	3.5%	23.4%
Total *Federal Register* rule documents	6,644	−4.4%	−11%	−9.3%
Federal Register final rule documents	4,132	−4.2%	−9.9%	−5%
Total rules in *Agenda*	4,509	−4%	2.3%	−8.1%
"Economically significant" rules in the pipeline	149	−5.7%	19.2%	NA
Rules impacting small business	996	−5.5%	35.9%	NA
Rules impacting state governments	608	−10.4%	−12.9%	NA
Rules impacting local governments	373	−11.2%	−15.6%	NA
Major rules finalized by agencies	72	−1.4%	20%	NA
EPA rules				
Total number of EPA rules in *Agenda*	416	−7.3%	−3.2%	NA
"Economically significant" EPA rules in *Agenda*	25	−19.3%	−34.2%	NA
Final rules issued by EPA	4	−20%	−33.3	NA
EPA rules impacting small business	185	9.7%	13.5%	NA

SOURCE: Clyde W. Crews, Jr. *Ten Thousand Commandments: An Annual Snapshot of the Federal Regulatory State* (2002), p. 3.

vary widely; for example, a single rule made by the Securities and Exchange Commission can have far-reaching economic consequences as opposed to the total of all the rules ever developed by the Peace Corps. Nonetheless, wherever they are executed, these administrative procedures must insure constitutional guarantees of due process and equal protection as well as follow provisions required in the Freedom of Information Act, The Government in Sunshine Act, and the Negotiated Rulemaking Act of 1990.

Structural Resources

These are the formal elements of bureaucracy that managers utilize to coordinate, control, and direct agency activities. The range of structural resources varies considerably from office to office, but as Jeffrey Pressman observed, at the local

Table 5.4 Federal Rules under Consideration by Agency in 2001

Agency	Total Rules	Agency	Total Rules
Dept. of Agriculture	312	Office of Management & Budget	5
Dept. of Commerce	342	Office of Personnel Management	91
Dept. of Defense	93	Peace Corps	9
Dept. of Education	8	Pension Benefit Guaranty Corporation	11
Dept. of Energy	61	Railroad Retirement Board	13
Dept. of Health & Human Services	277	Selective Service System	1
Dept. of Housing & Urban Development	89	Small Business Administration	37
		Social Security Administration	85
Dept. of the Interior	423	Tennessee Valley Authority	3
Dept. of Justice	229	Federal Acquisition Regulation	48
Dept. of Labor	141	Commodity Futures Trading Commission	30
Dept. of State	32		
Dept. of Transportation	511	Consumer Product Safety Commission	21
Dept. of the Treasury	458	Farm Credit Administration	17
Dept. of Veterans Affairs	164	Farm Credit System Insurance Corporation	1
Agency for International Development	6	Federal Communications Commission	145
Architectural and Transportation Barriers Compliance Board	5	Federal Energy Regulatory Commission	8
Commission on Civil Rights	1	Federal Housing Finance Board	12
Corporation for National & Community Service	9	Federal Maritime Commission	7
		Federal Reserve System	32
Environmental Protection Agency	416	National Credit Union Administration	22
Federal Emergency Management Agency	30		
General Services Administration	35	Nuclear Regulatory Commission	42
		Securities and Exchange Commission	80
National Aeronautics & Space Administration	17	Federal Trade Commission	13
National Archives & Records Administration	19	Federal Deposit Insurance Corporation	22
Institute of Museum Services	5	National Indian Gaming Commission	15
National Endowment for the Arts	5	Surface Transportation Board	4
Equal Employment Opportunity Service	3	Federal Mediation and Conciliation Commission	3
National Endowment for the Humanities	8	Udall Inst. for Environmental Conflict Res.	3
National Science Foundation	3	Court Services/Offender Supervision, D.C.	5
Office of Federal Housing Presidio Trust	2	Enterprise Oversight	9
Office of Government Ethics	11	Total	4,509

SOURCE: Compiled from Regulatory Information Service Center, *The Regulatory Plan and the Unified Agenda of Federal Regulations,* October 2001.

level several of the following structural resources are critical for effective managerial gamesmanship:

1. Sufficient financial and staff resources . . .

2. Programmatic jurisdiction over social programs—such as education,
    housing, development, job training, etc.

3. Administrative capacity within city government to implement programs
    within these various policy fields

4. A salary for (the official) which would enable him to spend full time on
    the job

5. Sufficient staff support . . . for policy planning, speech writing,
    intergovernmental relations . . .

6. Ready vehicles for publicity such as friendly newspapers or television
    stations

7. Internal and external groups . . . to help achieve particular goals[22]

On the federal level, Lester M. Salamon outlined and analyzed the important alternative structural resource "tools" available for implementing federal
programs in his *Beyond Privatization: The Tools of Government Action*. He writes
that there has been:

> A massive proliferation . . . in the instruments or tools the public sector
> uses to carry out its activities. These tools now include much more than
> direct service delivery by government bureaucrats. They also include
> project grants, formula grants, direct loans, loan guarantees, interest
> subsidies, social regulations, contracting-out, tax expenditures, vouchers,
> government corporations, franchises, price supports, entry restrictions, and
> many more. Indeed, a veritable technological revolution has taken place in
> the operation of the public sector in this country, characterized by a
> widespread expansion of the basic instruments used to carry out the
> public's business.[23]

Indeed, Figure 5.6 supports Salamon's contention that, comparatively speaking, only a small segment of federal government spending is in fact accomplished through the traditional "tool" of direct service delivery. As Table 5.5
underscores, however, each tool, according to Salamon has unique features, or
pros/cons, for applying it according to its visibility (or degree of transparency
to public accountability), directness (degree to which policy is carried out by
that entity alone), automaticity (degree to which tool responds to markets), and
coerciveness (degree to which tool must forcibly restrict individuals or groups).

The sufficiency or lack of such structural resources, or failure to consider alternative structural "tools," can make or break officials' abilities to carry out their
duties. As Graham Allison observes, "The fact that the fixed programs (equipment, men and routines that exist at the particular time) exhaust the range of
buttons that leaders can push is not always perceived by the leader. But in every
case it is critical for an understanding of what is actually done."[24] President

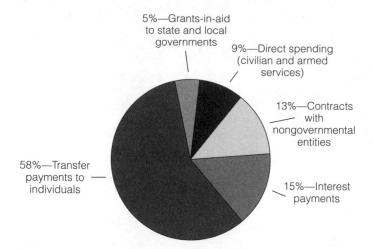

FIGURE 5.6   Major structural tools by which the federal government delivers services

Source: Donald F. Kettl et al. *Civil Service Reform: Building a Government That Works* (Washington, DC: The Brookings Institution, 1996), p. 12. Reprinted by permission of The Brookings Institution.

Carter's daring yet abortive helicopter raid to rescue American hostages in Iran failed precisely because Carter exhausted "the range of buttons" he could push to implement foreign policy in this case. The United States simply lacked the long-range mobile transports and combat personnel to carry out effectively such a complex, long-range rescue operation inside Iran. Jeffrey Pressman and Aaron Wildavsky's *Implementation* records a similar tragic tale at the local level (complete with Rube Goldberg cartoons) regarding the failure of the Economic Development Administration (EDA) to implement federal programs and public policies in Oakland, California, mostly because of the insufficiency of the basic structural resources necessary for the delivery of such community services. They point out how complexity of structures, short time frames, and an excessive number of missions defeated EDA's implementation plans in Oakland.

Process Resources

Such resources include managerial controls over hiring and firing, access to decision makers, opportunities to develop budgetary and fiscal resources (see Figure 5.7), utilization of and access to computer data and management information systems, and freedom from audit controls or direct oversight from other agencies and branches. Process resources are also essential for shaping various levels of bureaucratic games. Officials' control of process resources is critical for flexibility, discretion, and exercise of bureaucratic actions.

Francis Rourke has particularly stressed how information significantly contributes to bureaucratic power and influence: "Nothing contributes more to bureaucratic power than the ability of career officials to mold the views of other participants in the policy process. Bureaucracies are highly

Table 5.5 Common Tools of Public Action: Defining Features

Tool	Product/Activity	Vehicle	Delivery System	Degree of Visibility	Directness	Automaticity	Coerciveness
Direct government	Good or service	Direct provision	Public agency	High	High	Low	High
Social regulation	Prohibition	Rule	Public agency/regulatee	Low	Medium	Low	High
Economic regulation	Fair prices	Entry and rate controls	Regulatory commission	Low	High	Low	High
Contracting	Good or service	Contract and cash payment	Business, nonprofit organization	Medium	Medium	Medium	Medium
Grant	Good or service	Grant award/cash payment	Lower level of government, nonprofit	High	Low	Medium	Medium
Direct loan	Cash	Loan	Public agency	High	High	Low	Medium
Loan guarantee	Cash	Loan	Commercial bank	Medium	Low	Low	Medium
Insurance	Protection	Insurance policy	Public agency	Low	High	Low	Medium
Tax expenditure	Cash, incentives	Tax	Tax system	Medium	Medium	High	Low
Fees, charges	Financial penalty	Tax	Tax system	High	Medium	High	Medium
Liability law	Social protections	Tort law	Court system	Low	Low	High	Low
Government corporations	Good or service	Direct provision/loan	Quasi-public agency	High	High	Low	Medium
Vouchers	Good or service	Consumer subsidy	Public agency/consumer	High	Low	High	Medium

SOURCE: *The Tools of Government* by Lester M. Salaman, copyright ©2002 by Lester M. Salaman. Used by permission of Oxford University Press, p. 21. As well as data in Chapter 1, pp. 1–47.

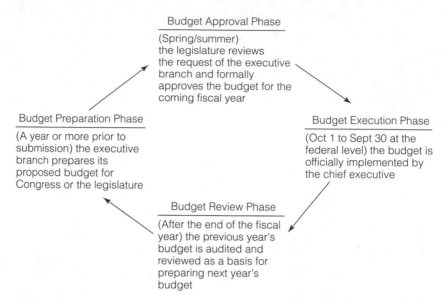

Budget Approval Phase

(Spring/summer)
the legislature reviews
the request of the executive
branch and formally
approves the budget for the
coming fiscal year

Budget Preparation Phase

(A year or more prior to
submission) the executive
branch prepares its
proposed budget for
Congress or the legislature

Budget Execution Phase

(Oct 1 to Sept 30 at the
federal level) the budget is
officially implemented by
the chief executive

Budget Review Phase

(After the end of the fiscal
year) the previous year's
budget is audited and
reviewed as a basis for
preparing next year's
budget

FIGURE 5.7   Budgets are an especially potent process resource and annually involve four basic continuous phases.

organized information and advisory processes. The data they analyze and transmit cannot help but influence the way elected officials perceive political issues and events. Herbert Simon has emphasized the importance of being able to shape the value or factual premises of decision makers as a means of insuring control over decisions themselves, and it is precisely in this way that bureaucratic information and advice commonly functions in the policy process."[25]

Rourke gives two prominent examples of how such elements contribute mightily to what happens in bureaucracy: George Kennan's post–World War II advisory role heading the policy planning unit at the State Department and his access to the ears of the secretary of state, the president, and the wider foreign affairs community decisively fashioned fundamental U.S. cold war programs and policies. Henry Kissinger likewise significantly shaped U.S. Vietnam and China policies through his prominent National Security Council advisory role. Access to top decision makers, namely the president, as well as to astute minds that marshaled and controlled foreign policy information and determined where and when decision makers got the information, was instrumental to both Kennan's and Kissinger's success stories. At the state and local levels, officials' advisory roles also serve as potent sources of bureaucratic power. Sometimes this is offered quietly in so-called back channels and other times it is offered up front in official briefing reports. By whatever manner, such process resources are critical to shaping outputs within every governmental jurisdiction.

Personal Resources

Individual qualities are equally important in shaping bureaucratic outputs, or what Yale's eminent political scientist Robert Dahl refers to as the individual attributes "to increase or combine resources through personal skills and abilities."[26] In essence, it is the person's own leadership capacity to combine and manipulate the resources of his or her bureaucratic office to achieve purposeful actions. As Bollens and Ries have noted, such personal leadership capabilities vary widely in city managers operating at the local level: "Depending upon their personality, individual managers will make more or less use of the resources attached to the position. Invariably managers are asked to present their views before civil and private organizations, that is, they are provided with many platforms for educating the public to municipal problems and can take the initiative in proposing programs for coping with them. A manager's sense of timing and tact will determine the extent to which he builds coalitions in support of his politics which, in turn, influence council's response to them."[27]

On the federal level, Gerald Garvey, in his recent "inside account" of workings of the Federal Energy Regulatory Commission (FERC) in *Facing Bureaucracy,* gives a good portrait of Bill McDonald, whom he calls a "remarkable civil servant" because of his unique leadership capacities that brought about innovative changes within FERC.

> McDonald was a master at accumulating and manipulating slack. The knowledge, skills, and loyalty of his inner entourage of staff subordinates represented slack in the FERC organization. So in a sense did McDonald's network of outside contractors, informants, and favor traders throughout the larger effective bureaucracy. McDonald considered these contacts and reserve resources as assets to be drawn upon when opportunities arose. . . .
>
> McDonald's aggressiveness and "field sense" were precisely the traits that Americans prize in business leaders, military tacticians, even professional athletes. He played a game of inches, as any civil servant must, but he played it aggressively, opportunistically and as close to the limits as he could . . . pushing opportunistically through apertures of change when they presented themselves.[28]

Ronald Loveridge[29] and others have classified four types of local-level leadership capacities and skills in bureaucracy at the grass roots: (1) *community leaders* who take the broadest, most creative view of their bureaucratic responsibilities and see themselves not merely as officials within government but as "doers," "change agents," and "activists" within the overall context of the community; (2) *chief executives* who confine their talents to executing in-house programs and policies and who prefer to work actively "behind the scenes" rather than up front in achieving actions within government agencies; (3) *administrative innovators,* managerial types found in local bureaucracies, who apply their administrative skills to technical and narrow roles in shaping the program outputs of an agency, especially in ways that improve its basic efficiency, effectiveness, and economy; and (4) *administrative caretakers* who exercise hardly *any* personal leadership capabilities at all, deferring to others' leadership, seeing their roles as simply to keep the doors of an agency open and the routines of government moving along, but little else.

Much of the exercise of personal leadership resources of course depends upon a manager's latitude of discretion within an agency. As Chapter 4 pointed out, the mix of competing internal subsystems within any given agency determines the scope, quality, and size of governmental outputs. This mix of subsystems also invariably determines the type of personal resources required by any manager to induce cooperation and cohesive direction within an agency. A bureaucracy dominated by political appointees requires personal leadership resources involving party loyalties, political influence, patronage, and even a large amount of salesmanship and charisma. Professional careerists respect, by contrast, personal leadership built upon expertise, education, experience within the agency, and "the right schools and assignments," plus a long-term "corporate identity" with the central missions, values, and perspectives of the dominant professional elite within the agency. General civil servants are a more heterogeneous group of individuals, who in part respond to the qualities professionals such as long-term subject-matter expertise and experience but also are driven by more complex sociopolitical-bureaucratic-economic motives of task, salary, grade, and position. Union and contractual subsystems demand bureaucratic managers with still different leadership traits and skills, namely, those who are able to negotiate well within business, nonprofit settings, persuade effectively often in lawyerlike ways, and who can drive hard bargains in contract negotiations and then see to it that these contracts are fulfilled in the best interests of their agencies.

While the necessary leadership skills therefore vary immensely depending on the mix of agency subsystems and the capabilities of individual managers, a good sense of timing as well as initiative, drive, creativity, tact, honesty, general good sense, level of trust by others, and specific knowledge of the job area are all critical personal resources at every level of bureaucracy (refer to Table 5.6). These attributes make things operate, *even at the very lowest levels.* As Kenneth C. Davis points out about police officers on the beat:

> The police are constantly confronted with problems of fairness to individuals and such problems are often intertwined with problems of policy. When should they not make an arrest that can properly be made? When should they stop and frisk? When should they say, break it up?
>
> When should they make deals with known criminals as the addict informers? What minor disputes should they mediate or adjudicate? These are tough questions which those on the lowest rungs of a police organization are asked to resolve everyday. No rule book holds the answers for each specific case. The individual patrolman must normally rely upon his own personal resources—i.e., experience, good judgment, common sense, etc.—for making such "calls."[30]

Books that have appeared underscore Davis's argument that significant choices take place at lower levels of public organization which are critical for enhancing or retarding overall agency effectiveness. John W. Gardner, after a lifetime of

Table 5.6 As One Moves up the Organizational Hierarchy Different Types of Leadership Skills Become Necessary

Role/Scope	Leading Change	Leading People	Managing for Results	Building Coalitions, Communications	Professional and Personal Growth	Customer Service
All employees including team leaders	Creativity and innovation Flexibility Resilience Adaptability	Conflict management Cultural awareness Integrity/honesty Teamwork Commitment to people	Accountability Decisiveness Problem solving Bias for action Judgement Technical skills	Interpersonal skills Communication	Willingness to learn Continuous learning Personal development	Commitment to veterans and families Responsive to veterans
First-Line Managers/Coaches	Encourages innovation Creative thinking Implements change	Empowers others Team building Develops people	Risk management Technical credibility Information-based management	Influencing negotiating Partnering	Promotes learning Coaches employees	Recognizes excellent customer service
Mid-Level Managers (e.g., Division Chiefs)	Strategic thinking Establishes direction	Develops managers/coaches	Implementing organizational performance goals	Networking	Provides opportunities for learning	Empowers others to take action
Directors/Executives	External awareness Vision Benchmarking	Modeling organization values	Goal setting Monitoring organizational performance	Political awareness	Creative learning environment	Breaks down barriers to good service Establishes customer-oriented culture

SOURCE: Ray Blunt, *Organizations Growing Leaders: Best Practices and Principles in the Public Service* (Arlington, VA: The Pricewaterhouse Cooper Endowment, December 2001), pp. 44–45.

both study and practice of public service leadership, makes that very point in the beginning of his book, *On Leadership.*

> Most leadership today is an attempt to accomplish purposes through (or in spite of) large, intricately organized systems. There is no possibility that centralized authority can call all the shots in such systems whether the system is a corporation or a nation. Individuals in all segments and at all levels must be prepared to exercise leaderlike initiative and responsibility, using their local knowledge to solve problems at their level. Vitality at middle and lower levels of leadership can produce *greater vitality in the higher levels of leadership.*[31] (Author's italics)

EXTERNAL SUPPORT FOR BUREAUCRATIC ACTION:
THE "WINDOWS OF OPPORTUNITY"

Important concepts that administrative theorists developed over many years focus on the internal sources for cooperation and cohesion within organizations. According to Chester Barnard's notion of "the economy of incentives,"[32] for example, much of the executive's functional role involves juggling and calculating many of the aforementioned internal resources of an organization in order to achieve purposeful actions. Herbert Simon added the useful concept of "the zone of indifference"[33] as an equally important aspect to achieving organizational goals; individual members of any organization willingly accept authority within various degrees of personal compliance. According to Simon, it is within these ranges of indifference that employees are willing to go along with directives for achieving the overall administrative missions of an agency.

These *internal* administrative attributes may be important and certainly cannot be overlooked. Yet seasoned bureaucrats know that something else is even more critical and necessary for achieving programmatic and policy outputs. Sometimes they refer to it as "windows of opportunity" or the chance "to move" on an issue, policy, or program that for a long time had remained "on the back burner." Machiavelli called it *fortuna,* for others it is simply "good luck." By whatever name, opportunities to take or not to take action are an essential ingredient—the other half of bureaucratic gamesmanship, one might say—of making things happen and of accomplishing purposeful activity.

Therefore, in playing bureaucratic gamesmanship, much of bureaucrats' time is spent looking around at the *external bureaucratic landscape:* judging other players and the politics of the situation; finding out where potential outside sources of power lie; and discovering how to gain access to these power sources and how to avoid the pitfalls and traps of "enemy players." Karl von Clausewitz, the great nineteenth-century German military strategist, emphasized that in warfare "the situation is everything." In other words, where the soldier finds himself—the geography, terrain, climate, population, deployment of both enemy and friendly forces—fundamentally determines the outcome of every battle.

Consequently, in the tradition of Clausewitz, modern U.S. Army officers who are destined to command battalions, regiments, divisions, and groups are sent to the U.S. Army Command and General Staff College at Fort Leavenworth, Kansas, for 6 months of intensive schooling directed primarily at case-by-case analyses of battlefield situations and strategies: Here future military leaders learn basic tactics through war games, computer simulations, and role-playing exercises. They study how to quickly analyze "the lay of the land" and how to take the best defensive position and to devise offensive strategies and strikes against the enemy. Knowing how to exploit the enemy's weak points and how to strengthen one's own position in the field under stressful, trying, and constantly shifting battlefield conditions in which information, logistical supplies, and time for analysis are frequently inadequate are the sort of practical skills acquired by officers in these war games. Essentially, fake battles are used to sharpen military leadership skills for the real battle. Top-flight business, medical, and law schools put their students through many of the same rigors of case-method analysis. They encourage students to analyze concrete situations in business, medicine, and law in order to foster their ability to grasp quickly the essentials of a situation and then to take action on it in the boardroom, clinic, or courtroom.

The distinguished administrative scholar John Gaus argued in one of his important books, *Reflections on Public Administration,* that public administrators as well should analyze "the ecological factors" in the administrative landscape—the people, place, physical and social technology, wishes of the population, ideas of the times, catastrophes of the moment, and personalities of the "players"—in order to properly undertake any effective bureaucratic activity. In his words, these ecological factors decisively determine "the ebb and flow of the functions of government."[34]

Louis Brownlow, one of the most outstanding city managers ever, certainly discovered this to be true in the field of local government. In his autobiography, *A Passion for Anonymity,*[35] he recounts how in the first community he managed, Petersburg, Virginia, his work had wide popular support. He consequently was able to accomplish many new capital works projects and to initiate many social programs for the city. This situation was a "bureaucrat's dream come true" (Brownlow was given not only a big salary but also a handsome house to live in as part of his "fringes"). His next managerial post was Knoxville, Tennessee, at a time when the city was being torn apart by competing political factions. As the new city manager, Brownlow found himself in the midst of political turmoil from the moment he stepped inside the city limits. Several rival courthouse factions made his every action a subject of heated political controversy. It was a no-win situation, and eventually it broke Brownlow's health. Under the circumstances he was soon forced to resign and move elsewhere.

Astute bureaucrats, therefore, size up situational possibilities and impossibilities quickly and use their evaluations as the basis for their actions. They learn when to move on projects and when not to move, depending on other events and other players in the bureaucratic game. Indeed, bureaucrats' very survival, as Brownlow's case in Knoxville illustrated, turns on how well or poorly they recognize and act upon the unique elements and configurations of any social, political, economic, or organizational landscape. Much of their time, therefore, is spent scouting the landscape. Learning who's who and what's what is essential to building support for an agency's administrative programs and missions. Bureaucrats learn how and when to tap the various "input factors" to public organizations, which were discussed in detail in Chapter 3. In other words, successful bureaucrats know that finding out and then working with the socio-economic, political, and institutional factors that surround all public officials and their organizations are fundamental to effective administrative action. Sometimes this knowledge is acquired in a few weeks or months. Sometimes it takes many years and is a continuous process of learning and relearning about the fluctuating environments within which bureaucracies swim. For all successful bureaucrats it is a long-term inductive course of study.

However this knowledge is acquired, it is critical for the success of bureaucratic work anywhere. Alan Greenspan, head of the Federal Reserve Board, spent a lifetime learning to read the economic and political "pulse rates" of the environment surrounding the Fed—the people, personalities, institutions, and critical economic forces that shape the board's missions and priorities. Consequently, he is generally credited today with being a highly successful board chairman. By contrast, President Jimmy Carter, although well intentioned and fired by lofty aims for his presidency, placed in top policy-making slots in the White House individuals who were largely inexperienced in the ways of Washington. These individuals did not have the background that would have enabled them to read either the highly complex Washington scene or the various players with whom the president had to work in building political bases of support. More than anything, Carter's loyalty to his own staff tended to isolate his administration from the significant political connections so essential for presidential leadership.

Furthermore, knowing the lay of the land helps any official not only to achieve purposeful actions but also to realize what *not* to do. In other words, recognizing fully the nature of the external situation is essential to understanding where the political land mines or roadblocks are located. Recognizing these limitations in any given situation aids the bureaucrat to set priorities for the best utilization of limited time and energy. Time and energy are always in short supply, and therefore understanding what *not* to do or what is simply impossible to achieve may well be as necessary to the accomplishment of purposeful actions as knowing what to do. Learning when to retreat can help avoid numerous disasters as well as personal frustration, wasted effort, and wasted lives, either on the battlefield or inside bureaucracy.

John W. Kingdon, a political scientist at the University of Michigan, has perhaps done the most serious scholarly work on how and why windows for policy action open or close in his book *Agendas, Alternatives, and Public Policies*. As the rough schema of Kingdon's model, shown in Figure 5.8, indicates, Kingdon envisions twin process streams continually constituting "alternatives" generated incrementally by "hidden participants" such as consultants, civil servants, and so on, and "agendas" generated by visible participants often "through a flurry of

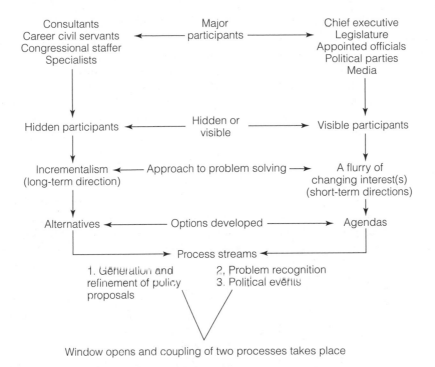

FIGURE 5.8   John W. Kingdon's model

Source: Adapted from John W. Kingdon, *Agendas, Alternatives, and Public Policies* (New York: HarperCollins, 1984).

changing interests" from the media, legislature, and others. When three things occur: (1) generation and refinement of policy proposals, (2) problem recognition, and (3) political events, windows can open and a "coupling" of the two process streams can take place. But, as Kingdon notes:

> Sometimes, windows open quite predictably. Legislation comes up for renewal on schedule, for instance, creating opportunities to change, expand, or abolish certain programs. At other times, windows open quite unpredictably, as when an airliner crashes or a fluky election produces an unexpected turnover in key decision makers. Predictable or unpredictable, open windows are small and scarce. Opportunities come, but they also pass.[36]

No one has yet invented the precise calipers that would accurately gauge the possibilities of any given situation of windows opening or closing. As Kingdon suggests, they may be predictable but also unpredictable. Yet, seasoned bureaucrats know by experience and intuition when windows of opportunity appear that enable them to take action within the shifting political landscape. These windows determine the scope, degree, and intensity of what they do or cannot do in performing agency missions. These windows come in various shapes and sizes and may be classified as follows.

Broad Windows for Action

Public agencies and their officials in small, homogeneous cities or large national organizations that operate during periods of strong national consensus involving their basic missions (as occurs during World War II or protracted national emergencies like the 9/11 terrorist attack) have comparatively broad windows for bureaucratic action. Windows of this type are created by fundamental long-term socioeconomic-political commitments by the electorate and by groups within the society that support the agency and its actions. Officials of a small-town police force or fire department often operate at their own discretion principally because of the backing of a stable, homogeneous council and of solid community support. Similarly, some of the great innovative bureaucratic achievements on the national level have been accomplished because of just such firm, deep, and broad windows for action. Admiral Hyman Rickover, who fathered the U.S. underwater atomic navy in the 1950s, and James Webb, who organized and headed NASA in the 1960s, when the United States landed men on the moon, accomplished their programmatic mission largely because of long-term popular acclaim and solid congressional–White House backing. The Manhattan Project, which built the first atomic bomb during World War II, was also successful largely because of this broad window for bureaucratic action, which gave it the funding, secrecy, and leadership necessary for rapid development. Most rapid, innovative, and highly productive actions in the public sector are based upon such instances of broad national support.

At the grass roots, enthusiastic, homogeneous backing from a community, as Brownlow did in Petersburg, Virginia, offers enormously broad windows of opportunity. Aaron Wildavsky's *Leadership in a Small Town* reports that city manager Richard Dunn found himself in just such a situation in Oberlin, Ohio.[37] The community was fairly small and homogeneous and gave strong backing across the board to Dunn, its full-time local administrator. As a result, Dunn achieved a great deal, according to Wildavsky, and had broad involvement with most local decisions as well as with the public policy-making and bureaucratic outputs across the spectrum of community affairs. Much of this success was caused by his expertise in municipal matters, which filled a void in which no one else had as much time to deal with or was quite as well informed.

In such situations where broad support exists, wide windows of opportunity frequently provide a great deal of discretion to an agency and its officials in conceptualizing, formulating, and implementing programs. Further, an agency operating under these conditions finds it can hire able professionals to staff and implement programs, devise complex, efficient service-delivery systems, and even perhaps extend and broaden services and overall mandates for public actions. General Eisenhower, for instance, was given staggering amounts of discretionary powers and logistical support for the World War II D-Day landings, as was General MacArthur for his island-hopping campaigns in the Far East and postwar occupation of Japan. Eisenhower and MacArthur, on the national level, and Brownlow and Dunn, on the local level, though, were operating under unusual and rare conditions that maximized the breadth of windows for bureaucratic action.

Shallow, Temporary Windows

By contrast, many agencies and bureaucrats have comparatively shallow, temporary windows for action. That is, they may have broad popular and interest group appeal, or they may have opportunities that are fleeting. Frequently national, state, or local catastrophes bring about such opportunities—or necessities—for fast bureaucratic actions. A classic case involves the 1942 Coconut Grove fire in Boston, in which 490 people died, largely because the club's fire doors opened inward rather than outward. This tragedy caused outrage and immediate legislative reaction across the country. It brought about quick but very fundamental changes in fire codes and building requirements. Thus a tragedy that results in mass popular reaction gives bureaucrats broad but temporary windows for bureaucratic action and enables them to move on matters that may have been blocked for many years. Mothers Against Drunk Drivers (MADD) campaigns to rid highways of drunk drivers and save thousands of lives (refer to Figures 5.9 and 5.10); the Three Mile Island nuclear mishap; the space shuttle *Challenger* explosion; the Hurricane Andrew devastation of South Florida; "the MOVE" disaster in Philadelphia; and the

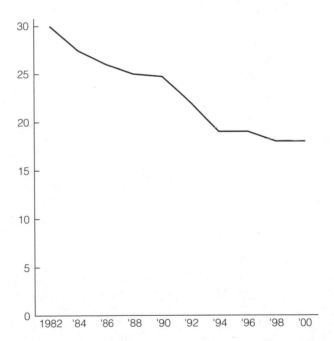

Short-term local MADD political campaigns to strengthen laws against drunk drivers influenced the decline of national fatality rates of traffic deaths.

FIGURE 5.9 Percentage of legally drunk drivers involved in fatal traffic accidents nationwide

Sources: National Highway Traffic Safety Administration; *New York Times,* May 22, 1994, p. 1. Reprinted by permission of The New York Times Agency. Updated from the Fatality Analysis Reporting System, National Traffic Highway Safety Administration (June 14, 2002).

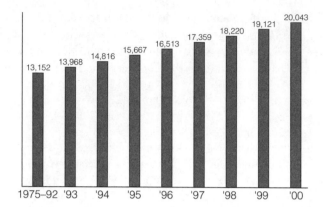

FIGURE 5.10 Cumulative estimated number of lives saved by minimum drinking age laws, 1975–2000

Source: National Center for Statistics and Analysis, NRD-31, *Traffic Safety Facts* (2000), p. 4.

massive 2002 Enron, Worldcom, and other corporate fraud cases brought similar short-term, intense popular demands for major bureaucratic responses to serious public problems and catastrophes. Creating limited delivery systems, temporary personnel, and short-term coping strategies are the norm for bureaucrats and their organizations in dealing with such issues. In these cases bureaucrats operate with the assumption that the window for action may close at any time, and so they must act fast.

In recent years, fiscal crises, particularly at the local level, have precipitated "crisis" situations that public managers have found challenging to cope with; but some have found in these situations new opportunities for taking actions that improve the overall organizational capabilities. Robert B. Denhardt, for example, in the book *The Pursuit of Significance,* describes what happened when Jan Perkins became city manager of Morgan Hill, California (pop. 25,000). Her finance officer resigned, and a $1.8 million deficit was suddenly discovered that no one knew of before:

> In the midst of this political chaos, Perkins was responsible for managing the city staff efficiently and responsibly. She began listening. A series of budget workshops were conducted in the community, providing Perkins with a chance to let people know what was happening with the city budget and to hear citizens' suggestions for solving the budget crisis. Internally, she talked with lots of people, asking them about the strengths and weaknesses of the city government and their concerns about their own work. She followed a fairly systematic game plan, going to their work areas, talking in fire stations, riding with police officers. The key question she asked was, "If you were city manager for a day, what would you do?"
>
> Listening to city employees provided helpful information to the new manager, but it also provided her an opportunity to model an important

behavior for supervisors and others—listening. . . . Whereas previously there had been no theme or continuity in the work of the city, Perkins began offering a common language and a common direction.[38]

Firm, Narrow, Long-Term Windows

Much more commonly, a federal, state, or local level of government has one sizable block of supporters that closely scrutinizes that bureaucracy and takes intense interest in its general affairs. Examples of such narrow, strong, continuous clientele backing include farmers' support of Agriculture Department programs; veterans and the Veterans Affairs Department; unions and the Labor Department; educators and the Education Department. These powerful, well-placed, and well-connected groups carefully watch over and cultivate their "captured" units of government. They carefully scrutinize the key political appointments (as was pointed out in Chapters 3 and 4, many of the appointees may in fact come from such pressure groups); secure favorable congressional programmatic and fiscal support (their representatives usually sit on the key legislative oversight subcommittees); gain favorable media and popular backing; and run interference on its behalf against external enemies and threats from other agencies or institutions. When an occasional critic does appear from within the ranks of "the protected agency," these support groups quickly see to it that the offending bureaucrat is removed or silenced. Robert Nimmo, who served in the early 1980s as President Reagan's first head of the Veterans Administration and who began to modestly criticize many of the VA's excessive expenditures, was quickly sent packing to his home in California after 1 year in office mostly because of various veterans group pressures (though, of course, the official reasons for his dismissal were quite different).

Defense contractors play similar roles in silencing DoD whistle-blowers within the ranks of the civil service. Such whistle-blowers learn quickly that special interests allied to the departments can play very hard ball and exercise enormous clout when they perceive the slightest threat to the status quo. After all, millions, indeed billions, of dollars may be jeopardized by such critics. So woe to the individual bureaucrat who runs afoul of such groups and who fails to nurture their support and blessings. On the other hand, with their backing, officials can often accomplish a wide range of bureaucratic activities that might include expanding their programmatic responsibilities; bringing on more and better-trained personnel to run those programs; inventing and implementing new effective service delivery systems; and possibly achieving a very high success rate of "favorable" customer support and clientele satisfaction for services rendered by the agency. As Table 5.7 points out, the growth of environmental groups in the 1980s ("green groups") was critical in increasing support for public environmental programs. In 1970, the Environmental Protection Agency (EPA) employed 4,000 people with a $1.3 billion budget. Today, the EPA has 18,000 employees with a $7 billion budget, thanks largely to a growing, well-placed cluster of environmental organization interest-group support.

**Table 5.7 Growth of America's Green Groups—
Increased Support for EPA**

	MEMBERSHIP (IN THOUSANDS)		
Organizational Growth	**1980**	**1990**	**2001**
Environmental Defense Fund	35	200	300
Greenpeace USA	250	2,500	250
National Audubon Society	412	578	550
Nature Conservancy	99	578	1 million
Natural Resources Defense Council	29	138	500
Sierra Club	181	622	700
Wilderness Society	50	404	200

SOURCE: Organizations, Web sites.

At the state and local levels, a stable clientele group such as the local business community as represented by the Chamber of Commerce, can frequently generate similar long-term, narrow special-interest backing for a state economic development corporation or a municipal downtown urban renewal project. Such firm, powerful pressure groups can often give managers wide latitude for undertaking creative community-wide actions. L. P. Cookingham, the highly successful city manager of Kansas City for 19 years, was installed by a reform group of business leaders who had ousted the old political machine. These business reformers retained control of city government for a number of years and kept Cookingham in office, thereby giving him enormous latitude for action and influence over most aspects of community life. His work there is something of a classic case history of how solid, enduring support form a sizable, well-placed faction in the community can offer a community-level bureaucrat widespread influence and programmatic discretion. Yet such long-term stability can shift suddenly as in the case of reforming New York City public schools. For decades teachers' unions blocked meaningful change by the mayor. Though in the wake of 9/11, the election of a new mayor, Michael Bloomberg, combined with support from New York City business and minority communities, mayoral control of NYC public schools was granted by the state legislature on June 30, 2002.

Tightly Closed Windows

On the other hand, bureaucrats know that some games are impossible to play because of widespread public opposition or narrow, intense interest group pressure that will block any initiatives in a policy or program area. Previous chapters have discussed such examples as the National Rifle Association's continuous efforts to keep the Bureau of Alcohol, Tobacco, and Firearms poorly staffed and financed and with limited oversight roles (indeed, in 1981 the NRA nearly shut down ATF entirely). Western ranchers play the same role vis-à-vis the Bureau of Land Management and antiabortion groups vis-à-vis the Department of Health and Human Services' abortion funding programs. Various anti-regulatory

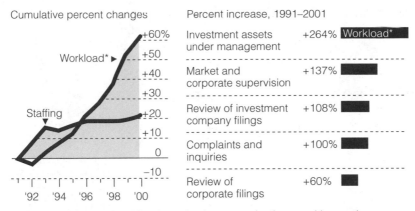

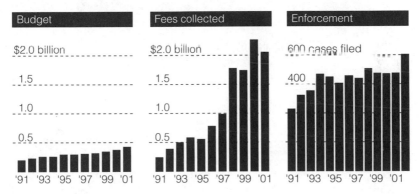

Years shown are fiscal years ending September 30.

FIGURE 5.11 SEC workload vs. resources 1991–2001

Source: General Accounting Office.

transportation interests actually terminated the Interstate Commerce Commission in the mid-1990s. Mexican-American groups in Congress and elsewhere largely inhibited legislative efforts to reform immigration laws and strengthen the Immigration and Naturalization Service's ability to cope with the flood of illegal aliens. During the 1990s, the SEC made repeated requests to increase its staff and budget for enforcement which was blocked by Congress. In December 1995, Congress even overrode a president veto of security legislation reform, thus making it harder for stockholders to file and win class action lawsuits proposed to the SEC against corrupt company officials. As Figure 5.11 points out while its workload rapidly increased sixty percent from 1991–2001, the SEC's staff resources remained roughly unchanged 1993–2001 in turn crippling its regulatory oversight capacity. At the local levels where tax limitation laws have been enacted, state, city, and county officials must grapple "just to survive," given public hostility toward government. In such agencies bureaucrats are often in a state of shellshock from protracted battles with their enemies, and must keep their heads down and learn to conduct holding actions or even strategic retreats because of the overwhelming strength, size, and intensity of their opponents. In such agencies morale is low, and ranks may have been thinned because of a steady string of defeats and defections. These are often unpleasant places in which to work, since little usually is accomplished, beyond the most mundane bureaucratic work routines. Though change can and does suddenly occur. Until 1964, limited scientific studies plus a tough tobacco lobby prevented government regulation of cigarettes. However, in January 1964, a U.S. Surgeon General's Committee Report linked smoking to health risks, and in July 1965, Congress enacted the Federal Cigarette and Labeling Act which began increasing regulation over the next three decades significantly that curbed cigarette consumption.

Limited Openings in the Windows

In some situations public agencies operate within an even split between opponents and allies. Such a standoff can sharply curtail agency actions and allow bureaucrats only narrow latitudes for taking new initiatives. If the division between the two groups is somewhat unstable, support for or opposition to the public organization can swing back and forth at any moment, and so agency directors must be very careful not to alienate either party, since either could one day gain the upper hand. The bureaucrats confronting these situations must constantly balance two contending interests, ensuring that neither is slighted or overlooked in terms of goods, services, policies, and other organizational outputs rendered to these groups by the agency. Indeed, given their limited room to maneuver, bureaucrats frequently retreat to mundane, perfunctory tasks that will not alienate either party and upset the balance of forces surrounding the agency.

Many county and city bureaucracies work with just such evenly divided interests. They may be called the "uptown" and "downtown" gangs or the "east" and "west" groups. Handling such contending forces can be a ticklish problem for local bureaucrats, giving them only limited leeway for action, as Frank Sherwood's classic administrative case study, "A City Manager Tries to Fire His Police Chief,"[39] illustrates. A small suburb of Los Angeles was divided roughly between "the Lemon Street gang" (long-time community residents) and newcomers (Hispanics, Catholics, and commuters to the center city). As Sherwood recounts, a controversy developed between the city manager and his newly appointed police chief, pitting one faction of the community against the other. The conflict soon became intense, protracted, and bitter, largely because both the manager and the chief mishandled matters. A stalemate ensued, and city government activities virtually ground to a halt until the chief was forced to resign at considerable cost and pain to everyone involved.

John Curry, a long-time city manager of Cambridge, Massachusetts, on the other hand, was a master at working out relations between Cambridge 39 (the blue collar, working-class section) and Cambridge 38 (the professional university crowd). He himself came from the Irish working-class background of Cambridge 39 yet also held a Harvard Ph.D. in linguistic philology, which placed him in good standing with Cambridge 38. He worked hard to avoid antagonizing either group, keeping the lines of communication open and giving both groups the municipal services they wanted—safe streets, good snow removal, and decent parking for the Cambridge 38 crowd and public employment, welfare, and recreation and the like for Cambridge 39. He balanced quietly, neatly, and conveniently the needs of each community group.

At the federal or state level some agencies also find themselves surrounded by evenly divided blocks of allies and opponents, which often gives them only marginal room for bureaucratic maneuver. As with a divided situation arising at the local level, the same situation at higher levels can lead to bureaucratic indecision or limited activity in favor of either competing party. The story of U.S. foreign policy efforts concerning the Shah of Iran as recounted by Scott Armstrong[40] reflects even splits between backers and opponents of the shah inside the Carter administration. Both groups repeatedly pressed opposing sides of the policy debate with equal intensity. The protracted policy struggles within the foreign affairs community over U.S. responsibilities in regard to the shah resulted in indecisiveness over what actions to take to protect U.S. national interests in the region, ultimately leading to the shah's downfall and to reduced U.S. power in the Middle East.

Unpredictable, Constantly Opening and Closing Windows

Many public bureaucracies in large, urban settings or in industrial states or at the national level work within a context of multiple shifting factions where numerous social, economic, and political groups compete for power and influence over their activities. These pluralistic, polycentric, political situations have been described and analyzed carefully by various community power studies. Noted political science scholars such as Wallace Sayre and Herbert Kaufman in their book *Governing New York City* observe that "no single ruling elite dominates the political and government system of New York City. . . . New York's huge and diverse system of government and politics is a loose-knit and multicentered network in which decisions are reached by ceaseless bargaining and fluctuating alliances among major categories of participants in each center and in which the centers are partially but strikingly isolated from one another."[41] At the Federal Level, Don Kettl makes much the same point about the operations of the Federal Reserve System. As he notes (see Figure 5.12), the rise of interest rates activated a flurry of "oversight interest" in the Fed's activities by Congress, as indicated in the number of bills introduced in Congress to oversee the Fed's actions. The uncertain changing economy thus decidely affects the Fed's freedom of action.

Hugh Heclo made much the same point recently regarding the diversity, openness, and instability of pluralistic interests operating at the national level, which he termed "issues networks." As Heclo writes, "Unfortunately, our standard conceptions of power and control are not very well suited to the loose-jointed play of influence that is emerging in political administration. We tend to

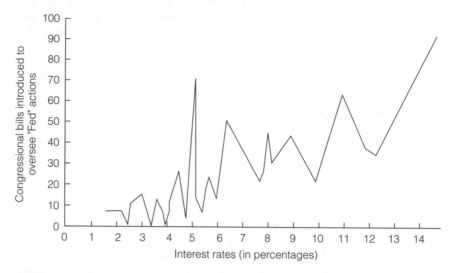

FIGURE 5.12   Interest rates compared to bills introduced in Congress as an indicator of intensity of oversight of federal reserve activities

Source: Adapted from Donald D. Kettl, *Leadership at the Fed* (New Haven, CT: Yale University Press, 1986), p. 164. Reprinted by permission.

look for one group exerting dominance over another, for subgovernments that are strongly insulated from other outside forces in the environment, for policies that get 'produced' by a few 'makers.' "[42]

Rather, as Heclo points out, "Looking for the few who are powerful, we tend to overlook the many webs, or what I will call 'issues networks.' "[43] These issues networks are open, shifting groups with numerous, temporary participants who move in and out of their circles, getting involved for a time and then "dropping out" of policy activities. They may suddenly "drop in" again on the policy-making processes quite unexpectedly. All this instability of surrounding interests tends to "complexify" matters for bureaucrats and their organizations. As Heclo points up, issues networks tend to complicate issues rather than simplify them: The spawning of zealots who are advocates of narrow programmatic and policy perspectives rather than of broad-minded compromise and conciliation produces further debate and argumentation.

Such diversity of opinion, shifting influence, and instability of people, policies, and their priorities create an extremely volatile, demanding situation within which public organizations formulate and implement their activities. Bureaucracy and bureaucrats caught in these turbulent, unpredictable environments must tread very cautiously, dealing with problems carefully, issue by issue, group by group. They must be able to put together coalitions on an ad hoc basis and be willing to compromise and entirely shift their organizational positions and activities quickly, even in the opposite direction, as new conditions arise. Managers of agencies operating under this uncertainty must be careful not to move ahead too quickly or to be too slow in adjusting to volatile shifting public policies and public opinion. Tact and sure-footedness are critical. Knowing

Table 5.8 Key Factors Maximizing or Minimizing Bureaucratic Output

Factors That Influence Bureaucratic Outputs	Maximize Outputs	Minimize Outputs
Specific assigned tasks for agency	Well-defined and within scope and competence of staff	Poorly defined and outside scope and competence of staff
Gamesmanship abilities	Managers committed, well-trained, experienced, and capable of selecting and playing games at *correct* levels	Managers untrained, uncommitted, inexperienced, and unable to select game level for play
Internal resources	Adequate for fulfilling assigned tasks	Inadequate for needs or demands on agency
External conditions	Optimal conditions for discretion, flexibility, and action	Little or no opportunities for discretion, flexibility, action
Overall time frame for program	Adequate for fulfilling assignments	Inadequate for fulfilling assignments
Institutional autonomy for agency's program operations	Public agency exercises institutional, political controls overall or most program operations and its authority equals responsibility for program operations	Public agency must share authority with many units, jurisdictions, interests, and therefore authority and responsibility is highly fragmented

when to move or not to move to take advantage of situations, positions, and opportunities is important. Little wonder then that lawyers abound in government bureaucracies today, for their training in the arts of bargaining, circumspection, compromise, negotiation, and deal making prepares them to deal well for just such uncertain conditions. In rapidly changing, pluralistic environments, public organizations in particular require these types of lawyer–like skills in their leaders in order to survive and prosper. In Robert Dahl's outstanding analysis of the pluralistic context of New Haven, Connecticut's, political life, *Who Governs?* he describes precisely these leadership capabilities in its highly able former chief executive, Mayor Richard Lee: "He rarely commanded. He negotiated, exhorted, beguiled, cajoled, pressed, appealed, reasoned, promised, insisted, demanded, even threatened, but most he needed support and acquiescences from other leaders who simply could not be commanded. Because he could not command, he had to bargain."[44]

SUMMARY OF KEY POINTS

Every public bureaucracy in the United States is created and sustained to perform some task or tasks. What these missions and duties are may be clearly evident or very hard to define. Generally, though, "the products" of every public agency

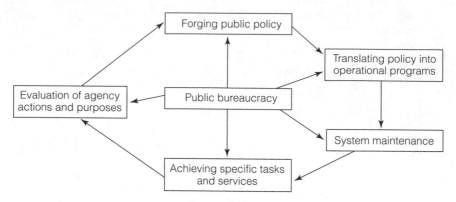

FIGURE 5.13   Public bureaucracies produce five varieties of outputs

depend upon the abilities, composition, and activities of its internal subsystems (see Figure 5.13): political appointees forge the broad political missions; bottom-level appointees along with top-level career professionals and civil servants translate these missions into operational programs; mid-level civil servants and professional careerists perform system maintenance; and the lower cadres of civil servants, union workers, and contractual employees are largely involved with implementing specific agency tasks. The processes by which these governmental outputs are performed vary significantly from private enterprise practices and, therefore, traditional generic models for understanding public agency outputs are inappropriate.

Rather, the bulk of this chapter presents a conceptual approach for understanding the dynamics of how bureaucratic outputs are performed. As Table 5.8 and Figure 5.14 indicate, the achievement of public organization outputs involves four components: first, the specific tasks of the agency; second, its gamesmanship capacities; third, its *internal resources*—the agency's legal, structural, process, and personal resources; and fourth, the *external conditions* within which agency operations take place. These *external conditions* were identified as essentially six varieties of windows for bureaucratic action, ranging from wide-open, long-term windows to tightly shut windows of opportunity.

KEY TERMS

bureaucratic outputs	legal statutes	bureaucratic routines
generic output models	high-stakes games	process versus structural resources
POSDCORB	low-stakes games	
fragmented authority	internal resources	constitutional limits on service delivery
"goldfish bowl" environment	windows of opportunity	

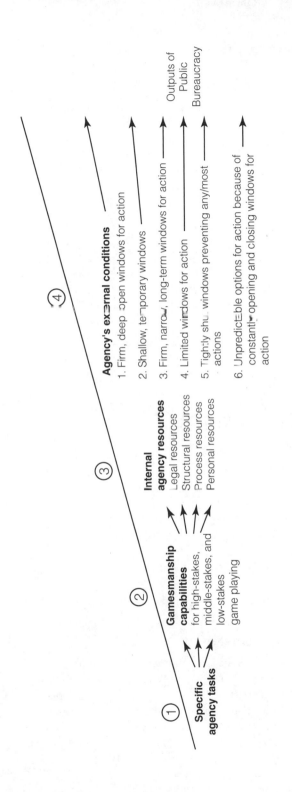

FIGURE 5.14 Achieving public agency outputs involves four components that all must work together at the same time.

REVIEW MATERIAL

Review Questions

1. Can you summarize some of the basic tasks public bureaucracies perform for society? What distinguishes these jobs from business or nonprofit organization tasks?

2. In what ways do generic output models differ from, or fail to explain fully, the actual accomplishment of public sector jobs? Why are they performed differently than in private enterprise organizations?

3. What is meant by the argument that public agencies carry out their duties through the use of gamesmanship? Do you agree?

4. Discuss the internal types of bureaucratic resources that public organizations can bring to the accomplishment of agency missions. Why is each resource important to achieve direction, cohesion, and cooperation in organizations?

5. Explain John Kingdon's concept of "windows of opportunity." Why are they critical to public security outputs? Does each window require a different set of public managerial skills to "seize the opportunity" that a window presents to an agency? If so, why and what are these managerial attributes?

Class Debate Pro/Con

Resolved that public bureaucracies ought to be required by law to be as specific as possible about the outputs they produce in order to make them accountable to the public(s) they serve.

Student Homework Exercise

Select one state or local public agency and research its enabling legislation that outlines its basic goals or purpose for being created. Then based upon brief, random surveys of its employees and clients, draw up a list of the actual functions it performs and compare and contrast these outputs with the agency's legislative mandates. Do the two differ? If so, why or why not?

Case Analysis

Read "The Blast in Centralia No. 5" in any edition of Richard Stillman's Public Administration: Concepts and Cases. The Department of Mines and Minerals had the legal requirement to regulate state mine safety, but for various reasons indicated throughout the case, it failed to perform these functions properly—or at all. What system would you propose to establish that would specifically prescribe the Department's regulatory outputs and then track their effective accomplishment? Explain why your new system would work better than the one that existed.

NOTES

1. An Act for Establishing an Executive Department to Be Denominated the Department of Foreign Affairs, July 27, 1789 (1 Stat. 4); refer to chapter 2, figure 2.

2. Organization for National Security, Title I, Section 102, 61 Stat. 343 (1947) and 63 Stat. 412 (1949).

3. Woodrow Wilson, "The Study of Administration," *Political Science Quarterly* 2 (June 1887): 197–220.

4. Grover Starling, *Managing the Public Sector,* 2d ed. (Homewood, IL: Dorsey Press, 1982), p. 1.

5. Luther Gulick and L. Urwick (eds.), *The Papers on the Science of Administration* (New York: Institute of Public Administration, 1937), p. 13.

6. Bertram Gross, *Organizations and Their Managing* (New York: Free Press, 1964).

7. Graham T. Allison, Jr., "Public and Private Management: Are They Fundamentally Alike in All Unimportant Respects?" in *Setting Public Management Research Agendas* (Washington, DC: Office of Personnel Management, February 1980), pp. 27–38.

8. Michael Barzelay with the collaboration of Babak J. Armajani, *Breaking Through Bureaucracy: A New Vision for Managing in Government* (Berkeley: University of California Press, 1992), pp. 8–9.

9. Allison, Jr., "Public and Private Management," p. 27.

10. Paul Appleby, *Big Democracy* (New York: Knopf, 1945), p. 1.

11. James W. Fesler and Donald F. Kettl, *The Politics of the Administrative Process* (Chatham, NJ: Chatham House, 1990), p. 244.

12. Elliot Richardson, *The Creative Balance* (New York: Holt, Rinehart, and Winston, 1976), p. 130.

13. As cited in Allison, "Public and Private Management."

14. *Federalist Papers,* No. 51.

15. Richard E. Neustadt, as cited in Laurence E. Lynn, Jr., see note 13.

16. Laurence E. Lynn, Jr., *Managing the Public's Business* (New York: Basic Books, 1981), chapter 6.

17. Ibid.

18. C. Wright Mills, *The Power Elite* (New York: Oxford University Press, 1956), p. 245.

19. Francis E. Rourke, *Bureaucracy, Politics, and Public Policy,* 2d ed. (Boston: Little, Brown, 1976), p. 15.

20. Lynn, Jr., *Managing.*

21. Herbert A. Simon, Donald W. Smithburg, and Victor A. Thompson, *Public Administration* (New York: Knopf, 1950), ch. 19.

22. Jeffrey L. Pressman, "Preconditions of Mayoral Leadership," *American Political Science Review* 2 (June 1972): 512.

23. Lester M. Salamon (ed.), assisted by Michael S. Lund, *Beyond Privatization: The Tools of Government Action* (Washington, DC: Urban Institute Press, 1989), p. 3.

24. Graham T. Allison, *Essence of Decision* (Boston: Little, Brown, 1971), p. 79.

25. Rourke, *Bureaucracy,* p. 19.

26. Robert Dahl, *Who Governs?* (New Haven, CT: Yale University Press, 1961), p. 225.

27. John C. Bollens and John C. Ries, *The City Manager Profession* (Chicago: Public Administration Service, 1969), p. 16.

28. Gerald Garvey, *Facing the Bureaucracy: Living and Dying in a Public Agency* (San Francisco, CA: Jossey-Bass, 1993), p. 216.

29. Ronald O. Loveridge, *City Managers in Legislative Politics* (Indianapolis, IN: Bobbs-Merrill, 1971), p. 17.

30. Kenneth C. Davis, *Discretionary Justice* (Baton Rouge: Louisiana State University Press, 1969), p. 212.

31. John W. Gardner, *On Leadership* (New York: Free Press, 1990), p. xiii.

32. Chester I. Barnard, *The Functions of the Executive* (Cambridge, MA: Harvard University Press, 1938), pp. 139.

33. Herbert A. Simon, *Administrative Behavior* (New York: Macmillan, 1947).

34. John Gaus, *Reflections on Public Administration* (University of Alabama Press, 1947), p. 43.

35. Louis Brownlow, *A Passion for Anonymity* (Chicago: University of Chicago Press, 1955), pp. 105–203.

36. John W. Kingdon, *Agendas, Alternatives, and Public Policies* (New York: HarperCollins Publishers, 1984), p. 213.

37. Aaron Wildavsky, *Leadership in a Small Town* (Totowa, NJ: Bedminister Press, 1964), pp. 215–35.

38. Robert B. Denhardt, *The Pursuit of Significance: Strategies for Managerial Success in Public Organizations* (Belmont, CA: Wadsworth, 1993), pp. 192–93.

39. Frank Sherwood, *A City Manager Tries to Fire His Police Chief,* ICP #76 (Syracuse, NY: Inter-University Case Program, 1960).

40. Scott Armstrong, "The Fall of the Shah," *Washington Post,* Oct. 25–Oct. 29, 1980, p. 1.

41. Wallace S. Sayre and Herbert Kaufman, *Governing New York City* (New York: Russell Sage, 1960), p. 710.

42. Hugh Heclo, "Issue Networks and the Executive Establishment," in Anthony King (ed.), *The New Political System* (Washington, DC: American Enterprise Institute for Public Policy Research, 1978), pp. 87–124.

43. Ibid.

44. Dahl, *Who Governs?*

45. Warner Mills and Harry Davis, *Small City Government* (New York: Random House, 1962), p. 32.

FURTHER READING

Several of Norton Long's insightful essays on bureaucracy first developed this notion of bureaucracy as gamesmanship. His book *The Polity* (Chicago: Rand McNally, 1962) is useful as well, as is Laurence Lynn, *Managing the Public's Business* (New York: Basic Books, 1981). Harold Seidman's *Politics, Position and Power,* 4th ed. (1986) develops these themes more fully. The best sources of gamesmanship ideas are found in biographical sketches of key masters of this art, including William Manchester, *American Caesar* (1978); Norman Polmar and Thomas B. Allen, *Rickover* (1982); Robert Caro, *The Power Broker* (1974); and Louis Brownlow, *A Passion for Anonymity* (1958); Thomas K. McGrew, *Prophets of Regulation* (1984); Donald F. Kettl, *Leadership at the Fed* (1986); Deborah Shapley, *Promise and Power: The Life and Times of Robert McNamara* (1993); and Bob Woodward, *Maestro* (2000). Several fine sketches of public servants are found in Norma Riccucci, *Unsung Heroes* (1995) as well as Jameson W. Doig and Erwin C. Hargrove (eds.), *Leadership and Innovation* (1990). John Gaus's *Reflections on Public Administration* (1947) remains the most sensitive treatment of the external environment within which public agencies must work in order to implement their programs.

In the past three decades, an impressive array of books on program implementation has appeared. Especially useful are Jeffrey L. Pressman and Aaron Wildavsky, *Implementation,* 2d ed. (1978); Walter Williams, *The Implementation Perspective* (1980); Walter Williams and Richard F. Elmore (eds.), *Social Program Implementation* (1976); Eugene Bardach, *The Implementation Game* (1977); Richard F. Elmore, *Complexity and Control* (1979); Martha Derthick, *New Towns In-Town* (1972); Beryl Radin, *Implementation, Change and the Federal Bureaucracy;* Malcolm L. Goggin, Ann O'M. Bowman, James P. Lester, and Laurence J. O'Toole, Jr., *Implementation Theory and Practice: Toward a Third Gen-*

eration (1990). See especially the excellent bibliography on this topic at the end of their book, perhaps the most up-to-date study of where we are today with implementation theory is found in the superb essay, "Synthesizing the Implementation Literature," by Richard E. Matland in *Journal of Public Administration Research and Theory* (April 1995). An increasing interest also involves the problems of overcoming organizational fragmentation; see especially Eugene Bardach, *Getting Agencies to Work Together* (1998).

Leadership has also been highly stressed in scholarly literature, a theme concerning the cause of success or failure of bureaucratic outputs. Some of the better recent books on this topic are: John W. Gardner, *On Leadership* (1990); Warren Bennis, *Why Leaders Can't Lead* (1989); James M. Kouzes and Barry Z. Posner, *The Leadership Challenge* (1987); Richard Lynch, *Lead!* (1992); Robert W. Terry, *Authentic Leadership* (1993); Dalton S. Lee and N. Joseph Cayer, *Supervision for Success in Government* (1994); Robert B. Denhardt, *The Pursuit of Significance* (1993); Barbara Kellerman (ed.), *Leadership* (1984); Steven Cohen and Ronald Brand, *Total Quality Management in Government* (1993); John M. Bryson and Barbara C. Crosby, *Leadership for the Common Good* (1992); Michael Barzelay with the collaboration of Babak J. Armajani, *Breaking Through Bureaucracy* (1992), Beryl A. Radin, *The Accountability Juggler* (2002); and Larry Terry, *Leadership of Public Bureaucracies* (2002). Perhaps the best of the prior political science generation's scholarship on the subject is found in James MacGregor Burns *Leadership* (1978). For a good collection of essays, see Patricia W. Ingraham and Donald F. Kettl, *Agenda for Excellence* (1992), as well as Mark Abramson and Kevin Bacon, *Leaders* (2002), and for a practical how-to-do-it manual, read the ICMA's *The Effective Local Government Manager,* 2d ed. (1993).

For a useful "insider" first-person account on the dilemmas of implementation inside public agencies today, read Gerald Garvey's *Facing the Bureaucracy* (1993), David Kessler, *A Question of Intent* (2001), General Wesley K. Clark, *Waging War* (2001), and Arthur Levitt, *Take on the Street'* (2002). For an excellent historical study of an agency's implementation of its activities throughout the Federal Government, see Paul C. Light's *Monitoring Government* (1993).

Beyond Privatization (1989), as well as his recent *The Tools of Government* (2002) edited by Lester M. Salamon, is "must reading" because of its important analysis and conceptualization of the alternative tools of government action. Also key to carrying out public programs is the support that bureaucrats receive from legislatures. Two of the best studies of this subject are, for the local level, James H. Svara, *Official Leadership in the City* (1990) and Christopher H. Foreman, Jr., *Signals from the Hill* (1988). For the federal level, John W. Kingdon's *Agendas, Alternatives, and Public Policies* (1984), though now somewhat dated, has excellent sections on "windows of opportunity." Although dealing primarily with personnel issues, three government reports are well worth reviewing in light of implementation questions: the Volcker Commission report, *Leadership for America* (1989), the Winter Commission report, *Hard Truths/Tough Choices: An Agenda for State and Local Reform* (1993), and the Hudson Institute's report, *Civil Service 2000* (1988). Finally, for a recent excellent summary of best leadership practices in public organizations, see Ray Blunt, *Organizations Growing Leaders: Best Practices and Principles in Public Service* (2001).

WEB SITES

http://www.asktheheadhunter.com/gv011219.htm: 9 Myths about Federal Jobs
http://www.townhall.com/issueslibrary/governmentreform/: Government Reform
http://www.statelocal.gov/: State and Local Government Gateway
http://www.privatization.org/: Privitization.org

6

■

The Feedback Loop in
the Bureaucratic System

❝ **M**ay you live in interesting times" is an ancient Chinese saying—*and a curse!* Constant change—both for good and ill—abounds throughout American society, decisively influencing the entire bureaucratic system. Making sense out of current changes in our immense administrative complex, now so central to U.S. governing processes and the functioning of society, is difficult. Indeed, generalizing about some of the swiftly moving major features of the bureaucratic system right now may well be risky, since exceptions can always be found that contradict any rule about bureaucratic changes—precisely because its entities are so vast and diverse. Further, change is so rapid within the system that what is apparent today may well disappear before the ink is dry on the page that attempts to describe it, not to mention knowing whether or not such change is a blessing or a curse.

At the risk of misperceiving some of the current trends—or missing others entirely—this chapter will scan the bureaucratic horizon and speculate about feedback sources directly shaping and reshaping the bureaucratic system today, particularly on three levels: First, how does feedback from the present turbulent socioeconomic-political environment influence the basic goals and purposes of public bureaucracy? Why does it recast the basic directions of bureaucratic institutions as well as future possibilities for their institutional development? Second, what feedback affects the political authority within public bureaucracies, given the surrounding environmental turbulence? In other words, how does the input from external environs reshape the internal bureaucratic processes to act effectively, or not? More specifically, how do the socioeconomic-political environs of today strengthen public bureaucracies foster agency weakness and decline? Third, in what ways do internal communication networks affect the operations of bureaucracy? Enhance or deter their managerial effectiveness? Act as building blocks or road blocks for allowing agencies to carry out their goals and legal mandates? In brief, this chapter will look at three critical dimensions of feedback to U.S. bureaucracy namely affecting its basic goals, its political authority, and its internal operations.

FEEDBACK AFFECTING BASIC BUREAUCRATIC
GOALS: OR, THE TWELVE TRENDS TRANSFORMING
THE PURPOSES OF MODERN BUREAUCRACY

Public bureaucracy has been rocked by several significant politico-economic-social trends during the past decade that profoundly affect their basic goals, objectives, and purposes. Some are obvious; others are not as apparent. Certainly no complete "still photo" of all these rapidly moving socio-economic-political forces is possible, but the following may provide an overview of twelve of these major forces and illustrate the profound dilemmas they raise for the modern bureaucratic system as a whole.

1. *The End of the Cold War and America as the Last Global Superpower*
The decade of the 1990s ushered in profound changes in the international order: the collapse of the former Soviet Union, the reunification of Germany, the introduction of democracy and free market reforms throughout Eastern Europe, the opening of new diplomatic and trade links with China and the Pacific Rim nations as well as throughout the entire North American Continent by means of the 1993 North American Free Trade Agreement (NAFTA). The list

of these global realignments could continue, but for America, the bottom line is: simply due to its political, economic, and military strength, America is now the last remaining global superpower. While the United States has less than 5 percent of the world's population, it generates 31.2 percent of the world's GDP (see Figure 6.1), greater than all of Western Europe, developing Asian countries, and Japan. This powerful industrial-economic strength is a direct source of America's political and military might. The technical inventiveness of U.S. industry gives the United States technological superiority in vital basic defense technologies, essential for maintaining global land, air, and sea military capabilities. Because of its unrivaled superiority in this field, America in the 1990s and at the dawn of the 21st century undertook critical leadership roles in foreign affairs on a number of fronts: in the Gulf war, in Somalia, in Iraq, in Russian relief efforts, in stopping nuclear proliferation, and in promoting free-trade and democratic reforms throughout the world. In the words of Joseph S. Nye, Jr., "America is bound to lead."[1] For American bureaucracy, specifically, the new imperatives of post-9/11 war on terrorism bring about numerous issues, such as: How should America's defenses be restructured to play effective and critical leadership roles against terrorism worldwide and at home? How can America work with and through international organizations to achieve its purposes of global stability, peace, and prosperity? Where should America place its national priorities and how can they be exercised on the world stage? What new forms of transnational organizations are necessary and how should they be created and staffed to achieve their goals?

   2. *Changing Demographics within the United States: The Increase in Population, the Old, and Minorities*
The old saw, "Demographics are destiny," may well explain America's future as well as its bureaucracy's future. According to the Census Bureau's mid-range projections, the total U.S. population will be 322.6 million in 2020—an increase

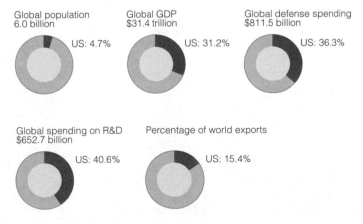

FIGURE 6.1   Measurements of USA power*

Sources: UN, World Bank; IISS: Institute for Management Development; Screen Digest and *The Economist,* June 19, 2002, p. 4.
*All figures are for 2000 but expected for 2001.

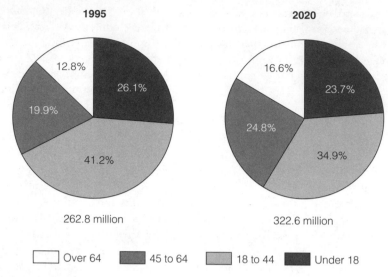

FIGURE 6.2 U.S. population

Source: *Washington Post* National Weekly Edition, March 28–April 3, 1994, p. 51. ©1994 The Washington Post, reprinted with permission.

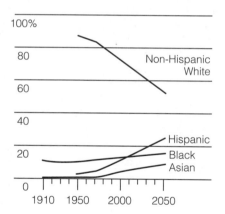

FIGURE 6.3 U.S. population by race and ethnicity, 1910–2050

Source: U.S. Census Bureau, 2002.

of 23 percent or 80 million people (see Figure 6.2). Aside from the absolute rise in total population, demographics show that the over-64 age group will grow by 3.8 percent, while the under-18 category will rise only 2.4 percent. Thus, the elderly will become the fastest growing age cluster and the young will shrink as a percentage of the overall population. Rates of change for minorities, as Figure 6.3 indicates, during the 1980s grew faster by significant margins than Americans as a whole. The Census Bureau therefore projects that about 79 percent of the total population increase between 1995 and 2020 will consist of minority group members. The number of non-Hispanic white Americans will increase by only 6.4 percent or 12.4 million people during this period. By contrast, over the next half century minority citizens will grow to 50 percent of the U.S. population: 18 percent Blacks, 26 percent Hispanics, and 6 percent Asians. The minority population will increase ten times faster than the white population, and by 2020, one in three Americans will be a member of a minority, and it will be one in two by 2050 contrasted to one in four today.

For public bureaucracies everywhere in the United States, the absolute increase in population will mean pressures to deliver more of all varieties of public services: mass transit, roads, bridges, water, sewers, housing, public planning for shopping and residential neighborhoods, new parks and recreation facilities, public education, and fire and police protection, to name a few. In particular, a growing elderly population requires minivan services, medical long-term care facilities, "senior citizen" recreation, and other social services. The increasing minorities will make new demands for public housing, job opportunities, public health, equal protection of the law, English language training, social services, and so on. Bureaucratic activities not only will expand significantly but will also be asked to deliver new and innovative programs to these emerging, influential groups in society.

3. *Population Shifts to the Suburbs and Outlying Areas and to the Western and Southern Regions*

Regionally, the West and South will grow faster than the Northeast and Midwest for two reasons: People will continue to move into these areas, and most migrations from abroad, mainly from Latin America and Asia, will settle in these locales. Las Vegas, Salt Lake City, Phoenix, Portland, Tucson, Boise, Denver, and San Antonio are expected to be among the fastest growing American communities (mid-sized, western/southern cities) over the next 25 years. Suburbs and outlying areas of metropolitan communities will capture most of the future population increase; so will counties on the rims of center cities. The farm population and older center-city populations in the Northeast and Midwest will continue to lose people, but southwestern and western cities will grow largely due to Asian and Hispanic migration (see Figure 6.4)[2]

Again, as noted in earlier chapters, these sociopolitical-economic shifts have caused many difficulties for state and local public bureaucracies, including problems of adjusting public services to the new influx or out-migrations of people; dealing with a rapidly shifting demographic composition of local populations and clientele groups' demands for those public services; coping with the strains of a growing or declining tax base and physical development/planning under conditions of cutbacks in federal expenditures, as well as increasing local constraints on raising public revenues such as statewide tax limitations and balanced budget requirements. While it is hard to predict the precise directions of these regional population shifts or when they will actually occur, it is certain that the tasks of coping with their aftershocks will be of long duration and profoundly difficult for various government agencies, especially at the local level.

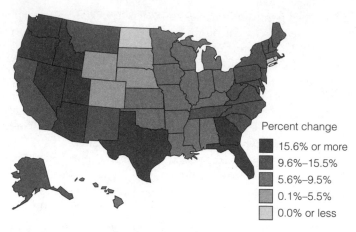

FIGURE 6.4 State population growth, 1990–1999

Source: U.S. Census Bureau, "State Population Estimates and Demographic Components of Population Change: 1990 to 1999," July 8, 1999.

4. *America's New Interdependence on the Borderless Global Economy, Increasingly Focused toward the Pacific Rim*

No longer is the United States self-sufficient in natural resources. This stark fact was brought home to most Americans with dramatic force when long lines snaked around gas stations during the energy crises of the 1970s. Today, more than half of the oil used domestically comes from abroad, mainly from the highly volatile Middle East, whose often-unfriendly nations are racked by political turbulence. Such is the case with many other natural resources Americans now consume. Even basic "Americana" such as baseball mitts are no longer American-made but come mainly from the Far Eastern industrial nations of Japan, Korea, and Taiwan, as do television sets, refrigerators, washing machines, and other commercial goods. As Table 6.1 points out, America's global interdependence increasingly means that familiar U.S. brand names are actually owned by foreign companies.

Further, cheap labor from abroad, especially the several million illegal immigrants arriving yearly because of higher wage rates, helps keep labor costs low in poorly paid service industries. For U.S. public organizations, this new interdependence with the global economy means that public sector agencies must now depend on the vagaries of the global economy, with its often wildly fluctuating prices for raw materials and finished goods, its cheap labor costs, and its uncertainties of supply and unpredictable quality of finished goods. For governmental organizations, these new economic uncertainties—such as rapid shifts in the money supply, interest rates, global demand for resources, prices for finished goods, cheap labor, sudden inflation or depression of costs—create enormously complex problems for long-term planning, efficient allocation of resources, and effective management of mandated programs. These new economic uncertainties also add profound insecurities for Americans, in turn

Table 6.1 U.S. Brands That Are Property of European Companies

Brand	Country	Company	Brand	Country	Company
Holiday Inn	U.K.	Six Continents Hotels	Burger King	U.K.	Diageo
			Amoco	U.K.	BP Amoco
Mellon Bank	Scotland	Royal Bank of Scotland	Snapple, Dr Pepper	U.K.	Cadbury Schweppes
Shell	U.K. Netherlands	Royal Dutch Shell	Mazola oil	U.K.	Associated British Foods
Kent cigarettes	U.K.	British American Tobacco	Pepsodent, Slim-Fast, Vaseline, Hellmann's mayonnaise, Chicken Tonight	U.K. Netherlands	Unilever
Baby Ruth	Switzerland	Nestle			
Random House	Germany	Bertelsmann			
Casual Corner, Brooks Brothers, U.S. Shoe	Italy	Retail Brand Alliance	Giant Food	Netherlands	Royal Ahold
			Jeep	Germany	Daimler-Chrysler
			Universal Studies, Sci-Fi Channel	France	Vivendi

SOURCE: *Washington Post National Weekly Edition* (May 27–June 2, 2002), p. 20.© 2002, the Washington Post. Reprinted with permission.

promulgating questions regarding the government's ability to cope adequately with homeland and international security.

5. *The Growth of Knowledge-Workers and Service-Sector Jobs and the Decline of Traditional "Smokestack" Industries and Farming*

Underlying these economic changes and population shifts is a fundamental realignment of the industrial base. Many of the aging smokestack industries are no longer competitive with third-world nations in Latin America and the Far East. Because of their significantly lower labor costs, these nations can produce industrial goods far more cheaply and efficiently in virtually every market sector from automobiles to television sets than the United States can. Hence, since the 1970s jobs and industry in goods-producing fields have declined, often moving outside the country to cheaper labor markets, and the service sector, particularly information-producing jobs, is now among the rapid growth areas of employment and industrial productivity in the United States. These jobs normally require considerably more skill, education, and technological expertise, as illustrated by the list of the fastest-rising and declining occupations in Figure 6.5. Note how, today one-quarter of workers are employed in professional, technical, and managerial/administrative occupations. In other words, Americans are increasingly "knowledge workers."

If these trends persist, as many experts expect they will, the U.S. workforce will require increasingly skilled, educated, and technologically competent workers. These economic and labor trends place enormous demands upon public bureaucracies at every level—preparing students for hi-tech careers; retraining older

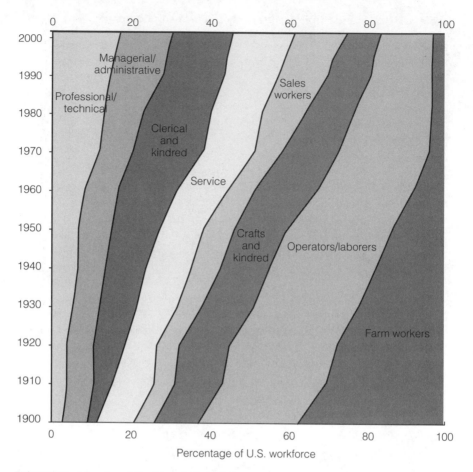

FIGURE 6.5   The rise of the knowledge worker

Source: Statistical Abstracts of the United States, 2001, U.S. Census Bureau

individuals in hi-tech skills; providing unemployment compensation and welfare support; and responding to the problems and pressures of those who for a variety of reasons cannot cope with or adapt to these rapid shifts in employment markets. Offering educational, welfare, and other vital human services that assist the job changes will no doubt be important priorities for public agencies in this era of rapid technological transformation.

6. *New Technologies: Challenges and Problems for Public Agencies*
Underlying both the sudden regional and occupational shifts in U.S. industry is a profound explosion of new technologies. As Figure 6.6 shows, by 1990 information-age capital spending had surpassed industrial-age spending. As a result, strikingly new developments in computers, word processors, telecommunications, integrated information systems, space shuttles, robotics, genetic engineering, undersea exploration, microchip processors, and space exploration—to name just a few—are examples of scientific and technological discoveries that are

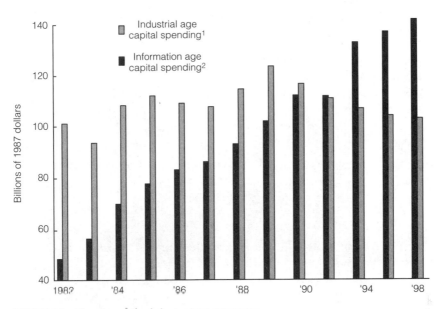

FIGURE 6.6   The rise of the information economy

Source: Adapted from *Fortune,* April 4, 1994, p. 77, with updated information from *Fortune Magazine* Web site.

1. On industrial equipment, machinery for services, mining, oil fields, agriculture, and construction (except tractors).

2. On computers and communications equipment.

fundamentally altering the way Americans live, work, and even think. For public bureaucracies, the impact of these discoveries and inventions is staggering. They create new, profound ethical questions (when can hospitals "pull the plug" that terminates a life?); diplomatic problems (should new high technology be exported to third-world nations and elsewhere?); regulatory issues (can the public ensure safe and proper experimentation with genetic research?); international security and defense issues (how shall we cope with the spread of nuclear technology, which makes the possibility of building small atomic bombs within the reach of many terrorists?); economic problems (who should profit from the taping of television programs by home video machines?); and complex internal management problems of bureaucratic services and resources (how can computers best be used by social service agencies to control costs and extend human services yet maintain the privacy of information on clients being served?). These and many more new questions raised by the unprecedented speed of scientific and technological change are being confronted by public agencies. Indeed, public agencies in many fields find themselves on the cutting edge of *both* scientific *and* ethical complexities of new and profound importance to the survival of the nation and the human race.

When the *Economist* asked readers to name the seven most important "wonders of the modern age," all of the top seven were technical innovations (see Figure 6.7). If the past is any guide to the future, it is a safe bet that tomorrow's technical innovations will be "prime movers" of societal change in the years ahead, thus, in turn, reshaping basic goals and directions for bureaucracy.

1. Jumbo jet
2. Micro-processor
3. Contraceptive pill
4. Deep-sea oil rig
5. World telephone network
6. Hydrogen bomb
7. "Tranquility Base" (site of the first moon landing)

FIGURE 6.7   The economist's poll of top seven wonders of the modern age

Source: *The Economist,* Feb. 19, 1994, p. 97.

7. *The Rise of a Hostile, Entrenched, Permanent Opposition to Government: Issue Networks, the Media, PACs, and Lawyers*

As Chapter 3 discussed, new groups have emerged in the past three decades that are a permanent source of hostility toward government in general and public bureaucracy in particular. Issue networks, for one, have evolved into thick webs of hostile critics surrounding every public agency. As Hugh Heclo noted (and which was discussed in Chapter 3), for the most part they serve *their own* interests by fueling debate and conflict over policy priorities, rather that promoting closure, compromise, and consensus. The media as well have become a major power in public affairs. Ratings of television news programs depend largely on how well they stimulate controversy, promote argument, expose corruption, and uncover wrongdoing within the public sector. Indeed, entire news shows, such as *60 Minutes,* one of the highest-rated programs on the networks, popular newscasters such as Dan Rather and Connie Chung, as well as talk-show hosts such as Rush Limbaugh and Larry King have gained popularity precisely because of the investigative, often hostile, "exposure" reporting with which they uncover "scandals" inside government and especially within bureaucracy.

In addition, Political Action Committees (PACs), narrow in policy focus and rich in resources, have largely replaced political parties as the source of campaign financing and candidate support. As Table 6.2 shows, the number of "nonconnected" and "other" PACs continues to grow; in 2002, PACs were the source of support of 47 percent of incumbents' political campaign funds: Altogether, PACs spent several billion dollars on each presidential election. PACs, in turn, promote candidates that are frequently tied to this or that single issue and, if elected, can be trusted to speak for, lobby for, and defend PAC supporters vis-à-vis the bureaucracy. Finding broad popular consensus and clear public mandates for action is therefore increasingly difficult for governmental bureaucracies, who are surrounded by a thick maze of powerful issue networks, media, and PAC forces, which are for the most part dedicated to promoting narrow criticism and self-interested controversy.

In 1960 there were 250,000 lawyers in the United States; in 1970, 355,000; in 1983, 622,000; and today, 723,000. In other words, while the total popula-

Table 6.2 Growth in PACs

Type	1974	1978	1982	1986	1990	1994	1998	2002
Corporate	89	784	1,467	1,744	1,795	1,660	1,567	1,514
Labor	201	217	380	384	346	333	321	313
Nonconnected	–	165	746	877	862	980	935	1,006
Other	318	487	778	952	869	792	821	882
Total	608	1,653	3,371	4,157	4,172	3,954	3,798	3,865

SOURCES: Ornstein, Mann, and Malbin, *Vital Statistics on Congress,* 1987–1988 (Washington, DC: American Enterprise Institute Congressional Quarterly Press), p. 103; U.S. Federal Election Commission press release, Jan. 20, 1992, and updated from the Federal Election Commission, *Semi-Annual Federal PAC Count,* News Release, July 15, 2002, p. 1.

tion since 1960 increased by roughly 50 percent, the number of lawyers almost tripled. While the causes of this "legal explosion" are numerous, the impacts upon government are profound. Argumentation, the promoting of causes and cases, debate, and the "complexifying" of issues are lawyers' stock in trade. Rather than promoting closure, improving productivity, and securing results, lawyers tend to find methods of delaying procedures, slowing down action, and reducing outputs of organizations; in short, of making them less-effectively managed. As the number of lawyers has grown, so have the issues involving government liability for actions, once thought to be beyond the bounds of court involvement. Court actions involving the military's use of Agent Orange in Vietnam and the fallout from nuclear tests conducted in the Nevada desert during the 1950s are only two recent examples of the broadening scope of legal liability and lawyer/judicial activism affecting public bureaucracies.

Courts themselves have fostered the widening scope of litigation and liability. Society as a whole has become much more willing, "to take legal action" against government for perceived or real wrongs inflicted by bureaucracy. The specific impacts of the litigiousness of society upon public bureaucracy are many, but on the whole the trend in this area has probably made public agencies more cautious and less prone to take initiative, even if those actions by public agencies benefit the majority of citizens. Fear of legal action, often involving large sums of money and public criticisms, is a sound reason for such inaction.

8. *More Households: Smaller and Less Self-Sufficient*
Americans tend to live longer, divorce more frequently, delay marrying or remain single more often, as well as have fewer children or no children at all in order to pursue a two-career marriage. The result is both a marked increase in the number of households and smaller household size. Between 1970 and 2000 the number of households jumped from 63.4 to 95.7 million, for an average growth rate of 1.7 million annually. By the end of the 1990s there should be another 20 million households. The average household size declined substantially during the same period, from 3.14 to 2.62 persons; the number of persons living alone nearly doubled, and the number of one-parent families doubled also. Ninety percent of one-parent families were headed by women; and 51 percent were black. For public agencies, the changing composition and size of households in America are

Table 6.3 Children of Two-Parent Families and Families Headed by One Parent (mother)

Children Who:	Biological Mother and Father	Biological Mother Only
Live in Poverty	11%	38%
Show some health vulnerability	38	45
Show antisocial behavior	24	40
Have repeated a grade	12	24
Have been expelled or suspended	4	11
Have had emotional counselling	3	7

SOURCE: U.S. Public Health Service.

significant, particularly from the standpoint of increasing dependency upon and need for government services by growing groups of elderly living alone and single parents, especially poor, female-headed, minority households, which require public assistance in order to survive. The continued decline of the self-sufficient family unit places enormous burdens and strains upon public-bureaucracies. The declining size of households also means greater dependency on public services in a variety of areas such as education, welfare, and recreation. As Table 6.3 emphasizes, the disparity is striking between children who live in conventional two-parent families and those who do not.

9. *The Widening Young/Old Poverty Gap*

As Figure 6.8 stresses, since 1974, there has been a widening gap between the young and old in poverty. Fewer elderly over 65 years of age are impoverished as compared to children under 18 years old. Why this recent phenomenon has occurred is largely a cumulative effect of governmental policies since the 1960s. Between 1965 and 1979, federal spending on the elderly quadrupled through indexing Social Security payments to cost of living increases and creating Medicare/Medicaid programs and other entitlements aimed at reducing elderly impoverishment and improving their overall quality of life. In addition, states and localities since the 1970s have helped by introducing special tax limitation measures, such as Proposition 13 in California, which holds down property tax increases for long-time homeowners while newer, often younger homeowners must pay property taxes at current market rates. Also, income tax breaks for special senior social services add numerous "hidden benefits." This growth of such benefits from every level of government is a byproduct of increased application of "grey-power" political muscle. Seniors are far better organized than the young. They have more talent and time to devote to AARP-style lobbying to promote retirees' interests, not to mention the financial means to support sympathetic legislators or punish those who are not supportive of senior's demands. The young have neither the time, skills, or money to equal this "grey power," hence the emergence of "the young/old poverty gap" (see Figure 6.8.). This gap is likely to expand, given that the 10 "growth occupations" during 1995–2005 will be fairly low-level service jobs (Table 6.4).

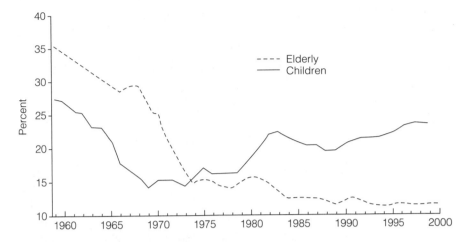

FIGURE 6.8   Official poverty rates for children (under age 18) and the elderly (over age 65), 1960–2000

Source: U. S. Bureau of the Census.

Table 6.4 Ten Occupations Adding the Most U.S. Jobs

Occupation	Jobs Added (1992–2005)
1. Sales persons, retail	786,000
2. Registered nurses	765,000
3. Cashiers	670,000
4. General office clerks	654,000
5. Truck drivers	648,000
6. Waiters/waitresses	637,000
7. Nurses aides/orderlies	594,000
8. Janitors/cleaners	548,000
9. Food preparation workers	524,000
10. Systems analysts	501,000

SOURCE: U.S. Dept. of Labor, cited in *The Futurist,* May–June 1994, p. 5.

For public bureaucracies, this "young/old gap" raises serious generational equity issues: How do we balance the affluence of one generation against the needs of another? In what ways can federal, state, and local resources be combined to deal effectively with a wide range of youth issues such as education, health, job training, unemployment, and crime? Is it possible for public resources to be coordinated and targeted on this single age category, given the dispersed, fragmented programs related to this group? And particularly, where does the political support come from, since the young are so poorly equipped to "play the political game," at least compared to the elderly?

10. *The Federal Deficit and State Budget Crises*

David S. Broder, a senior *Washington Post* columnist, reports of a town meeting in Newburgh, New York, he attended that was convened by U.S. Representative Maurice Hinchey (Dem., NY) to listen to voters views during the congressional recess:

> The most poignant moment came when a high school student said her ambition was to be a teacher, but "I'm the oldest of three in my family, and I can't ask my parents to help me with college." The prospect of repaying college loans from a teacher's salary scares her, she said.
>
> Hinchey said Congress has approved a Clinton initiative that will let some people pay back college loans by doing community service, "but it's woefully inadequate. The problem is the deficit." Then he explained how the national debt had exploded during the years this young woman was growing up. "Now, we're on track to cut the deficit by 40 percent," he said, in part by starving programs like college aid.[3]

The increasing federal deficit that puts constraints on many programs, such as the college aid program so badly needed by that young woman in Newburgh, is a product of many factors of deep cuts in the federal revenue base due to a recession, continued entitlement growth, plus a rapid build-up of defense expenditures after 9/11 terrorist attacks, thereby quickly shifting from a 1 percent of GDP federal budget surplus in 2000 to 1 percent of GDP deficit in 2001. While the Gramm-Rudman-Hollings Act of 1986 and the 1993 Clinton Budget Initiative both cut soaring deficit that led to surpluses in FY 1997 to FY 2000. Today, however, $40 billion in entitlements, or those federal benefits that are automatically paid to anyone who qualifies as well as increases in FY 2002 Pentagon Budget to fight terrorism along with the $50 billion economic stimulus package passed for 2001 and a $1.5 trillion farm aid bill in 2002 fosters is rising federal deficits projected to be 160 billion in FY 2002 and $110 billion for FY 2003. The major entitlements (excluding Social Security) are: Medicare, Medicaid, Supplemental Security Income, government employees' benefits and pensions, welfare, farm price supports, student loans, military pensions and veterans' benefits, and unemployment compensation. The larger deficit now requires 15 percent of the annual federal budget simply to pay interest on the growing debt, leaving less and less money for other discretionary federal programs (or those federal programs that are not entitlements). From an economic standpoint, the deficit drains the economy of resources for private investment, limiting employment and industrial growth. It also serves to erode the dollar's value abroad, increasing the difficulties of American competitiveness in overseas markets and the overall exercise of America's leadership in world affairs. At the state level, the 2000–2002 recession also caused a serious fiscal crisis as Figures 6.9 and 6.10 emphasizes. Though unlike the federal government, states cannot run deficits and so must make deep cuts in basic state services such as higher education, health, welfare, and safety.

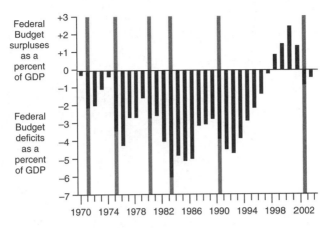

FIGURE 6.9   Federal budget position as share of GDP

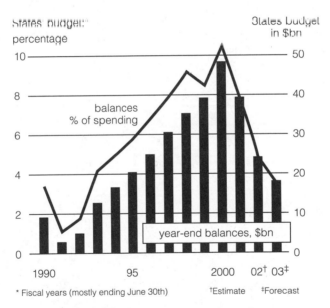

FIGURE 6.10   State budget balances as a percentage of spending

Source: National Association of State Budget Officers.

11. *The Environmental Challenge*

According to World Watch, our long-term global environmental vital signs are not encouraging: Forests are shrinking; desert areas are expanding; lakes are dying; underground water levels are declining; water quality is in jeopardy in many areas; world-wide temperatures and sea levels are rising; and the hole in the ozone layer is expanding, causing increased penetration of deadly radiation.[4] As a nation's prosperity grows, as Figure 6.11 indicates, the rates of pollution

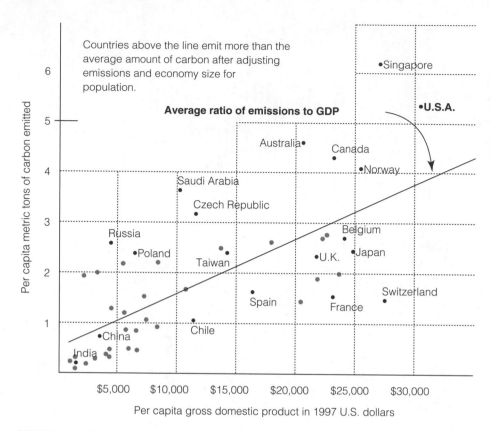

FIGURE 6.11   Pollution vs. prosperity among selected countries

Sources: C.I.A.; Carbon Dioxide Information Analysis Center.

increases in turn causing greater damage to the environment worldwide. Table 6.5 ranks the top 26 "environmental risks" according to the general American public's perception of risk compared to what the EPA experts determine is "real risk factors." What is surprising is the large difference between what the general public believe constitutes serious environmental risk and the actual risk according to the EPA experts. For example, the danger from "indoor radon" is listed high by the experts but next to last, in twenty-fifth place, by the general public. Hazardous waste sites are ranked first by the public but "medium-low" by experts.

Clearly, public bureaucracies face enormous challenges on the environmental front: How can they educate the general public as to the "real threats" facing the world and nation in this area? Indeed, what are the "real risks" in the environment we should focus upon? How can bureaucracies apply their expertise to solve or even learn about these issues? In what ways can American organizations work across national boundaries to deal with serious growing global environmental threats? What new forms of organizations, talent, and authority are required to cope with these massive challenges that require global cooperation on a scale never before conceived of in human history?

Table 6.5 Where Danger Lurks

Public Ranking of Risks	EPA Experts' Rankings
1. Hazardous waste sites	Medium-to-low
2. Exposure to workplace chemicals	High
3. Industrial pollution of waterways	Low
4. Radiation from nuclear accidents	Not ranked
5. Radioactive waste	Not ranked
6. Chemical leaks from underground storage tanks	Medium-to-low
7. Pesticides	High
8. Pollution from industrial accidents	Medium-to-low
9. Water pollution from farm runoff	Medium
10. Tap water contamination	High
11. Industrial air pollution	High
12. Ozone-layer destruction	High
13. Coastal water contamination	Low
14. Sewage-plant water pollution	Medium-to-low
15. Vehicle exhaust	High
16. Oil spills	Medium-to-low
17. Acid rain	High
18. Water pollution from urban runoff	Medium
19. Damaged wetlands	Low
20. Genetic alteration	Low
21. Non-hazardous waste sites	Medium-to-low
22. Greenhouse effect	Low
23. Indoor air pollution	High
24. X-ray radiation	Not ranked
25. Indoor radon	High
26. Microwave oven radiation	Not ranked

SOURCE: Frederick Allen, U.S. EPA, as cited in *Governing*, April 1994, p. 64. Reprinted with permission, *Governing* magazines, copyright 1994.

12. *Shifting Fundamental Values*

The revolution in personal morality that began in the 1960s, spread in the 1970s, and continued into the 1980s and 1990s has many important ramifications for public bureaucracies. Attitudes toward drug use, pornography, homosexuality, crime, suicide, abortion, and premarital and teenage sex are considerably more tolerant today than they were three decades ago. Surveys point up that on the whole Americans are also more tolerant toward minorities, the poor, the handicapped, and women than they were in the 1960s. As a result, important advances have been made among these groups in social legislation and in economic and political status. Yet strong moral reactions from the political right and religious fundamentalists are also evident in the twenty-first century in regard to these changing national mores and morals. In other words, concepts of the American Dream and the Good Society are being hotly debated today.

Should the Good Society include a much broader spectrum of activities and groups than it did only a few decades ago? Should it reflect only the ideals of white traditional Americans? Or should it become more pluralistic in scope, encompassing many new groups and lifestyles?

U.S. society today includes a rich texture of multiple subcultures from communities like San Francisco or West Hollywood, which are dominated by gays, to cities in south Florida where a Spanish-speaker can pass a lifetime without speaking English. As futurist John Naisbitt writes, we've moved from "an either/or" society to a society of "multiple options."[5] Or, from one that offers only chocolate and vanilla to one that offers 31 flavors. This new diversity of cultures and subcultures—and its many definitions of morality and of THE GOOD—is no doubt a two-edged sword in regard to the activities of public bureaucracies. Like the fragmented electorate discussed earlier, increased societal diversity often makes collective action on the part of public agencies more difficult to undertake on behalf of *the public*. What is good and correct public action in a society of increasingly diverse interests, views, and values? This multiple-option society, on the other hand, may be an important force in making public agencies more tolerant and open to the various groups that surround their activities. Competing claims of pluralistic demands and values pressing in on every public organization today may well be a powerful, perhaps the most powerful, check on their activities and behavior. More will be said about this subject in Chapter 7 on the future of American bureaucracy.

FEEDBACK AFFECTING PUBLIC BUREAUCRATIC AUTHORITY: SOURCES OF WEAKNESS VERSUS SOURCES OF STRENGTH

More mega-socioeconomic-political trends affecting bureaucratic goals and purposes no doubt could be added to the aforementioned list of 12 (see Figure 6.12). This list is nowhere near complete. Yet the more critical issue for this book is, what are the effects of many of these trends upon the contemporary bureaucratic authority to take action? If the broad socioeconomic-political environment sets overall direction of U.S. bureaucracy today, how do these trends influence public bureaucracy capacity to exercise its power and influence as an institution? As a system? As a group of public officials? As a central activity of government? The changing sociopolitical-economic environment is reshaping and redirecting the internal systems of public organizations, their institutions, their people, and their activities in many new, profound, and significant ways. In particular, some innovations have already been addressed in previous chapters serve on the whole to strengthen public bureaucracies by promoting clear organizational direction, institutional cohesion, managerial effectiveness, swift action, and decisive exercise of administrative authority. On the other hand, some recent forces promulgate precisely the reverse: indecision, fragmentation,

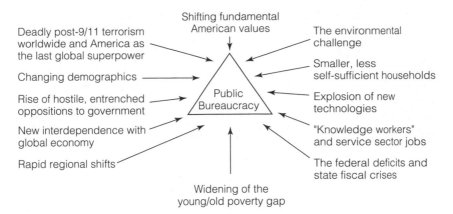

FIGURE 6.12   Summary of twelve current mega-trends influencing America's public bureaucracy's basic goals and purposes

ineffectiveness, inaction, and limits on administrative authority. In short, its institutional decline. First let us review those that tend to promote the latter.

Forces Fostering Institutional Decline and Fragmentation

Rising Bureaucratic Governance by Temporary Amateurs Erodes Neutral Experience As Chapter 4 underscored, in many areas of the federal government as well as in state and local agencies, there is an increasing reliance upon staffing bureaucracies not just at the very top level but at two, three, four, or more levels down the bureaucratic hierarchies with temporary political amateurs. In turn, this generally has meant a declining support for and dependence upon professional expertise within agencies for long-term planning, personnel efficiency, innovative ideas, institutional memory, and managerial effectiveness. Many of these amateurs not only lack the necessary long-term commitment, skills, and experience in government but also exhibit a strong distrust of and even hostility toward professionals and a disdain for their values and their competence. As the late Frederick C. Mosher once observed: "This is no new phenomenon in American governmental life, but the recent attacks by candidates and political office holders upon the civil service, the foreign service, the military services, and other systems built up over the years to assure merit, loyalty, and institutional memory have been particularly extreme. They are unfortunate, not only in their effect on the morale of public servants and the future attractiveness of government as a career, but also for the political appointees themselves who must ultimately depend upon the career people to help them make policy and carry out their directions."[6]

At the federal level during the last two decades, governmental units such as the Office of Management and Budget, the Office of Personnel Management,

Table 6.6 Federal Service Noncareer Appointees, 1980–2000

Category of Employee	1980		1990		2000	
	Number	Percent of Total	Number	Percent of Total	Number	Percent of Total
Presidential appointees	488	7.6	557	8.9	1345	21
Noncareer SES	582	9.1	675	10.9	720	11.1
Total Noncareerist	6,379	100	6,190	67.9	6,478	100%

SOURCE: Office of Personnel Management monthly reports.

the Department of the Interior, indeed most major federal departments, witnessed politicization in their career ranks to a far greater extent than ever before (though the trends of politicization began long ago in the Johnson, Nixon, Ford, and Carter administrations). Throughout all units, the Reagan-Bush-Clinton administrations staffed SES with the maximum number of political appointees planned by law. As Table 6.6 shows, between 1980 and 2000, the numbers of presidential appointees, noncareer SES, as well as the total numbers of noncareerist posts grew though their percentage composition varied within each decade.

This politicization of policy levels not only can reduce government in-house competence and neutral application of expertise to broad, public service goals, but also affects professional and civil service subsystems in many ways. First, many "pros" leave government service dissatisfied at working for less-than-competent bosses. The SES careerist members who joined in 1979 left in large numbers in the 1980s due to this feeling of lack of support for their professionalism. Aside from the obvious problems of reducing managerial and policy expertise when senior and mid-level policy posts are staffed largely by politicians or newly promoted careerists, more profoundly it is increasingly hard to separate the "pros" from the "pols" inside bureaucracy. For example, "the heads-up-get-ahead" officers of the army, air force, and navy know that they must not only have "their tickets punched" as field commanders and staff officers to succeed in their respective career services, they must also be adept at using the jargon of systems analysis, Pentagon bureaucratic infighting techniques, and playing politics on the hill with the various armed services committees, subcommittees, and staffs. This mingling of politics and professionalism may well foster greater degrees of political responsiveness, but it may also incite greater activism among officers, as the example of Vice Admiral James (Ace) Lyons clearly points up. His outspoken criticism of the War Powers Resolution at the Naval War College during the mid-1980s raised a storm of congressional and media criticism,[7] which was repeated when military professionals, such as Lieutenant Colonel Oliver North, housed at National Security Council, were used to gain conservative political support for Latin American conservative causes. This mixing of "pros" with "pols" raises other more profound problems. As former Secretary of State Henry Kissinger suggested, "On some levels it has eased civilian-military relations, on a deeper level, it deprived the policy process of the simpler, cruder but perhaps more relevant assessments needed when issues are reduced to a test of arms."[8]

Increasing Complexity Fragments the Bureaucratic System   Once upon a time not very long ago, U.S. public bureaucracy at the local level came in essentially two varieties—a mayor-council and a council-manager form (with a few commission-type governments as well). Despite their institutional differences, their local functions were fairly clear-cut—to provide the basic public services at the community level, such as police, fire, welfare, and public works. Other services were left to private or nonprofit agencies. Federal and state intervention was limited. The revenue base—property taxes—for supporting these local activities was similarly well defined and largely separate from other levels of government. Thus functional and support responsibilities were fairly evenly divided among local, state, and federal agencies. Each had its own specific tasks, public organizations to carry out these tasks, and revenue bases for support. This may be called "the layer-cake model of federalism."

As prior chapters in this book have explained, such simple institutional arrangements have disappeared from U.S. government. Particularly in recent decades, the layer-cake conception of federalism with its neat division of functional assignments has given way to a system of great complexity. Public organizations at every level of government are deeply intertwined and interrelated with one another. They are often hard to differentiate at any level of government. A state public health department, for instance, often secures most of its funds from federal sources and in turn depends entirely upon local agencies to actually administer its programs. Its personnel and buildings may be located in the state capital, but this state bureaucracy may be little more than a transfer point for federal funds that flow downward to local sources. The state agency may thus serve as an extended arm of federal and local bureaucracy— that is, as a regulatory checkpoint for ensuring that local authorities indeed comply with state health codes and procedures. Numerous other examples abound. In practice, often not much distinction exists between federal, state, and local entities, because they are so operationally interdependent. Perhaps in legal fiction they remain different agencies, but certainly not in institutional practice. The same complex and intertwined interrelationships between bureaucratic agencies are the norm in virtually every policy field today.

As Figure 6.13 emphasizes, much of the complexification within government agencies, such as the U.S. Department of Agriculture, has occurred gradually through the addition of new tasks and responsibilities over more than a century, with many programs not necessarily fitting well into the overall original design of the department. The piecemeal, often haphazard addition of programs creates serious coordination problems, as illustrated in Figure 6.14. The emerging policy challenges facing America in biotechnology, rural development, marketing, and water quality cut across several U.S.D.A. departments (not to mention many others throughout the federal, state, and local levels).

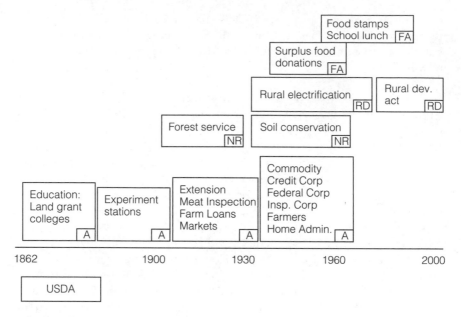

FIGURE 6.13   Chronology of major events in the creation of the U.S. Department of Agriculture

Source: U.S. Dept. of Agriculture.

The complexification of the entire bureaucratic system, such as in the U.S.D.A., generally works to make its actions more difficult, cumbersome, and problematic. Where more personnel, layers of hierarchy, units of government, vested interests, and regulations enter into the decisional and implementation processes, more opportunities for delay, indecision, and inaction or even contradictory actions occur. There are more points for "veto groups" to hold up action as the system "complexifies." Further, fixing responsibility for action or inaction becomes more difficult. Establishing who is at fault for a breakdown or delay becomes harder as more parties are involved and as the system grows in size and complexity. There are limits to what the human mind can comprehend and manage—even with the aid of supercomputers.

Too Many Promises and Ill-Conceived Demands Overburden the Bureaucratic System   Elected officials today increasingly rely on television to get their messages across to voters. The 30-second spot has become perhaps the most powerful vote-getter and source of political education for Americans nowadays. Heavy reliance upon simplistic commercials tends to make candidates exaggerate their claims. Furthermore, funding from various PACs and special interests, now so critical to the financing of these expensive campaigns, fosters a plethora of often very narrow and ill-conceived campaign promises, which often cause the electorate to make specific demands for bureaucratic action after the election. Again to cite Frederick Mosher:

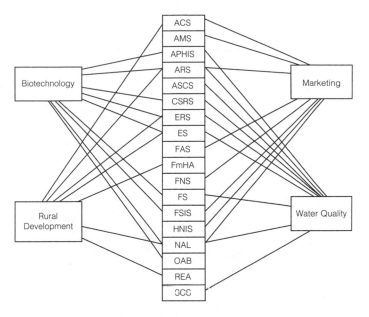

Note: The following abbreviations are defined as follows:

Key:
ACS = Agricultural Cooperative Service
AMS = Agricultural Marketing Service
APHIS = Animal and Plant Health Inspection Service
ARS = Agricultural Research Service
ASCS = Agricultural Stabilization and Conservation Service
CSRS = Cooperative State Research Service
ERS = Economic Research Service
ES = Extension Service

FAS = Foreign Agricultural Service
FmHA = Farmer's Home Administration
FNS = Food and Nutrition Service
FS = Forest Service
FSIS = Food Safety and Inspection Service
HNIS = Human Nutrition Information Service
NAL = National Agricultural Library
OAB = Office of Agricultural Biotechnology
REA = Rural Electrification Service
SCS = Soil Conservation Service

FIGURE 6.14   Complexities of coordination in four emerging cross-cutting policy issues due to fragmentation within U.S. Department of Agriculture

Source: GAO Report, *Revitalizing USDA* (GAO/T-RCED-93-62), p. 6.

Candidates for the presidency are tempted, almost compelled, to make promises and commitments to those whose support they seek, long before the nominating convention is held. The pressure for promises increases right up to (and after) the inaugural address; pressure for jobs, for favors, for support on policies and programs. But once in office, things look a great deal different from their appearance outside. Commitments on programs and policies in particular, once seen as ideologically desirable and politically inviting, may later appear quite unwise, damaging, or

Public school teachers, like most public servants, are increasingly being asked to do more with less.

downright impossible. If the successful candidate, once in office, abides by them, he may be doing himself and his country a grave disservice.[9]

In particular, as Mosher also observes, the pressure to put these demands into action is particularly acute during the first hundred days of a new administration, precisely at the time when it is least able to act with care and deliberation:

> There is no period when a president is as ill-prepared to launch a comprehensive program of legislation as during the months immediately following his first inauguration. He and his major advisers are still in the process of education. Unless he himself is a graduate of Congress his acquaintance with and channels to the appropriate fishing holes in Congress are still underdeveloped. The majority of his political appointees in various departments and agencies are not yet even named, let alone confirmed and in office. This means that contacts between top administration officials and the more knowledgeable career officers have not yet begun. It is hard to imagine a situation more conducive to mistakes—perhaps terribly damaging mistakes—than when a new administration, riding the crest of popularity, pushes through a program based on the ideological rhetoric of a heated political campaign without benefit of the wisdom and the skepticism of officials who have had prior experience in government.[10]

The Growth of the Contractual Subsystem Causes Numerous Oversight Problems   As Chapter 4 stressed, the contracting out of services at every level of government today results from a mixture of economic pressures to keep costs down, and political pressures to reward specific local commercial groups with lucrative government contracts. Contracting out for services also coincides with the general public sentiments that government be cut, squeezed, and trimmed. As Chapter 4 underscored, the contractual subsystem is one of the hidden major growth areas today in government. Its growth has, however, tended to accelerate numerous problems and dilemmas of managerial efficiency, oversight, and accountability. One only needs to read the newspaper headlines to discover some of these major issues of accountability:

Army Probes a Computer Firm on Charges of Contract Misconduct

Local Cable Contractor Defaults on Contract with County

GAO Finds Difficulties in Fast Food Contract Services

Navy Sub-contractors Face Fraud Charges Due to Cost-Overruns

FDA Cites Phony Evidence in Contracted Drug Experiments

As these headlines point up, serious ethical, managerial, and accountability problems arise as public jobs get done out of house rather than in-house. Long chains of not-so-interconnected private contractors and subcontractors, driven frequently by the pressures of only the bottom line rather than by the broad moral concerns of the public good, have raised enormous problems involving the legal use of funds, programmatic efficiency and effectiveness, and security safeguards for classified defense work. Contracting out stretches and lengthens enormously the size of the bureaucratic system as more people and firms are involved with government work. Indeed, pin-pointing who is responsible for delays, cost overruns, quality controls, and other failures, becomes increasingly complicated and difficult to determine. This is especially true when multibillion-dollar contracts for highly sophisticated public programs are at stake.

Lester Salamon sums up the central dilemma of contracting-out government services: "Third-party government creates serious problems of management accountability for which standard public administration fails to prepare us. This is so because . . . third party government places significant shares of the authority for running federal programs into the hands of nonfederal, often nonpublic, institutions over which federal managers have imperfect control at best. . . . In other words, federal managers are often forced to accept, for reasons of political expediency, forms of government action that complicate program management and create serious problems of accountability."[11] Or as Don Kettl has underscored, the increase of what he terms "government by proxy" (or, third-party government through contracting-out) makes the success of government more dependent "on all Americans and their sense of citizenship." Kettl writes:

All of those responsible for the performance of government—whether part of government or not—must recognize their broader responsibility to the public for their behavior. Accountability thus has to extend beyond creating government mechanisms to detect and cure problems. Whether filling out an income tax form, taking out a government loan, following a federal regulation, or working for a government contractor, each citizen plays an important role in making programs work. Each of our individual actions, added together, determines the results of governmental policy. Government by proxy thus emphasizes with great clarity the obligations of citizenship, for, as its strategies grow, government and its performance depend increasingly on all of us.[12]

Adding External and Internal Checks Increases System's Inflexibility
Since the 1970s many legal checks at every level of government have been "invented" to curb bureaucracy—and now most public agencies labor under these constraints, which were originally designed and approved by legislatures to improve public accountability. Examples are numerous: The Legislative Reorganization Act of 1970 significantly increased congressional oversight capacities; the War Powers Resolution of 1973 placed important curbs on presidential warmaking powers; the Congressional Budget and Impoundment Act of 1974 substantially increased congressional involvement within executive budget-making processes; the Freedom of Information Act as amended in 1973 sharply expanded public access to executive department records and information sources; the creation and expansion of Inspector General offices in every major federal department in 1978 provided new internal institutional checks upon agency practices (see Table 6.7); the Ethics in Government Act of 1978 toughened and extended financial disclosure and conflict-of-interest laws involving government employees. Likewise at the state and local levels, new restrictions were placed upon public bureaucracy through "sunshine" and "sunset" laws as well as through strict revenue limitations brought about by constitutional changes such as Proposition 13, which was passed by voters in California in June 1978, or Amendment One passed by Colorado voters in 1992.[13]

Bureaucracy at every level lives in the aftershocks of these and many other influential and significant measures. Often they affect public agencies in unforeseen and unintended ways, even in ways that are contradictory to their framers' intentions.

Veterans preference in federal jobs is a case in point (see Figure 6.15). Part of the Veteran's Act of 1944 to assist returning World War II veterans to find jobs gave them five to ten extra "bonus points" over nonveterans in federal civil service hiring and retention during reductions in force. However, today it severely limits the discretion of managers in retaining or hiring "the most capable individuals" as well as staffing with women and minorities, who are less likely to be veterans. Thus, this "veterans preference" works to give preference to one group over another, limiting "merit" and "representative" values.

Another good illustration is the Freedom of Information Act (FOI). It was originally intended to open up government. By the twenty-first century it was apparent that this seminal piece of reform legislation may well be doing precisely the reverse—opening up government for *private interests, not the general public.* Eighty-five percent of FOI requests processed at the Food and Drug Administration, for example, came from businesses that it regulates. Of the 72,534 FOI requests FDA processed, 22 percent came from law firms, 18 percent from the

Table 6.7 Expansion of the Inspectors General (IG) Concept, 1976–1989

Year	Statute (P.L. number)*	Establishment
		Presidentially appointed IGs
1976	94-505	Health, Education, and Welfare
1977	95-91	Energy
1978	95-452	Agriculture, Commerce, Housing and Urban Development, Interior, Labor, Transportation, Community Services Administration, Environmental Protection Agency, General Services Administration, National Aeronautics and Space Administration, Small Business Administration, Veterans Administration
1979	96-88	Education
1980	96-294	U.S. Synfuels Corporation
1980	96-464	State
1981	97-113	Agency for International Development
1982	97-252	Defense
1983	98-76	Railroad Retirement Board
1986	99-399	U.S. Information Agency
1987	100-213	Arms Control and Disarmament Agency
1988	100-504	Justice, Treasury, Federal Emergency Management Administration, Nuclear Regulatory Commission, Office of Personnel Management
1988	100-504	ACTION, Amtrak, Appalachian Regional Commission, Board of Governors of the Federal Reserve System, Board for International Broadcasting, Commodity Futures Trading Commission, Consumer Product Safety Commission, Corporation for Public Broadcasting, Equal Employment Opportunity Commission, Farm Credit Administration, Federal Communications Commission, Federal Deposit Insurance Corporation, Federal Election Commission, Federal Home Loan Bank Board, Federal Labor Relations Authority, Federal Maritime Commission, Federal Trade Commission, Government Printing Office, Interstate Commerce Commission, Legal Service Corporation, National Archives and Records Administration, National Credit Union Administration, National Endowment for the Arts, National Endowment for the Humanities, National Labor Relations Board, National Science Foundation, Panama Canal Commission, Peace Corps, Pension Benefit Guaranty Corporation, Securities and Exchange Commission, Smithsonian Institution, Tennessee Valley Authority, United States International Trade Commission, United States Postal Service
1989	101-73	Resolution Trust Corporation
1989	100-193	Central Intelligence Agency
		Nonpresidentially appointed IGs

SOURCE: Frederick M. Kaiser, "Inspectors General: Establishing Statutes and Statistics," in Paul C. Light, *Monitoring Government* (Washington, DC: The Brookings Institution, 1993), p. 26. Reprinted by permission of The Brookings Institution.

*Each public law number refers to a separate statute or to the act that contained the respective amendment to the Inspector General Act of 1978.

By law, veterans who are disabled or who served on active duty in the United States Armed Forces during certain specified time periods or in military campaigns are entitled to preference over non-veterans both in Federal civil service hiring and in retention during reduction in force.

Hiring Preference in Civil Service Examinations
- Candidates who pass an examination are ranked by their scores. Veterans eligible for preference are entitled to have 5 or 10 extra points (explained below) included in their scores if they pass an examination. A passing score is 70 or higher.
- Regardless of their scores, qualified veterans with a compensable service-connected disability of 10 percent or more are placed at the top of most civil service examination lists of eligibles, except for scientific and professional jobs at GS 9 or higher.
- A Federal agency hiring candidates from an examination list must consider the top three available candidates for each vacancy.
- An agency may not pass over a candidate with preference and select an individual without preference who has the same or lower score, unless the Office of Personnel Management approves the agency's reasons.
- Veterans may apply within 120 days after discharge for any examination open during their military service.

5-Point Hiring Preference
Five points are added to the passing examination score of a veteran who served:
- During the period December 7, 1941, to July 1, 1955; or
- For more than 180 consecutive days, any part of which occurred after January 31, 1955, and before October 15, 1976; or
- In a campaign or expedition for which a campaign medal has been authorized, including Lebanon, Grenada, Panama, and Southwest Asia (Desert Shield/Storm).

  Medal holders who enlisted after September 7, 1980, or entered on active duty on or after October 14, 1982, must have served continuously for 24 months or the full period called or ordered to active duty. The service requirement does not apply to veterans with compensable service-connected disabilities, or to veterans separated for disability in the line of duty, or for hardship.

10-Point Hiring Preference
Ten points are added to the passing examination score of:
- A veteran who served at any time and who (1) has a present service-connected disability or (2) is receiving compensation, disability retirement benefits, or pension from the military or the Department of Veterans Affairs. Individuals who received a Purple Heart qualify as disabled veterans.
- An unmarried spouse of certain deceased veterans, a spouse of a veteran unable to work because of a service-connected disability, and a mother of a veteran who died in service or who is permanently and totally disabled.

  Ten-point preference eligibles may apply for any job for which (1) a list of examination eligibles is (or is about to be) established, or (2) a nontemporary appointment was made in the last 3 years.

General Requirements for Preference
- Preference applies in hiring from civil service examinations, for most excepted service jobs, and when agencies make temporary appointments, or use direct hire and delegated examining authorities from OPM.
- An honorable or general discharge is necessary.
- Military retirees at the rank of major, lieutenant commander, or higher are not eligible for preference unless they are disabled veterans.
- Guard or Reserve active duty for training purposes does *not* qualify for preference.
- When applying for Federal jobs, eligible veterans should claim preference on their job applications. (Applicants claiming 10-point preference must complete form SF 15, *Application for 10-point Veteran Preference.*)

FIGURE 6.15 Veteran preference for federal jobs

Thirty Percent or More Disabled Veterans
Veterans with 30 percent or higher compensable service-connected disability ratings are eligible for direct appointments without examination, which may lead to conversions to career appointments. Veterans should contact the Federal agencies where they would like to work for job opportunity information.

If rejected for employment or retention because of disability or if passed over for hiring, these veterans are entitled to be notified by the agency, to respond to the agency's action, and to receive a copy of OPM's final determination. Once hired, disabled veterans can participate in the Disabled Veterans Affirmative Action Program and receive assistance in development and advancement opportunities.

Credit for Military Service
When a candidate's work experience is evaluated in an examination, full credit is given for military service. Such service is either considered as an extension of the work the veteran did before entering the Armed Forces, or it is rated on the basis of the actual duties performed in the Armed Forces, whichever is more beneficial to the veteran. Also, military time may count toward civil service retirement and vacations.

Retention Preference
Generally, employees who have preference in examinations and appointments also have preference over other employees in retaining their jobs in a reduction in force (RIF). However, certain employees who retired from military service are not eligible for preference for job retention purposes.

When layoffs are necessary, each nontemporary employee competes for retention with other employees who do similar work at the same pay grade and who serve under similar conditions. Among competing employees, the order of separation is determined by type of appointment, veterans' preference, length of service, and performance ratings.

Veterans have preference in retention over nonveterans. Veterans with disability ratings of 30 percent or higher and whose performance has been rated acceptable have preference over nonveterans and other veterans.

FIGURE 6.15   *Continued*

SOURCE: *U.S. Office of Personnel Management, August, 1991.*

press, 11 percent from business, foreign governments, research groups, and special interests; very few came from the general public. The estimated FDA costs for processing FOI requests were over $10 million. As Antonio Scalia observes, FOI and its amendments "were promoted as a boon to the press, the public, the little guy; they have been used most frequently by corporation lawyers."[14]

Whether proposed changes in FOI legislation will result in curbing such "excesses" is hard to predict. In general, such laws have created more legal complications, operational dilemmas, personnel costs, new budget requirements, and institutional management problems. These laws have also led to an increase in the number and power of lawyers *inside and outside* public agencies, who interpret and contest these legal requirements. In many cases, more alarmingly, the laws have given special interests a wider influence over internal bureaucratic operations and policies.

Yet the real impact of increasing "rule-boundedness" throughout bureaucracy serves ultimately to impede overall government performance. Professor Steven Kelman, in his thoughtful analysis, *Procurement and Public Management,* makes that very point in regard to federal government procurement practices: namely, that detailed requirements intended to promote competition in contracting have made the performance of government worse, not better.

When most government procurement involved simple, standard products such as paper to write on or coal to heat the buildings—and when most government action involved straightforward tasks such as accurately collecting statistics or correctly determining veterans' pensions—it is understandable that the quality of performance was not considered as problematic as it might be today. Either good quality performance was easily seen as more or less coterminous with the observance of rules to ensure equity, economy, and integrity or else it was easily seen as something that substantive rules in the form of organizational standard operating procedures could achieve.

In procurement, more of what the government now buys is complex and hence ill-suited to the kind of complete specifications in contractual language that the original system used as the way to achieve good substantive performance by vendors. Vendors can serve more and more as sources of ideas, not merely as instruments to satisfy simple wants that government has determined. . . . The complex or experimental nature of what is being undertaken or the new expectations of citizens from government increase the difficulty of attaining excellence.

Existing rules become inappropriate as the world changes. . . . Yet, despite their inappropriateness to changed circumstance, rules are difficult to change. To achieve good substantive performance in a changing world, an organizational design relying heavily on rules of any sort becomes increasingly inappropriate.[15]

Broad, Sustained Public Hostility Coupled with Effective, Narrow Special Interest Intrusion into Bureaucracy Thwarts Public Action

The late U.S. Senator Stephen M. Young from Ohio was well-known for his caustic replies to constituent letters. In one letter that Young received, the writer complained of "federal handouts to the poor." Young's response was:

A young man lived with his parents in a low-cost public-housing development in Hamilton County. He attended public school, rode the free bus, enjoyed the free-lunch program. Following graduation from high school, he entered the army and upon discharge kept his National Service Life Insurance [sic]. He then enrolled in an Ohio university, receiving regularly his GI check. Upon graduation, he married a public-health nurse and bought a farm in southern Ohio with an FHA Loan.

Later, going into the feed and hardware business, in addition to farming, he secured help from the Small Business Administration when his business faltered. His first baby was born in the county hospital, built in part with Hill-Burton federal funds. Then he put part of his land under the Soil Bank Program and used the payments for not growing crops to help pay his debts.

His parents, elderly by now, were living comfortably in the smaller of his two farm homes, using their Social Security and Old Age Assistance checks. Medicare covered most of their doctors' and hospital bills. Further, the young man received help from the Rural Electrification Administration, the Farmers

Home Administration, the Federal Housing Administration, and the National Student Loan Program, which financed his children's college education.

Then, a little later, it was rumored that he had joined a cell of the John Birch Society and also the Liberty Lobby, both right-wing extremist groups. He wrote his congressman denouncing excessive government spending, Medicare, big government, the United Nations, high taxes, etc. He wrote:

"I believe in rugged individualism. People should stand on their own two feet, not expect government aid. I stand on my own two feet. I oppose all those socialistic trends you have been voting for and demand return to the free enterprise system of our forefathers."

Young's letter to his disgruntled constituent points out well the central paradox of modern America: For better or worse, or better *and* worse, throughout our lives we are deeply dependent on the services provided by numerous public agencies for our survival but at the same time many Americans hold damning views of the very institutions that serve their basic needs. We cannot live without public bureaucracy today, but we are contemptuous of its existence!

As Figure 6.16 emphasizes, compared to business and labor in "what it takes to succeed," the overall negative attitudes toward government remain high, according to a Roper survey. For example, only 13 percent of the public believes "sheer hard work" brings success in government, compared to 33 percent in business and 22 percent in labor. Such hostility not only engenders broad public opposition to bureaucratic activity, it also prevents governmental organizations from attracting capable individuals to staff their programs at all levels and from improving overall agency morale and managerial effectiveness.

Along with broad and sustained public hostility to bureaucracy, we see the rise of well-organized, aggressive special interest groups. Increasing numbers of sophisticated hostile political interests surround many government organizations, thereby limiting public agencies' room to maneuver in many cases. These PACs have continued to flower and grow (see Table 6.2). They are well financed and highly influential. These political groups and other interests tend to complexify issues rather than simplify them; prolong debate rather than push for closure; and impede the implementation of programs rather than promulgate their effective and speedy administration. In short, they promote delay, not action. Further, they tend to push for particular interests rather than the general public welfare. Their sophistication, size, and influence over bureaucracy have tended to increase for many reasons—increased funding, more expertise, and advanced use of technologies, to name only a few.

Take, for instance, two of the most powerful pressure groups in Washington, DC: the Heritage Foundation and Gray and Company. Probably few Americans outside the nation's capital have heard of either, yet today they decisively influence the course of national politics and bureaucratic actions through spinning fine, invisible webs of influence around many public agencies. They tend to press for special interests rather than for the collective general welfare. Highly skilled lawyers and lobbyists in growing numbers tend to dominate, direct, and influence these groups.

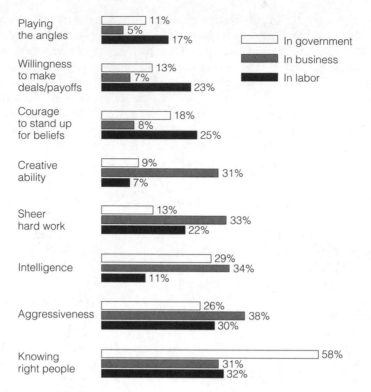

FIGURE 6.16 What Americans believe it takes to succeed in government, labor, and business

Source: Roper ASW, NOP World Company. Reprinted with permission.

The Heritage Foundation, a nonprofit conservative think tank, has also been especially influential. It succeeded in placing many of its key personnel in major political posts in the Reagan–Bush administrations. It closely monitors the progress of various executive agencies in achieving conservative laissez-faire doctrines and openly criticizes any laxness in adhering to the conservative ideological line. Conservative lawyers and lobbyists who head this organization focus their efforts on educating the public and members of Congress about bureaucratic activities adverse to their point of view through frequent press conferences, testimony at public hearings, and brief, fact-filled reports passed out to the public and press. Heritage is well financed by wealthy individuals and businesses, highly sophisticated in public relations, well connected within the administration, and staffed with able specialists in various policy fields of foreign and domestic affairs that advocate and cultivate intensively the conservative view.

Gray and Company, a Washington, DC-based lobbyist agency, is powerful, well connected, well financed, and extremely sophisticated in the arts of persuasion, media campaigning, computer capabilities, data analysis, and public opinion surveys. Gray represents 130 firms, foreign governments, and other groups and operates with a multimillion-dollar budget, making it the largest

Washington lobbying firm. Gray's personal connections run throughout Washington. Gray uses many sources to acquire inside information for the gain of its clients (such as American Express, Republic of Turkey, and Zana Corporation). Much of its work is simply in opening the right doors, gaining access to information, and creating the right impression through public presentations and media campaigns aimed at influencing favorable bureaucratic decisions or outcomes. Sometimes Gray is not successful; for example, in its urging of the Justice Department to file a brief in favor of Reverend Sun Myung Moon in a Supreme Court case of tax fraud or in its support of American Express in opposing the Transportation Department's "scatter plan" for the Washington National Airport. Often, however, Gray is quite successful in pressuring Congress and the bureaucracy, as in a major media effort to improve Turkey's national image in order to secure increased foreign aid for that country. In short, personal friendships, PR expertise, high-speed computer capabilities, direct mailings, and ample finances make Gray and Company and other pressure groups potent forces that intrude into bureaucratic operations and influence public agencies on the federal scene.

James A. Smith, who studied these groups in some depth in his book *The Idea Brokers,* sees the relationship of these groups and government as the most serious question we face as a democracy. Smith writes:

> Woodrow Wilson feared the notion of a "government of experts." The powerful allure—especially strong in a democracy, with its ingrained respect for science—of a rational, efficient decision-making process would always outweigh the attractions of the messy and passionate conflict of interests envisioned by the founders of the American government. But democracy depended, in his vision, on the dedicated amateur who understood the concrete applications of a policy initiative and who could speak the common language of the ordinary citizen. "What are we for," he asked, "if we are to be scientifically taken care of by a small number of gentlemen who are the only men who understand the job?"
> Contemplating our present vast and complex knowledge sector, one finds it hard to resist the conclusion that much of what Wilson feared has come to pass. The expert class has interposed itself between the average citizen and the deliberations of government, often confusing and overcomplicating straightforward issues with its arcane vocabularies and giving politicans a way to duck their obligations by leaving politically difficult problems to expert commissions and study groups. It is sometimes hard to fix responsibility in such a system, and in the broader context of American political culture it is hard for the citizen to assess the often sharp disputes within the expert class. . . . The most serious questions cannot even be posed, let alone answered, in the language of common sense.[16]

Table 6.8 indicates that interest groups are prevalent at the "grass roots level" as well, but according to the city council members' perceptions of group influence in their respective cities, groups vary significantly in exercising power and influence over local governments' policy and administrative affairs. Similarly, on

Table 6.8 Council Members' Perceptions of Group Influence in Their Cities

	CITY SIZE			
Group	Average	Small	Medium	Large
Neighborhoods	66	61	66	69
Businesses	56	50	57	59
Elderly citizens	39	38	40	40
Realtors/developers	27	16	26	38
Racial minorities	26	18	20	39
Environmentalists	22	19	25	23
Labor unions	22	9	21	32
Municipal employees	21	21	20	22
Ethnic groups	17	12	14	23
Women	16	13	14	21
Good-government organizations (e.g., LWV)	13	14	13	13
Antipornography/anti-vice groups	10	9	12	10
"Pro-choice" groups	5	4	3	8
"Right to life" groups	4	4	3	4

SOURCE: Charldean Newell (ed.), *The Effective Local Government Manager,* 2nd ed. (Washington, DC: ICMA, 1993), p. 38. Reprinted by permission.

Note: The figures indicate the percentage of council members who felt that each group had *considerable* influence on council decisions. 904 council members were interviewed. City size: small = 25,000 to 70,000; medium = 70,000 to 199,999; large = more than 200,000.

Table 6.9, "The Power 25 in Washington, DC," the annual ranking by *Fortune Magazine* of the most influential lobbyists show considerable variation in their perceived power rankings within only one year.

The Rise of "The Uncontrollables" in the Public Budgetary Process

Naomi Caiden pointed out in her excellent essay "The New Rules of the Federal Budget Game" in the *Public Administration Review* that we no longer create government budgets by making annual authorizations through public managers, with incremental bargains struck between various bureaucratic and political players. Neither is budget making as isolated as it once was. Rather, budgeting has become "prey to the vagaries of assumptions about a fluctuating economy." Much of what is spent in the federal budget, which in turn fuels the size, shape, and purpose of public bureaucracy, is now tied to "uncontrollables"—formula-driven entitlements, long-term contracts with private enterprise, and interest payments on debt. As Chapter 5 emphasized, these "uncontrollables" as a percentage of the total federal budget have steadily risen over the past 30 years, while discretionary spending percentages have fallen. These uncontrollable costs, furthermore, have become highly unpredictable and largely beyond the reach of traditional institutional budgetary controls. For the most part, their costs are driven by shifting groups/individuals qualifying for entitlements, by free market fluctuation of interest rates, by inflationary or deflationary trends

Table 6.9 The Power 25 Elite in Washington, DC
(Number in parentheses is last year's ranking.)

1 American Association of Retired Persons (1)

2 National Rifle Association of America (4)

3 National Federation of Independent Business (3)

4 American Israel Public Affairs Committee (2)

5 AFL-CIO (5)

6 Association of Trial Lawyers of America (6)

7 Chamber of Commerce (11)

8 National Right to Life Committee (9)

9 National Education Association (21)

10 National Restaurant Association (15)

11 American Bankers Association (20)

12 National Governors' Association (26)

13 American Medical Association (10)

14 National Association of Manufacturers (13)

15 National Association of Realtors (17)

16 National Association of Homebuilders (16)

17 Motion Picture Association of America (19)

18 Credit Union National Association (8)

19 National Beer Wholesalers Association (24)

20 National Association of Broadcasters (18)

21 American Farm Bureau Federation (14)

22 American Federation of State, County, and Municipal Employees (29)

23 International Brotherhood of Teamsters (46)

24 United Auto Workers Union (39)

25 Health Insurance Association of America (22)

SOURCE: *Fortune,* December 6, 1999, p. 208.

affecting business contracts, and by sudden global shifts in the supplies of natural resources or finished manufactured goods used by government—all hard
to predict or foresee. These same forces make governmental revenues hard to
budget. As Caiden writes, even though "figures for budgetary allocations still
march across the pages of the budget document in neat ranks by a function
and by agency to all appearances the results of conscious annual decisions,"
the reality is far different: "in seeking to control the economy, the budget has
become its prisoner."[17]

The result is that not only the budget but also public bureaucracy—as a
whole and as individual agencies— are now prisoners of economic forces
beyond their control. Public managers must now *respond* to these forces, not
exercise a measure of control over them. Bureaucratic functions and purposes
are thus intermeshed, intertwined, and driven by complex global and national
economic forces, which often are not easily seen or for that matter understood
even by experts. No one knows for certain how these interrelationships work or

influence society. Yet the interrelationships are there—*and are highly influential*. Here are some examples from recent newspaper stories:

- A slump in Detroit auto sales triggers slowing production, rising unemployment in primary- and secondary-supplier industries, and an automatic surge of federal-state-local unemployment and welfare benefits to the jobless, in turn pushing up demands upon social service agencies.

- A one-cent increase in the cost of gasoline because of a cut in Saudi Arabian oil production automatically triggers a half-a-million dollar increase in a large metropolitan school district's annual operating budget, forcing, in turn, cutbacks in various extracurricular activities and sports programs in order to balance the educational budget.

- The Rural Electrification Administration, which makes low interest loans to a thousand small rural cooperatives for agricultural development, is going broke because the loans were negotiated at far below current market interest rates; hence program cuts are required.

- Chicago's Continental Federal Bank is saved by the Federal Savings and Loan Insurance Corporation because of bad loans made to failing third-world Latin American nations that might trigger a crisis in the entire banking industry.

- Shortfalls in the Social Security's Medicare program are expected in the twenty-first century as the number of retirees who are automatically entitled to Social Security payments climb steadily— lower benefits or higher payroll taxes therefore will be needed.

- Fifteen percent of the federal budget goes to pay for the national debt. If $175 billion (approximately) was added to this debt, a 2 percent increase or decrease in the interest rates charged on this debt will automatically add or subtract $17.5 billion to the federal budget— which in turn will add pressures (or lessen them) on various other programmatic expenditures in defense and social programs.

- As cheaper third-world steel is dumped on U.S. markets, national production of steel slows, unemployment rises, and unemployment- welfare benefits to the jobless grow, thereby pushing up budget costs and social service demands.

- The number of 65 years and older veterans, automatically entitled to free care at VA's 175 hospitals and 119 nursing homes, rises from 10 percent in 1980 to 45 percent in 2015, with significantly increased costs to government (see Figure 6.17).

Automatic economic-budget ratchets work on state and local levels with equally profound effects upon city, county, and state public bureaucracies and the people they serve. In 1978, for example, Prince George's County in Maryland overwhelmingly authorized the TRIM Amendment (Tax Reform Initiative by Marylanders) to its constitution. Much like California's Proposition 13, TRIM put a permanent freeze upon county property taxes—*without room for in-*

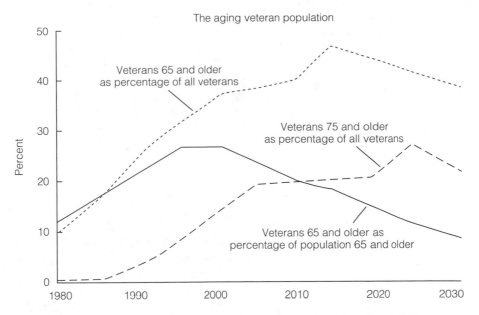

FIGURE 6.17   How socioeconomic pressures drive agency needs—future trends in the aging of the veteran population as a case in point

Sources: Veterans Administration; Social Security Administration.

flationary increases. Two decades later, local newspapers reported that county fire trucks were arriving understaffed at the scenes of fires; police cars were being used long after national standards required them to be replaced; road mainte-nance trucks and county roads were in disrepair; public schools had eliminated free driver education classes, free athletic events, and free textbooks, among other services; and that even student desks were in short supply.

In brief, the rise of these "uncontrollables" works to reduce bureaucratic au-thority, long-term planning, efficient use of resources, agency autonomy, and general public management effectiveness.

Forces Promoting Bureaucratic Cohesion
and Effectiveness

Certainly the prospects for public bureaucracy today are not all bleak. There is another side to the story, namely, forces at work supporting organizational co-hesion, decisive agency direction, institutional effectiveness, administrative ac-tion, and the increased exercise of bureaucratic authority. At times these trends may be harder to see or at least are less obvious than those just outlined, but they are present nonetheless.

Insistent Demands for Effective "Multiple-Optioned" Governmental Action and Services   Not too long ago, voters in Miami rejected by an almost two-to-one margin a proposal to replace the current professional manager-council form of city government with a strong mayoral system. According to newspaper accounts, the strong-mayor plan "was opposed by black and Hispanic groups, who feared the measure would further politicize city government"[18] and reduce the effective delivery of public services. Perhaps the Miami election is symbolic of the enduring strong support of voters for effective public institutions— those that are professional, free of politics, well managed, and dedicated to the public interest—to deliver a wide variety of goods and services. The public expectation, not always realized, is that these public goods and services will be provided promptly, fairly, and efficiently. Like the larger U.S. society, U.S. bureaucracy has moved from offering only a choice of chocolate or vanilla to offering many choices of flavor. Bureaucracy comes in many forms and serves many purposes. Public organizations perform a staggering array of services that were not even dreamed of a few years ago: Public libraries in some regions routinely rent out video games and do nationwide computer searches for virtually any kind of information; U.S. defense planners are preparing to fight warfare in space in the twenty-first century while working today to keep oil tankers in the Persian Gulf safe from terrorist attack; the Federal Emergency Management Agency offers enormous low interest disaster-relief loans while running all sorts of training programs for dealing with fire emergencies, nuclear attack, and other emergencies. Meteorologists of the National Oceanographic and Aeronautics Administration use sophisticated satellites, planes, and computers to map the weather all over the world. The list of new programs and services that have been added at the state level alone since 1959 is staggering, as depicted in Figure 6.18, but the point is apparent: Public bureaucracy mirrors U.S. thirst for multiple options *and answers* to its problems. As John Naisbitt pointed up, just as U.S. society is now multiple-optioned, so too is its bureaucracy.

What multiple-option bureaucracy means in practice is that institutions must show a surprisingly high capacity for producing diverse goods and services, for diverse interests in society, in turn requiring increased professional competence by public agencies to deliver the goods. Increasing numbers of Americans are now also directly affected by public agencies and *expect* these public products to be delivered to them. Statistics show that one-fourth of the U.S. population received direct personal benefits from the federal government (66 million persons in 36 million households). Much of government now touches citizens directly in ways heretofore unknown, heightening citizen demands for effective public services. They have, in other words, a greater vested interest than ever before in seeing to it that programs directly benefiting them are implemented well.

Bureaucratic Innovation Bubbling Up from the Grass Roots Is a Positive Force for Changing the System While there remains broad, intense hostility toward bureaucracy, surprisingly strong support for innovation on the part of many local governments is evident in recent surveys. For example, a 1999 survey (see Figure 6.19) asked, "From which level of government do you feel you get the most for your money—federal, state, or local?" Since 1972, the federal level has steadily lost popular support—from 39 percent down to a current 23 percent of the population—while at the same time local levels have steadily

Traditional Agencies: Present in Thirty-Eight or More States since 1959

Adjutant General
Aeronautics
Aging
Agriculture
Alcoholic Beverage Control
Attorney General
Banking
Budgeting
Child Welfare
Corrections
Education
Emergency Management
(Civil Defense)
Employment Services
Fire Marshal
Fish and Game
Food (inspection/
purity)
Forestry

Geology
Health
Higher Education
Highways
Insurance
Labor
Labor Arbitration and
Mediation
Law Enforcement
Library
Mental Health
Mining
Motor Vehicles
Oil and Gas
Parks and Recreation
Parole
Personnel
Planning

Post Audit
Public Utility Regulation
Purchasing
Revenue
Secretary of State
Securities (regulation)
Soil Conservation
Solid Waste (Sanitation)
Tourism (Advertising)
Treasurer
Unemployment Insurance
Veterans Affairs
Vocational Education
Water Quality
Water Resources
Welfare
Workman's
Compensation

Second-Generation Agencies: Present in Thirty-Eight or More States since 1969[a]

Administration
Air Quality
Commerce
Community Affairs
Comptroller

Court Administration
Criminal Justice
Planning
Economic Development

Federal-State Relations
Highway Safety
Juvenile Rehabilitation
Natural Resources

Third-Generation Agencies: Present in Thirty-Eight or More States since 1979[a]

Alcohol and Drug Abuse
Archives
Art Council(s)
Child Abuse
Civil Rights
Consumer Affairs (Protection)
Energy
Environment
Ethics
Exceptional Children
Finance

Historic Preservation
Housing Finance
Human Resources (Human
Service)
International Trade
Manpower
Mass Transit
Medicaid
Occupational Health and
Safety
Public Lands

Railroad
Savings and Loan
Social Services
State-Local Relations
Telecommunication
Transportation
Veterinarian
Vocational
Rehabilitation
Women's Commission

Fourth-Generation Agencies: Present in Thirty-Eight or More States in 1989[a]

Emergency Medical Services
Equal Employment
Opportunity

Ground Water Management
Hazardous Waste
Small and Minority Business

Training and Development
Underground Storage Tanks

Emergent Agencies: Present in Twenty-Five or More States in 1989[a]

Coastal Zone
Management
Horse Racing
Licensing (occupations)

Lotteries
Mining Reclamation
Ombudsman

Public Broadcasting System
Public Defender
Victim Compensation

FIGURE 6.18 Proliferation of state agencies, 1959 to the present

Source: Council of State Governments, 1959, 1969, 1979, and 1989, as cited in Herbert, Wright, and Brudey, "Challenges to State Governments," *Public Productivity Review,* 16(1) (1990):p 12. Reprinted by permission of Sage Publications.

a. Agencies listed in these sections are in addition to those in previous sections, which continued to be present in 38 or more states.

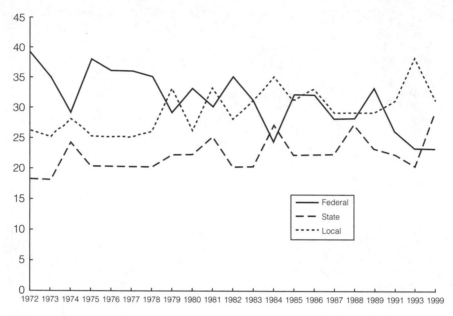

FIGURE 6.19   Which level of government gives you the most for your money? (1972–1999).

Source: Richard L. Cole and John Kincaid, "Public Opinion and American Federalism: Perspectives on Taxes Spending, and Trust—An ACIR update," *Publius* 30, 1–2 (Winter/Spring 2000), p. 192. Reprinted by permission of *Publius: The Journal of Federalism.*

gained popular support. Though as Table 6.10 emphasizes, there is a considerable variation of support among different genders, races, ages, levels of education, and ethnic groups. As an ACIR report explains, "In a period of high and continuing deficits, part of the sharp decline in public support for the federal government can be attributed to recent publicity highlighting wasteful spending by the federal government. . . ." The increase in public support for all kinds of local governments may also reflect public perceptions that local governments are doing a far better job of getting their budget acts together than is the federal government.

However, cities and localities seem at times to be more directly responsive and innovative in handling immediate policy problems and public agendas. Many of the national policy solutions to pressing issues today have seemingly bubbled up from experimentation at the state and local levels, for example, preferred provider health care options to reduce health costs; recent campaigns to rid the roadways of drunk drivers; home day care for elderly; barring the use of nonreturnable bottles and cans; requiring nonsmoking sections in places of business and in public buildings; competency testing for teachers; placing moratoriums on the construction of nuclear facilities; and workfare programs to reduce welfare costs. State and local bureaucracies also have been highly innovative in developing new nonadministrative devices to achieve their policy objectives, such as "down zoning" for stimulating new types of land use in

Table 6.10 Demographic Characteristics of "Most for Your Money" Respondents, 1999

Characteristics	Federal	State	Local	Sig.[1]	CC[2]
Gender				NS	.06
Female	28.5%	37.4%	34.1%		
Male	26.6	33.4	40.0		
Race				.000	.21
Black	51.2	34.5	14.3		
White	24.2	36.9	38.9		
Ethnicity				NS	.04
Hispanic	30.8	29.2	40.0		
Non-Hispanic	27.3	36.4	36.4		
Education				NS	.12
Less than High School	35.8	35.8	28.5		
High School Graduate	29.3	35.7	35.0		
Some College	23.9	35.2	40.8		
College Graduate	22.6	35.6	41.8		
Post-Graduate	21.3	34.0	44.7		
Party Identification				.000	.23
Democrat	36.9	35.5	27.6		
Independent	27.1	26.5	46.4		
Republican	15.7	40.4	43.9		
Region				NS	.08
Northeast	29.8	32.3	37.9		
North Central	25.6	35.2	39.2		
South Atlantic	29.3	37.3	33.3		
South Central	26.1	37.3	36.6		
Mountain	35.2	33.3	31.5		
Pacific	24.6	35.2	40.2		

[1] Level of significance reported is based on the chi-square value.

[2] Contingency coefficient.

SOURCE: Richard L. Cole and John Kincaid "Public Opinion and American Federalism: Perspectives on Taxes, Spending, and Trust—an ACIR update," *Publius*, 30, 1–2 (Winter/Spring 2000), p. 192. Reprinted by permission of *Publius: The Journal of Federalism*.

communities; "targeted differential code enforcement" to promote business development; new sorts of tax differentials to promote investment; imaginative use of public procurement policies to increase internal efficiency; alternative uses of schools and public buildings to promote community activities; and streamlining of permit procedures to expedite local construction.

A noteworthy case in point was the government's response to rebuilding the Los Angeles freeway system after the earthquake on January 17, 1994, which caused massive damage throughout the city. Because the city's freeway system, especially the East–West Santa Monica Freeway, is so vital to its economy, the California Department of Transportation (Caltrans) scrapped all of its bidding

The National Center for Patient Safety (NCPS), **Department of Veterans Affairs (VA):** Created guidelines to empower staff to report adverse events involving patients, which are underreported for fear of punishment. This systematic change will prevent future mistakes from recurring thus saving lives.

The OK-First Program, **Oklahoma:** Uses state of the art computer technology to give public workers up-to-the-minute information about severe weather. This allows safety workers to make lifesaving decisions quickly and effectively and to broadcast emergency warnings in a timely manner to the public regarding tornados, high winds, wild fires, and other weather related hazards.

Ho-Chunk, Inc., **Winnebago Tribe, Nebraska:** Reinvested profits from gaming enterprises to develop new businesses, thus ensuring a diversified economic platform for Native Americans in Nebraska. The program increased employment, decreased poverty, and increased the Tribe's annual revenues.

Mathematics, Engineering, Science Achievement (MESA), **California:** A staff team of teachers, parents, industry leaders, and higher education staff provide academic support and positive reinforcement to help educationally disadvantaged students to excel in math and science. Eighty-five percent of high-school graduates who participate in MESA attend college—much higher than the state average of 50 percent.

The Toledo Plan, **Toledo, Ohio:** This plan presents a unique method of peer review to evaluate and monitor teachers in Toledo public schools. The teacher to teacher method has proven to be less confrontational than previous review methods and fosters better teaching.

FIGURE 6.20 2001 winners of the Innovations in American Government Award given by the Institute for Government Innovation at Harvard University's John F. Kennedy School of Government

and contract procedures. Firms were given only days, not months, to bid for the repair work, and for the first time, had to include *both costs and time* to get the job done. In addition, they had to agree to work round-the-clock and pay $200,000 per day fines for every day work continued past the deadline and receive $200,000 bonuses for every day that work was completed ahead of schedule. The result: The Santa Monica Freeway was reopened in a record 66 days instead of the anticipated 140 days! In short, the grass roots level of bureaucratic innovation and responsiveness in recent years has been impressive (see, for example, Figure 6.20, which lists the 2001 winners of the Innovation Awards in American Government) may account in large part for higher levels of public support. Public agencies at the local level *seem* to the general public to be more innovative, more in touch with the public they serve, responsive by comparison with their federal counterparts today. The reverse was true just a few decades ago when it was the federal level that was seen as more progressive.

Increasing Specialization and Professionalism Strengthens Government Effectiveness Despite the apparent intrusions of politics into the bureaucratic ranks and the attendant problems it poses for appointee and careerist subsystems, the drive for specialization, expertise, and professionalization at all levels of the public service and in virtually every policy field seems to continue unabated. Gifford Pinchot, for example, the first chief of the U.S. Forest Service, defined the job of a professional forester as simply "tree farming." That was in the early 1900s. Today, largely because of the National Forest Management Act of

1976 (which amended the Resources Planning Act of 1974), an ever-widening body of specialists is found in the ranks of the U.S. Forest Service. In order to run the nation's forests properly, the National Forest Management Act directs the Forest Service to use "a systematic, interdisciplinary approach intended to integrate the knowledge of the physical, biological, economic and social sciences, and design arts." This legal mandate translates into a plethora of new specialists with advanced training in statistics, genetics, archaeology, petroleum engineering, chemistry, microbiology, and other fields—specialists who simply were not there a decade ago. Within the last decade, the growth rate of several selected professional specialities within the Forest Service has been as follows: hydrologists, +86.4 percent; wildlife biologists, +15.2 percent; soil scientists, +10.5 percent; range conservationists, +6.7 percent; and landscape architects, +6.1 percent. During the same period, the number of general foresters ("tree farmers") increased by only 0.8 percent. The Forest Service reflects the broad trends of professionalization throughout government, favoring specialized expertise over administrative generalists.

The growth of professionalism can also be seen in a sample list of federal government job requirements (see Table 6.11). Note the increases in all categories of highly technical expertise compared to the declining percentage of the federal work force in "worker," "helper," or "laborer" categories. Even grass roots bureaucracies demand is increasing for highly specialized, diverse skills in order to function.[19]

The drive for professional specialization and expertise within public bureaucracy is now stimulated by many factors: (1) legislation (as in the case of the Forest Service, which mandates the use of experts); (2) new technologies (for example, in health or defense fields, where new inventions spur the growth of new expertise to understand and cope with them); (3) new problems for social action (recent mandates to deal with acid rain, chemical spills, and unsafe landfills force agencies to hire a whole new set of experts); and (4) the professions themselves create new types of professions when they press to subdivide their ranks into clearly defined new varieties of subspecialties (teachers who today are "reading specialists" or "remedial teachers"—categories created in large part by the demands of professional educators). Professional associations are particularly vocal in pressing for separate, identifiable status, high recognition, unique training programs, special certification, and new subfield identities. Every professional association involved in the public sector exhibits these tendencies today. The Code of Ethics of the National Association of Social Workers, for instance, argues at the outset: "The social workers should strive to become and remain proficient in professional practices and proficient in professional functions." The emphasis throughout is upon uniquely differentiated roles, specialized expertise, advanced training, higher status, and *professionalism* as the unique hallmarks of the modern-day social worker.

New Technologies Inside Bureaucracy Improve Public Organizations' Efficiency   As has been said, much of the pressure for hiring new professionals and creating new professional subfields inside public organizations today is promoted by the technological imperative. As new problems confront U.S.

Table 6.11 The Federal Government Will Employ More Professionals and Management Related Workers in the Twenty-First Century

Share of Total U.S. Employment	Share of Federal Employment 1986	2000	Net Change (+ or −)
Management Related Occupations	14.1%	15.2%	+1.1
Engineers, Architects, and Surveyors	5.2	6.0	+0.8
Natural and Computer Scientists	5.2	5.4	+0.2
Social Scientists	0.8	0.8	—
Social, Recreational, and Religious Workers	0.4	0.4	—
Lawyers and Judges	0.9	1.0	+0.1
Teachers, Librarians, and Counselors	1.1	1.1	—
Health Treatment Occupations	4.1	4.2	+0.1
Writers, Artists, and Entertainers	0.7	0.7	—
Technicians	8.9	10.0	+1.1
Other Professionals and Paraprofessionals	6.9	7.0	+.01
Marketing and Sales Occupations	0.5	0.5	—
Administrative Support Occupations	25.1	21.4	−3.7
Service Occupations	6.2	6.3	+0.1
Agriculture, Forestry, and Fishing	1.1	1.1	—
Blue-collar Worker Supervisors	1.9	2.0	+0.1
Construction Trades	2.2	2.3	+0.1
Extractive and Related Workers	0.0	0.0	—
Mechanics, Installers, and Repairers	6.2	6.6	+0.4
Precision Production Occupations	2.0	2.0	—
Machine Setters, Operators, and Tenders	0.8	0.8	—
Working Occupations and Assemblers	0.7	0.7	—
Plant and System Occupations	0.4	0.5	+0.1
Material Moving and Vehicle Operators	1.6	1.6	+0.1
Helpers and Laborers	3.1	2.9	—
Total	100.0%	100.0%	

SOURCE: U.S. Bureau of Labor Statistics, *Current Population Report.*

government—such as fighting terrorism worldwide, aiding refugees in Africa, or combating new forms of disease—increasingly sophisticated technologies are needed by government agencies, which in turn necessitates the hiring of personnel who can "invent" and apply these technologies on behalf of the public. Government itself has become the spawning ground for new technologies on a vast scale within virtually every policy field. DoD's little-known Defense Advanced Research Planning Agency (DARPA) is today promoting the fifth generation of computers necessary to fight complex battles, and this will no doubt have important spillovers in industrial-economic-social development across the United States. The FBI has developed innovative uses for behavior research through its behavior science research unit at Quantico, Virginia, which can "profile" psychological portraits of serial killers with amazing accuracy. Further, the FBI has invented new high-speed automated fingerprint-reading devices that increase the speed with which police departments can "read" prints, enabling them to make arrests in cooperation with local police all across the country. Many large public university programs today, such as those at the University of California and the University of Texas, are developed and enhanced by state legislators to attract industrial and regional development. Through high-tech research, universities are becoming "magnets" for industrial growth. The Internal Revenue Service is using new supercomputers in its regional centers throughout the country to increase their collection rates, reduce their labor-intensive manpower costs, and achieve higher taxpayer compliance. Table 6.12 lists another example: vital basic technologies that give the United States military superiority in global defense. On the other hand, at the local level, as Table 6.13 underscores, the development of E-government has brought many advantages, depending on the stages of its development in cities and towns.

The application and use of new technologies by public organizations are reshaping public services in profound and important ways. Like their private enterprise counterparts, public sector agencies are using applied technologies to extend their range of services, reduce costs, improve the timeliness and efficiency of services rendered, and increase internal analytical and control capabilities. The complexities of these new technologies reshape the fundamental nature of the public workforce by fostering increased specialization, expertise, and professionalization. The ethical implications are apparent, too. The computerization of the IRS, for example, has created enormous ethical and security problems for the agency.

Perhaps the White House organization best epitomizes these contemporary trends involving technological impacts inside government. For although the White House has always been a highly political entity, it has been restructured in ways that draw upon a wide range of hard and soft management technologies to extend its influence and control over its staff. Through numerous skilled assistants, the White House employs a highly sophisticated cluster of technologies for strategic planning through its various planning and evaluation offices, and those for survey research through public opinion polling. Besides drawing on these technologies and specialized experts, the White House has innovatively utilized several unique organizational formats (or soft technologies) to implement its programs and policies, such as employing insiders, temporary "outside" private commissions, and temporary internal task forces to push through its various policy priorities and initiatives.

Application of New Expertise and Knowledge Bases from the Outside Also Aid Efficiency The negatives of contracting out government services were cited earlier in this chapter. There are also positive aspects to the increased reliance upon the contractual subsystem; namely, it brings into government fresh perspectives and new talent that could not normally be tapped for long-term governmental service or that government agencies could not afford to hire. It

Table 6.12 U.S. Defense Superiority

Basic Technologies for Maintaining Defense Superiority	U.S. Superiority
Microelectronic circuits and their fabrication	X
Preparation of Gallium Arsenide (GaAs) and other compound semiconductors	X
Software producibility	X
Parallel computer architectures	X
Machine intelligence/robotics	X
Simulation and modeling	
Integrated optics	X
Fiber optics	X
Sensitive radars	
Passive sensors	
Automated target recognition	X
Phased arrays	X
Data fusion	X
Signature control	X
Computational fluid dynamics	X
Air breathing propulsion	X
High-power microwaves	
Pulsed power	X
Hypervelocity projectiles	X
High-temperature/high-strength/lightweight composite materials	X
Superconductivity	X
Biotechnology materials and processing	X

SOURCE: U.S. Dept. of Defense, *Critical Technologies Plan for the Committee on Armed Services, United States Congress* (Washington, DC: U.S. Government Printing Office, 1989), app. A, pp. A1–A94.

also tends to break up traditional professional relationships and create broader, more diversified and democratic pools of expertise for solving public problems.

In the words of William Bacchus, we may now have "professionals without professions."[20] His point: we now have many professionals in the public service whose formal links to particular professional groups or specific professional educational programs are tenuous at best. Indeed, many public professionals are not even housed in one place as a unified, identifiable group of people but are rather "nested" all over government, even outside government, in odd and curious places. Witness the professional intelligence community (see Figures 6.22 and 6.23). The National Security Act of 1947 and 1949 set up the Central Intelligence Agency to unify all intelligence operations under one roof and, consequently, during the 1950s a highly professional cadre of intelligence personnel grew up within the CIA. In 1953 the agency contained most government in-

Table 6.13 As E-Government Develops in Stages, Great Internal and External Benefits Accrue Throughout Local Governments

| | | ADMINISTRATIVE FUNCTIONS | | | | POLITICAL FUNCTIONS |
		Stage 1	Stage 2	Stage 3	Stage 4	Stage 5
	Types of government	Information: dissemination/ catalogue	Two-way communication	Service and financial transaction	Vertical and horizontal integration	Political participation
Internal	Government to government	Agency filing requirements	Requests from local governments	Electronic funds transfers	One-stop job, grade, vacation time, retirement information, etc.	N/A
	Government to public employees	Pay dates, holiday information	Requests for employment benefit statements	Electronic paychecks	All services and entitlements	N/A
External	Government to individual—services	Description of medical benefits	Request and receive individual benefit information	Pay taxes online	Register and vote: federal, state, and local (file)	N/A
	Government to individual—political	Dates of elections	Receive election forms	Receive election funds and disbursements	All regulatory information on one site	Voting online
	Government to business—citizen	Regulations online	SEC filings	Pay taxes online, receive program funds (SB, etc.), agricultural allotments	Marketplace for vendors	Filing comments online

STAGES OF E-GOVERNMENT

Table 6.13 *Continued*

| | STAGES OF E-GOVERNMENT | | | | POLITICAL FUNCTIONS |
| | ADMINISTRATIVE FUNCTIONS | | | | |
	Stage 1	Stage 2	Stage 3	Stage 4	Stage 5
Government to business—market-place	Posting request for proposals	Request clarification or specs	Online vouchers and payments	Marketplace for vendors	N/A
Technologies used	Basic Web technology, bulletin boards	Electronic data interchange, email	Electronic data interchange, electronic filing system, digital signature, interoperable technology, public key infrastructure	Integration of the technologies required for phase 1, 2, and 3.	Public key infrastructure, more sophisticated interface and interoperable technologies, chatrooms

SOURCE: *Public Administration Review,* July/August 2002, 62, no. 4, p. 426. Reprinted by permission of the American Society of Public Administration.

telligence agents *within its own house* and within a highly structured professional career system, as depicted in Figure 6.21.

By the twenty-first century, however, all that was changed, as Figure 6.22 illustrates. Intelligence activities—and intelligence professionals—are spread out across the federal government, even outside the CIA because of contracts with major think tanks such as Brookings and Rand and with large companies, such as Hughes, that are involved with developing intelligence-gathering techniques and inventions. The CIA's nowadays employs only 4,000 people, and controls a few billion dollars, whereas "the broad intelligence community" involves tens of thousands of people, spending over $30 billion. These intelligence "pros" today lack a common home, clear lines of advancement, "elite controls," the "right" schools for professional preparation, and a commonly agreed upon set of skills, values, and expertise—in short, an overall corporate identity. On the other hand, the CIA significantly influences the course of policy choices in this particular field, even though its informal ranks and operational activities cut across many organizational lines, subareas, and specialties—even beyond the traditional boundaries of government. However, as recent critics point out, this tangled intelligence community structure, with competing organizations, purposes, and priorities without a boss with real clout led to systematic flaws that caused the massive intelligence failure to dedect ahead of time the 9/11 Terrorist Attack.

Such is also the case at the state and local levels, where the neat, precise boundaries and contours of public professions have faded or been erased entirely. The "pros" influencing the public sector have become fluid, hard-to-identify clusters of men and women (and women in recent years have grown in numbers and prominence in these ranks). For professionals in government, the route to success or to failure is increasingly difficult to pinpoint. There are no longer clear guideposts or road maps that direct individuals toward the one best way to succeed. But the diversity among these skilled employees that this ambiguousness fosters may well be a new source of institutional strength that promotes new perspectives, taps fresh talent, creates better research opportunities, and on the whole strengthens expertise in government agencies and their delivery capabilities.

Small Is Beautiful Compared to the rest of the industrial world, the United States ranks third from the last in public expenditures on its bureaucracy as a percentage of its GDP, 36.1 percent. Only Japan and Switzerland are lower, 32.4 percent and 30.7 percent, respectively. Overall, as a percentage of the total population, federal sector employment declined during the past decade (see Figure 6.24). Several policies in the Reagan-Bush-Clinton eras fostered this trend, such as reduction of federal personnel thanks to "reinventing government" reforms; deregulation of various sectors of the economy; shifting federal programmatic responsibilities to state, local, and private sector organizations; reduction in federal grants, loans, and subsidies; easing federal regulations attached to intergovernmental aid programs to states and localities; and accelerating nongovernmental solutions to public problems through tax and private sector incentives.

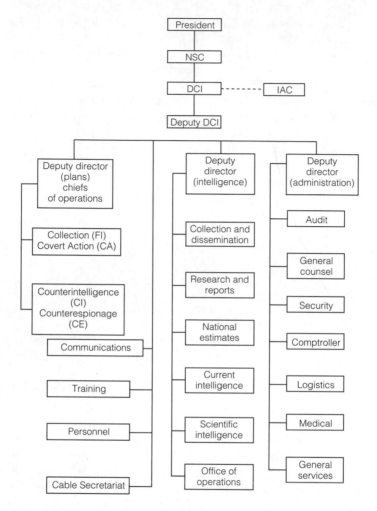

FIGURE 6.21   1953 CIA organization chart shows that most intelligence operations were housed in-house.

In addition, the last decade saw major shifts in international affairs, as discussed at the outset of this chapter. The decline of the Cold War meant a decline of military strength. In one year, 1992–93, over 100,000 personnel were cut from the Department of Defense. The secretary of defense estimated that, by 1996, the Department of Defense was reduced by 40 percent compared to its 1990 personnel level.

Not only have international political changes caused "down sizing" in the military-industrial complex of America's bureaucracy, but the application of new technologies is also shrinking the workforce significantly. The Hudson Institute report, *Civil Service 2000* (refer to Figure 6.23), stressed that clerical and blue-collar jobs will continue to decline well into the twenty-first

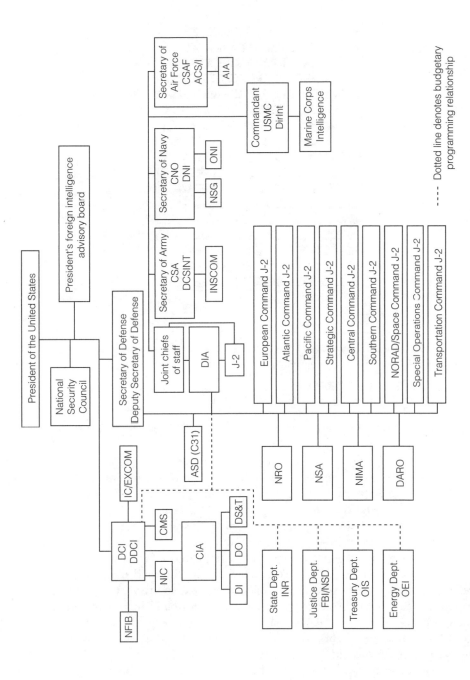

FIGURE 6.22 Today, the CIA is only one among numerous major federal intelligence gathering agencies spending 30 billion annually with various overlapping duties and functions that form the intelligence community. Note: This figure does not include the new Department of Homeland Security which also includes many intelligence units.

Source:The Economist, April 20, 2002, p. 24. ©2002 The Economist Newspaper Ltd. All rights reserved. Reprinted with permission. Further reproduction prohibited. www.economist.com.

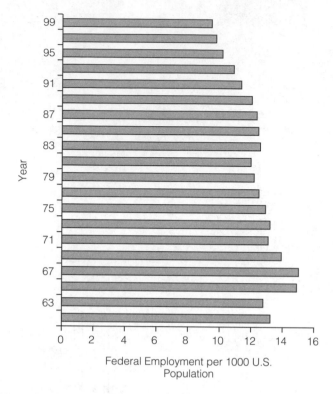

FIGURE 6.23   Federal employment per 1,000 population

Source: *Statistical Abstract of the United States*, 2002.

century: "The relatively high proportion of professionalism in the federal sector and the impact of automation in such formerly labor-intensive fields as data processing make this trend likely to continue. For example, the Internal Revenue Service is moving steadily toward electronic income tax filing, and the Social Security Administration is converting to electronic payroll data filing and benefits payments."[21]

As discussed earlier in this chapter, the trend toward increased reliance on privatization and contracting-out is likely to continue, bringing not only reduced full-time government personnel but improved efficiency and the advantages of economies of scale. Politically, privatization and contracting-out offer opportunities for expanding or maintaining expenditures, while seeming to reduce federal employment and agency costs. Administratively, these practices enhance the government's ability to hire highly skilled scientists, engineers, and technical workers who could not otherwise be attracted to government employment. It also allows agency managers to bypass restrictive, cumbersome, and burdensome administrative systems, such as procurement and personnel.

Overall, what can we make of these twin trends within public bureaucracies—those enhancing its authority and those promoting its weakness and decline?

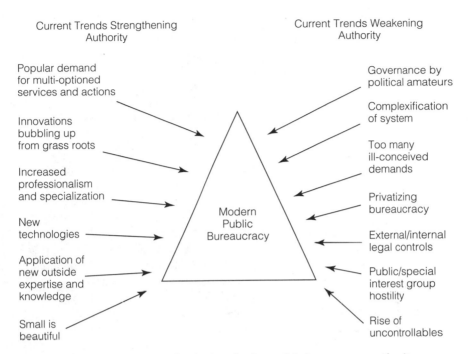

FIGURE 6.24   Feedback strengthening/weakening public bureaucracy authority

Certainly, as we have already observed, the picture is mixed. Both trends are at work today. As Figure 6.24 indicates, these previously enumerated forces exhibit significantly different impacts upon various elements of the bureaucratic system. In reality, then, nowadays American bureaucracy is being neither totally transformed nor allowed to remain a stable institution; rather, important elements of the system are simultaneously being weakened and strengthened by powerful feedback forces of change.

FEEDBACK AFFECTING INTERNAL OPERATIONS: CRITICAL COMMUNICATIONS NETWORKS WITHIN PUBLIC AGENCIES

No bureaucratic unit in the United States is oblivious to its general environment. All operate with formal and informal communications links, some quite elaborate, for assessing and responding to the changing social-political-economic conditions in which they function. As the previous sections of this chapter emphasized, survival may well depend on these links to the outside. These feedback mechanisms range from informal receipt of citizen complaints about their performance to formal, complex procedures for public budget hearings or legislative oversight of agency affairs. The range between the small and informal to large-scale formal feedback mechanisms is normally quite broad and diversified in most public agencies. Procedures include such techniques as citizen survey questionnaires, ombudsman offices, FAX or email numbers, inspector general units, "complaint hotlines," and various special offices and personnel devoted to obtaining and giving out general citizen information. Today the press and media play a major role in this feedback process (refer to Chapter 3).

Increasingly, as well, various elements of public organizations are required to respond to rapidly fluctuating economic conditions through modern use of a variety of contractual arrangements discussed in Chapter 4. OMB Circular A-76, for example, now requires competitive bidding for a broad range of federal contracts, which in turn makes many federal agencies highly dependent upon and responsive to private firms' costs and pricing requirements. Formulas and entitlements, which increasingly drive public budgets today at the federal level and which will be discussed more fully in the next chapter, "lock in" agency programmatic needs and demands directly and automatically to specific requirements. United States public bureaucracy is now so intertwined with and directly responsive to changing economic conditions that it is often hard to separate the public and private dimensions of economic life today.

Table 6.14 shows how various factors of communication networks can play an important role in influencing the effectiveness of the informal feedback process. Also, the various windows within which bureaucratic action happens or fails to happen, which were discussed earlier in Chapter 5, shape the special nature and scope of the feedback mechanisms employed by any given agency. Within stable, homogeneous settings, much of the public agency feedback may be conducted entirely on the basis of quite informal relationships between the citizenry and bureaucrats. Warner Mills and Harry Davis captured well this informality in the small town of Beloit, Wisconsin, in which city manager Archie Telfer "knows from long experience that city councils do not always know their own will. This is likely to occur with a problem whose political dimension is not clear. In such a case councilmen may either ignore the issue in the hope that it will go away, or offer some informal authorization for action to avoid going officially on record. Telfer knows that a nod of the head from a key councilman, or an oblique remark in informal conversation, may (or may not) be as significant a clue to action as a formal resolution."[22] Similarly, where there is a shallow, temporary window for bureaucratic action, the game signals from the citizenry and feedback employed may be entirely informal and improvised, responses to the immediate demands and conditions of the moment. Certainly this is the case in bureaucratic responses to disasters, such as a downed aircraft or a railway accident. Such community disasters force public agencies to cope as best they can within the limits of their resources and personnel. Their responses to such mishaps are frequently haphazard and catch-as-catch-can.

Firm but narrow long-term windows are different. Since well-placed and strong clientele groups serve as the basis for agency survival and prosperity, gauging and responding to these groups' interests undoubtedly must be the principal bureaucratic concern. Hence, many of the feedback mechanisms em-

Table 6.14 Bureaucratic Feedback Mechanisms Can Be Helped or Hindered by Various Factors of Communication Networks

Factors	Helping Feedback	Hindering Feedback
Language	Use of understandable and shared vocabulary	Use of language that is incomprehensible to parties involved
Perception of problems/issues discussed	"On same wavelength"	Mental perceptions of sender and receiver different
Geographic or status distance	Sender and receiver in close proximity	Geographic distance with many chains of intermediaries
Communication techniques	Face-to-face interchange	Impersonal exchange highly dependent upon inadequate technology that can break down
Volume	Adequate for needs	Excessive or insufficient volume for needs
Freedom to communicate	Free flow of ideas and information	Institutional censorship or personal self-protection of initiator distorts communication
Pressures of time and work	Adequate time and work load to receive, "digest," and comprehend communications	Time pressures and overload of work distorts or destroys effective communications between sender and receiver

ployed by the agency are targeted and directed at its specific clientele groups. Usually quite a full range of such techniques is utilized to gauge consumer satisfaction, from informal speaking engagements to citizen surveys to formal public hearings. The opposite, of course, is the case where public agencies are opposed by large, overwhelming pressure groups. Neither side communicates with the other very much, and if it does, it is only via the most antagonistic, formalized routes.

Public organizations operating within either evenly divided interest groups or constantly fluctuating, pluralistic groups are prone to be highly communicative with their publics. Their leaders need to keep an attentive eye on the changing needs, demands, and requirements of such interests and then to respond as needed. Under these conditions, as exemplified by Robert Dahl's portrait of Mayor Lee, a full range of feedback mechanisms must be employed by bureaucratic agencies to keep their programs responsive to shifting, or potentially shifting, conditions. Perhaps these agencies will even employ a sizable staff of public relations experts and policy or program planners, whose job is to stay alert to these changing trends and respond accordingly. Much also depends on the special leadership abilities of the managers of these agencies. Often they need to be highly verbal, mobile, and adept at adjusting and shifting their priorities according to changing social contexts.

What is especially apparent from recent research, conducted in various public bureaucratic settings, is that communications can make or break implementation processes for government. As Malcolm L. Goggin, Ann O'M. Bowman, James P. Lester, and Laurence J. O'Toole, Jr., concluded in their book *Implementation Theory and Practice: Toward a Third Generation,* communication serves "as the glue that holds the pieces together. Messages, their senders, and message recipients are the critical ingredients. Decoding these messages and absorbing them into agency routines is what implementation is all about."[23]

This thesis is underscored by Professor James L. Garnett at the beginning of his book, *Communicating for Results in Government: A Strategic Approach for Public Managers:* "Communication often makes the difference between government success and failure, sometimes between life and death."[24] Clearly, Maureen Hogan Casamayou's *Bureaucracy in Crisis* offers some poignant examples from both the space shuttle *Challenger* and Three Mile Island disasters about how bureaucratic communication failures occur when, in her words, "early warnings were blocked by structural or procedural deficiencies so that key people were not alerted. . . ."[25]

THE FEEDBACK LOOP IN AN ERA
OF DISSENSUS: WHAT IS THE PLACE
OF BUREAUCRACY
WITHIN A DEMOCRACY?

How can we sum up the wide diversity of feedback trends described in this chapter? Is there an overriding concept that aptly characterizes the present era in which feedback loop functions with respect to public bureaucracy as a core institution of U.S. government?

Perhaps there are too many forces around today to be summarized neatly in a single phrase. Perhaps we are too close to them to accurately gauge such matters. More distance from events may well be required for a clearer understanding of their lasting importance and significance for feedback affecting bureaucracy.

From our chapter review of the diverse variety of feedback influencing contemporary public bureaucracy, perhaps "The Era of Dissensus" would most aptly sum up the dominant mood of the times. It is a period without apparent consensus or overriding paradigm to explain public bureaucracy's role or place within the American democracy. Many socio–political–economic forces and points of view jostle for support and acceptance. No one view has been settled upon as "the truth." Ironically, American bureaucracy *de facto* may well be the "core of modern government," yet Americans *de juri* have yet to legitimize its place as being so central to running society. Indeed, most would probably prefer to do without it, that is, if repeated polling surveys on such questions are to be believed. And yet, in practice, no other institution in America is capable of addressing the critical twelve socio-economic–political trends, outlined at the outset of this chapter, that are significantly influencing America's future. So once again, we return to the theme that was stressed in the opening chapter—America's bureaucracy may well be the core of its government, yet Americans have not figured out its role, or even if it *ought* to have role in government!

Chapter 7 will focus directly upon this peculiar American dilemma of finding a place for its bureaucracy within its democracy. The legitimacy issue is rooted in the U.S. Constitution, which is largely silent on this issue. However, three founding fathers advanced very different enduring normative models that addressed this question. Throughout our two-hundred-plus years of history, these models have competed for support but none has achieved dominance over the others. These shifting value-models are critical to understanding the current unsettled legitimacy debate now—and in the future—over the place of bureaucracy in our democracy.

SUMMARY OF KEY POINTS

U.S. public bureaucracy at the dawn of the twenty-first century is affected by feedback from three important sources: First, the turbulent external environment in which government agencies operate has undergone rapid changes that shaped new and important basic goals and directions for public agencies at all levels of government. The twelve socioeconomic-political forces outlined at the beginning of this chapter work in many ways to "complexify," reshape, and enlarge the tasks and responsibilities of bureaucracy while at the same time working to make basic socioeconomic-political support for those tasks and responsibilities harder to achieve. The paradox is that today U.S. sociopolitical *and* economic responsibilities of a global nature require more diverse and complex actions from government agencies, but popular opinion on the home-front offers, at times, diminished political support for those public agencies.

As a result of these external forces, the internal dynamics of the bureaucratic system are rapidly changing to adapt to these severe pressures which influence its political authority to act effectively. Some pressures serve to strengthen elements of the bureaucratic authority by enhancing organizational cohesion, institutional effectiveness, and administrative action. Some trends today do precisely the reverse. The picture is mixed.

Also decisively influencing internal operations of U.S. public bureaucracies right now are critical communications networks which serve to enhance or deter agency managerial effectiveness. Formal as well as informal networks of communications are both vital to shaping internal operational effectiveness and bureaucratic outputs. All form in profound and provocative ways, which has stimulated critical changes and important redirections within the bureaucratic system—both its particular parts and as a whole. "The Era of Dissensus" may indeed be the term that most aptly sums up these trends at the end of the 21st century.

KEY TERMS

global superpower

demographic change

global economy

issue networks

privatization of bureaucracy

external/internal legal checks

bureaucratic goals

PACs

think tanks

knowledge workers

information economy

young/old poverty gap

uncontrollables

multioptioned bureaucratic authority

feedback loop

grass-roots innovations

professionals without professions

hard versus soft technologies

communications networks

era of dissensus

REVIEW MATERIAL

Review Questions

1. Why is the feedback loop so critical to the bureaucratic system's overall performance?

2. Which of the dozen critical environmental feedback pressures outlined in the opening of this chapter that impact the basic goals of public agencies strike you as being the most significant ones? The least significant? And why?

3. How are some of these pressures perhaps affecting you and your future? In what ways will they act in positive or negative ways in shaping your future career choices and personal development?

4. Given those critical and significant environmental pressures upon bureaucracy that you outlined in question one, think about how some of these might influence the design and structure of particular public agencies. Take a specific government agency you know or have had experience with (say, a public school or post office or motor vehicle department) and outline at least three effects these environmental trends might have today upon that unit of government.

5. What are some of the "unintended consequences" of several of these aforementioned trends on bureaucracy? For example, on the contractual subsystem? Or the imposed legal constraints upon public agencies?

Class Debate Pro/Con

Resolved that the single most important source of feedback today affecting the future of American Public Bureaucracy results from the 9/11 terrorist attack on the United States.

Student Homework Assignment

Select a state or local public agency and outline its feedback loop: 1) What major socio-political-economic feedback shapes its basic goals and directions? Where do these factors come from and how do they influence the broad purposes of that organization? 2) In what ways does feedback affect its bureaucratic authority by strengthening or weakening its organizational capability to act? What are these factors? Specifically how and where do they impact on the agency's institutional capacity? 3) What feedback influences its internal communications networks? From where does this sort of feedback derive and how does it directly affect this agency's managerial operations?

Case Analysis

"The Blast in Centralia No. 5" in any edition of Richard Stillman's Public Administration: Concepts and Cases: Sketch the feedback loop evident at the Department of Mines and Minerals, especially on three levels: Feedback that shaped the agency's general goals and purposes? Feedback affecting its bureaucratic authority to act? Feedback affecting its internal communication networks? Which feedback source in your view was the most influential for determining the department's regulatory actions (or rather its inaction) and why?

NOTES

1. Joseph S. Nye, *Bound to Lead* (New York: Basic Books, 1991).

2. Data drawn from an interview with Anthony Downs, Senior Fellow, Brookings Institution, as reported in *Washington Post Weekly Edition*, March 28–April 3, 1994, p. S-1

3. David S. Broder, "Seen from Far Away," *Washington Post National Weekly Edition*, April 11–17, 1994, p. 4.

4. As outlined in Lester R. Brown, Christopher Flavin, and Edward Wolf, "Earth's Vital Signs," in Edward Cornish (ed.), *The 1990s and Beyond* (Bethesda, MD: World Future Society, 1990), p. 138.

5. John Naisbitt, *Megatrends* (New York: Warner Books, 1984), ch. 10.

6. Frederick C. Mosher, "Presidential Transitions and Foreign Policy: The American Experiences," *Public Administration Review*, July/Aug. 1985, p. 470.

7. "Admiral Decries Military Restraints," *Washington Post*, June 23, 1984, p. 1+.

8. "Can We Fight a Modern War?" *Newsweek*, July 9, 1984, p. 48.

9. Mosher, "Presidential Transitions," p. 471.

10. Ibid.

11. Lester M. Salamon (ed.), *Beyond Privatization: The Tools of Government Action* (Washington, DC: Urban Institute Press, 1989), pp. 11–12.

12. Don Kettl, *Government by Proxy* (Washington, DC: CQ Press, 1988), p. 161. For other useful discussions of the problems of contracting-out government services, read John A. Rhefuss, *Contracting Out in Government* (San Francisco, CA: Jossey-Bass, 1989); Susan R. Bernstein, *Managing the Contracted Services in the Non-Profit Agency* (Philadelphia, PA: Temple University Press, 1991); R. DeHoog, *Contracting Out for Human Services* (Albany: State University of

New York, 1984); Lawrence K. Finley, *Public Sector Privatization* (New York: Quorum Books, 1989); John D. Donahue, *The Privatization Decision* (New York: Basic Books, 1989); William J. Gormley (ed.), *Privatization and Its Alternatives* (Madison: University of Wisconsin Press, 1989); Donald F. Kettl, *Sharing Power* (Washington, DC: Brookings Institution, 1993); and Jonas Prager, "Contracting Out Government Services: Lessons from the Private Sector," *Public Administration Review,* 54(2) (1994): 176–84.

13. For a comprehensive collection and discussion of these seminal documents affecting U.S. bureaucracy in the 1980s, see Richard Stillman II (ed.), *Basic Documents of American Public Administration Since 1950* (New York: Holmes and Meier, 1982), section 4.

14. Antonio Scalia, "The Freedom of Information Act Has No Clothes," *Legislation,* 6(2) (1982): 16.

15. Steven Kelman, *Procurement and Public Management: The Fear of Discretion and the Quality of Government Performance* (Washington, DC: AEI Press, 1990), pp. 88–89.

16. James A. Smith, *The Idea Brokers: Think Tanks and the Rise of the New Policy Elite* (New York: Free Press, 1991), p. 238.

17. Naomi Caiden, "The New Rules of the Federal Budget Game," *Public Administration Review,* Nov./Dec. 1984, p. 643.

18. *PA Times,* Sept. 15, 1985, p. 1.

19. For a discussion of the recent trends of increasing professionalism and politicization at the local level, read Richard Stillman II, "Local Public Management in Transition," *1982 Municipal Yearbook* (Washington, DC: International City Management Association, 1982).

20. William Bacchus, "Foreign Affairs Officials: Professionals without Professions?" in Richard Stillman II and Frederick C. Mosher (eds.), *Professions in Government* (New Brunswick, NJ: Transaction Pubs. 1981); pp. 11–20.

21. The Hudson Institute, *Civil Service 2000* (Washington, DC: U.S. Office of Personnel Management, 1988), p. 8.

22. Warner Mills and Harry Davis, *Small City Government* (New York: Random House, 1962), p. 32.

23. Malcolm L. Goggin, Ann O'M. Bowman, James P. Lester, and Laurence J. O'Toole, Jr., *Implementation Theory and Practice: Toward a Third Generation* (New York: HarperCollins, 1990), p. 40.

24. James L. Garnett, *Communicating for Results in Government: A Strategic Approach for Public Managers* (San Francisco, CA: Jossey-Bass, 1992), p. 3.

25. Maureen Hogan Casamayou, *Bureaucracy in Crisis: Three Mile Island, the Shuttle Challenger, and Risk Assessment* (Boulder, CO: Westview Press, 1993), p. 167.

FURTHER READING

Feedback literature should be considered broadly and so several books and essays cited in this chapter are good sources. Some of the futurist literature, even though it may be popularly oriented and sometimes uneven, provides at times a good guide to socioeconomic-political feedback influencing U.S.

bureaucracy. In particular, see such writings as John Naisbitt, *Megatrends,* as well as his more recent *The Global Paradox,* Edward Cornish (ed.), *The 1990s and Beyond,* Neil Howe and Bill Strauss, *13th Gen,* Peter Drucker, *Frontier's of Management,* Charles Handy, *The Age of Paradox,* Alvin Tofler, *Future Shock,* and Daniel Bell, *The Coming of the Post-Industrial Society.* Theodore White's *America in Search of Itself* is a keen historical insight into the present by a contemporary student of history and a respected journalist. For a readable summary of the 2000 American census data and its key demographic trends, see Sam Roberts, *Who We Are* (2001). For a highly negative view of our future, read Robert D. Kaplan, "The Coming Anarchy," *Atlantic Monthly* (Feb. 1994), pp. 44–76. For a dark view of American government's future, see Jonathan Rauch, *Demosclerosis* (1994). Reading some of the outstanding national newspapers, such as the *New York Times,* the *Wall Street Journal,* the *Washington Post,* and the *Los Angeles Times* and thoughtful periodicals such as *Newsweek, The Economist, The Futurist, American Demographics, Fortune,* and *Time Magazine* can be helpful, as can some of the journals that are more focused on bureaucratic activities, such as the *National Journal, Governing, Administration and Society, The American Review of Public Administration, Administrative Science Quarterly,* and *Public Administration Review.*

One should not overlook government reports, particularly from the GAO and the Census Bureau, on trends in government or special studies on critical issues such as the Bureau of Alcohol, Tobacco and Fire Arms' *Investigation of Vernon Wayne Howell, also known as David Koresh* (1993). In recent years five important general studies on the public service have been issued and are well worth reading in regard to highlighting key bureaucratic trends in the 1990s: OPM, *Civil Service 2000* (1988); the Volcker Commission Report, *Leadership for America* (1989); the Winter Commission Report, *Revitalizing State and Local Public Service* (1993); the Gore Report, *Creating a Government That Works Better and Costs Less* (1993); and ACIR, *Changing Public Attitudes on Governments and Taxes* (1993).

WEB SITES

http://www.diplomatswithoutborders.org/: Private, Business Diplomacy

http://www.socialsecurity.org/: Social Security Privatization

http://www.edweek.org/context/topics/issuespage.cfm?id=15: Privatization of Education

http://www.townhall.com/issueslibrary/governmentreform/: Government Reform

7
■

The Future
of the American
Bureaucratic System

What is the future of the bureaucratic system in the United States? Will it become more effective and efficient in delivering public goods and services for society? More equitable and fairer in distributing those goods and services? Will it be more accountable to the public at large as well as more responsive to individual and group needs? Will it retain its significant core functions in U.S. society? Will it grow or decline in influence? In short, what is tomorrow's role for public bureaucracy within America's democracy?

This final chapter will attempt to answer these and other critical questions by arguing that the future of U.S. public bureaucracy is fundamentally a normative value problem, one rooted in a unique, changing triad of historic national values. In other words, the central thesis of this concluding chapter is that our peculiar past national values will shape our future bureaucratic institutions. The chapter will be devoted to understanding these values and how they have influenced U.S. bureaucracy. It will begin by outlining the essential nature and content of these historic norms that are labeled Hamiltonianism, Jeffersonianism, and Madisonianism and explain how these values decisively influenced the course of American bureaucracy over the last two centuries. The chapter will conclude by stressing that the future role of U.S. bureaucracy will ultimately be determined by "trade-offs" among these competing values.

THREE FOUNDING FATHERS' NORMATIVE MODELS
FOR BUREAUCRACY IN A DEMOCRACY

The U.S. Constitution largely ignored the existence of *or need for* a bureaucratic system. It was mostly silent on this subject. But three of the founding fathers did give some attention to the subject in their writings—Alexander Hamilton, Thomas Jefferson, and James Madison.

Alexander Hamilton: Maximizing
Administrative Efficacy

Of all the founding fathers, none displayed more interest in and enthusiasm for administration and organization than Alexander Hamilton. Hamilton was a man of action from the time he was the brilliant 23-year-old aide-de-camp to General Washington during the Revolution. Throughout his tenure as the first secretary of the treasury in President Washington's Cabinet, he demonstrated masterful planning, control, and organization of national finances. As Leonard White writes, "In the Federalist Papers, Hamilton set out the first systematic exposition of Public Administration, a contribution which stood alone for generations. In his public life, he displayed a capacity for organization, system, and leadership which after a century and a half is hardly equalled."[1]

The role Hamilton saw for bureaucracy in government as well as in society was an expansive one. He was an ardent, enthusiastic nationalist who envisioned a big, bold, broad role for the American nation—politically, economically, and militarily. His writings are studded with glowing ideas for promoting "the public interest," "the public good," "the good of the general society," and "the national interest." Some say he valued the nation more than its people. At least there was nothing timid or modest about Hamilton's vision for the future of the United States, for he was a very early believer in positive government framed essentially to promote a strong nation and its interests. He argued for setting up a national bank, a national university, a professional army and navy, a public school system, and a variety of national public works projects, such as building roads, ships, canals, and dams and mining metals for industrial development. In short, he laid out a bold blueprint for the nation's future.

Hamilton favored a strong, energetic administration[2] based on maximizing the efficiency and effectiveness of public organizations to bring about his expansive vision of the future of the country. His normative model of the place of bureaucracy within a democracy thus contained these elements: (1) broad discretionary and activist roles for public agencies, characterized by strong, decisive leadership that evidenced "energy" and "tone" (words he repeatedly used); (2) unified public organizations with responsibility for administrative action undivided and preferably concentrated in one individual (as opposed to being spread out among boards or committees); (3) administrative power allocated to individuals and governmental units commensurate with the responsibility for the tasks assigned; (4) adequate time in office to ensure administrative effectiveness, long-term planning, and operational stability for implementing public programs; (5) preference for paid, trained professionals (as opposed to part-time volunteers) in staffing governmental positions; (6) emphasis on national planning, sound fiscal management, and responsible exercise of creative public leadership; and (7) popular control of public organizations achieved by means of the election of responsible, capable chief executives with adequate political power and support in order to ensure that tasks are performed competently and well.

Thomas Jefferson: Maximizing Administrative Accountability to the Public at Large

If the values of nationalism fired Hamilton's conception of administration, Jefferson's values were shaped primarily by concerns for THE PEOPLE. His commitment to individual liberty, freedom for humanity, and the pursuit of personal happiness was evident throughout his writings, but never more forcefully than in the Preamble to the Declaration of Independence, which dedicated the United States to popular values of "life, liberty and the pursuit of happiness." Unlike Hamilton, Jefferson exhibited an abiding faith in human nature and its unlimited potential for growth and development unfettered by governmental authority. And unlike Hamilton, who repeatedly spoke of "administrative discretion," "energy," and "tone," Jefferson stressed "limits on government," "individual rights," "freedom," and "liberty." As he said, "I am for a government that is frugal and simple." The New England town meeting perhaps came closest to his ideal of a polity that *was* "simple" and "frugal" and maximized citizens' participation in governing their own affairs.

A Jeffersonian normative model regarding the relationship of bureaucracy to democracy therefore, as Lynton Caldwell observed,[3] placed a heavy emphasis upon numerous devices to ensure bureaucracy's strict accountability to the general public and included such elements as: (1) extensive popular participation, especially voluntary mass involvement in administration (as opposed to staffing administration with paid, full-time professionals); (2) maximum decentralization of functions in order to limit activities and bring public activities under close and constant popular scrutiny; (3) operational simplicity and economy—simplicity so that administrative activities could be easily understood by the average citizen, and economy so it would not be economically burdensome to the public; (4) strict legal limitations that clearly spell out organizational purposes and restrict administrative discretion and authority in order to protect human rights; (5) a weak leadership role for public administrators through defining them as narrow functional specialists and technicians rather than as broad-ranging general managers or educated professionals exercising wide discretionary powers; (6) lack of concern for promulgating national planning, long-term operational stability, and effective program implementation but rather a focus on developing voluntary citizen efforts, private initiatives, and the free market alternatives to the performance of public tasks; and (7) administrative power in public organizations that flows from the bottom up, not from the top down, in order to sharply limit administrative outputs and ensure public oversight.

James Madison: Balancing Administrative
Interest Group Demands

James Madison shared many of Jefferson's concerns about protecting human liberty through limitations placed upon government, but he also held little enthusiasm for his fellow Virginians' idealization of the broad abstraction THE PEOPLE, which served as Jefferson's basic value premise and upon which his normative conceptions of bureaucracy-democracy relationships were founded. Madisonian analysis of U.S. government and the exercise of political authority rested instead upon the faction (or in modern terms, the interest group) which he saw as the chief fount of government's authority.

Federalist 10 indicates that while Madison saw factions as the prime movers of U.S. politics, he had little liking for any sort of faction. He defined a faction as "a number of citizens whether amounting to a majority or a minority of the whole, who are united and actuated by some common impulse or passion, or of interests adverse to the rights of other citizens, or the permanent and aggregated interests of the community."[4]

Madison "fathered" a Constitution that employs numerous "checks and balances" to mitigate the pernicious influence of factions upon governing institutions. As he underscores in Federalist 51, while the root causes of factions can never be eliminated, a framework of government can be designed so that their harmful influence over government institutions and public decisions is reduced. His fundamental advice in Federalist 51 on the framing of a stable, enduring government is well known: "Ambition must be made to counteract ambition," so that "you first enable the government to control the governed; in the next place, oblige it to control itself."[5]

Madisonian analysis basically was oriented toward structuring a process that would reduce but not eliminate factional influence to enable government *both* to govern adequately *and* to ensure its public accountability. Hence, he sought a "mixed government" that would balance competing interest group demands. His genuine contribution to political philosophy was his conception of "an extended republic" that would broaden geographic size and diversity in order to balance competing interests and thus protect human liberty and promote social stability. Indeed, throughout his writings, unlike either Hamilton or Jefferson, Madison, as historian Ralph Ketchum indicates,[6] places a special premium on achieving the values of organic social balance, political equilibrium, and the Aristotelian "Golden Mean."

Yet, unlike either Hamilton or Jefferson, Madison says little *explicitly* about the role of administration in the context of U.S. politics. But from what he said about the executive branch, the execution of public policies, and his conceptions of faction-based politics, we can conclude that Madison conceived of a very different role for bureaucracy in democracy. The normative elements of this Madisonian model include the following elements: (1) public organizations that are involved in a pluralistic political process rooted in the divergent, changing factional interests of society; thus, their administration and relationship to politics can be neither static nor clear-cut but rather are dynamic, complex, intertwined, and interconnected with a diversity of organic social interests; (2) bureaucracies are political in that they share in the processes of exercising political authority with other branches of government—courts, executive, and legislature—and thus they should, like the other branches, engage in balancing social interests to promote consensus, stability, and representation of divergent points of view; (3) public agencies, though they may formally be separate bodies because of functional differentiation, in practice share power with executive, legislative, and judicial branches in order to undertake effective action and to operate within a continuous, complex *vertical* system of checks and balances upon the other three branches; (4) public entities that operate in a continuous, complex set of *horizontal* power-sharing arrangements between federal, state, and local units and acquire power to take effective action as well as to operate checks and balances upon one another; (5) in this fragmented world of political authority, public administrators exercise the "art of the possible" in dealing with these competing interests and so their roles would principally entail political negotiation, compromise, and bargaining; (6) social consensus and equilibrium between competing interest groups, not organizational efficacy nor accountability to an abstract will of THE PEOPLE; should be the primary aim of public officials; and (7) administrative power to drive actions comes from neither the top down nor the bottom up but must be picked up piecemeal by public administrators from the top, bottom, and sides of government agencies within a politically fragmented, constantly changing fluid environment.

In sum, these three founding fathers produced three very different normative models of bureaucratic-political relationships. They are summarized in Table 7.1.

Table 7.1 Three Founding Fathers' Normative Models

Topic	Hamilton	Jefferson	Madison
Overall goal	strong, sustained; focused organizational efficacy to promote national interests	strict public accountability to maximize personal liberty	organic balancing of interest group demands to promote social stability (i.e., finding "the golden mean")
Key method	unified administrative processes	decentralized, participatory processes	horizontial/vertical checks and balances; an extended republic
Degree of administrative discretion	broad	narrow	mixed and interdependent with other branches
Degree of centralization	high	low	varied with the capacity to acquire power
Organizational autonomy	high	low	interdependent with societal interests
Ideal public official	professional careerist—i.e., "a doer"	citizen volunteer—i.e., "a servant of the people"	negotiator and compromiser—i.e., interest brokers
Sources of power	flows from top down	flows from bottom up	flows from all around—top down, bottom up, and side to side
Agency outputs and capacity to shape future of the nature	strong	strong	mixed—driven by diverse conflicting needs of special interests
Degree of separation of politics from administration	sharp—to promote agency efficiency	sharp—to promote public control	complex, mixed and unclear, depending upon many processes
Social status of bureaucrats	high-status "professionals"	low status "technicians"	mixed status as "interest brokers"
Basic unit of social analysis	the nation	the people	the faction

HISTORIC PATTERNS OF BALANCING
ADMINISTRATIVE EFFICACY, PUBLIC
ACCOUNTABILITY, AND INTEREST GROUP DEMANDS

Americans have never made up their minds throughout their 200-plus-year national history as to which of the three normative models they prefer. They have
remained uncertain about finding a place for their bureaucracy within their

democracy. From time to time, the stress has been placed on promoting the values of administrative efficacy over the other two values; at other times, accountability to the general public has predominated; and at still other times, responding to diverse interest group demands has been clearly an overriding priority. Yet within any single historic period where one value has held sway over the other two, the others have never been entirely neglected or ignored. Calibrating the proper emphasis has never been easy nor have the results ever been permanent, though four distinct eras where one value has tended to predominate over the other two can be discerned.

The Nineteenth-Century Dominance
of Jeffersonian Values

As Chapter 2 emphasized, during most of its first century the U.S. government operated with little bureaucracy (with the exception of the Civil War era). Hence its Constitution, erected upon republican ideals, was largely compatible with its limited bureaucratic institutions. Limited functions were demanded from government. Accident of geography had much to do with creating these conditions. High agricultural productivity made the nation largely self-sufficient, and continental isolation made a large standing army unnecessary. Further, there was virtually no popular demand for extensive social services. Rural farmers and small communities that dotted the landscape were relatively independent from public institutions for key support services. Only briefly, in the 1790s, did an activist (Alexander Hamilton) favoring rapid national modernization seriously press the case for an expansionist positive government, complete with a large professional army and a trained civil service to perform a broad array of nation-building tasks. The rapid decline of the Federalists and the rise of Jeffersonian-Jacksonian Democrats committed to the political dogma that "government governs best that governs least" ensured the continuation of the Jeffersonian ideals supporting negative government throughout most of the nineteenth century.

Ideology and geographic accident that sharply restricted administrative functions were external constraints on bureaucracy. They, in combination with three other important internal constraints in this era, maximized the Jeffersonian values favoring tight controls and public accountability of bureaucracy. First, direct popular controls over administrative machinery waxed because of the rapid growth of a party system that awarded administrative jobs based upon party loyalty and activism. Particularly after the election of Andrew Jackson, the spoils system grew and became a deeply ingrained institutional process. The belief that any job in government could and should be done by the average person was accepted as a given. Thus party affiliation was stressed over professional expertise as a central requirement for holding public office. Most of the federal government jobs were with the post office and required the performance of menial and repetitive tasks that could indeed be performed by the lay citizen, making bureaucratic expertise unnecessary. Further, the lack of serious external threats, except for those from Native Americans, meant that the United States

could rely upon untrained citizen-soldiers in state militias for its primary defense. Even the top military posts in this era were largely filled by political appointees; of the 37 generals appointed between 1802 and 1861, not one was a
West Pointer and 23 were without any military education or experience.[7] Political appointment became common practice in most civil administrative offices as well (with citizen-volunteers providing most public services at the local
level). Probably these personnel trends peaked in the 1860s when Lincoln used
patronage more effectively than any previous president to run a government and
to fight the Civil War.

Money, or more precisely tight fiscal constraint, was the second critical instrument ensuring the primacy of public accountability. Despite Alexander
Hamilton's early efforts to develop a comprehensive executive budget in order
to strengthen executive branch autonomy and managerial planning, Congress,
not the chief executive, firmly grasped the reins of budgetary controls over public agencies. Surprisingly, presidents gave up this authority over the purse without much of a fight.[8] In his first annual message to Congress, Thomas Jefferson
recommended that appropriations be made as "specific sums to every purpose
susceptible of definition;[9] and each public agency operated through a complex
voucher system expending funds incrementally authorized by Congress in the
absence of centralized treasury oversight. This fiscal pattern of legislative control made the nation's financial system unique by comparison with that of every
other nation (both then and today) by giving Congress, not the president, authority over policy formulation and internal administrative matters of agencies.
The multiplicity of fiscal controls over public agencies by legislatures at every
level of government was further extended by dividing up responsibility for fiscal oversight among several special committees and subcommittees. Not only
was it customary for several legislative subcommittees to exercise financial oversight over the same public agency—thereby serving to fragment bureaucratic
fiscal integrity—but the process of financial oversight was further divided into
two elements: first, legislative authorization to approve the programs, and second, appropriations to fund the programs.

A third significant strategy for extending public accountability over public
organizations throughout the nineteenth century involved the structuring of
their organizational designs so as to prevent organizational autonomy and enhance their dependency upon other branches in order to function. From the
earliest period onward, public agencies, their organizations, and their procedures
were subject to intense congressional scrutiny. Nothing was considered beyond
the bounds of legislative concern. As Don Price notes, "The term executive
branch . . . is a misleading metaphor. Organization charts and television pundits
to the contrary, there is no such thing as an executive branch of the U.S. government. The Constitution gives the President certain executive powers, but it
does not mention the executive branch. Instead, it lets the Congress by legislation set up executive departments and control their organization and procedures
to any degree it likes."[10]

Beginning with Jefferson, Congress developed the habit of setting up governmental organizations through highly detailed legislative statutes that exhibited

minute technical controls over their designs, purposes, internal procedures, and external relationships. The general thrust of these legislative mandates was not only to make these agencies creatures of the legislature but also to foster functional specialization. The military, for example, was, throughout much of the nineteenth century, organized around strong specialized bureaus—cavalry, infantry, engineers, and ordnance—rather than around a unified command structure staffed with military professionals who were servicewide generalists, not technical specialists. Officers identified with bureaus in which they served since they were not general military professionals with increasingly advanced training and progressively broader experience. Not until the National Security Act of 1947 was this preference for bureau specialists over military generalists altered. The same was true for civilian agencies where specialized bureaus rather than broad departmental interests were of paramount influence and concern. Institutional fragmentation served not only to inhibit unity of purpose and generalized public professionalism but also to divide and conquer. By creating small "bureau governments," staffed with political appointees in various specialized fields, Congress easily controlled these numerous small bureaucratic entities through detailed subcommittee oversight.

Throughout most of the nineteenth century, U.S. public agencies were creatures of Congress, not the President. President James Garfield in 1882, for example, could enumerate *all* of his presidential duties without ever mentioning "administration of the executive branch" as a significant responsibility. And the young Woodrow Wilson in 1885 wrote his political science Ph.D. dissertation, which became a best-selling book entitled *Congressional Government,* as a criticism of legislative control over most federal administrative machinery. The irresponsible actions that ensued from fragmented, haphazard political oversight by congressional subcommittees were Wilson's primary target. Indeed, most of the great leaders of federal departments during this period were lawyers and legislators—Albert Gallatin, Jefferson's secretary of the treasury; John C. Calhoun, Polk's secretary of war; and William Seward, Lincoln's secretary of state—who knew the workings of the law and Congress and gained most of their fame in legislative halls. Bureaucracy offered little opportunity for bolstering one's reputation in that century.

But were the other values—administrative efficacy and interest group demands—entirely neglected during this era? Hardly, but they were not predominant values. Flashes of concern for administrative efficacy appeared in various parts of government from time to time in the nineteenth century, such as during Amos Kendall's tenure as postmaster general in Jackson's presidency, described in Mathew Crensen's *Federal Machine,*[11] and during the Civil War, when professionals gained prominence in Lee's army, as described in Douglas Southall Freeman's *Lee's Lieutenants.*[12] The organization of special interests, such as farmers, who pressed their case for the first clientele department, the Department of Agriculture (1862), also began in the nineteenth century.[13] However, political authority was exercised by fairly homogeneous political communities, not by organized special interests.[14] There were, of course, sectional interests that loomed large over the entire century's politics, especially prior to the Civil War, but the organization of government services *around or directed at* particular special interest group demands had to await the twentieth century and a fundamental shift in the underlying nature of U.S. political authority.

The Dominance of Neo-Hamiltonian Values, 1883–1945

The year 1883 saw the passage of the Civil Service Act. It also marks the beginning of a decisive shift in national values, away from the Jeffersonian ideal of limited government and its attendant emphasis upon strict administrative accountability to THE PEOPLE. Instead, stress upon neo–Hamiltonian values favoring administrative efficacy began to appear. Not that Hamiltonianism ever entirely eclipsed Jeffersonianism, only that new methods, outlooks, and perspectives tended to give priority during this period to improving overall efficacy of public institutions.

If Jeffersonianism favored limited functions, popular representation, fiscal constraints, and organizational dependency as the keys to "marrying" bureaucracy with democracy, Hamiltonianism sought to broaden the range of public action, enhance public professionalism, and strengthen executive management and organizational autonomy. This decisive shift in national values did not come all at once but grew gradually over time and was to a great extent caused by a rapidly changing sociopolitical and economic environment that required a new approach to national governance.

The nation itself was rapidly modernizing from an agrarian republic to a contemporary industrial society with significantly differentiated and expanded functions. A modernizing nation required a modernized government. Industry during this era replaced agriculture as the major employer, thus creating needs for new public regulatory agencies such as the Interstate Commerce Commission. Growing international responsibilities required a standing military and diplomatic presence abroad; and a vast influx of immigrants to the United States turned towns into cities, creating heterogeneous urbanized communities requiring effective local administrative services of many kinds. These new socioeconomic and political realities of life at the turn of the century made Jeffersonian values less relevant to the growing responsibilities of a modernizing nation. Jeffersonian values, for most Americans at the dawn of the twentieth century, just did not make sense nor contain much meaning in a rapidly changing society that suddenly demanded that new tasks be performed with efficiency and dispatch (though some political leaders, such as William Jennings Bryan, clung steadfastly to the old Jeffersonian values). Effective public organizations were now required to carry out the myriad and expanding responsibilities of a modernizing nation-state. On the eve of this transformation of values, in 1871, only 51,020 civilians worked for the federal government, of whom 36,696 (73 percent) were postal employees. The remaining 14,424 constituted the entire national government for 40 million Americans. By 1940, nearly 1 million federal workers were employed in a wide range of social, economic, regulatory, and public services, with a mere 5 percent employed in the post office.

This period 1883–1945 witnessed not only the rapid expansion and differentiation of governmental services but also the development of skilled, specialized public personnel. Any effective public bureaucracy must contain, at its heart, a career service, with dedicated employees who are offered opportunities for career development and have advanced education, specialized expertise, and at least some degree of freedom from politics in order to exercise bureaucratic responsibilities. The Civil Service Act of 1883 was a first important step in that direction. Drawn largely from the British experience but adapted to American circumstances, the act developed merit criteria as opposed to political criteria for appointment to public office. While it took nearly a half-century to extend merit protection to most elements of government (helped by the passage of other such important laws as the Classification Act of 1923), the growth in the size and scope of skilled expertise inside government agencies was perhaps the most significant factor enhancing and extending administrative efficacy during this era. Also critical to strengthened public agencies was the establishment of various specialized professional groups, such as the foreign service, which was established by the Rogers Act of 1924. The extension upward, downward, and outward of professional expertise came gradually and piecemeal during this era with the growth of new specialists in various fields, such as public health, personnel, teaching, and city planning (refer to Chapter 4).

Along with growing expertise, professionalization, and specialization, modernization of key management institutions and techniques was also instrumental in furthering the goal of administrative efficacy. Among the important management reforms were the establishment of the general staff by Elihu Root in 1902 to improve management planning, coordination, and control of the military (later extended to most civilian agencies); and the development of an executive budget, first used by the New York Bureau of Municipal Research for the New York Public Health Department and later established in the federal government through the 1921 Budget and Accounting Act. Also, new staff offices such as the Bureau of the Budget (established by the Treasury Department in 1922) and the post of chief of naval operations, created in 1915, were important organizational devices for centralizing executive control. At the grass roots level, the reorganization of state government pursued by Governors Lowden in Illinois and Byrd in Virginia set new patterns for increasing executive management effectiveness and centralizing state-level functions. The council-manager government in cities and towns, spurred on especially through the work of the National Municipal League, as well as the "bureau movement" modernized, centralized, and rationalized local institutions by putting trained management expertise at the core of expanding municipal functions. City government with city managers in charge soon equipped cities with new financial management and with budgeting, planning, and civil service capacities (as cited in Chapter 2).

Equally critical to the enhancement of overall administrative efficacy during this period was the increasing institutional autonomy of executive branch agencies at every level of government. Separation of politics and administration was advocated as good government practice by reformers and theorists. In practice, though, institutional autonomy from congressional subcommittee oversight was promoted by Congress itself. Independent regulatory agencies, beginning with the ICC in 1887, and the first government corporations, starting with Panama Railway Company in 1905, were designed as autonomous units that could do what Congress either could not do or did not want to do (see Chapter 2). World War I particularly accelerated the trends toward organizational autonomy and centralization of authority in executive agencies. Wartime emergencies, as always, necessitated rapid troop mobilization, national economic planning, press censorship, and emergency nationalization, as well as regulation of various sectors of industry.

The Hatch Act (refer to Figure 7.1) formalized the separation of "administration" from "politics," thereby serving to strengthen administrative autonomy and discretion at the federal as well as at state and local levels.

While peacetime in the 1920s saw the return of many of these administrative powers to private authority, the Great Depression and World War II saw another set of emergencies that created overnight new bureaucratic institutions with autonomous authority for dealing with these crises. Perhaps the strongest influences in achieving organization autonomy and administrative independence from congressional oversight were the Reorganization Act of 1939 and Reorganization Plan No. 1, which implemented several of the Brownlow Commission's recommendations.

Brownlow synthesized most forcefully the neo-Hamiltonian values in arguing for the creation of a strong, energetic presidency by means of (1) placing the president in charge of an independent executive branch; (2) establishing adequate staff assistance in the White House in order that the executive branch functions could be properly managed; (3) transferring authority for budgeting, personnel, and planning to the White House in order to strengthen the managerial capacity of the president; (4) professionalizing civil service personnel by extending upward and downward merit protection to cover all nonpolicy-determining posts; (5) reducing the president's control and the lines of authority by reorganizing the more than 100 agencies reporting to him into 12 major departments; (6) giving the executive "complete responsibility for accounts and current financial transactions" while providing a genuine independent post-audit of all fiscal transactions by an auditor general reporting to Congress.

Here, in short, was the "high energy" model for the federal government that had been in the making since 1883—professional personnel, executive budgets, rationalized organizational span of control, "pre-audit" authority, autonomous executive units, general management and planning capacity, and political authority concentrated in political executives while leaving administrative work to the "pros" to allow maximum administrative efficacy. Brownlow, as Barry Karl observed,[15] transferred upward to the federal level many ideas that 20 years earlier had become the model for effective local government practices, especially as exemplified by the council-manager plan. And certainly long after the Brownlow Report, these neo-Hamiltonian ideals favoring administrative efficacy echoed in many postwar recommendations for governmental reorganization, such as the two Hoover Commission Reports

Be it enacted by the Senate and House of Representatives of the United States of America in Congress assembled, That it shall be unlawful for any person to intimidate, threaten, or coerce, or to attempt to intimidate, threaten, or coerce, any other person for the purpose of interfering with the right of such other person to vote or not to vote as he may choose, or of causing such other person to vote for, or not to vote for, any candidate for the office of President, Vice President, Presidential elector, Member of the Senate, or Member of the House of Representatives, Delegates or Commissioners from the Territories and insular possessions.

"Sec. 2. It shall be unlawful for (1) any person employed in any administrative position by the United States, or by any department, independent agency, or other agency of the United States (including any corporation controlled by the United States or any agency thereof, or any corporation all of the capital stock of which is owned by the United States or any agency thereof), or (2) any person employed in any administrative position by any State, by any political subdivision or municipality of any State, or by any agency of any State or any of its political subdivision or municipalities (including any corporation controlled by any State or by any such political subdivision, municipality, or agency and any corporation all of the capital stock of which is owned by any State or by any such political subdivision, municipality, or agency), in connection with any activity which is financed in whole or in part by loans or grants made by the United States, or by any such department, independent agency, or other agency of the United States, to use his official authority for the purpose of interfering with, or affecting, the election or the nomination of any candidate for the office of President, Vice President, Presidential elector, Member of the Senate, Member of the House of Representatives, or Delegate or Resident Commissioner from any Territory or insular possession."

Sec. 3. It shall be unlawful for any person, directly or indirectly, to promise any employment, position, work, compensation, or other benefit, provided for or made possible on whole or in part by any Act of Congress, to any person as consideration, favor, or reward for any political activity or for the support of or opposition to any candidate or any political party in any election.

Sec. 4. Except as may be required by the provisions of subsection (b), section 9 of this Act, it shall be unlawful for any person to deprive, attempt to deprive, or threaten to deprive, by any means, any person of any employment, position, work, compensation, or other benefit provided for or made possible by any Act of Congress appropriating funds for work relief or relief purposes, on account of race, creed, color, or any political activity, support of, or opposition to any candidate or any political party in any election.

Sec. 5. It shall be unlawful for any person to solicit to receive or by in any manner concerned in soliciting or receiving any assessment, subscription, or contribution for any political purpose whatever from any person known by him to be entitled to or receiving compensation, employment, or other benefit provided from or made possible by any Act of Congress appropriating funds for work relief or relief purposes.

Sec. 6. It shall be unlawful for any person for political purposes to furnish or to disclose, or to aid or assist in furnishing or disclosing, any list or names of persons receiving compensation, employment, or benefits provided for or made possible by any Act of Congress appropriating, or authorizing the appropriation of funds for work relief or relief purposes, to a political candidate, committee, or campaign manager, and it shall be unlawful for any person to receive any such list or names for political purposes. . . .

FIGURE 7.1   The Hatch Act erected an influential legal barrier for separating "politics" from "administrative" activities at federal and state levels (1939).

(referred to by Herman Finer as "Mr. Brownlow's children"), the continued growth of the council-manager plan, the Ash Commission Report (1970), and, significantly, National Academy of Public Administration's report, *A Presidency for the 1980s* (1981). But in the post–World War II United States, neo-Hamiltonian values were no longer in ascendancy, having given way to a very different amalgam of values for designing "ideal" political-bureaucratic relationships.

Madisonian Value Patterns in the Post–World War II Era

World War II proved to be another turning point in political–bureaucratic relationships. The crisis of wartime not only centralized political authority in the United States to unprecedented degrees, but the new postwar global responsibilities of an economic-political superpower also required the maintenance of a complicated international and military apparatus in order to carry out tasks imposed by free world leadership. Further, a welfare state, largely begun by the New Deal in the 1930s, required numerous administrative agencies in order to carry out growing social tasks that Americans deemed essential.

The lives of millions of Americans in this period were directly touched for the first time by the activities of an expanded bureaucracy at every level of government; for payment of social security checks, auto licensing, FHA/VA home mortgages, regulating most sectors of the economy, and furthering new scientific developments, such as the atomic bomb. As a result, bureaucratic institutions became more numerous and more complicated. Their interconnections and relationships with politics likewise became more complex. Hence, the underlying American values associated with these relationships shifted as well. Compare, for example, two bureaucracies—both considered highly successful in accomplishing their particular missions during World War II—the Manhattan Project and the Selective Service System. By means of quite different institutional processes, both organizations achieved their objectives.

The purpose of the Manhattan Project was to develop an atomic bomb quickly. The complexity of this task (no one really knew if the bomb would work or even if it could be built in the first place), the diversity of personnel and material resources required for it (spanning a continent), and the requirements of speed and secrecy (only a chosen few, those at the very highest policy level, could know about its existence), forged a public entity that was unprecedented. U.S. bureaucracy showed remarkable inventiveness in designing this new public organization. The project was organized in such a way as to ensure tight control at the top by secretary of war Henry Stimson, chief of staff General George C. Marshall, and General Leslie Groves as operational director. A wide range of expert personnel and highly specialized material resources were pulled together from across the United States in the production of the bomb. Dispersion of resources prevented many individuals from knowing the overall extent and purpose of the operations. A highly restricted group composed of top scientists of that day, such as Vannevar Bush from MIT and James B. Conant of Harvard, and military officers such as navy Admiral Parnell and army General Styer, served as a joint sciences-military advisory policy committee for the project. Requirements for competitive bidding for contracts were eased to permit sole-source suppliers to build specialized parts of the bomb. The project maximized administrative efficacy—speed, secrecy, efficiency of implementation—through limiting, though not entirely neglecting, accountability requirements.

By contrast, the complex system for drafting individuals developed in World War II (which operated until 1973), the Selective Service System, created by Congress and directed by General Hershey, proved an equally effective bureaucratic instrument for inducting 12 million soldiers during World War II.

Whether one agreed with its purposes or not, the draft system functioned well in World War II by maximizing public involvement at the grass roots. While there was a national headquarters, the bulk of its work was delegated to state headquarters and 6,443 local boards composed of three or more volunteer community citizens. In contrast with the highly centralized, scientifically driven institutional processes involved with the Manhattan Project, voluntary grass roots participation, coupled with federal- and state-level procedural controls, mobilized men rapidly and implemented the draft laws successfully and economically—it cost only $22.50 to draft a soldier during World War II.

The complexification and differentiation of bureaucratic processes continued in the postwar era, as described in Chapter 2, with the establishment of large, unique entities for achieving the varied tasks of governance. Americans invented superdepartments at the federal level, such as the Departments of Defense and of Health and Human Services, as well as small but critical coordinative units, such as the Advisory Commission on Intergovernmental Relations, and units to control and extend scientific knowledge, such as the Atomic Energy Commission, and the National Science Foundation—each highly complicated, differentiated institutional processes deemed vital for servicing complicated, diverse national interests. As Herbert Simon, Dwight Waldo, and other postwar theorists stressed, simple pre–World War II principles of economy and efficiency (à la Brownlow) no longer applied to organizational life. The "one-best-way" gave way to "multiple-best-ways" of organizing and formulating political-administrative relationships.[16] Thus institutional complexity became the hallmark of bureaucratic operational processes after 1945.

The development and growth of postwar U.S. bureaucratic institutions, as "realistic" political scientists point out, involved numerous special interest groups. As administrative agencies touched more Americans in this era, more groups and individuals, out of self-interest, came to influence the course of administrative processes. In *The Governmental Process* (1951), David Truman depicted the reality of government as *a process,* a seamless web of competition and compromise between competing social interests, each pressing its claims on existing public institutions and creating new ones to service its needs. Like Madison, Truman analyzed in realistic and behavioral terms U.S. society as based upon interest groups and their interaction. According to Truman, "The behavior that constitutes the processes of government cannot be adequately understood apart from groups, especially the organized and powerful interest groups."[17] Truman, echoing Madison, postulated that government provides social equilibrium through establishing and maintaining a "measure of order between groups." Bureaucracy became but one of "a multiplicity of points of access" for groups seeking to influence public policies.

Like Madison, Truman and other political scientists of this period viewed the problem of governance essentially in terms of *structuring access* of groups to government so that none gains the upper hand and so that, overall, balanced points of view are heard. Thereby, in turn, the public interest would be well served. Implicit within their writings was a faith that the processes of bargaining and compromise between interests over administrative goods and services would work out for the good of the total society or at least for *most of those within society*. As Truman writes, "Government functions to establish and maintain a measure of order in the relationship between groups." We find this evidenced also in Robert Dahl's classic, *A Preface to Democratic Theory*, where he writes: "The vast apparatus that grew up to administer the affairs of the American welfare state is a decentralized bargaining bureaucracy. This is merely another way of saying that bureaucracy has become a part of . . . the 'normal American political process.' "[18] Most Americans probably concurred with this uncritical, benevolent view of the self-regulating pluralistic system of interest groups operating in, around, and through bureaucracy. Theodore Lowi coined the phrase "interest groups liberalism"[19] to symbolize the postwar mood in general support of these arrangements.

Perhaps no one has captured the spirit, attitudes, and faith in interest group liberalism as well as Charles E. Lindblom did in his famous 1959 essay, "The Science of 'Muddling Through,' "[20] Here, the bureaucrat is not a "doer" governed by the Hamiltonian values of promoting efficacy or efficiency, but rather an official, one of many, who practices "the art of the possible" in a complex world of competing interests. Negotiation and compromise are the tools of his trade, with which he tries to produce "agreeable compromise to all parties concerned." He "muddles," rather than manages. Yet in this difficult, confused act of incremental decision making, argued Lindblom, he produced the best pragmatic results for society as a whole. He achieved social harmony and political equilibrium through compromises in a fluid, unstable sea of ever-changing interest groups. Here were Madisonian values stated in their clearest, most concise, and most persuasive manner in the postwar United States. In the relatively calm period of the 1950s, when the United States enjoyed both superpower status and industrial prosperity, these Madisonian values stressing interest-group balance fitted hand in glove with the social stability and conservativism of the times.

Hence, the debate over how best to control bureaucracy in a democratic society between Carl Friedrich and Herman Finer,[21] which dominated the thinking of political scientists and government specialists after 1940 (i.e., were internal or external controls the most effective instruments for controls?) was largely an irrelevant question. *Both* Friedrich and Finer's ideas were in practice used. Both at times were highly effective. Both at times were highly ineffective. In the postwar world of Madisonian institutional complexity, built upon a liberal faith in self-regulating interest groups, a wide variety of institutional controls were put into place and found to be effective *and* wanting at the same time. The prior examples of the Manhattan Project and Selective Service point out this diversity quite well. But there were others. The Veterans Preference Act of 1944 created the Veterans Administration as an independent agency built upon open access to single-interest veterans groups. The act catered to veterans' interests, often at the expense of the interests of others. Conversely, new postwar institutions were created, such as the Department of Defense at the federal level, which merged the army, navy, and air force under one superdepartment, and the Council of Governments (CoGs), which administered 701 grants to grass roots organizations that fostered planning on a regional basis. These two organiza-

Table 7.2 Political-Bureaucratic Relations in Three Eras

	Nineteenth Century (Jefferson Era)	Late Nineteenth/Early Twentieth Century (Hamiltonian Era)	Post–World War II (Madisonian Era)
Socioeconomic setting	largely rural, stable, isolationist	predominantly nation-building	mature welfare state with global responsibilities
Political authority basis	homogenous community life	rapid sociopolitical-economic change	interest group liberalism, scientific changes, and international responsibilities
Bureaucratic duties	limited	expanding	diverse
Generalist/specialist personnel	generalist political personnel	growth of professional/specialized staffs	mixed generalist/specialist personnel
Fiscal controls	sharp limits imposed by legislatures	increased executive control/authority through executive budgets	mixed controls on finances depending upon agency and policy area
Organizational autonomy/dependency	highly dependent upon legislature	increasing autonomy	mixed organization autonomy, and dependence
Use of external or internal controls	primarily external controls utilized, based upon laws	increasing reliance upon internal controls, based upon public professions and their norms	highly complex mix of *both* external and internal controls
Ideological basis of political-bureaucratic relationship	"best government governs the least"	"politics—administrative dichotomy"	"interest group liberalism"

tions, which are decidedly important postwar bureaucratic innovations, promote diverse points of view on defense and metropolitan policy matters. But DoD did not prevent the rise of—and controls by—the military–industrial complex. Nor did CoGs solve critical political problems of postwar center-city decay. No absolute "objective" controls for bureaucracy by democracy seemed to exist; some only promoted certain values over others. The diversity of means *and* ends were evident and practical. In short, Madisonianism thrived.

Table 7.2 sums up elements of bureaucratic-political relations in each of the three historic eras discussed so far in this chapter.

THE PERSISTING RIVALRY OF THE
THREE VALUE TRADITIONS

In the words of Samuel P. Huntington, the late 1960s and early 1970s witnessed a "democratic surge"[22] that characterized past eras of Jeffersonian-Jacksonian democracy and progressive reform, in which there was a vital reassertion of democratic idealism in all phases of life in the United States. As Huntington argues, the era reflected

> a general challenge to the existing system of authority, public and private. In one form or another, this challenge manifested itself in the family, the university, business, public and private associations, politics, the governmental bureaucracy and the military service. People no longer felt the same compulsion to obey those whom they had previously considered superior to themselves in age, rank, status, expertise, character or talents. Within most organizations, discipline eased and differences in status became blurred. Each group claimed its right to participate equally—and perhaps more equally in the decision making which affected itself. In American society, authority had been commonly based on organizational position, economic wealth, specialized expertise, legal competence, or electoral representation. Authority based on hierarchy, expertise and wealth all obviously ran counter to the democratic and equalitarian temper of the times.[23]

Was the reassertion of Jeffersonian idealism due to the Vietnam war? The rise of a "youth culture"? The demands for equal rights by women and minorities? The television age? The Great Society programs? The reactions to Watergate and the Nixon presidency? While the reasons for the sudden "democratic surge" were complex and are even now still unclear, Huntington points to a number of significant consequences of the "democratic surge":

1. Increase in the size and scope of governmental activity, though with a concomitant decline in governmental authority.

2. Increased public interest and concern about government, coupled with a sharp decline in public trust and confidence in government.

3. Increased public activism in politics, yet with a commensurate decay in the traditional two-party system.

4. A noticeable shift away from coalitions supporting government to those in opposition to it.[24]

Popular in this period was a philosophical treatise by John Rawls, *A Theory of Justice,*[25] which defined justice in egalitarian terms. In the fields of history and politics, Arthur Schlesinger's *The Imperial Presidency*[26] found a wide, enthusiastic post-Watergate audience for its criticism of the flagrant abuses of strong executive institutions in the United States. This book stood in sharp contrast to a popular text on the presidency a decade earlier by Richard E. Neustadt, *Presidential Power,*[27] which had praised the values of a strong chief executive. Egalitarian themes found their way into the literature of economics, particularly in E. F. Schumacher's *Small Is Beautiful,*[28] which proposed that the goods and services in society be distributed more equitably and, in the words of its subtitle, *As If People Mattered.* In public administration, books such as that of Frank Marini (ed.), *Toward a New Public Administration,*[29] and Vincent Ostrom's *The Intellectual Crisis in American Public Administration,*[30] though

grounded in radically different methodological traditions, argued for the similar popular values of broader participation, decentralization of authority, and
social equality.

Throughout the 1960s and 1970s many of these Jeffersonian values
were translated into institutional reality by means of new legislation directly
affecting the internal operation of most public agencies.[31] First, there was a
sharp increase in formal and informal controls placed upon bureaucratic
operations to improve public accountability. The Legislative Reorganization
Act of 1970 began a rapid expansion of congressional oversight staff and
functions aimed at improving public accountability. New legislation, such as
the War Powers Resolution (1973), the Freedom of Information Act as
amended in 1974, the Congressional Budget and Impoundment Control
Act of 1974, the Ethics in Government Act of 1978, and Codes of Ethics
for Public Services (1983) sought to place important new external controls
on executive branch activities. New internal procedural controls, such as
the extension of the Office of Inspector General throughout the federal executive branch, were approved in 1978, as were the various ombudsman offices and "sunset" and "sunrise" laws instituted with state and local
bureaucracies during this same period. Such legislation tended to reduce
public organizational autonomy, flexibility, and discretion and to increase
institutional fragmentation and legislative oversight. Furthermore, efforts
were made by the late 1970s to limit sharply bureaucratic functions. At the
local level, Proposition 13 in California (1978) and Proposition 2½ in Massachusetts served as "model legislation" for those who advocated reducing
the role of the public sector through placing tight revenue-raising lids in
state constitutions. On the federal level, the movement toward deregulation
of various economic sectors begun in the Carter administration, combined
with sharp cutbacks in federal expenditures inaugurated by the Reagan administration in 1981, reflected these popular Jeffersonian values favoring
less government. Furthermore, the scope of popular representation *within*
public organizations at every level of government was extended and enlarged during this era. Generally, the roles of professionals and professional
groups such as city managers, foreign service officers, and public health officials were not enhanced or supported by the public but rather gave
ground to expanded groups of political appointees, minority group representation, citizen volunteers, public review boards, and contractual employees. Administration efficacy yielded to extended public accountability, on
many fronts, throughout the 1970s and 1980s.

By the dawn of the twenty-first century, however, the picture has become mixed. Strong concerns about finding effective means of achieving
broader public accountability over bureaucracy are still expressed by many.
The dominant ideological environment, though once sharply hostile to
public bureaucracy, exhibiting values that favored squeezing, cutting, and reducing bureaucracy has yielded to more support for public servants after the
9/11 terrorist attacks. Police, fire, emergency, and military personnel, indeed
all government workers, have gained new respect for their effective, swift re-

sponses to deadly terrorism. However, to be fair, the competing demands of Madisonian interest groups on governmental activities and its bureaucracy have hardly declined. Indeed, as Chapter 6 suggested, there is strong indication that PACs, issue networks, and pressure groups have strengthened their influence throughout the executive branch. Yet since the 9/11 tragedy, we see perhaps a renewed stress on Hamiltonian values for increased administrative efficacy as pervasive in order to promote national security, fight terrorism abroad, and homeland security domestically, not to mention environmental protection, conduct international diplomacy, enhance national competitive capabilities in international trade and economics, revitalize U.S. industry, rebuild local infrastructure, employ the unemployed, stimulate hi-tech industries, and improve educational opportunities. These and other insistent public demands for action by liberals, moderates, and conservatives turn on the capacity of some public agency to ultimately deliver the goods.

PUBLIC BUREAUCRACY IN AMERICA TOMORROW: THE NECESSITY FOR RECOGNIZING THE VALUE OF TRADE-OFFS

Americans have never quite made up their minds about the place of bureaucracy in their democracy. Certainly this confusion over values is apparent today. As with numerous other unsettled constitutional issues, the genius of the founding fathers in writing the U.S. Constitution was precisely in allowing succeeding generations of Americans to determine the shape of their government. Throughout the nineteenth century, when Jeffersonian values predominated, institutional arrangements affecting bureaucratic-democratic relationships were fashioned to stress the value of public accountability. In the late nineteenth and first half of the twentieth century, when the United States was in a nation-building mode, administrative efficacy replaced accountability as the overriding priority. As a mature superpower and welfare state in the socially stable era after World War II, a benign Madisonian liberalism favored an interplay of interest groups stressing organic social balance and institutional equilibrium.

No single value for structuring political-bureaucratic relations is inherently right or wrong. Each of the three has worked successfully in its own time and place. Each of the three also contains inherent limitations and problems. The dilemma the United States faces today is that all three of these values have come to the forefront of national debate and attention. Strong ideological currents and political interests in society loudly press their cases for Jeffersonian, Hamiltonian, and Madisonian perspectives. The issue of which *one* historic value should predominate over the others remains unresolved to this day. Americans run their government with a confusing amalgam of all three value-emphases, which creates a situation of enormous confusion and complexity—and frustration. Realistically, one cannot expect

the United States to suddenly decide to adopt one value perspective and neglect the others entirely. The problem is a matter of emphasis and accent.

The U.S. system of governance throughout its history has given at least some
attention and concern to all three values as a basis for fashioning bureaucratic-
democratic relations. But throughout most of its 200-year plus history, only one
value approach at a time has tended to predominate over the other two. What
is perhaps most important for the future of bureaucracy in U.S. society is a frank
appreciation of the strengths and limits of each value and of what trade-offs or
consequences ensue from the adoption of one value over the others. Understanding the trade-offs can help clarify the alternatives facing Americans today
as they fashion tomorrow's bureaucratic-democratic relationships.

Hamiltonian Values Maximizing Administrative Efficacy

A modern system of public bureaucracy constructed upon Hamiltonian values
is depicted as a generalized model in Figure 7.2. The system focuses on producing high-energy outputs rather than on maximizing public accountability
or interest group demands. A bureaucratic system reflecting these values (1) ensures the adequacy of economic and political inputs in order to undertake the
required tasks; (2) permits clear political objectives and policy directions from
the top; (3) contains a highly professionalized cadre of public officials to carry
out the tasks; (4) possesses the essential tools of effective leadership, broad administrative discretion, institutional autonomy, and unified orderly procedures
to deliver public goods with speed and dispatch; and (5) manages and restricts

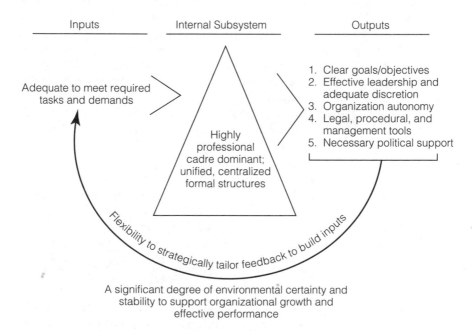

FIGURE 7.2 Public bureaucracy (Hamiltonian Model)

feedback, communications, and publicity in such a way as to enhance, not detract from, the efficient programmatic outputs. Table 7.3 depicts representative public agencies today that approximate this model.

The values that ultimately shape the overall design of this bureaucratic system, however, are not purchased without some costs:

1. Doing a particular job is given precedence over temporary popular concerns or individual group demands. This perspective assumes that there is a fixed task that can be understood and accomplished. It thus tends to be rigid and inflexible in its pursuit of these goals.

2. The emphasis upon achieving administrative efficacy—getting the job done effectively and quickly by focusing on achieving certain objectives, sometimes at any cost, tends to ignore other important, though possibly secondary, tasks. Adaptability to multiplicity of goals is thus sacrificed or reduced.

3. Hamiltonian values demand the attainment of adequate inputs of economic and political power to perform the required tasks. In other words, authority must equate with responsibility. This ideal is considered sound management practice for fashioning any high-energy bureaucratic model. Yet more often than not, public bureaucracy today involves dealing with fragmented institutions, shifting interest groups, with radically opposing ideologies. Power to operate agencies usually must in real life be picked up piecemeal, and available input resources normally are never adequate to do any job.

4. The internal dynamics of this system place a premium upon maximizing professional expertise and limiting political oversight. Increasing the autonomy of professionals assumes a degree of faith in their competency to make impor-

Table 7.3 Representative Public Agencies Approximating Hamiltonian Model

	U.S. Marine Corps	New York Port Authority
Purposes	clear-cut combat missions and defense preparedness	broad metropolitan transportation projects
Organizational designs	centralized military hierarchy—power flows from top down	independent special district with autonomous funding/personal authority
Source of inputs	strong popular support and congressional backing	autonomy for revenue raising and fiscal directions
Internal subsystem control	highly professionalized military cadre of officers	highly professional engineering and transit planners
Outputs—the strengths	swift combat force prepared for demanding, single missions of national need	effective regional-wide transit planning and building
Outputs—the weaknesses	complex missions, with multigoals or unclear political goals offer problems in implementation	single-mindedness in transportation development; neglects other urban needs or broad citizen participation

tant judgment calls. Ultimately, professionalizing bureaucracy involves increasing discretionary authority of experts over lay citizens.

5. A high-energy model achieves efficient output levels by building unified, stable administrative delivery systems with the necessary administrative discretion and staffing levels. The following elements are critical for inducing high-level outputs: limiting the span of control, clear lines of nonfragmented authority, authority for reorganization, internal systems for long-range planning, and tight hierarchical control. However, such centralized management tools for speeding service delivery reduce opportunities for political participation, decentralized community involvement, and intrusion of particularistic demands by interest groups.

6. Hamiltonian values also stress the importance of bold, creative, and decisive leadership as central to making things happen in order to maximize administrative efficacy. Robert Moses, General George Patton, J. Edgar Hoover, and Alexander Hamilton exemplify this sort of high-energy public leader. But this high-octane leadership frequently is purchased at the price of individual rights, due process, and the accommodation of interest group demands.

7. Feedback mechanisms necessary to achieve administrative efficacy require limits on communication, secrecy, and news restrictions to a high degree in order to gain agency publicity, popular support, future resources, and political approval. Openness, access to information, and public scrutiny are, therefore, sacrificed in adopting Hamiltonian values.

Jeffersonian Values Maximizing Public Accountability

By contrast, a modern bureaucratic system constructed upon Jeffersonian values can be abstractly illustrated as in Figure 7.3. Here the emphasis is upon maximizing accountability to the public as a whole, often at the expense of administrative efficacy or satisfying special interest group demands. Important elements of the model include (1) strict legal limitations placed upon economic and political inputs; (2) a high degree of political oversight and popular participation *within* the bureaucratic system; (3) emphasis on decentralizing delivery of outputs as far as possible; (4) weak overall executive leadership; and (5) constant public scrutiny over the entire system. Public organizations exhibiting these features are outlined in Table 7.4. Some of the costs apparent in using this type of value-orientation to structure bureaucratic-democratic relations are as follows.

1. Extensive popular participation, expanded oversight, and political involvement serve to lengthen the time needed to achieve agreement upon organizational goals and create delay in the implementation of services, thereby reducing the overall administrative efficacy.

2. This model assumes that there *is* a single, undifferentiated *public* to be served, not many groups, or that the PEOPLE, not groups, are paramount in making democracy work. It is often "blind" to the essential requirements and problems of operating in a pluralistic society.

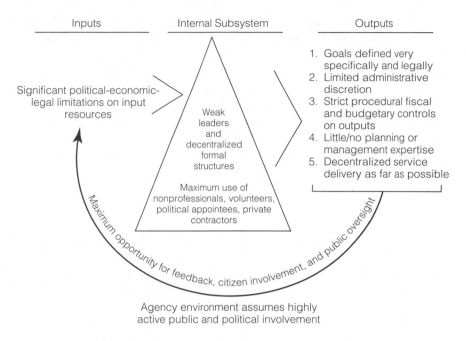

FIGURE 7.3   Public bureaucracy (Jeffersonian Model)

Table 7.4 Representative Public Agencies Approximating Jeffersonian Model

	Executive Offices of the Mayor, Governor, President	**New England Town-Meeting Government**
Purposes	re-election of chief executive	representation of community interests
Source of inputs	voters selection	decisions of town meeting
Internal subsystem control	political appointees	citizen-volunteers
Outputs—the strengths	responsiveness to public opinion	mass citizen involvement in community life
Outputs—the weaknesses	little long-term planning/management capacity	little or no expertise in dealing with complex citizen demands or urban problems
Organizational design	fluid and changing according to electoral needs	simple organizations with few employees

3. Legal limitations on inputs, particularly economic resources, reduce the flexibility and ability of the governmental agency to meet changing and expanding demands, frequently leading to situations where responsibilities *exceed* the authority to act. This can lead to irresponsible, even corrupt, bureaucratic actions.

4. The internal dynamics of such a bureaucratic system emphasize expanding the roles for political appointees, citizen volunteers, and nonprofessionals, thus frequently reducing knowledge, expertise, skilled planning, and management competency, as well as rationality and operational consistency.

5. Decentralization of public services promotes flexibility and adaptability to different local and regional needs, but this also can create frequent opportunities for political intrusion by special interests as well as lack of uniform standards in services rendered and laws enforced.

6. Strict legal internal procedures to ensure public accountability related to program implementation, staffing, budgeting, and organizing service delivery can reduce the likelihood of bold, creative, and innovative public leadership.

7. Public scrutiny, ample information, and media publicity can enhance "honest" feedback to citizens about agency actions, but not without possibly jeopardizing national security, personal privacy, law enforcement, security, and the confidentiality that is necessary for frank appraisals and thoughtful deliberations within the inner councils of government. Economic costs to government may increase because of procedural delays required by more public oversight.

Madisonian Values Maximizing Balanced Interest Group Demands

A third alternative for modeling bureaucratic systems on Madisonian values is depicted in Figure 7.4. Madisonian values stress attaining a social equilibrium through balancing interest group demands. The generalized elements of this system include (1) inputs principally based upon interest groups' demands; (2) bureaucratic outputs incrementally adjusted to meet special interest needs; (3) putting the principal focus of the internal bureaucratic subsystem upon "satisficing" the interest groups; (4) directing feedback towards promoting interest group satisfaction; and (5) devoting the bureaucracy, not to efficiency, effectiveness, or to public service to the nation or the community as a whole, but to promotion of social equilibrium. Some of the typical units of government that operate in this mode are depicted in Table 7.5, but there are costs in adopting this bureaucratic model:

1. The goal of maintaining social equilibrium through satisfying interest group demands is an essentially conservative doctrine favoring the status quo over change and innovation. The model implicitly assumes that the present arrangement of social interests is adequate and that their "caring and feeding" at present levels are acceptable, *and* that nonincremental change upsetting the existing status quo is unacceptable.

2. The model thus favors the powerful and organized groups over the "voiceless," unorganized, weak, and underrepresented ones.

3. The Madisonian system, by its very nature, is a complex, fragmented, interconnected system of institutions operating with numerous checks

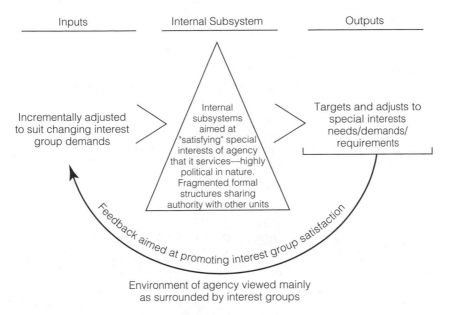

Inputs | Internal Subsystem | Outputs

Incrementally adjusted to suit changing interest group demands

Internal subsystems aimed at "satisfying" special interests of agency that it services—highly political in nature. Fragmented formal structures sharing authority with other units

Targets and adjusts to special interests needs/demands/ requirements

Feedback aimed at promoting interest group satisfaction

Environment of agency viewed mainly as surrounded by interest groups

FIGURE 7.4   Public bureaucracy (Madisonian Model)

Table 7.5 Representative Public Agencies Approximating Madisonian Model

	Veterans Administration	**Local, State, Road Department**
Clear purpose	fulfill veterans needs	transportation functions
Organization design	permits limited executive control; maximizes veteran group oversight	permits limited executive control; maximizes highway interests control over department
Sources of inputs	large veterans organizations	powerful highway and transportation groups
Internal dynamics	highly political	highly political
Outputs—strengths	high amounts of social services for veterans	promotion of various state road-building and transit programs
Outputs—weaknesses	largely ignores other interest group needs and requirements	promotes road-building and major capital projects at expense of alternatives

and balances upon one another, but it also induces a high degree of institutional fragmentation and dispersal of authority, thereby making bureaucratic accountability and responsibility much harder to establish. To whom does the individual citizen turn to for help or justice when administration becomes so complicated? Which institution or public agency can be held accountable when power becomes so fragmented, interdependent, and shared? Public accountability tends to be reduced as fragmentation increases.

4.   Where inputs and outputs of the system turn largely upon "satisficing" special group demands, what ensures that *national* needs are considered, international economic or global security functions accomplished, and long-term future policy responsibilities for such imperatives as the fiscal deficit or environmental problems met? The narrow perspectives and short-term agendas of particular groups tend to drive out priorities for preparing the long-term, broad public agendas. The big picture, in short, is sacrificed often for the immediate needs of special interests.

5.   The internal dynamics of agencies that maximize representation of special interests inside agencies tend to open up agencies to political fun and games, "smoke and mirrors" misrepresentation of reality not to doing work. Appearance of representation of interests, political diversity, and participation are given frequently more emphasis than what happens in reality.

6.   Leadership of these public organizations, from top to bottom is measured in terms of an individual's capacities to bargain, negotiate, and compromise effectively as opposed to his or her ability to make things happen and efficiently produce goods and services. Important institutional elements *necessary to lead* and deliver services are often overlooked. Gaining agreement, rather than achieving tangible goals, becomes an end in itself.

7.   Feedback, and indeed all agency activity, is judged by essentially political perspectives—will it strategically enhance the short-term interests of the agency? Gain bargaining chips? How will it "play" to the media? Build political support? Enhance reputations? The general public welfare or institutional efficacy for the long term tends to be disregarded.

THE FUTURE OF U.S. PUBLIC BUREAUCRACY
AS A VALUE PROBLEM: THE WORTH
OF A SYSTEMS PERSPECTIVE

At the end of a seminal book, Don Price recalled an incident that happened during his service as vice chairman of the Weapons Research and Development Board in the Pentagon.[32] Price was being flown in a navy plane out to Cape Hatteras (off the coast of North Carolina) to an aircraft carrier, where he was to watch the testing of new naval weapons. The weather was cloudy and the sea was rough. The navy lieutenant flying the plane had trouble finding the carrier. While cruising in search of the ship, he tuned in a radio station that announced the appointment of a new secretary of defense. While Price and others aboard expressed surprise at the appointee's selection, the navy lieutenant expressed little interest and then said, "By the way, who is the secretary of defense now?" Price tells how he felt a sense of outrage at a naval officer having so little comprehension of the broad governmental picture that he did not even know the name of his civilian superior. "But then," explains Price, "came a break in the clouds and far below—it seemed miles below—we could see the carrier on which we were to land. It looked about as big as a teacup, bouncing on the waves. And all of a sudden I did not want that navy pilot to have the slightest concern with the policies or the identity of his political superiors. I only wanted him to know how to land that plane."

In real life, especially when *our* lives depend upon it, we, like Don Price, want public bureaucrats to do what they are supposed to do, when they are supposed to, as effectively as possible. Knowingly or not, we depend upon numerous public agencies to do such important jobs as protecting the nation from terrorism, inspecting the food we eat, the roadways we use, and the drinking water we consume, fighting fires, teaching the young, and regulating the market place as well as the safety of workers on the job. In real life, also, we want these numerous agencies to be responsible to the public they serve, protect the rights of citizens, obey the law, follow legally prescribed due processes, allow for popular oversight of their actions and, above all else, be responsive to the general welfare and needs of the citizenry. In short, we prize public accountability as well. *And* in real life, too, we form associations to press our claims upon government as groups of farmers, veterans, steel workers, teachers, and many others who lay legitimate claim to benefits and services from one or several public agencies. The right to associate and secure *our group's interests* from government is regarded as important and essential by most Americans.

The point is that in reality Americans are not pure Jeffersonians, Hamiltonians, or Madisonians. Rather, we take public action based on bits and pieces of all three value systems, often contradictory and confused, regarding public bureaucracy. And such has been true throughout the course of U.S. history as Figure 7.5 suggests. While one value may have predominated over the other two for long periods, the others have never been entirely neglected nor ignored. All three are vital to knitting together democracy with bureaucracy.

But, as the foregoing analysis suggests, there are always important trade–offs associated in the pursuit of one value over the other two. By maximizing one, sacrifices are required from the other two. All three cannot be obtained at the maximum levels simultaneously—nor would we want that to happen if could be. How ghastly is the prospect of living with (or under) the perfectly efficient bureaucracy! Or under one that is perfectly accountable to the public! Or perfectly responsive to all interest group demands!

And in real life, too, public agencies must operate with the constant dilemma of adjusting and juggling these three competing values in the course of carrying out their affairs. As long as they operate within the U.S. governmental system, they must constantly balance concerns for administrative efficacy, public accountability, and interest group demands in order to govern justly and well. No one value can entirely eclipse the other two. Certainly so far no one has dis-

Neo-Hamiltonian Values Strengthening Administrative Efficacy	Non-Reauthorization of the Independent Counsel (1999)
Creation of General Staff (1902)	*Report,* U.S. Commission on National Security for the 21st Century (2001)
Taft Commission on Economy and Efficiency (1912)	**Neo-Jeffersonian Values Strengthening Administrative Accountability**
Model City Charter (1916)	Freedom of Information
Budget and Accounting Act (1921)	Act (1967)—FOIA
Classification Act (1923)	Amendments (1974)
Brownlow Report (1937)	Legislative Reorganization Act (1970)
Reorganization Act (1939)	War Powers Resolution (1973)
Hatch Acts (1939 and 1940)	State "Sunset and Sunshine" Laws (mid-1970s)
Government Corporation Act (1945)	Privacy Act (1974)
Employment Act (1946)	Budget Impoundment and Control Act (1974)
First Hoover Report (1949)—Performance Budgeting	Civil Service Reform Act (1978)
Organization for National Security Act (1947 and 1949)	Inspector General Act (1978)
	Proposition 13 (California, 1978)
Second Hoover Report (1955)	Ethics in Government Act (1978)
Kestnbaum Report (1955)	President's Council on Integrity and Efficiency (1984)
Creation of ACIR (1959)	Federal Quality Institute (1988)
PPBS Applied to DoD (1961)	Ethics Reform Act (1989)
BoB Circular A-95 (1969)	Financial Officers Act (1990)
Reorganization Plan No. 2 (1970)	Hatch Act Reform Amendments (1993)
ZBB established (1977)	**Neo-Madisonion Values Strengthening Special Interest Roles**
Civil Service Reform Act (1978)	Veterans' Preference Act (1944)
Reagan's Cabinet Councils (1981)	Administrative Procedure Act (1946)
REFORM 88 Management Improvement Initiative (1982)	Federal Labor-Management Program established by E.O. 10987 and 10988 (1962)
President's Private Sector Survey on Cost Control (1983)	Title VII of Civil Rights Act of 1964
President's Council on Management Improvement (1984)	Equal Employment Opportunity Act (1972)
	Legislative Reorganization Act (1970)
Federal Employees Retirement System Act (1986)	Freedom of Information Act Amendments (1974)
Federal Employee Pay Comparability Act (1990)	Budget and Impoundment Control Act (1974)
National Commission on the Public Service (1989)	Privacy Act (1974)
Government Performance and Results Act (1993)	Creation of Expansion of PACs by Campaign Reform Act (1974)
Social Security Independence and Improvement Act (1994)	Department of Education (1977)
	Department of Veterans Affairs Act (1988)
Government Management Reform Act (1994)	National Partnership Council (1993)

FIGURE 7.5 Significant legislative and executive actions in shaping values of U.S. bureaucracy

covered a magic tool with which to fine tune the "correct" relationship among the three values.

What is most important for citizens and public officials to appreciate is that important costs and benefits are associated with each value. And here, taking the broad systems perspective, as this book does, can offer a better understanding of what happens to any public organization, to its inputs, outputs, and feedback, and to the general environment when a certain value is emphasized over others. In the imperfect world in which we live, there always will be trade-offs, costs, and benefits resulting from actions based upon particular value orienta-

The unending search for responsible government may be considered to be "The Capitol Cornerstone."

Reprinted by permission of Roger Harvel, *Greenville (SC) News.*

tions. Being conscious of the results of our actions before they are taken makes not only good horse sense but wise public policies as well.

SUMMARY OF KEY POINTS

The U.S. Constitution of 1787 is largely silent on the subject of bureaucracy. However, nowadays, the United States operates with a large public bureaucracy as its core system of governance. How to knit together our democratic ideals embodied in the written document and operational reality involving bureaucratic practices has been a recurring dilemma throughout U.S. history. No perfect "fit" between the two has yet been discovered. The issue involves a fundamental question of values: what is the place of bureaucracy in our modern democracy? Three value-approaches were outlined in this chapter—Jeffersonian, Hamiltonian, and Madisonian normative models—that have, in very different ways, served to answer this question. Throughout much of the nineteenth century, Jeffersonianism, emphasizing public accountability, dominated American bureaucratic-political relations. It fit hand in glove with the largely rural, self-sufficient, isolationistic nation. The nation-building, expansionist forces of the late nineteenth and early twentieth centuries led to a strong assertion of Hamiltonian values reshaping fundamental democratic-bureaucratic relationships. Mid-20th Century United States, with the creation of a mature welfare state and global international responsibilities, found Madisonian values, embodied in interest group liberalism, formulating the design of democratic-bureaucratic relations. Today, all three values find prominence and support. The chief theme of this chapter is that the selection of *any one* value over the other two involves certain costs and benefits. A frank recognition of the trade-offs adopting one value over the other two is essential. A systems perspective can be an invaluable tool for improving our knowledge about these potential trade-offs.

KEY TERMS

administrative efficacy	Brownlow Commission Report	Hamiltonian values
public accountability		Jeffersonian values
administrative interest groups	interest group liberalism	Madisonian values
	value trade-offs	systems perspective

REVIEW MATERIAL

Review Questions

1. What briefly are the nature and content of Jeffersonian, Hamiltonian, and Madisonian values?

2. Why is the problem of relating bureaucracy to democracy so complicated within the context of U.S. politics?

3. Can you describe the key periods in U.S. history that were important turning points in political-administrative relations? Why were they significant?

4. Why does the author argue that the future of U.S. bureaucracy concerns recognizing trade-offs associated with different values involving political-bureaucratic relationships? What ways can we better calculate potential trade-offs for any bureaucratic reform?

5. Briefly, how did the three founding fathers—Hamilton, Jefferson, and Madison— conceive of connecting bureaucracy with democracy? If they returned today, how do you think the founders would view their ideas operating within the context of contemporary U.S. bureaucracy? Positively or negatively? Or, both?

Class Debate: Pro/Con

Resolved that the 21st Century with the rise of global terrorism, economic interdependence, instant media coverage, internet email and so on has made past American Values, i.e., Hamiltonianism, Jeffersonianism, and Madisonianism, irrelevant for shaping future U.S. bureaucracy and its actions.

Student Homework Assignment

Research one of the significant legislative/executive actions listed in figure 7.5. What were the value prescriptions of its authors? Their motivations for proposing it? The reasons for its enactment and/or implementation? Its continuing influence on bureaucracy and society today? Do impacts now conform to the original values or purposes of its framers? Why or why not?

Case Analysis

Read "The Blast in Centralia No. 5" in any edition of Richard Stillman's Public Administration: Concepts and Cases. Reflect upon each of the major participants in the case study and generalize how their value orientations towards public bureaucracy influenced their actions: The Governor? The Director of Mines and Minerals Department? Bell and Zoller? The UMW Union? Where did these values or outlooks come from? How did they effect the outcome of the case? Would you classify them as Hamiltonian, Jeffersonian, Madisonian, or what sort of other values?

NOTES

1. Leonard D. White, *The Federalists: A Study in Administrative History* (New York: Macmillan, 1948), p. 478.

2. Clinton Rossiter, *Alexander Hamilton and the Constitution* (New York: Harcourt Brace Jovanovich, 1964), p. 162.

3. Lynton K. Caldwell, *The Administrative Theories of Hamilton and Jefferson: Their Contribution to Thought on Public Administration* (Chicago: University of Chicago Press, 1944), pp. 236–41.

4. James Madison, "The Federalist, No. 10," in Edmund M. Earle (ed.), *The Federalist* (New York: Random House, 1937), p. 54.

5. Madison, "The Federalist, No. 51," ibid., p. 337.

6. Ralph Ketchum, *James Madison: A Biography* (New York: Macmillan, 1971), p. 301.

7. Samuel P. Huntington, *The Soldier and the State* (Cambridge, MA: Harvard University Press, 1957), p. 206.

8. Don K. Price, *America's Unwritten Constitution: Science, Religion, and Political Responsibility* (Baton Rouge: Louisiana State University Press, 1983), p. 83.

9. Ibid.

10. Ibid., p. 86.

11. Mathew Crenson, *The Federal Machine* (Baltimore, MD: Johns Hopkins University Press, 1975).

12. Douglas Southall Freeman, *Lee's Lieutenants: A Study in Command,* 3 vols. (New York: Scribners, 1942–44).

13. Refer to Chapter 2 of this text for an extended discussion of this subject.

14. Robert H. Wiebe, *The Search for Order, 1877–1920* (New York: Hill and Wang, 1967).

15. Barry Karl, *Executive Reorganization and Reform in the New Deal* (Cambridge, MA: Harvard University Press, 1963).

16. See especially Dwight Waldo, *The Administrative State* (New York: Ronald Press, 1948), and Herbert Simon, *Administrative Behavior* (New York: Macmillan, 1947).

17. David B. Truman, *The Government Process* (New York: Knopf, 1951), p. 501.

18. Robert A. Dahl, *A Preface to Democratic Theory* (Chicago: University of Chicago Press, 1956), p. 145.

19. Theodore J. Lowi, *The End of Liberalism*

(New York: Norton, 1969), p. 37.

20. Charles E. Lindblom, "The Science of 'Muddling Through,' " *Public Administration Review* 19 (Summer 1959): 79–88.

21. Carl J. Friedrich, "Public Policy and the Nature of Administrative Responsibility," *Public Policy* (1940), pp. 3–24, and Herman Finer, "Administrative Responsibility in Democratic Government," *Public Administration Review* 1 (Summer 1941): 335–50.

22. Samuel P. Huntington, "The United States," in Michael Crozier, Samuel P. Huntington, and Joji Watanuki (eds.), *The Crisis of Democracy* (New York: New York University Press, 1975), pp. 74–75.

23. Ibid.

24. Ibid.

25. John Rawls, *A Theory of Justice* (Cambridge, MA: Harvard University Press, 1971), p. 25.

26. Arthur Schlesinger, *The Imperial Presidency* (Boston, MA: Houghton Mifflin, 1973).

27. Richard E. Neustadt, *Presidential Power* (New York: Wiley, 1960).

28. E. F. Schumacher, *Small Is Beautiful: Economics as If People Mattered* (New York: Harper and Row, 1973).

29. Frank Marini (ed.), *Toward a New Public Administration: The Minnowbrook Perspective* (Scranton, PA: Chandler, 1971).

30. Vincent Ostrom, *The Intellectual Crisis in American Public Administration* (University of Alabama Press, 1973).

31. For a useful summary of these seminal pieces of legislation framing political-administrative relationships in the 1970s, refer to Part Four of Richard J. Stillman II (ed.), *Basic Documents of American Public Administration Since 1950* (New York: Holmes and Meier, 1982).

32. Price, *Unwritten Constitution,* pp. 177–78.

FURTHER READING

The historic problems associated with bureaucratic-political relationships have been discussed by scholars for some time. The earliest and best discussion is between Carl J. Friedrich, "Public Policy and the Nature of Administrative Responsibility," *Public Policy,* 1 (1940), pp. 3–24, and Herman Finer, "Administrative Responsibility in Democratic Government," *Public Administration Review* 1 (Summer 1941), pp. 335–50. A summary of both these essays can be found in Alan A. Alshuler (ed.), *The Politics of Federal Bureaucracy* (1968). Also useful are Paul H. Appleby, *Morality and Administration in Democracy* (1952); Frederick C. Mosher, *Democracy and the Public Service,* 2d ed. (1982), especially Chapter 8; and Arthur A. Maass and Laurence I. Radway, "Gauging Administrative Responsibility," *Public Administration Review* 9 (Summer 1949), pp. 182–92. Some useful recent treatments include Hugh Heclo, *A Government of Strangers* (1977); Douglas Yates, *Bureaucratic Democracy* (Cambridge: Harvard University Press, 1982); Louis Fisher, *The Politics of Shared Power* (1981); Samuel Krislov and David H. Rosenbloom, *Representative Bureaucracy and the American Political System* (New York: Praeger, 1981); Francis E. Rourke, *Bureaucracy, Politics and Public Policy,* 3d ed. (Boston: Little, Brown, 1984), especially Chapter 7; Judith Gruber, *Controlling Bureaucracies* (1987); Dennis D. Riley, *Controlling the Federal Bureaucracy* (1987); John P. Burke, *Bureaucratic Responsibility* (1986); Harold Seidman and Robert Gilmour, *Politics, Position, and Power,* 4th ed. (1986); Michael Barzelay,

Breaking Through Bureaucracy (1993); Gerald Garvey, *Facing the Bureaucracy* (1993); Frank J. Thompson (ed.), *Revitalizing State and Local Public Service* (1993); Bernard Rosen, *Holding Government Bureaucracies Accountable,* 3rd ed. (1999); and Robert Behn, *Rethinking Democratic Accountability* (2001).

For several useful articles, see Kenneth John Meier, "Representative Bureaucracy: An Empirical Analysis," *American Political Science Review* (June 1975), pp. 526–42; James Q. Wilson, "The Rise of the Bureaucratic State," *The Public Interest* (1975); Herbert Kaufman, "Emerging Conflicts in the Doctrines of Public Administration," *American Political Science Review* (Dec. 1956), pp. 1057–73; David H. Rosenbloom, "Public Administration Theory and the Separation of Powers," *Public Administration Review* (May/June 1983), pp. 213–27; Lynton K. Caldwell, "Novus Ordo Seculorum: The Heritage of American Public Administration," *Public Administration Review* (Sept./Oct. 1975), and in the same issue, Barry D. Karl, "Public Administration and American History: A Century of Professionalism," pp. 476–505; Mark T. Lilla, "Ethos, 'Ethics' and Public Service," *The Public Interest* (Spring 1981), pp. 3–17, and in the same issue, Thomas C. Shelling, "Economic Reasoning and the Ethics of Policy," pp. 37–61. Several of Norton Long's insightful essays wrestle with the problems of bureaucratic oversight and accountability and can be found in a collection of his writings, *The Polity* (Chicago: Rand McNally, 1962). Also see Francis E. Rourke, "American Bureaucracy in a Changing Political Setting," *Journal of Public Administration Research and Theory* (1991); Barbara S. Romzek and Melvin J. Dubnick, "Accountability in the Public Sector: Lessons from the Challenger Tragedy," *Public Administration Review* (1987); Terry Moe, "Control and Feedback in Economic Regulation: The Case of the NLRB," *American Political Science Review* (1985); B. Dan Wood and Richard W. Waterman, *Bureaucratic Dynamics: The Role of Bureaucracy in a Democracy* (1994); and several essays in Richard J. Stillman (ed.), *The American Constitution and the Administrative State* (1989). For a useful comparative overview of this subject, see B. Guy Peters, *The Politics of Bureaucracy,* 4th ed. (1995), especially Chapter 8. A good summary of recent models of legislative-administrative interaction, is Jeff Gill, "Formal Models of Legislative/Administrative Interaction: A Survey of the Subfield," *Public Administration Review* (Jan./Feb. 1995).

Jeffersonian, Hamiltonian, and Madisonian perspectives continue to be represented in various books about bureaucracy. Jeffersonianism is found in "hard right polemics" such as Martin L. Gross, *A Call for Revolution: How Washington Is Strangling America—and How to Stop It!* (1993), or "public choice scholars" like John E. Chubb and Terry M. Moe, *Politics, Markets, and American's Schools* (1990). Hamiltonians frequently appear in the ranks of public administration scholars who advocate stronger, more effective management practices such as Hal Rainey, *Understanding and Managing Public Organizations,* 2nd ed. (1997) or applied texts such as the ICMA, *The Effective Local Government Manager,* 2nd ed. (1993). Madisonians today most often are among political scientists and include such writings as James Q. Wilson's general overview of this subject, *Bureaucracy* (1989), or Martha Derthick's realistic, single agency analysis, *Agency Under Stress: The Social Security Administration in America* (1990). One should not miss sensitive historical treatments of the overall dilemmas of balancing these competing perspectives in various administrative settings, such as Thomas K. McCraw's *Prophets of Regulation* (1984); Donal F. Kettl's *Leadership at the Fed* (1986); John T. Tierney's, *The U.S. Postal Service* (1988); Theda Skolpol's *Protecting Soldiers and Mothers* (1992); or Mark Huddleston and William Boyer's *The Higher Civil Service in the United States* (1996).

Serious students of the topic of administrative efficacy, accountability, and interest groups should also examine primary materials—executive orders, congressional acts, and official reports as contained in Frederick C. Mosher (ed.), *Basic Documents of American Public Administration, 1776–1950* (New York: Holmes and Meier, 1976), and Richard J. Stillman II (ed.), *Basic Documents of American Public Administration since 1950* (New York: Holmes and Meier, 1982).

Recent studies of cultural values and their impacts upon institutions are also important: Paul Light, *The Tides of Reform* (1997); Christopher Hood, *The Art of the State* (1998); Camilla Stivers, *Bureau Men, Settlement Women* (2000); Richard Stillman, *Creating the American State* (1998); and Lawrence Harrison and Samuel P. Huntington (eds.), *Culture Matters* (2000).

WEB SITES

http://www.andromeda.rutgers.edu/~ditomaso/obl_4/: Changing Bureaucratic Models
http://www.albany.edu/~dkw42/barnard.html: Brownlow Commission Excerpts

Index